©1988   Nissan Motor Co., Ltd.
All rights reserved. No part of this publication may be reproduced or used in any form or by any means without the written permission of the publisher.

Published by Gloview Co., Ltd., 2-60-6, Nihonbashi-Hamacho, Chuo-ku, Tokyo 103, Japan.

Distributors:
UNITED STATES: Kodansha International/USA, Ltd., through Harper & Row, Publishers, Inc., 10 East 53rd Street, New York, N.Y. 10022. CANADA: Fitzhenry & Whiteside Ltd., 195 Allastate Parkway, Markham, Ontario L3R 4T8. BRITISH ISLES: Premier Book Marketing Ltd, 1 Gower Street, London WC1E 6HA, England. EUROPEAN CONTINENT: European Book Service PBD, 63 Strijkviertel, 3454 PK De Meern, The Netherlands. AUSTRALIA AND NEW ZEALAND: Bookwise International, 1 Jeanes Street, Beverley, South Australia 5007, Australia THE FAR EAST: Japan Publications Trading Co., Ltd., 1-2-1, Sarugaku-cho, Chiyoda-ku, Tokyo 101, Japan.

First Printing: May 1988

ISBN 0-87040-763-5

Printed in Japan

BUSINESS JAPANESE

a guide to improved communication

PREFACE

We are very pleased to present the second edition of BUSINESS JAPANESE. In the two years since BUSINESS JAPANESE was first published, the text has exceeded all expectations by becoming an international best-seller. This, we feel, is because BUSINESS JAPANESE filled such an important gap in the exchange of information between East and West. Although we as a nation have always been eager to learn about and even adopt the traditions and business strategies of the rest of the world, we have been less diligent about introducing our own country to others. Tourist information was readily available, certainly, but few efforts were made to give students overseas a rounded, up-to-date image of our nation's very active business community.

We at Nissan have been concerned with correcting this imbalance of information for a long time. Indeed, BUSINESS JAPANESE grew out of the training programs that Nissan has been conducting at our manufacturing plants in Japan for over 10 years. Working closely with the engineers and executives who came from all over the world to participate in these programs, we were able to discover the special instruction requirements of professionals aspiring to learn Japanese. These findings, confirmed by our experiences in the more than 150 countries where we maintain business ties, finally came together in 1984 in the BUSINESS JAPANESE Project.

BUSINESS JAPANESE was the first Japanese language text to focus on contemporary business vocabulary, and the first also to feature inside information about the business practices of our country. On popular demand, we subsequently provided cassette tapes and a volume for advanced students, BUSINESS JAPANESE II. BUSINESS JAPANESE is used today at language institutions throughout the world; but perhaps the ultimate testament to its success is the number of Japanese courses that have since followed in its footsteps by providing lessons and information similarly targeted at the business community.

For all of us at Nissan, BUSINESS JAPANESE represents a significant step in our ongoing efforts to enhance the flow of information between East and West. We are therefore proud of the textbook's popularity and determined also to regularly update and revise our series to reflect the fast-evolving language and customs of our nation. We trust that our efforts have been successful and that this new edition will continue to meet your language needs, and with your approval.

Yoshio Arakawa
Director
Nissan Motor Co., Ltd.

Tokyo
March, 1987

ACKNOWLEDGMENTS

The lessons in this text are adapted from the curricula that I have been offering to the diplomatic community in Japan for over 20 years. I am honored to contribute my experiences to such an important and timely project as BUSINESS JAPANESE. It is indeed rewarding to know that what started out as a course primarily for diplomats is now used widely in the business community; and that, as a result of this text, the study of Japanese itself is becoming increasingly popular in the United States and Europe.

I am deeply indebted to the management of Nissan Motor Co., Ltd., without whose vision and support BUSINESS JAPANESE would never have been realized, much less introduced to such a wide audience. I am especially grateful to the staff of the International Division for their guidance in the production of this second edition.

I also wish to thank Mr. Masaaki Nakamori and Mr. Yuji Nakazato for their help in designing the language sections of this book; and to express my special appreciation to Ms. Madalena Velasquez whose "Business Information" sections provide such a meaningful backdrop to each lesson, and to the other staff of Asian Advertisers, Inc. for their assistance throughout this project.

> Hajime Takamizawa
> Chief Instructor
> Japan Field School
> U.S. State Department

Yokohama
March, 1987

CONTENTS

Preface
Acknowledgments
Introduction

Lesson	Language Section	Page	Business Information	Page
1	Meeting People I	1	Exchanging Business Cards (meishi)	11
2	Meeting People II	13	Ranks and Titles	23
3	Using the Phone	25	Communicating over the Phone	35
4	Telling Time	39	The Life of the Expatriate Manager	49
5	Visiting I	51	Visiting	63
6	Visiting II	65	Polite Expressions (keigo)	79
7	At the Office	81	The Japanese Writing System	92
8	At the Store	95	Borrowed Words	107
9	Making Appointments	109	The Business Luncheon I	123
10	Business Luncheons	125	The Business Luncheon II	137

Lesson	Language Section	Page	Business Information	Page
11	On the Way to the Showroom	139	Getting Around by Taxi	151
12	At the Showroom	153	Japanese Language Word Processors	165
13	Extending Invitations for a Party	167	Giving a Business Party	177
14	Messages	179	Making Speeches	190
15	Hiring People	193	The Recruitment Process	205
16	Interviews	207	The Interview	219
17	Business Negotiations I	221	Starting Negotiations	233
18	Business Negotiations II	235	Negotiations	246
19	Business Negotiations III	249	Reading Business and Financial Documents	261
20	Japanese Business Practices	265	Dealing with Failure— or with Success	276

Appendix

Verbs 278

Adjectives 279

Counters 279

Verb Inflections 280

Bibliography 282

Index 284

INTRODUCTION

Objective

BUSINESS JAPANESE offers a new orientation to the study of the Japanese language. Unlike the generalized approach of most Japanese textbooks, the aim of BUSINESS JAPANESE is to help the foreign business person meet his or her specific needs in everyday business situations in Japan:

BUSINESS JAPANESE will assist you in mastering all fundamentals of grammar and vocabulary essential for normal business activities.

BUSINESS JAPANESE will equip you with a wealth of background information about Japanese companies, local business protocol, customs, etc. to enable you to understand, and operate with confidence in, your new business environment.

Organization of the Text

BUSINESS JAPANESE is divided into twenty lessons, each with the same easy-to-follow format:

a. Statement of lesson objectives.
b. List of target expressions and grammatical points to master.
c. Description of business situation to be covered.
d. Dialogue utilizing target expressions in business situations. New vocabulary which you should pay particular attention to is listed before every conversation.
e. Full dialogue provided in Japanese writing, for reference.
f. Full dialogue provided again in Roman letters, by way of summary.
g. Related and additional useful expressions for business situation.
h. Notes on grammar and vocabulary introduced in the dialogue.
i. Practices, exercises and self-testing.
j. Background information pertaining to business situation ("Business Information").

Special Features

In BUSINESS JAPANESE, the level of language skills is closely coordinated with that of the business activities being described in order to provide the most coherent structure for the gradual acquisition of business-related skills:

    a. As the narrative proceeds from relatively simple business situations, e.g. phone calls and introductions, to more complex ones like contract negotiations, the student is taught correspondingly more sophisticated expressions and grammatical patterns.

    b. Grammar rules and new terminology are introduced systematically so that each new chapter reinforces and expands the skills covered in the previous one.

    c. Alternate expressions and uses are provided wherever possible to allow the student maximum opportunity to tailor newly-acquired skills to his/her individual needs.

    d. Each dialogue in the text is based on a single business situation in Japan. Each lesson can therefore also serve as a handy phrase-book for the student when searching for specific words, expressions, etc. appropriate for a given business situation.

This integrated format ensures that, by the end of the course, the student will not only have mastered the fundamentals of Japanese grammar, but will also be self-sufficient in basic, daily conversation with his Japanese affiliates and familiar with the idiosyncracies of his new working environment.

How to Use This Text

BUSINESS JAPANESE has been designed so that the busy foreign professional can learn Japanese either in class or at home, with a minimum of preparation and review. Students are of course recommended to proceed at their own pace, as best suits their individual schedules and skills. The following guidelines, however, have been provided for your benefit to ensure thorough and rapid mastery of the material covered in this volume:

Step 1: Introduction to the Dialogue
1) instructor explains new target expressions, grammar and vocabulary (with reference to Notes as necessary).
2) student practices pronunciation.
3) student practices the dialogue.
4) role-playing exercises based on the dialogue to develop initial familiarity with new words and patterns.

Step 2: Introduction to Related Expressions
1) instructor explains related and additional expressions (with reference to Notes as necessary) for systematic expansion and enrichment of core expressions.
2) student practices pronunciation.
3) role-playing exercises as in Step 1.

[Please note that instead of routinely memorizing new expressions, etc. students are encouraged to acquire mastery over them through repeated use and varied application.]

Step 3: Practices and Exercises
1) completion of all practices and exercises provided.
2) exercises also draw upon preceding lessons in order to assure depth of understanding. Thorough comprehension of each exercise is recommended before proceeding to the next.

Step 4: Applied Conversation
1) rewording and adaptation of exercises, etc. to relate target expressions as much as possible to student's own experiences.
2) students are encouraged to request additional drills from the instructor to tailor new expressions to their personal business needs.

Step 5: Review
Review of the business dialogue and business information to place narrative into broader perspective.

Step 6: Preparation for Next Lesson
Students are encouraged to read notes on grammar, idiomatic expressions and business information prior to the actual lesson.

If the above guidelines are faithfully observed, even at the pace of one Step per day (approximately one lesson a week), the most time-pressed business person will still be able to acquire a practical working knowledge of the Japanese language in less than 6 months.

Special Note Concerning Self-Study

It is of course preferable that a teacher be available to explain to you the more tricky aspects of grammar, and other special characteristics of the Japanese language. However, for those who will be studying the course on their own, the following are recommended in addition to the standard guidelines:

1) Examination of the pronunciation chart provided on the following pages.
2) Close reading of the dialogue and additional expressions for *basic* comprehension. Heavy reliance on the English translations is not recommended, as Japanese expressions frequently have no real equivalent in any other language. Wherever possible, literal (but awkward) translations have been provided to facilitate comprehension.
3) Careful study of all notes on grammar and vocabulary.
4) Diligence in completing all practices, exercises and drills. Repetition of key exercises is strongly recommended for the independent student, and you should not move on to the next exercise until absolutely confident of the preceding one. Model answers have been provided for most exercises for your guidance.

Note: All company names, except for Nissan Motor Co., Ltd. and all personal names used in this text are purely fictional. Any coincidences with real-life companies or personalities are unintentional.

A TABLE OF JAPANESE SOUNDS
Showing the **Katakana** and **Hiragana** Syllabaries

The romanization system used in this text is basically the system used in ordinary dictionaries (i.e. the Hepburn system). The letters **a, i, u, e,** and **o** represent the five basic vowels in Japanese, pronounced as follows, with crisp, short breaths: **a** as in B**a**ch, **i** as in p**i**ano, **u** as in h**u**la, **e** as in b**e**t, and **o** as in h**o**pe. Vowels can be doubled resulting in almost exactly twice the length of the same sound as the single short vowel. However, note that, in this text, there are the following three exceptions to the Hepburn system:

1. Doubled (long) vowels are indicated as **aa, ii, uu, ee,** and **oo,** instead of **ā, ī, ū, ē,** and **ō.**

Examples:	Hepburn System	This Text	Meaning
	Kachō	**Kachoo**	'Manager'
	Tōkyō	**Tookyoo**	'Tokyo'

The vowel cluster **ei** is represented as the doubled (long) vowel, **ee.**

Examples:	Hepburn	This Text	Meaning
	Keiyaku	**Keeyaku**	'contract'

a B**a**ch — あ ア	**i** p**i**ano — い イ	**u** h**u**la — う ウ	**e** b**e**t — え エ	**o** h**o**pe — お オ	
ka — か カ	**ki** — き キ	**ku** — く ク	**ke** — け ケ	**ko** — こ コ	**ga** — が ガ
sa — さ サ	**shi** — し シ	**su** — す ス	**se** — せ セ	**so** — そ ソ	**za** — ざ ザ
ta — た タ	**chi** — ち チ	**tsu** — つ ツ	**te** — て テ	**to** — と ト	**da** — だ ダ
na — な ナ	**ni** — に ニ	**nu** — ぬ ヌ	**ne** — ね ネ	**no** — の ノ	
ha — は ハ	**hi** — ひ ヒ	**hu** — ふ フ	**he** — へ ヘ	**ho** — ほ ホ	**ba** — ば バ
ma — ま マ	**mi** — み ミ	**mu** — む ム	**me** — め メ	**mo** — も モ	**pa** — ぱ パ
ya — や ヤ		**yu** — ゆ ユ		**yo** — よ ヨ	
ra* — ら ラ	**ri*** — り リ	**ru*** — る ル	**re*** — れ レ	**ro*** — ろ ロ	«Doubled
wa — わ ワ	**n** — ん ン				**aa**

* The Japanese "r" sound is the only consonant that does not closely correspond to any English consonant. It is pronounced by flicking the tip of the tongue against the roof of the mouth, to produce a sound resembling the English "d".

2. The consonant **n,** when it is pronounced as an independent syllable preceding a **y** or a vowel within a word, is indicated as **n'** for additional clarity.
Examples: Hepburn   This Text   Meaning
              honya   **hon'ya**   'bookstore'

When three or more vowels follow each other, an apostrophe is used to indicate word formation.
Example: Kee'eegaku   'business administration'

3. **Fu,** the "fricative *h*", is indicated as **hu.**
Examples: Hepburn   This Text   Meaning
               Furansu **Huransu**   'France'
               fune   **hune**   'ship'

KEY

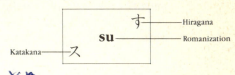

ぎ gi ギ	ぐ gu グ	げ ge ゲ	ご go ゴ
じ ji ジ	ず zu ズ	ぜ ze ゼ	ぞ zo ゾ
		で de デ	ど do ド

び bi ビ	ぶ bu ブ	べ be ベ	ぼ bo ボ
ぴ pi ピ	ぷ pu プ	ぺ pe ペ	ぽ po ポ

(long) Vowels»

ii	uu	ee	oo

きゃ kya キャ	きゅ kyu キュ	きょ kyo キョ
ぎゃ gya ギャ	ぎゅ gyu ギュ	ぎょ gyo ギョ
ひゃ hya ヒャ	ひゅ hyu ヒュ	ひょ hyo ヒョ
びゃ bya ビャ	びゅ byu ビュ	びょ byo ビョ
ぴゃ pya ピャ	ぴゅ pyu ピュ	ぴょ pyo ピョ
にゃ nya ニャ	にゅ nyu ニュ	にょ nyo ニョ
りゃ rya リャ	りゅ ryu リュ	りょ ryo リョ
しゃ sha シャ	しゅ shu シュ	しょ sho ショ
じゃ ja ジャ	じゅ ju ジュ	じょ jo ジョ
ちゃ cha チャ	ちゅ chu チュ	ちょ cho チョ

Special Symbols:

(   ) in the English version indicates: (a) words which do not actually appear in the Japanese, but are provided for a more natural translation; (b) words that further clarify English translation; (c) references to other parts of the text; (d) a description/clarification of the business situation. (exception: the word 'it,' when used in idiomatic expressions about time, weather, etc. is not found in parentheses.)

(   ) in the Japanese version indicates words that are not always necessary, and that may be dropped depending either on the context or on the style of the individual speaker.

[lit.   ] indicates literal translation.

[imp.   ] indicates implied meaning.

«   » indicates general category or person/thing/grammatical term to be inserted.

/   / indicates: (a) terms pertaining to grammar; (b) cue(s) to be used in the following Practice.

...   indicates that the sentence is incomplete, and requires the insertion of a word, phrase or clause for completion.

-    clarifies the formation of words, and does not affect pronunciation. In this text, "-" has been inserted in the following cases:

      a) between a personal name and **san/sama**/job title.
         Example: Yamada-san
      b) preceding "counters."
         Example: ichi-dai
      c) between noun and **suru/dekiru.**
         Example: benkyoo-suru
      d) compound words.
         Example: denwa-suru

Lesson 1

Meeting People I

OBJECTIVES

1   to introduce yourself in the Japanese way.

2   to use Japanese greetings.

3   to introduce one person to another.

Lesson 1

TARGET EXPRESSIONS AND PATTERNS

1 I'm «name X».   **Watakushi wa «X» desu.**

2 I'm «name X» from «company Y».   **Watakushi wa «Y» no «X» desu.**

3 This is Mr./Ms. «name X».   **Kochira wa «X»-san desu.**

4 I'm not «name X».   **Watakushi wa «X» ja arimasen.**

SITUATION

William Brown is an employee of the American consulting company, P & C, Ltd. He is visiting Japan to conduct market research. Today he is going to visit Mr. Yamamoto of Keidanren (Federation of Economic Organizations). He has a letter of introduction to Mr. Yamamoto from a common friend, Mr. Jack Miller, Manager of P & C, Ltd.

DIALOGUE

(Mr. Brown has been shown to the reception room. When Mr. Yamamoto comes in, Mr. Brown stands up and greets him.)

| | | hello | **konnichi wa** |
| **Brown** | | Mr./Ms. Yamamoto | **Yamamoto-san** |

1	Hello! Are (you) Mr. Yamamoto?	**Konnichi wa. Yamamoto-san desu ka.**

| | how do you do? | **hajimemashite** |
| **Yamamoto** | [lit. this is the first time] | |

2	Hello! (I) am Yamamoto. How do you do?	**Konnichi wa. Yamamoto desu. Hajimemashite.**

| | P & C (Ltd.) | **Pii-ando-shii** |
| **Brown** | William Brown | **Uiriamu Buraun** |

3	How do you do? (I) am William Brown of P & C.	**Hajimemashite. Pii-ando-shii no Uiriamu Buraun desu.**

— 2 —

Lesson 1

(Mr. Brown takes out his business card.)

	this	**kore**
	I	**watakushi**
	business card	**meeshi**
	my business card	**watakushi no meeshi**
Brown	pleased to meet you [lit. please treat me favorably]	**doozo yoroshiku**

4	This is my business card. Pleased to meet you.	**Kore wa watakushi no meeshi desu. Doozo yoroshiku.**

Yamamoto	thank you very much	**arigatoo gozaimasu** (polite)
	please	**doozo**

5	Thank you very much. This is my card. Please (take this.)	**Arigatoo gozaimasu. Watakushi no meeshi desu. Doozo.**

(Bowing slightly to Mr. Yamamoto, Mr. Brown takes his business card with both hands.)

	oh	**aa**
	(Mr.) Miller	**Miraa**
Brown	letter of introduction	**shookaijoo**

6	Oh, Mr. Yamamoto. This is Mr. Miller's letter of introduction.	**Aa, Yamamoto-san. Kore wa Miraa no shookaijoo desu.**

	thanks	**doomo**
Yamamoto	(in good) health	**genki, ogenki** (respectful)

7	Thanks. Is Mr. Miller well?	**Doomo. Miraa-san wa ogenki desu ka.**

	yes	**ee**
Brown	very	**totemo**

8	Yes, (he) is very well.	**Ee, totemo genki desu.**

Yamamoto	so	**soo**

9	Oh, is that so?	**Aa, soo desu ka.**

Lesson 1

JAPANESE WRITING

1	ブラウン：	こんにちは。山本さんですか。
2	山　本：	こんにちは。山本です。はじめまして。
3	ブラウン：	はじめまして。ピー・アンド・シーのウィリアム・ブラウンです。
4	ブラウン：	これは私の名刺です。どうぞよろしく。
5	山　本：	ありがとうございます。私の名刺です。どうぞ。
6	ブラウン：	ああ、山本さん。これはミラーの紹介状です。
7	山　本：	どうも。ミラーさんはお元気ですか。
8	ブラウン：	ええ、とても元気です。
9	山　本：	ああ、そうですか。

READING

1	Brown:	Konnichi wa. Yamamoto-san desu ka.
2	Yamamoto:	Konnichi wa. Yamamoto desu. Hajimemashite.
3	Brown:	Hajimemashite. Pii-ando-shii no Uiriamu Buraun desu.
4	Brown:	Kore wa watakushi no meeshi desu. Doozo yoroshiku.
5	Yamamoto:	Arigatoo gozaimasu. Watakushi no meeshi desu. Doozo.
6	Brown:	Aa, Yamamoto-san. Kore wa Miraa no shookaijoo desu.
7	Yamamoto:	Doomo. Miraa-san wa ogenki desu ka.
8	Brown:	Ee, totemo genki desu.
9	Yamamoto:	Aa, soo desu ka.

ADDITIONAL USEFUL EXPRESSIONS

1　Greetings

a)	Good morning.	**Ohayoo (gozaimasu).**
b)	Good evening.	**Konban wa.**
c)	Good-bye.	**Sayoonara/Shitsuree-shimasu.**
d)	Good night.	**Oyasumi nasai.**
e)	You're welcome.	**Doo itashimashite.**

2

A:　Mr. Brown. How are (you)?	**Buraun-san, ogenki desu ka.**

— 4 —

Lesson 1

	thank you (for asking) [lit. thanks to you (All is well)] you	okagesama de anata
B:	Thank you. (I)'m fine. And you?	Okagesama de, genki desu. Anata wa.

3	this person company	kochira kaisha
A:	Mr. Brown, this [lit. This person] is Tanaka of my company.	Buraun-san. Kochira wa watakushi no kaisha no Tanaka desu.
B:	Mr. Tanaka? (I)'m Brown. How do you do?	Tanaka-san desu ka. Buraun desu. Hajimemashite.
C:	(I)'m Akira Tanaka. Nice to meet you.	Tanaka Akira desu. Doozo yoroshiku.

4	excuse me [lit. (it's) a rudeness] but	shitsuree ga
A:	Excuse me, but are you Mr. Smith?.	Shitsuree desu ga, anata wa Sumisu-san desu ka.

	no	iie
B:	No, (I)'m not Smith.	Iie, Sumisu ja arimasen.
A:	Excuse me.	Shitsuree-shimashita.

NOTES

1 Japanese Pronunciation

Japanese pronunciation is quite simple for native English speakers, with only a few exceptions. The spelling system used in this text is designed to enable you to communicate in Japanese in the shortest time.

Listen carefully to the teacher's pronunciation as some sounds may be difficult for you in the beginning. If you cannot master the exact pronunciation, do not be too concerned, as the slight mispronunciation of certain words will not interfere with communication. If you cannot master the Japanese **r** pronunciation right away, for example, you can still be understood by using the English **r** sound. In other cases, it will be essential for you to pronounce the word correctly in order to make yourself understood, especially when distinguishing between words with a single consonant and those with double (e.g. **kata** 'person' vs. **katta** 'bought').

— 5 —

Lesson 1

The Japanese language has five vowels. They are pronounced approximately as they are in Spanish. In English, **a, e, i, o** and **u** have various pronunciations, depending on the word. In Japanese, there is only one way to pronounce each of these sounds. As you study this lesson, you will learn all of the sounds normally encountered in the Japanese language.

In Japanese, each syllable in a word takes an equal amount of time to pronounce. Since each syllable (normally consisting of a vowel or consonant plus vowel) in a Japanese word requires one "beat." Therefore, a word like **anata** 'you' takes three "beats": **a na ta.**

Words containing the "**aa**," "**ii**," "**uu**," "**ee**," or "**oo**" vowels express long vowels and should be pronounced as one continuous sound, roughly equal in length to two identical short vowels.

Note the pronunciation of the following sounds in Japanese.

a	as in "father," but shorter
i	as in "bee," but shorter
u	as in "put," but with unrounded lips
e	as in "bet"
o	as in "caught," but shorter
tsu	as in "Pittsburgh"

The Japanese **r** is different from the English **r** and, to a native speaker of English, sounds like **l, r** or **d.** It is in fact a "flapped" **r,** in which the tip of the tongue briefly touches the roof of the mouth directly behind the teeth and is drawn away quickly.

One other sound which does not occur in English is **h** before **u.** This sound, often represented in romanization by **f** (i.e. **Mt. Fuji**), is closer to **h** than **f. Hu** is pronounced by blowing air out between the unrounded lips. Do not rest the upper teeth against the lower lip, as in the English **f.**

Japanese is normally not stressed in the same manner as English. That is to say, certain syllables are not louder or stronger as in English.
However, Japanese is accented through pitch, or voice level. Some syllables are higher in pitch than others. You should try to duplicate the pitch while listening to your teacher's pronunciation. However, if you find it difficult, the safest pronunciation is a relatively even one, with little modulation and without emphasis on any one syllable or syllables.

In Tokyo dialect, you will encounter a nasalized **g,** which may sound like **n** to you. If you can not master it, don't worry about it excessively. You can manage with an ordinary "hard" **g,** as in "gun."

There are two cases in Japanese when the vowel is "whispered," or not pronounced. These are **i** and **u** between voiceless consonants (i.e. **t, h, k, p** and **s**) or at the end of a word, following a voiceless consonant.

Lesson 1

Therefore, a word like **ikimasu** '(someone) goes' sounds more like **ikimas.** Also, the word **sukiyaki** is pronounced as though it were spelled **skiyaki.** When in doubt, verify the pronunciation of any word by listening to your teacher's pronunciation. Rely on your ear, not your eye!

2 Copula **desu**
Desu is the copula 'to be' and can mean 'am/is/are.'

«subject A» **wa***	**B desu.**
A	is B.
Watakushi wa	**Yamamoto desu.**
I	am Yamamoto.

In this pattern, particle* **wa** indicates that the preceding noun is the subject of the sentence. In the above example, **watakushi** 'I' is the subject. Particle **wa** will be discussed in detail in the following lesson.

Examples: a) **Kore *wa* Jakku Miraa-san no shookaijoo *desu.***
          (**Kore** is the subject)
          "This is a letter of introduction from Mr. Jack Miller."
   b) **Miraa-san no shookaijo *wa* kore *desu.***
          (**Miraa-san no shookaijoo** is the subject.)
          "Mr. Miller's letter of introduction is this (one)."

**Particles are non-inflective words which follow words or phrases to indicate the relationship of the preceding word(s) to the rest of the sentence. Particles also include the equivalent of prepositions in English as will be explained later.*

Ja arimasen is the present negative form of **desu,** meaning 'am/is/are not.'

«subject A» **wa**	**B ja arimasen.**
A	is not B.
Kochira wa	**Tanaka-san ja arimasen.**
This «person»	is not Mr. Tanaka.

Examples: a) **Kore wa watakushi no meeshi *ja arimasen.***
          "This is not my business card."
   b) **Watakushi no kaisha wa Pii-ando-Shii *ja arimasen.***
          "My company is not P & C, Ltd."

3 Particle **no** 'of'
Particle **no** occurs between nouns like "A **no** B" and usually means "A's B" or "B of A." Depending upon context, it is also used in the sense of " located in A," "B related to A," etc.**

Examples: a) **Tanaka-san *no* meeshi**   'Mr. Tanaka's business card'
   b) **anata *no* kaisha**   'your company'
   c) **Shikago *no* Jakku**   'Jack in/from/of Chicago'
   d) **tenisu *no* hon**   'a book about tennis'

***Please note that **no** functions in much the same way as the English preposition **of.** However, since the word order is different from that of English, **no** has been included under the category of particle.*

Lesson 1

4 Question Particle **ka**

In Japanese, it is not necessary to change the word order to make an interrogative sentence. You can do so just by adding **ka** to the end of a sentence.

Compare: **Kore wa Yamamoto-san no meeshi desu.**
"This is Mr. Yamamoto's business card."

and

Kore wa Yamamoto-san no meeshi desu *ka*.
"Is this Mr. Yamamoto's business card?"

Note: Not all questions end with **ka**, e.g. **"Anata wa."** in ADDITIONAL USEFUL EXPRESSIONS **2** in this lesson. Any phrase can become a question when pronounced with rising intonation.

5 -san

-san is attached to a family name (i.e. **Yamamoto-san**), a given name (i.e. **Jakku-san**), or a family name plus a given name (i.e. **Tanaka Akira-san***), and means either Mr., Mrs., Miss or Ms. It is the polite form of addressing/referring to an individual. However, you cannot use **-san** with your own name, or with the names of others in your group, when speaking with a person who is not a member of this group. See Business Information, Lesson 2, for more details.

*In Japanese, one's family name is always mentioned first. In the above example, **Tanaka** is a family name and **Akira** is a given name.

6 Watakushi

Watakushi is often contracted to **watashi,** which is less formal.

7 Greetings

Konnichi wa "Hello," "Good day" is usually used from late morning to a little before dark. It literally means "How about today?"

Ohayoo gozaimasu "Good morning" is a formal greeting used when addressing a superior or a client in the morning. **Gozaimasu** is dropped when addressing a colleague or subordinate. The literal meaning of **ohayoo** is "It is early."

Konban wa "Good evening" is usually used after it gets dark. It literally means "How about this evening?".

Note that the above greetings are commonly used when meeting for the first time that day. In responding to those greetings, you can use the same expressions.

Sayoonara "Good-bye" is sometimes contracted to **sayonara.** But in business situations **shitsuree-shimasu** is used to mean "good-bye," although it literally means "I commit a rudeness."

Oyasumi nasai "Good night" literally means "Go to sleep," so it is usually used when you are going to sleep, or when someone is going to sleep. When you are leaving someone late in the evening and going directly home, this expression is also used for "good-bye."

— 8 —

Lesson 1

Okagesama de indicates the speaker's appreciation for interest in his personal affairs ("thanks for asking") or for assistance ("thanks to you"). This expression usually accompanies favorable or pleasant information.

Doomo alone is an informal expression of thanks.

PRACTICE

1 Pronunciation Practice

Directions: The teacher reads the following Japanese words borrowed from English. Guess the meaning of each word and check with your teacher to see if correct. Ask for additional words if necessary.

Example: Teacher: **Koohii.**
Student: Coffee.

a) **suutsu**	c) **beruto**	e) **juusu**	g) **naihu**	i) **hoteru**
b) **nekutai**	d) **suteeki**	f) **hanbaagu**	h) **nooto**	j) **terebi**

2 Communication Practice

Directions: Practice correctly introducing yourself.

Patterns: 1 **Watakushi wa** «your family name/full name» **desu.**

2 **Watakushi wa** «company» **no** «name» **desu.**

3 Communication Practice

Directions: Teacher and student introduce themselves to each other.

Example: Teacher: **Watakushi wa** «name» **desu. Doozo yoroshiku.**
Student: **Watakushi wa** «company» **no** «name» **desu. Hajimemashite. Doozo yoroshiku.**

4 Communication Practice

Directions: Student introduces his acquaintances to the teacher.

Example: Student: «teacher's name»**-san.**
Kochira wa «acquaintance's company» **no** «name» **desu.**
Teacher: «Name»**-san desu ka.**
Watakushi wa «name» **desu. Hajimemashite.**

Lesson 1

5 Communication Practice

Directions: Student and teacher exchange business cards.
Practice appropriate Japanese expressions and rituals, as follows:
(1) bow, and then (2) hand over card while introducing yourself. However, it is also good to say **kore wa watakushi no meeshi desu** "This is my business card", while handing over your card, to let the person know that you are going to give him your card. It's more polite to receive the card with both hands.

Example: Student: **Watakushi wa «name» desu. Kore wa watakushi no meeshi desu. Doozo yoroshiku.**
                 Teacher: **Doomo arigatoo gozaimasu. Watakushi wa «name» desu.** (While handing over his card), **Hajimemashite.**

6 Response Practice

	Teacher's Greetings or Questions	Student's Responses
a)	**Ohayoo gozaimasu.**	**Ohayoo gozaimasu.**
b)	**Konnichi wa.**	**Konnichi wa.**
c)	**Konban wa.**	**Konban wa.**
d)	**Sayoonara.**	**Sayoonara.**
e)	**Oyasumi nasai.**	**Oyasumi nasai./Sayoonara.**
f)	**Doomo arigatoo.**	**Doo itashimashite.**
g)	**Doozo.**	**Arigatoo gozaimasu.**
h)	**Ogenki desu ka.**	**Okagesama de genki desu. (Anata wa.)**

EXERCISES

What do you say in the following situations?   **Model Answers:**

1	You have just met someone in the morning.	**Ohayoo gozaimasu.**
2	You have just met him in the afternoon.	**Konnichi wa.**
3	You have just met him in the evening.	**Konban wa.**
4	He gave you his business card.	**Arigatoo gozaimasu.**
5	He has just thanked you for something.	**Doo itashimashite.**
6	He is leaving.	**Shitsuree-shimasu./Sayoonara.**
7	You are going to retire for the night.	**Oyasumi nasai.**

Lesson 1

BUSINESS INFORMATION

Exchanging Business Cards (meishi)

The first step in any business relationship in Japan is the exchange of business cards (名刺 **meeshi**). Even if your paths have already crossed at industry or social gatherings, many Japanese businessmen will not acknowledge an official channel of communication between their company and yours until this obligatory first step has been taken. When doing business in Japan, therefore, you should always be equipped with a generous supply of meishi printed in both English and Japanese and be prepared also to trade these at every opportunity. If you are seriously interested in pursuing a business relationship, you should follow up on this initial meeting with regular calls and traditional summer and new year greetings (暑中見舞 **shochuumimai,** and 年賀状 **nengajoo)** or, in the case of foreign affiliates, Christmas cards (クリスマスカード **kurisumasu kaado).** It is of course also proper to advise your contacts of any change of address, title or other basic information, and to present them with a new card when you have the first chance to do so in person.

A meishi can sometimes even function as an introduction in its own right. A personal introduction or phone call is of course the best way to bring two parties together, but when neither is possible, a few words scribbled on an intermediary's meishi and "signed" with his seal (はんこ **hanko),** are perfectly acceptable substitutes. In fact, this practice is far more common than the formal letter of introduction.

From the above, it will be obvious that exchanging meishi in Japan is not just a preliminary formality that can be disposed of quickly. Rather, since it is the initial step in any business relationship, proper manners while exchanging cards are essential in order to create the best possible first impression. Many Japanese companies even provide meishi guidelines for new employees, such as the following:

1) Have your meishi handy at all times so you can hand it out immediately upon meeting someone, without fumbling around.
2) Stand when you give your meishi, and do so with one hand.
3) Hold out your meishi with the writing facing the recipient and be sure to pronounce your name and that of your company clearly. Since surnames are usually mentioned first in Japan, this reminder is especially important for the foreign businessman, as otherwise your counterpart is likely to confuse your first name with your last.
4) The visiting party should be the first to give his meishi.
5) When you are accompanying your boss or superior, you should hand out your meishi only after he has introduced you. If there are three or more persons in your party, introductions should be made in order of seniority.
6) If possible, receive your new acquaintance's card with both hands, and scan it immediately for the vital information.
7) Try to address your new acquaintance by name in the course of the conversation.
8) Do not play around with the meishi once received. Instead, lay the meishi in front of you during that first meeting and refer to it from time to time to show polite interest in your new acquaintance's position and responsibilities. At the end of the meeting, put the meishi away safely in your card holder.

Lesson 1

The standard business meishi in Japan features conservative black type against a white or cream background. It measures 9cm × 5.5cm and contains the following information:

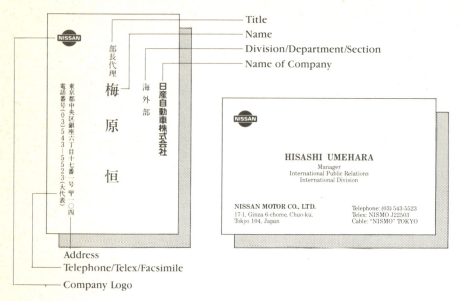

If you wish to include special degrees and qualifications, e.g. "Ph.D.", on your card in addition to the standard company information, it is best to do so only on the English side since academic qualifications are sometimes considered pretentious in Japan. Please note too that, although fashionable stationers now offer "designer" cards in all colors of the rainbow, they have not yet been so bold as to tamper with the prescribed dimensions of business meishi. For the convenience of your acquaintances, therefore, you should have your card made accordingly so it will fit comfortably into standard meishi boxes and files.

Department/Section names:

Eegyo-bu	営業部	Sales Department
Kaigai-bu	海外部	International/Overseas Department
Kikaku-shitsu	企画室	Corporate Planning Office
Koohoo-shitsu	広報室	Public Affairs Department
Senden-bu	宣伝部	Advertising Department
Choosa-bu	調査部	Business Research Department
Soomu-bu	総務部	General Affairs Department
Hooki-bu	法規部	Legal Department
Jinji-bu	人事部	Personnel Department
Roomu-bu	労務部	Labor Relations Department
Keeri-bu	経理部	Budget and Accounting Department
Zaimu-bu	財務部	Finance Department
Koobai-bu	購買部	Purchasing Department
Gijutsu-bu	技術部	Engineering Department
Seesan-kanri-bu	生産管理部	Production Control Department
Shoohin-kaihatsu-shitsu	商品開発室	Product Development Office

Lesson 2

Meeting People II

OBJECTIVES

1 to discuss professional relationships.

2 to indicate where someone works.

3 to ask or inform someone where a company is.

Lesson 2

TARGET EXPRESSIONS AND PATTERNS

1 Mr./Ms. «name X» is(my)friend/ acquaintance.

«X»-san wa tomodachi/shiriai desu.

2 Mr./Ms. «name X» is an employee of «company Y».

«X»-san wa «Y» no shain desu.

3 Mr./Ms. «name X» was an employee of «company Y».

«X»-san wa «Y» no shain deshita.

4 Mr./Ms. «name X» was not an employee of «company Y».

«X»-san wa «Y» no shain ja arimasen deshita.

5 Where is «company X»?

«X» wa doko desu ka.

6 «Company X» is in «place Y».

«X» wa «Y» desu.

SITUATION

The conversation between Mr. Brown and Mr. Yamamoto shifts to a discussion of their mutual acquaintance, Mr. Takada, who is working for JETRO (Japan External Trade Organization).

DIALOGUE

	by the way	tokoro de
	JETRO	Jetoro
	Mr./Ms. Takada	Takada-san
Yamamoto	acquaintance	shiriai, oshiriai (respectful)

1	By the way, is Mr. Takada of JETRO (your) acquaintance?	**Tokoro de, Jetoro no Takada-san wa oshiriai desu ka.**

Brown

2	Mr. Takada?	**Takada-san desu ka.**

(Mr. Brown is trying to recall Mr. Takada.)

| | friend | tomodachi |
| Yamamoto | a male given name | Yoshio |

3	Yes. (He) is Mr. Yoshio Takada, Mr. Miller's friend.	**Ee. Miraa-san no tomodachi no Takada Yoshio-san desu.**

— 14 —

Lesson 2

he	**kare**
CBM	**Shii-bii-emu**
company employee	**shain**
Brown but	**ga**

4 Ah, Yoshio! He was an employee of CBM, but [imp. he is not with CBM anymore.] — **Aa, Yoshio-san. Kare wa Shii-bii-emu no shain deshita ga...**

formerly	**izen**
sales and marketing department	**eegyoo-bu**
staff of a department	**buin**
staff of the sales and marketing department	**eegyoo-buin**
now	**ima**
International Communication Department	**kokusai-kooryuu-bu**
Yamamoto general manager	**buchoo**

5 Yes, (he) was formerly a staff member of the Sales and Marketing Department of CBM, but now (he) is General Manager of the International Communication Department of JETRO. — **Ee, izen wa Shii-bii-emu no eegyoo-buin deshita ga, ima wa Jetoro no kokusai-kooryuu-bu no buchoo desu.**

office	**jimusho**
Brown where?	**doko**

6 Oh, is that so? Where is JETRO's office? — **Aa, soo desu ka. Jetoro no jimusho wa doko desu ka.**

Yamamoto a place name in Tokyo	**Toranomon**

7 JETRO is in Toranomon. — **Jetoro wa Toranomon desu.**

Brown

8 Oh, is that so? — **Aa, soo desu ka.**

— 15 —

Lesson 2

JAPANESE WRITING

1　山　本：　ところで、ジェトロの高田さんはお知り合いですか。
2　ブラウン：　高田さんですか。
3　山　本：　ええ。ミラーさんの友達の高田良夫さんです。
4　ブラウン：　ああ、良夫さん。彼はCBMの社員でしたが…
5　山　本：　ええ、以前はCBMの営業部員でしたが、今はジェトロの国際交流部の部長です。
6　ブラウン：　ああ、そうですか。ジェトロの事務所はどこですか。
7　山　本：　ジェトロは虎の門です。
8　ブラウン：　ああ、そうですか。

READING

1　Yamamoto:　Tokoro de, Jetoro no Takada-san wa oshiriai desu ka.
2　Brown:　Takada-san desu ka.
3　Yamamoto:　Ee. Miraa-san no tomodachi no Takada Yoshio-san desu.
4　Brown:　Aa, Yoshio-san. Kare wa Shii-bii-emu no shain deshita ga…
5　Yamamoto:　Ee, izen wa Shii-bii-emu no eegyoo-buin deshita ga, ima wa Jetoro no kokusai-kooryuu-bu no buchoo desu.
6　Brown:　Aa, soo desu ka. Jetoro no jimusho wa doko desu ka.
7　Yamamoto:　Jetoro wa Toranomon desu.
8　Brown:　Aa, soo desu ka.

ADDITIONAL USEFUL EXPRESSIONS

1

| | she | kanojo |
| | Mr./Ms. Yamada | Yamada-san |

| A: | Is she Ms. Yamada? | Kanojo wa Yamada-san desu ka. |

| | secretary | hisho |

| B: | Yes, that's right. (She) is Mr. Brown's secretary. | Ee, soo desu. Buraun-san no hisho desu. |

2

| | that person (he/she) | ano hito |

| A: | Is that person an employee of your company? | Ano hito wa anata no kaisha no shain desu ka. |

| | staff member | shokuin |

| B: | No, he is a staff member of JETRO. | Iie. Kare wa Jetoro no shokuin desu. |

Lesson 2

3

A:	Was Mr. Takada an employee of P & C, Ltd.?	**Takada-san wa Pii-ando-shii no shain deshita ka.**
B:	No, (he) wasn't.	**Iie, soo ja arimasen deshita.**

4

A:	Where is your company?	**Anata no kaisha wa doko desu ka.**

head office	**honsha**
America, USA	**Amerika**
Chicago	**Shikago**

B:	The head office is in Chicago, USA.	**Honsha wa Amerika no Shikago desu.**

Japan	**Nihon, Nippon**
branch office	**shisha**

A:	How about branch offices in Japan?	**Nihon no shisha wa.**

a place name in Tokyo	**Marunouchi**

B:	(We have one in) Marunouchi. [lit. (It) is in Marunouchi.]	**Marunouchi desu.**

REFERENCE

Foreign Countries (popular version)		Foreign Cities	
Chuugoku	China	**Amusuterudamu**	Amsterdam
Doitsu	Germany	**Berurin**	Berlin
Huransu	France	**Nyuuyooku**	New York
Igirisu	U.K.	**Pari**	Paris
Itaria	Italy	**Pekin**	Beijing
Kanada	Canada	**Rondon**	London
Kankoku	Korea	**Rooma**	Rome
Kita-Choosen	North Korea	**Rosu (Anjerusu)**	Los Angeles
Oosutoraria	Australia	**Shidonii**	Sydney
Oranda	Holland	**Souru, Sooru**	Seoul
Sobieto, Soren	U.S.S.R.	**Toronto**	Toronto

— 17 —

Lesson 2

Factories in Japan belonging to corporations financed with foreign capital*

Major Japanese corporations invariably attract a lot of attention when they establish manufacturing plants overseas, but the same interest is not always generated when the reverse occurs, i.e. when foreign firms establish facilities in Japan. The map below shows a cross-section of foreign-owned facilities throughout the country, together with each factory's country of origin and main item(s) of production. [Note: This information has been selected at random and is not intended as a comprehensive list. Names provided are those of the mother company.]

① *Hokkaido*
NOVO Industri A/S, Denmark: *Biotechnology*
The Dow Chemical Co., USA: *Styrofoam*

② *Miyagi Prefecture*
Sandvik AB, Sweden: *Drill parts*

③ *Fukushima Prefecture*
Motorola Inc., USA: *Semiconductors*

④ *Tochigi Prefecture*
E.L. Dupont de Nemaurs Co., USA: *Cereals*
The Dow Chemical Co., USA: *Chemicals*

⑤ *Gunma Prefecture*
The M.W. Kellogg Co., USA: *Cereals*
The Procter & Gamble Co., USA: *Detergents*

⑥ *Ibaragi Prefecture*
Nabisco Inc., USA: *Biscuits*
Nestle S.A., Switzerland: *Malted milk drinks*
Texas Instruments Inc., USA: *Semiconductors*

⑦ *Saitama Prefecture*
Garrett Corp., USA: *Turbo-chargers*
Rank Xerox Ltd., UK: *Facsimiles and workstations*
Sandoz A.G., Switzerland: *Pharmaceuticals*
Texas Instruments Inc., USA: *Semiconductors*

⑧ *Tokyo*
Hewlett-Packard Co., USA: *Electronics*
Honeywell Inc., USA: *Electronics*

⑨ *Kanagawa Prefecture*
Avon Products Co., USA: *Cosmetics*
Cie. Gervais Danone, France: *Yogurt*
Dow Corning Corp., USA: *Chemicals*
Honeywell Inc., USA: *Electronics*
IBM Corp., USA: *Computers*
NCR Corp., USA: *Electronics*
NOVO Industri A/S, Denmark: *Pharmaceuticals*
Rank Xerox Ltd., UK: *Copiers*
Scott Paper International, USA: *Tissue paper*
3M Inc. (Minnesota Mining Mfg.), USA: *Magnetic products*

⑩ *Shizuoka Prefecture*
E.L. Dupont de Nemaurs Co., USA: *Plastic coatings*
Nestle S.A., Switzerland: *Coffee*
Revlon International Corp., USA: *Cosmetics*
Texas Instruments Inc., USA: *Controller equipment*
The Procter & Gamble Co., USA: *Soaps*
Unilever N.V., Netherlands: *Margarine*

⑪ *Aichi Prefecture*
Pfizer Inc., USA: *Feed additives*
The Dow Chemical Co., USA: *Urethane materials*

⑫ *Mie Prefecture*
General Foods Corp., USA: *Coffee*

⑬ *Shiga Prefecture*
Boehringer Ingelheim International, GmbH, West Germany: *Pharmaceuticals*
IBM Corp., USA: *Computers*
Max Factor & Co., USA: *Cosmetics*

⑭ *Hyogo Prefecture*
Ciba-Geigy Ltd., Switzerland: *Pharmaceuticals*
Gadelius & Co., AB, Sweden: *Ship equipment*
General Foods Corp., USA: *Pet foods*
Nestle S.A., Switzerland: *Coffee*
The Procter & Gamble Co., USA: *Disposable diapers*

⑮ *Okayama Prefecture*
The Dow Chemical Co., USA: *Plastics engineering*

⑯ *Oita Prefecture*
Texas Instruments Inc., USA: *Semiconductors*

⑰ *Nagasaki Prefecture*
Fairchild Semiconductor Corp., USA: *Semiconductors*

*Including joint ventures

Lesson 2

NOTES

1 **Deshita** is the past affirmative form of copula **desu** and **ja arimasen deshita** is the past negative form. The inflection of copula is as follows:

Tense	Form	Meaning
Present/Affirmative	**desu**	am/is/are
Present/Negative	**ja arimasen**	am/is/are not
Past/Affirmative	**deshita**	was/were
Past/Negative	**ja arimasen deshita**	was/were not

Examples:

a) **Yamada-san wa hisho** *desu.*   "Ms. Yamada is a secretary."
b) **Yamada-san wa hisho** *ja arimasen.*   "Ms. Yamada isn't a secretary."
c) **Yamada-san wa hisho** *deshita.*   "Ms. Yamada was a secretary."
d) **Yamada-san wa hisho** *ja arimasen deshita.*   "Ms. Yamada wasn't a secretary."

2 Particle **ga** is used between independent clauses and means 'but' or 'however'.

Examples:
    a) **Ano hito wa shiriai desu** *ga,* **tomodachi ja arimasen.**
       "That person is my acquaintance, but not my friend."
    b) **Takada-san wa watakushi no kaisha no shain deshita** *ga,* **Yamamoto-san wa shain ja arimasen deshita.**
       "Mr. Takada was an employee of my company, but Mr. Yamamoto wasn't an employee."

3 O- in **ogenki** (introduced in Lesson 1) and **oshiriai** is a respectful prefix, attached to the beginning of a noun or adjective in polite speech. Therefore, the combination "**o** + noun/adjective" rarely refers to the speaker's own situation.

Compare:
    a) **Watakushi wa genki desu.**   "I'm fine."
       and
    Takada-san wa *o***genki desu.**   "Mr. Takada is fine."

    b) **Kanojo wa watakushi no shiriai desu.**   "She's my acquaintance."
       and
    Kanojo wa Yamada-san no *o***shiriai desu.**   "She's Ms. Yamada's acquaintance."

Lesson 2

4 **Shain** (社員) is usually used to refer to an employee/employees of so-and-so Company. (**Watakushi wa Pii-ando-shii no shain desu.** "I'm an employee of P & C, Ltd.") However, when you wish to tell someone you are a company employee (as an occupation), you should say **kaishain** (会社員).

Shokuin (職員) is commonly used to describe the staff of a nonprofit organization, like JETRO and Keidanren.

PRACTICE

1 Transformation Practice

Example: Teacher: **Watakushi wa Buraun desu.** (Affirmative)
"I'm Brown."
Student: **Watakushi wa Buraun ja arimasen.** (Negative)
"I'm not Brown."

a) **Kanojo wa Yamada-san desu.**   **Kanojo wa Yamada-san ja arimasen.**
b) **Yamamoto-san wa shiriai desu.**   **Yamamoto-san wa shiriai ja arimasen.**
c) **Kore wa watakushi no meeshi desu.**   **Kore wa watakushi no meeshi ja arimasen.**

2 Transformation Practice

Example: Teacher: **Takada-san wa Shii-bii-emu no shain deshita.** (Affirmative)
"Mr. Takada was an employee of CBM."
Student: **Takada-san wa Shii-bii-emu no shain ja arimasen deshita.** (Negative)
"Mr. Takada was not an employee of CBM."

a) **Yamada-san wa hisho deshita.**   **Yamada-san wa hisho ja arimasen deshita.**

b) **Kare wa eegyoo-buin deshita.**   **Kare wa eegyoo-buin ja arimasen deshita.**

c) **Tanaka-san wa Jetoro no shokuin deshita.**   **Tanaka-san wa Jetoro no shokuin ja arimasen deshita.**

3 Response Practice

Directions: Answer the questions according to cues given by the teacher.

Example: Teacher: **Kore wa anata no meeshi desu ka. /Iie/**
"Is this your business card?" /No/
Student: **Iie, watakushi no meeshi ja arimasen.**
"No, (it) is not my card."

— 20 —

Lesson 2

a) **Buraun-san wa Shii-bii-emu no shain deshita ka. /Iie/**   **Iie, Shii-bii-emu no shain ja arimasen deshita.**

b) **Kore wa Miraa-san no shookaijoo desu ka. /Iie/**   **Iie, Miraa-san no shookaijoo ja arimasen.**

c) **Anata no jimusho wa Toranomon desu ka. /Ee/**   **Ee, Toranomon desu.**

d) **Yamada-san wa hisho deshita ka. /Iie/**   **Iie, hisho ja arimasen deshita.**

4 Communication Practice

Directions: Practice telling the teacher where your office/company is by using the following patterns:

Patterns:
a) **Watakushi no jimusho wa** «place» **desu.**
b) **Kaisha wa** «name of country» **no** «place» **desu.**
c) **Honsha wa** «place» **desu ga, Nihon no shisha wa** «place» **desu.**

Examples:
a) **Watakushi no jimusho wa Marunouchi desu.**
b) **Kaisha wa Igirisu no Rondon desu.**
c) **Honsha wa Amerika no Nyuuyooku desu ga, Nihon no shisha wa Shinjuku desu.**

5 Communication Practice

Directions: Using maps and the Japanese cities and place names given on page 18, ask the teacher where the various cities or places are. The teacher will point out the city or place on the map, so try to remember where it is.

Example: Student: **Kyooto wa doko desu ka.**
Teacher: **Koko** ('here') **desu.**

EXERCISES

a) Supply the following information for the teacher.
1   Name of your company.
2   Place where your company's head office is located.
3   Place where your company's branch office in Japan is located.
4   Name of your secretary.

Lesson 2

b) Inform your teacher that:

    1   Mr. Takada is Mr. Miller's acquaintance.
2   Mr. Brown was an employee of P & C, Ltd.
3   JETRO's office is in Toranomon.
4   Ms. Yamada was not Mr. Yamamoto's secretary.
5   The branch office of P & C, Ltd. is in Shinjuku.

Model Answers:

a)

1   **Watakushi no kaisha wa «company» desu.**
2   **Watakushi no kaisha no honsha wa «place» desu.**
3   **Watakushi no kaisha no Nihon no shisha wa «place» desu.**
4   **Watakushi no hisho wa «name» desu.**

b)

1   **Takada-san wa Miraa-san no shiriai desu.**
2   **Buraun-san wa Pii-ando-shii no shain deshita.**
3   **Jetoro no jimusho wa Toranomon desu.**
4   **Yamada-san wa Yamamoto-san no hisho ja arimasen deshita.**
5   **Pii-ando-shii no shisha wa Shinjuku desu.**

Lesson 2

BUSINESS INFORMATION

Ranks and Titles

Although a number of Japanese social customs have succumbed to Western influence, the society itself remains highly stratified. There is always *some* distinction in rank between any two Japanese, whether of age, sex, company position or family background. The rank of an individual will determine how he is expected to behave towards another, the manner of speech he will choose and, of course, the way in which he will address, and be addressed by, others.

In normal social and business situations, it is quite proper to address another person—though never yourself—as "So-and-so-**san.**" "**San**" is the most common polite equivalent of "Mr./Mrs./Miss/Ms." and is used regardless of the age, sex or marital status of the person being addressed. The title indicates respect, but is equally appropriate in intimate relationships.

In formal situations, however, or when you are speaking with an important person whose rank is higher than your own, it is usually better to address the person by his professional title. When meeting Mr. Arakawa, the general manager of a client company, for instance, you should address him as "Arakawa **buchoo**" instead of "Arakawa-**san.**" This rule of etiquette also holds true when you are speaking of a famous person, or one highly regarded in society—unless, of course, it is understood by all listeners that that person is a close friend of yours. Consequently, when referring to the president of a well-known company, you should say "So-and-so **shachoo** (president)" to indicate your awareness of his important position as well as your respect.

Given the hierarchical nature of Japanese society, you will no doubt appreciate the strategic significance of the initial exchange of meishi. Business cards inform new acquaintances of the others' ranks right from the start. As a result, everyone will know his or her place in the new relationship and behave accordingly from then on.

When you first meet your Japanese business counterpart, you should pay particular attention to his title. Should you accidentally bump into a high-ranking acquaintance at some professional or formal gathering, and cannot for the life of you recall his actual position, you can take refuge in the English language and safely call him "Mr." So-and-so. This would in most cases be preferable to "**-san,**" which might sound too familiar.

Another word of caution is that you should avoid trying to become too familiar too soon. Many Westerners are accustomed to a very casual atmosphere back at home, where they can comfortably call everyone inside and outside their organization—from janitor to president—by his or her first name. In Japanese professional circles, however, the "first-name basis" relationship exists only among close friends in a company, and even then only among those of the same age group. And while you may be hoping to put everyone at ease by dispensing with formalities and insisting that your Japanese colleagues or counterparts call you John or Mary, as the case may be, you will actually be rocking the boat and disrupting the normal hierarchy of social conduct. For some foreign visitors, it may be unsettling to have to remember ranks and titles all the time, especially when

— 23 —

Lesson 2

they themselves are used to familiarity and equality for all. But this is part and parcel of cultural exchange. In order to keep the gears of business well lubricated, it would be good to remember that in Japan, (to borrow from Orwell) "some are more equal than others."

A typical ranking system in a Japanese company is provided below, in order of seniority, with approximate English equivalents:

Kaichoo	会長	Chairman
Shachoo	社長	President
Huku-shachoo	副社長	Vice President
Senmu Torishimariyaku	専務取締役	Senior Managing Director
Joomu Torishimariyaku	常務取締役	Managing Director
Torishimariyaku	取締役	Director
Buchoo	部長	General Manager
Jichoo	次長	Deputy General Manager
Kachoo/Buchoo Dairi	課長/部長代理	Manager/Acting General Manager
Kakarichoo/Kachoo Dairi	係長/課長代理	Group Chief/Acting Manager
Buin/Kain	部員/課員	Staff
Hirashain	平社員	Title-less staff (slang)

Note also the following structure of a typical Japanese company.

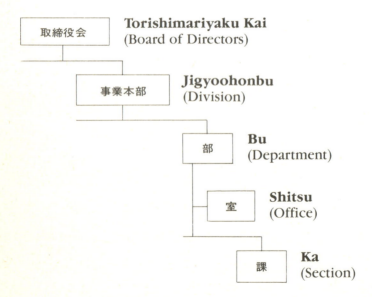

— 24 —

Lesson 3

Using the Phone

OBJECTIVES

1 to pronounce and understand Japanese numbers.

2 to ask someone for his phone number and inform him of yours.

3 to start a telephone conversation.

4 to ask the caller to identify himself.

Lesson 3

TARGET EXPRESSIONS AND PATTERNS

1	Do you know (about) «item X»?	«X», wakarimasu ka.
2	«Name X»'s telephone number is...	«X» no denwa-bangoo wa...desu.
3	Hello.	Moshimoshi.
4	Who's calling, please?	Dochirasama desu ka.
5	May (I) speak to Mr./Ms. «name X»?	«X»-san onegaishimasu.

SITUATION

Mr. Brown asks his secretary, Ms. Yamada, for the telephone number of JETRO (Japan External Trade Organization). He calls Mr. Takada, General Manager of JETRO.

DIALOGUE

	telephone	denwa
	number	bangoo
	telephone number	denwa-bangoo
Brown	to understand, to know*	wakarimasu

> **1** Ms. Yamada, do (you) know the telephone number of JETRO?
>
> Yamada-san, Jetoro no denwa-bangoo, wakarimasu ka.

	yes	hai
	five	go
	eight	hachi
	two	ni
	one	ichi
Yamada	582-5511	go-hachi-ni no go-go-ichi-ichi

> **2** Yes, (I) know (it). JETRO('s number) is 582-5511.
>
> Hai, wakarimasu. Jetoro wa go-hachi-ni no go-go-ichi-ichi desu.

Brown	thank you very much	doomo arigatoo

> **3** Thank you very much.
>
> Doomo arigatoo.

*Although verbs in this text are translated in the infinitive (i.e. to know) for ease of reference, they are actually in the non-past formal form, meaning "know(s)/will know." There is no real infinitive form in Japanese.

Lesson 3

(Mr. Brown telephones JETRO)

Operator

| 4 | (This) is JETRO. | **Jetoro desu.** |

| | Mr./Ms. Takada | **Takada-sama** (respectful) |
| **Brown** | May (I) speak to [lit. please] | **onegai-shimasu** |

| 5 | May (I) speak to Mr. Takada, General Manager of the International Communication Department? | **Kokusai-kooryuu-buchoo no Takada-sama, onegai-shimasu.** |

Operator   who?   **dochirasama** (respectful)

| 6 | Who's calling, please? | **Dochirasama desu ka.** |

Brown   person   **mono**

| 7 | (I)'m with P & C, (Ltd). [lit. (I)'m a person of P & C, (Ltd).] | **Pii-ando-shii no mono desu.** |

| | a little, for a while | **shooshoo** |
| **Operator** | please wait | **omachi kudasai** |

| 8 | Just a moment, please. [lit. Please wait a while.] | **Shooshoo omachi kudasai.** |

Takada   hello   **moshimoshi**

| 9 | Hello, (this) is Mr. Takada. | **Moshimoshi, Takada desu.** |

Brown   for a long time   **shibaraku**

| 10 | Hello, (this) is (Mr.) Brown of P & C, (Ltd). (I) haven't seen (you) for a long time. | **Moshimoshi, Pii-ando-shii no Buraun desu. Shibaraku deshita.** |

Takada   really   **hontoo ni**

| 11 | Are (you) Mr. Brown? It's really been a long time. | **Buraun-san desu ka. Hontoo ni shibaraku deshita.** |

— 27 —

Lesson 3

JAPANESE WRITING

1 ブラウン：　山田さん、ジェトロの電話番号わかりますか。
2 山　　田：　はい、わかります。ジェトロは582の5511です。
3 ブラウン：　どうもありがとう。
4 オペレーター：　ジェトロです。
5 ブラウン：　国際交流部長の高田様お願いします。
6 オペレーター：　どちら様ですか。
7 ブラウン：　ピー・アンド・シーの者です。
8 オペレーター：　少々、お待ち下さい。
9 高　　田：　もしもし、高田です。
10 ブラウン：　もしもし、ピー・アンド・シーのブラウンです。しばらくでした。
11 高　　田：　ブラウンさんですか。本当に、しばらくでした。

READING

1　Brown:　Yamada-san, Jetoro no denwa-bangoo, wakarimasu ka.
2　Yamada:　Hai, wakarimasu. Jetoro wa go-hachi-ni no go-go-ichi-ichi desu.
3　Brown:　Doomo arigatoo.
4　Operator:　Jetoro desu.
5　Brown:　Kokusai-kooryuu-buchoo no Takada-sama, onegai-shimasu.
6　Operator:　Dochirasama desu ka.
7　Brown:　Pii-ando-shii no mono desu.
8　Operator:　Shooshoo, omachi-kudasai.
9　Takada:　Moshimoshi, Takada desu.
10　Brown:　Moshimoshi, Pii-ando-shii no Buraun desu. Shibaraku deshita.
11　Takada:　Buraun-san desu ka. Hontoo ni, shibaraku deshita.

ADDITIONAL USEFUL EXPRESSIONS

1

0	zero, ree	15	juugo
1	ichi	16	juuroku
2	ni	17	juushichi, juunana
3	san	18	juuhachi
4	shi, yon	19	juuku
5	go	20	nijuu
6	roku	30	sanjuu
7	shichi, nana	40	shijuu, yonjuu
8	hachi	50	gojuu
9	ku, kyuu	60	rokujuu
10	juu	70	nanajuu, shichijuu
11	juuichi	80	hachijuu
12	juuni	90	kyuujuu
13	juusan	100	hyaku
14	juushi, juuyon		

Lesson 3

200 nihyaku	800 happyaku
300 sanbyaku	900 kyuuhyaku
400 yonhyaku	1,000 sen
500 gohyaku	10,000 ichiman
600 roppyaku	100,000 juuman
700 nanahyaku	

2   what number   **nan-ban**

A:	What's Mr. Tanaka's telephone number?	**Tanaka-san no denwa-bangoo wa nan-ban desu ka.**

543-5523   **go-yon-san no go-go-ni-san-ban**

B:	It's 543-5523.	**Go-yon-san no go-go-ni-san-ban desu.**

(telephone) extension   **naisen**

A:	How about (his) extension (number)?	**Naisen wa.**

(I) don't know   **wakarimasen**

B:	(I) don't know the extension.	**Naisen wa wakarimasen.**

3   your house   **otaku**

A:	Hello. Is (this) Mr. Tanaka's residence?	**Moshimoshi. Tanaka-san no otaku desu ka.**

to be wrong   **chigaimasu**
my house   **uchi**

B:	No. Wrong number. This [lit. my house] is Takada.	**Iie, chigaimasu. Uchi wa Takada desu.**
A:	(I)'m sorry.	**Shitsuree-shimashita.**

that's OK   **doo itashimashite**

B:	That's OK.	**Doo itashimashite.**

Lesson 3

4	(the person addressed)	**sochira**
A:	Hello. Is this Mr. Yamamoto's office?	**Moshimoshi. Sochira wa Yamamoto-san no jimusho desu ka.**
B:	Yes, it is.	**Hai, soo desu.**
A:	May (I) speak to Mr. Yamamoto?	**Yamamoto-san, onegai-shimasu.**

	away from home or office	**gaishutsu-chuu**
B:	(He)'s out now, but [imp. may I help you?]	**Ima gaishutsu-chuu desu ga...**
A:	Oh, (I) see. [lit. (I) understood.]	**Aa, wakarimashita.**

	well	**jaa**
	later	**ato de**
A:	Well, (I)'ll call (you) later.	**Jaa, ato de denwa-shimasu.**

5 Useful Idiomatic Expressions

Please give (me) a call.	**Odenwa kudasai.**
(He)'s not at home now.	**Ima rusu desu.**
(He) has just stepped out for a moment. [lit. (He) has left (his) seat now.]	**Ima seki o hazushite imasu.**

NOTES

1 Wakarimasu

Wakarimasu is a verb meaning 'to understand' or 'to know.' The **-masu** in **wakari-masu** is a verb inflection used in a normal style statement. It indicates the affirmative non-past tense.* Its four main forms are as follows:

Tense	Form	Meaning
non-past affirmative	**wakari*masu***	understand or will understand
past affirmative	**wakari*mashita***	understood
non-past negative	**wakari*masen***	do/will not understand
past negative	**wakari*masen deshita***	did not understand

*A non-past tense represents either a future action or a habitual present action, depending on the context.

— 30 —

Lesson 3

Japanese verbs can occur by themselves as complete sentences.

Example: **Wakarimasu ka.**   "Do (you) understand?"

                     Ee, wakarimasu.   "Yes, (I) understand."

As in the DIALOGUE, **wakarimasu** is often used to ask someone if he understands something.

X,	wakarimasu ka
As for «item X»,	do you understand it? or do you know it?

Examples: a) **Takada-san no denwa-bangoo, *wakarimasu ka.***
              "Do (you) know Mr. Takada's telephone number?"
              [lit., "As for Mr. Takada's telephone number, do (you) know (it)?"]

            b) **Nihongo, *wakarimasu ka.***
              "Do (you) understand Japanese?"
              [lit., "As for Japanese, do (you) understand (it)?"]

2 Chinese-origin numerals

The numerical expressions introduced in this lesson are Chinese in origin. Higher numbers (above 100,000) are as follows:

1,000,000	**hyaku man**
10,000,000	**sen man**
100,000,000	**ichi oku**
1,000,000,000	**juu oku**
10,000,000,000	**hyaku oku**
100,000,000,000	**sen oku**
1,000,000,000,000	**itchoo**

In addition to the expressions which are Chinese in origin, there are also expressions unique to the Japanese language (1 through 10, and 20). These numbers will be introduced in Lesson 6.

Bangoo in **denwa-bangoo** refers to 'number' in the sense of 'assigned number' or 'serial number' not 'mathematical numeral.'

Therefore, **nan-ban** literally means 'what assigned number?' or 'what serial number?' and **gosen-gohyaku-nijuusan-ban** means 'No. 5523.'

Ban is a counter for telephone numbers, seat numbers, check numbers, etc.

Lesson 3

3 Moshimoshi

Moshimoshi is the most common way to say 'hello' on the telephone. As you see in this lesson, the person who makes a telephone call usually says **moshimoshi** first, to start a telephone conversation. Psychologically, you are verifying that the other party is on the line.

4 Onegai-shimasu

Onegai-shimasu literally means, "(I)'d like so-and-so" or "please give (me) so-and-so", but on the telephone, «name»-**san**/«name»-**sama, onegai-shimasu** is used to signify, "May (I) speak to Mr./Ms. «name»?" «Name»-**sama** is more formal than «name»-**san.** This pattern is also used when ordering food at a restaurant.

Huraido-chikin, *onegai-shimasu.*   "(I)'d like fried chicken."

Orenji juusu, *onegai-shimasu.*   "Please give (me) orange juice."

5 Mono

Mono 'person' is often used as a substitute for the speaker's name when he feels it is not necessary to tell his name.

PRACTICE

1 Please read the following telephone numbers.

Example: 543-5523   **'Go-yon-san no go-go-ni-san'**

a) 971-6904	c) 803-1616	e) 941-7639	g) 409-8386
b) 456-7141	d) 622-6514	f) 583-7141	h) 351-5270

2 Practice informing others of your telephone number by using the following patterns.

a) **Uchi no denwa-bangoo wa** ☐ **no** ☐ **desu.**

b) **Watakushi no kaisha no denwa-bangoo wa** ☐ **no** ☐ **desu.**

c) **Jimusho no naisen wa** ☐ **desu.**

3 Ask your teacher to provide the telephone numbers of the following organizations and write them down.

Example: JETRO

   Student: **Jetoro no denwa-bangoo wa nan-ban desu ka.**

— 32 —

Lesson 3

a) MITI

b) Japan Air Lines

c) Keidanren

d) Your teacher's office or home number

Note: Telephone numbers of the organizations listed above are as follows:

a) JETRO: 582-5511   c) Japan Air Lines: 248-2081

b) MITI: 501-1511   d) Keidanren: 279-1411

4 Read the following numbers:

Example: 123   'hyaku nijuu san'

a) 77   f) 1,500

b) 29   g) 5,070

c) 308   h) 37,000

d) 640   i) 80,088

e) 192   j) 103,000

5 Communication Practice

Directions: You call Keidanren and ask for Mr. Yamamoto.
Teacher asks who is calling.
You respond by mentioning your company and your name.
Teacher asks you to wait a moment.

Example: Student: **Moshimoshi.**
Teacher: **Keedanren desu.**
Student: **Yamamoto-san, onegai-shimasu.**
Teacher: **Dochirasama desu ka.**
Student: «company» **no** «name» **desu.**
Teacher: **Shooshoo omachikudasai.**

After practicing the conversation above, practice similar conversations by using the names of your acquaintances and their companies.

— 33 —

Lesson 3

6 Communication Practice

Directions: Teacher makes a phone call to you.

You answer as in a real situation, giving your full name.

Teacher does likewise and greets you.

You greet teacher and inquire after the teacher's health.

Teacher answers that he is very well and asks about you.

You thank him and tell him that you are also very well.

Example: Teacher: **Moshimoshi.**

Student: «Name» **desu.** (Use real name.)

Teacher: **Watakushi wa «name» desu. Konnichi wa.**

Student: **Konnichi wa. Ogenki desu ka.**

Teacher: **Ee, genki desu. Anata wa?**

Student: **Okagesama de, genki desu.**

EXERCISES

You have just received a telephone call. Please express the following in Japanese.

1 Who is calling?
2 Just a moment.
3 Mr. Yamamoto is out now.
4 No. Wrong number.
5 Oh, Mr. Yamamoto. I haven't seen you for a long time.

Model Answers:

1 **Dochirasama desu ka.**
2 **Shooshoo omachi kudasai.**
3 **Yamamoto-san wa ima gaishutsu-chuu desu.**
4 **Iie, chigaimasu.**
5 **Aa, Yamamoto-san, shibaraku deshita.**

Lesson 3

BUSINESS INFORMATION

Communicating over the Phone

In Japan, as anywhere else, effective communication over the phone is an invaluable tool in all business transactions. In addition to the expressions and vocabulary already introduced in this Lesson, the following typical conversations are provided to enable you to hold your own while exchanging greetings and formalities over the telephone.

1 Calling an Office

Scenario 1: Identifying yourself

Williams:	Hello, this is Williams calling. Could (I) please speak to Mr. Ohsawa of the International Division?	**Moshimoshi. Watakushi wa Uiriamusu to mooshimasu. Kaigai-bu no Oosawa-san onegai-shimasu.**
Operator:	Excuse me (for asking you this), but which organization do you belong to, Mr. Williams?	**Osoreirimasu ga, dochira no Uiriamusu-sama deshoo ka.**
Williams:	(I) am from ABC Trading.	**Ee-bii-shii Toreedingu desu.**

[Note: It is normal for the operator, or any other person who answers the call, to ask the name of your organization. Therefore, it is usually more convenient to identify yourself fully right from the beginning, i.e. **"Ee-bii-shii Toreedingu no Uiriamusu desu."**]

Scenario 2: When the party is out

Operator:		
Ans. #1:	(I) am sorry, but Ohsawa has stepped out for a moment [lit. ... "left his seat"].	**Mooshiwake arimasen ga, Oosawa wa seki o hazushite orimasu ga...**
Ans. #2:	...Ohsawa is not in at the moment.	**...Oosawa wa gaishutsu shite orimasu ga...**
Ans. #3:	...Ohsawa hasn't come in yet.	**...Oosawa wa mada shussha shite orimasen ga...**
Williams:	Do (you) know when he will be back?/in?/	**Itsugoro okaeri/shussha ni naru ka wakarimasu ka.**
Operator:	One moment please... (He) is scheduled to be back/in the office/in around two hours.	**Shooshoo omachi kudasai... Nijikan kurai de modoru/shussha suru yotee desu.**

— 35 —

Lesson 3

Williams:

Ans. #1:	OK. Then, (I) will call back around that time.	**Wakarimashita. Sonokoro mata kake naoshimasu.**
Ans. #2:	(I) will call back in a little while.	**Nochihodo kake naoshimasu.**
Ans. #3:	Could (I) speak to someone else in the International Division?	**Kaigai-bu no hoka no kata onegai-dekimasu ka.**

Scenario 3: When the party is absent

Operator:

Ans. #1:	(I) am sorry, Mr. Ohsawa has already gone home.	**Mooshiwake arimasen ga, Oosawa wa moo kitaku shimashita.**
Ans. #2:	...Mr. Ohsawa is on holiday today.	**...Oosawa wa kyuuka-chuu desu.**

Williams:	OK, (I)'ll call back tomorrow.	**Wakarimashita, ashita mata kakemasu.**

Scenario 4: When the party is away on business

Operator:	(I) am sorry, Mr. Ohsawa is away on business.	**Mooshiwake arimasen ga, Oosawa wa shucchyoo-chuu desu.**

Ans. #1:

Williams:	Is there a number at which I could contact him?	**Renraku-saki o oshiete itadake-masen ka.**
Operator:	You can call him at «number» in Osaka.	**Oosaka «number» desu.**

Ans. #2:

Williams:	When will (he) be back?	**Itsu okaeri ni narimasu ka.**
Operator:	(He) will be in on Wednesday afternoon.	**Suiyoo no gogo kara shussha itashi-masu.**

Scenario 5: When the party has been transferred

Ans. #1:

Operator:	Mr. Ohsawa has been trans-ferred to our Brussels office.	**Oosawa wa Burasseru jimusho e tenkin shimashita.**
Williams:	Is that so? Could (I) please have (his) new phone number?	**Soo desu ka. Atarashii renraku-saki o oshiete kudasai.**

Lesson 3

Ans. #2:

Operator:	Mr. Ohsawa has been transferred to another department.	**Oosawa wa tabusho e utsurimashita.**
	He is now in the Export Department, at extension «number».	**Ima wa Yuushutsu-bu no naisen «number» -ban desu.**
Williams:	Could (you) please put me through to (him)?	**Tsunaide itadakemasu ka.**

Scenario 6: Leaving messages

Operator:	(I) am sorry, but Ohsawa is at a meeting now.	**Mooshiwake arimasen ga, Oosawa wa tadaima kaigi-chuu desu.**

Williams:

Ans. #1:	Could (you) ask (him) to call back Mr. Williams at «number», please?	**«Number» -ban no Uiriamusu made odenwa kudasaru yoo, otsutae kudasai.**
Ans. #2:	Could (you) ask (him) to call (me) back urgently?	**Isogimasu no de sugu odenwa kudasaru yoo, otsutae kudasai.**
Ans. #3:	Could (I) leave a message?	**Meseeji o onegai dekimasu ka.**

Operator:	Yes, please (go ahead).	**Hai, doozo.**
Williams:	The lunch tomorrow will be postponed. Please call (me) back.	**Asu no chuushoku wa enki-shimasu. Odenwa kudasai.**

Scenario 7: When you get stuck

Williams:

Ans. #1:	Could (you) repeat (that), please?	**Moo ichido yutte kudasai.**
Ans. #2:	Could (you) say (that) more slowly, please?	**Moo sukoshi yukkuri onegai-shimasu.**
Ans. #3:	(I) am sorry, but (I) don't understand Japanese very well.	**Sumimasen ga, nihongo wa yoku wakarimasen.**
Ans. #4:	Could (I) please speak to somebody who understands English?	**Donata ka eego no dekiru kata to ohanashi dekimasu ka.**

— 37 —

Lesson 3

Scenario 8: The wrong number

Operator:

| Ans. #1: | This is «number». What number are you calling? | **Kochira wa «number» desu. Nanban ni okake desu ka.** |
| Ans. #2: | (I) am sorry. There is no one by that name in this office. Perhaps (you) have got a wrong number. | **Osoreirimasu ga, sono yoo na mono wa toobu ni wa orimasen. Omachigai de wa nai deshoo ka.** |

2   Calling in an Emergency

In case of an emergency, dial the following numbers for help:

110   Police
119   Fire Department/Ambulance

You should be prepared to explain in Japanese who you are, where you are calling from, and what assistance you need, as follows:

Uchi wa «ward»**-ku** «section»**-cho** «number»**-banchi desu.**   My address is ☐

Watakushiwa ☐ **desu.**   My name is ☐

Keekan, onegai-shimasu.   Please send the police.

Kyuukyuusha, onegai-shimasu.   Please send an ambulance.

Kaji desu.   Fire!

Lesson 4

Telling Time

OBJECTIVES

1   to tell time.

2   to indicate where someone is.

3   to ask where someone is.

4   to use time words.

Lesson 4

TARGET EXPRESSIONS AND PATTERNS

1 (I will) telephone Mr. «name X».   **(Watakushi wa) «X»-san ni denwa o kakemasu.**

2 It's «time X» now.   **Ima «X» desu.**

3 What time is it now?   **Ima nan-ji desu ka.**

4 Where is Mr./Ms. «name X»?   **«X»-san wa doko ni imasu ka.**

5 Mr. «name X» is in «place Y».   **«X»-san wa «Y» ni imasu.**

6 «Phrase X», so/therefore «phrase Y».   **«X** (cause)» **kara,** «**Y** (result)».

SITUATION

Mr. Brown talks with his secretary, Ms. Yamada, about making an international call to Mr. Smith, Manager of the Research Dept. at the head office. Ms. Yamada explains to Mr. Brown about the time difference between Tokyo and Detroit. As Mr. Brown has only recently arrived in Tokyo, he doesn't yet know what the difference is.

DIALOGUE

	section chief, manager	**kachoo**
	Mr. Smith [lit. Manager Smith]	**Sumisu-kachoo**
Brown	to place a telephone call	**denwa o kakemasu**

1	Did (you) telephone Mr. Smith [lit. Manager Smith]?	**Sumisu-kachoo ni denwa o kake-mashita ka.**

	Detroit	**Detoroito**
	night	**yoru**
	so	**kara**
	to be, exist	**imasu**
Yamada	/particle of emphasis/	**yo**

2	No, (I)'ll call (him) later. Now it's night in Detroit, so the manager isn't at the office.	**Iie, ato de kakemasu. Ima Detoroito wa yoru desu kara, kachoo wa jimu-sho ni imasen yo.**

— 40 —

Lesson 4

Brown what time? **nan-ji**

3	Oh, that's right. [lit. it was so.] What time is it now in Detroit?	**Aa, soo deshita. Detoroito wa ima nan-ji desu ka.**

	well	**eeto...**
	here, this side	**kochira**
	morning	**asa**
	11:00	**juuichi-ji**
	there, the other side	**achira**
	9:00	**ku-ji**
Yamada	about 9:00	**ku-ji goro**

4	Well, now it's 11:00 in the morning here, so it's about 9:00 at night there.	**Eeto, ima kochira wa asa juuichi-ji desu kara, achira wa yoru no ku-ji goro desu.**

Brown

5	Oh, is (that) so?	**Aa, soo desu ka.**

	therefore	**desu kara**
	this evening	**konban**
Yamada	to telephone	**denwa-shimasu**

6	Therefore, (I)'ll call (him) this evening.	**Desu kara, konban denwa-shimasu.**

Brown

7	About what time are (you) going to call this evening?	**Konban nan-ji goro denwa-shimasu ka.**

	time difference	**jisa**
Yamada	14 hours	**juuyo-jikan**

8	The time difference between Tokyo and Detroit is 14 hours, so (I)'ll call (him) at about 10.	**Tookyoo-Detoroito no jisa wa juu-yo-jikan desu kara, juuji-goro denwa-shimasu.**

— 41 —

Lesson 4

JAPANESE WRITING

1　ブラウン：　スミス課長に電話をかけましたか。
2　山　　田：　いいえ、後でかけます。今デトロイトは夜ですから、課長は事務所にいませんよ。
3　ブラウン：　ああ、そうでした。デトロイトは今何時ですか。
4　山　　田：　ええと、今こちらは朝11時ですから、あちらは夜の9時ごろです。
5　ブラウン：　ああそうですか。
6　山　　田：　ですから、今晩電話します。
7　ブラウン：　今晩何時ごろ電話しますか。
8　山　　田：　東京―デトロイトの時差は14 時間ですから10時ごろ電話します。

READING

1　**Brown:**　**Sumisu-kachoo ni denwa o kakemashita ka.**
2　**Yamada:**　**Iie, ato de kakemasu. Ima Detoroito wa yoru desu kara, kachoo wa jimusho ni imasen yo.**
3　**Brown:**　**Aa, soo deshita. Detoroito wa ima nan-ji desu ka.**
4　**Yamada:**　**Eeto, ima kochira wa asa juuichi-ji desu kara, achira wa yoru no ku-ji goro desu.**
5　**Brown:**　**Aa, soo desu ka.**
6　**Yamada:**　**Desu kara, konban denwa-shimasu.**
7　**Brown:**　**Konban nan-ji goro denwa-shimasu ka.**
8　**Yamada:**　**Tookyoo-Detroito no jisa wa juuyo-jikan desu kara, juuji-goro denwa-shimasu.**

ADDITIONAL USEFUL EXPRESSIONS

1　　　　　　　　　　　where　　**doko**

A:　Where is Mr. Takada now?	**Ima Takada-san wa doko ni imasu ka.**

　　　　　　　　　　　London　　**Rondon**

B:　Mr. Takada is in London.	**Takada-san wa Rondon ni imasu.**

2　　　　　　　　　　　today　　**kyoo**
　　　　　　　　　the president　　**shachoo**

A:　Are (you) going to call the president today?	**Kyoo shachoo ni denwa-shimasu ka.**

Lesson 4

tomorrow	**ashita**

B: No. (I)'ll call tomorrow.	**Iie, ashita shimasu.**

3

A: Did (you) phone JETRO?	**Jetoro ni denwa-shimashita ka.**

yesterday	**kinoo**

B: Yes, (I) did (it) yesterday.	**Ee, kinoo shimashita.**

4

this morning	**kesa**
who	**dare**

A: Who did (you) call this morning?	**Kesa dare ni denwa-shimashita ka.**

an international call	**kokusai-denwa**

B: (I) made an international call to Mr. Smith in Detroit.	**Detoroito no Sumisu-san ni kokusai-denwa o kakemashita.**

5

A: What time is it now?	**Ima nan-ji desu ka.**

a.m. (before noon)	**gozen**
1:30	**ichi-ji han**

B: It's 1:30 a.m. now.	**Ima gozen ichi-ji han desu.**

p.m. (after noon)	**gogo**
2:10	**ni-ji jup-pun**

C: It's 2:10 p.m. now.	**Ima gogo ni-ji jup-pun desu.**

15 minutes to 4	**yo-ji juugo-hun mae**

D: It's 15 minutes to 4 now.	**Ima yo-ji juugo-hun mae desu.**

— 43 —

Lesson 4

	20 minutes after 7	shichi-ji nijup-pun (sugi)
E:	It's 20 minutes after 7 now.	**Ima shichi-ji nijup-pun (sugi) desu.**

6

	everyday about how many hours?	**mainichi** **nan-jikan gurai**
A:	About how many hours are (you) in the office everyday?	**Mainichi nan-jikan gurai jimusho ni imasu ka.**

	usually	**taitee**
B:	(I)'m usually (in the office) about eight and a half hours.	**Taitee hachi-jikan han gurai imasu.**

NOTES

1 Location Particle **ni** and Direction Particle **ni**

Particle **ni,** which follows a noun of place and is usually followed by **imasu,** is a location particle to indicate the location of something animate (or inanimate, which will be introduced later) and means 'in, on, at.'

(Person) **wa**	(Place) **ni**	**imasu.**
Sumisu-san wa	**Detoroito *ni***	**imasu.**
Mr. Smith is in Detroit.		

Examples:

a) **Buraun-san wa Tookyoo *ni* imasu.**   "Mr. Brown is in Tokyo."
b) **Shachoo wa kaisha *ni* imasen.**   "The president isn't at the company."
c) **Takada-san wa Amerika *ni* imashita.**   "Mr. Takada was in America."
d) **Yamada-san wa otaku *ni* imasen deshita.**   "Ms. Yamada wasn't at her home."
e) **Jakku wa doko *ni* imasu ka.**   "Where is Jack?"

Particle **ni** used in the sentence **Sumisu-kachoo *ni* denwa o kakemasu** "(I)'ll phone Mr. Smith [lit. Manager Smith]" shows direction of the action; its English equivalent is 'to.' Therefore, the literal translation of the above sentence is, "(I)'ll make a telephone call to Mr. Smith [lit. Manager Smith]."

2 Particle **kara** 'so'

Kara directly following a phrase indicates that the phrase is the reason or cause of the following phrase (result), and it is usually translated as 'so,' 'because' or 'since.'

— 44 —

Lesson 4

Phrase 1 (reason) + **kara,**	Phrase 2 (result)
Detoroito wa ima yoru desu *kara,*	**shachoo wa jimusho ni imasen.**
Now it's night in Detroit, so	the president isn't at the office.

3 Time Counters
Ji combined with numerals shows the hour of the day.
Jikan following numerals is used to measure the number of hours.

Compare:	**Ichi-*ji* desu.**	"It's 1:00."
		and
	Ichi-*jikan* desu.	"It's one hour long."
		or "It takes one hour."

On the other hand, **hun** with numerals is used both to indicate the time of day and the length of time in minutes. (**h** sound sometimes changes to **p**.)

Compare:	**Ni-ji jup-*pun* desu.**	"It's 2:10."
		and
	Ni-jikan jup-*pun* desu.	"It's 2 hours and 10 minutes long."
		or "It takes 2 hours and 10 minutes."

As you have already learned, in order to tell the time of day in hours only, a numeral + counter **-ji** is used. However, to tell time in terms of both hours and minutes, three patterns are used.
The simplest one is made up of the hour + the minute (i.e. **ni-ji jup-pun,** which corresponds to the English expression of 2:10).
Other patterns consist of (a) the hour + minute + **mae** 'before' and (b) the hour + minute + **sugi** 'after.'

Examples:	a) **Ni-ji jup-pun *mae* desu.**	"It's 10 minutes to 2."
	b) **Ni-ji jup-pun *sugi* desu.**	"It's 10 minutes after 2."

4 Particle **yo**
Yo, occuring at the end of sentences, is used for emphasis. It gives assurance to the sentence to which it is attached.

PRACTICE

1 Time Telling Practice

Directions: Practice pronunciation by repeating after the teacher.

a)	**ichi-ji**	1 o'clock	g)	**shichi-ji**	7 o'clock
b)	**ni-ji**	2 o'clock	h)	**hachi-ji**	8 o'clock
c)	**san-ji**	3 o'clock	i)	**ku-ji**	9 o'clock
d)	**yo-ji**	4 o'clock	j)	**juu-ji**	10 o'clock
e)	**go-ji**	5 o'clock	k)	**juuichi-ji**	11 o'clock
f)	**roku-ji**	6 o'clock	l)	**juuni-ji**	12 o'clock

Lesson 4

2 Time Telling Practice

Directions: Read the following in Japanese.

Example: 2:10 "Ni-ji jup-pun"

a) 3:30   d) 8:01   g) 10:15   j) 10:49 p.m.
b) 5:55   e) 11:19   h) 12:32   k) 15 to 5
c) 7:25   f) 4:47   i) 1:24 a.m.   l) 11 after 4

3 Comprehension Practice

Directions: The teacher will give various readings of time in Japanese, which please write down in numerical form.
(To teachers: Please prepare ten readings of different times of the day, and examples of measuring length of time.)

a) _____   f) _____
b) _____   g) _____
c) _____   h) _____
d) _____   i) _____
e) _____   j) _____

4 Communication Practice

Directions: The teacher asks you what time it is. Respond by reading in Japanese each of the times indicated below.

Example: Teacher: **Ima nan-ji desu ka.**   "What time is it now?"
Student: **Ima «time» goro desu.**   "It's about «time» now."

a) 6:20   c) 11:05   e) 7:30   g) 12:00   i) 8:45

b) 10:15   d) 9:50   f) 3:25   h) 1:55   j) 7:35

— 46 —

Lesson 4

5 Response Practice

Directions: Answer the teacher's questions, following the cues provided.

Example: Teacher: **Ima Takada-san wa doko ni imasu ka. /kare no otaku/**
"Where is Mr. Takada now?" /his house/
Student: **Ima Takada-san wa kare no otaku ni imasu.**
"Mr. Takada is at his house."

a) **Ima shachoo wa doko ni imasu ka. /Detoroito no honsha/**
Ima shachoo wa Detoroito no honsha ni imasu.

b) **Ima Yamamoto-san wa doko ni imasu ka. /Keedanren/**
Ima Yamamoto-san wa Keedanren ni imasu.

c) (On the telephone)
Ima anata wa doko ni imasu ka. /Toranomon/
Ima watakushi wa Toranomon ni imasu.

6 Response Practice

Directions: Give negative answers to the teacher's questions.

Example: Teacher: **Jakku wa Tookyoo ni imasu ka.** "Is Jack in Tokyo?"
Student: **Iie, kare wa Tookyoo ni imasen yo.** "No, he isn't in Tokyo."

a) **Kesa Yamada-san wa kaisha ni imashita ka.**
Iie, kanojo wa kaisha ni imasen deshita yo.

b) **Ashita Tanaka-san wa jimusho ni imasu ka.**
Iie, kare wa jimusho ni imasen yo.

c) **Sumisu-san wa Shikago no honsha ni imashita ka.**
Iie, kare wa Shikago no honsha ni imasen deshita yo.

d) **Kyoo anata wa Jetoro ni imasu ka.**
Iie, watakushi wa Jetoro ni imasen yo.

7 Communication Practice

Directions: Inform the teacher where your friends/acquaintances presently are (5 different persons).

Example: **Watakushi no tomodachi/shiriai no «name» -san wa ima «place» ni imasu.**

8 Communication Practice

Directions: Tell the teacher where you were/are, by using real place names.

Examples: a) **Watakushi wa kinoo «place» ni imashita.**
b) **Watakushi wa kesa «place» ni imashita.**
c) **Watakushi wa ima «place» ni imasu.**
d) **Watakushi wa kyoo «place» ni imasu.**
e) **Watakushi wa ashita «place» ni imasu.**

— 47 —

Lesson 4

EXERCISES

a) Teacher asks what time it is. Give the following answers in Japanese.
1   It's about 6:30.
2   It's 8 to 12.
3   It's 7 minutes after 10.
4   It's 8:11 a.m.
5   It's 3:55 p.m.
6   It's 11:00 at night.

b) Give the teacher the following information.
1   Mr. Brown will telephone Mr. Yamamoto this evening.
2   The time difference between Tokyo and Paris is 8 hours.
3   Mr. Takada is my friend, so I know his telephone number.
4   You will make an international call to Mr. Smith in Chicago.
5   Ms. Yamada called Mr. Takada, General Manager of JETRO, this morning.

Model Answers:

a) 1   **Roku-ji sanjup-pun/han goro desu.**
2   **Juuni-ji hap-pun mae desu.**
3   **Juu-ji nana-hun sugi desu.**
4   **Gozen hachi-ji juuip-pun desu.**
5   **Gogo san-ji gojuugo-hun desu.**
6   **Yoru juuichi-ji desu.**

b) 1   **Buraun-san wa Yamamoto-san ni konban denwa-shimasu.**
2   **Tookyoo-Pari no jisa wa hachi-jikan desu.**
3   **Takada-san wa watakushi no tomodachi desu kara, denwa-bangoo ga wakarimasu.**
4   **Shikago no Sumisu-san ni kokusai-denwa o kakemasu.**
5   **Yamada-san wa kesa Jetoro no Takada-buchoo ni denwa-shimashita.**

Lesson 4

BUSINESS INFORMATION

The Life of the Expatriate Manager

The expatriate manager in Japan of course faces all the standard problems that overseas assignments entail, e.g. moving, finding appropriate housing and educational facilities for the family, and adjusting to new business and social customs. These problems are compounded in Japan by astronomical prices for everything from accommodation to parking space to recreation, and by the demands of this exceptionally competitive marketplace. But for many foreign executives, the greatest difficulty of all lies in mastering the Japanese language. To make matters worse, while your head office may be prepared to assist in all other phases of the adjustment process in Japan, this is one obstacle you will have to overcome on your own.

Everyone knows that there are advantages to mastering the local tongue. It has been said, for example, that the chances of a successful business transaction increase five-fold if you can speak the Japanese language, and ten-fold if you can also read it. However, for the expatriate manager who already has a host of other problems to contend with, it is easy to conclude that (1) he simply cannot afford the time to study Japanese; (2) English is in any case *the* universal language; and (3) besides, he can always get an interpreter. Sometimes, it is the head office that decides that, with the thousand and one "more pressing" projects still pending, you should certainly waste neither time nor company money on an exotic oriental language which you could never *really* master anyway.

If you or your senior officers harbor any doubts about the necessity or benefits of learning Japanese, it would be helpful to remember the following points:

1) Despite wide exposure to the English language, not everyone in Japan does in fact speak it. Moreover, even if a businessman has a fairly good command of English, he may still insist on an interpreter during negotiations. This may be partly because he lacks confidence in his linguistic abilities, but it may also be a negotiation tactic. It has often been suggested that, because the English-speaking visitor depends on—and has to wait for—the interpreter to shed light on a discussion, his Japanese counterpart (who might well understand *both* sides of the conversation) thereby gains extra time to observe, listen, formulate questions and prepare rejoinders. Consequently, although you have the apparent advantage of negotiating in your mother tongue, your counterpart is actually the one in better control of the discussion.

2) Sometimes, the foreign visitor makes the mistake of identifying the one fluent English-speaker in a group of Japanese businessmen as the most important or most intelligent, simply because this person is the only one with whom he can establish any sort of rapport. He consequently focuses his attention on this English-speaking member of the group when, in fact, that person is the lowest-ranking of the group, e.g. an export trainee who just happens to have spent time abroad. By concentrating on him, the visitor would simply be wasting a lot of breath; more important, in a status-conscious company, he would also be violating the hierarchical standards of conduct and snubbing the *real* powers-that-be.

— 49 —

Lesson 4

Examples of the benefits of knowing Japanese while in Japan could fill an entire text. Suffice it to say at this point, however, that in Japan—as anywhere else in the world—a little respect for the language and customs goes a long way. Whatever time and effort you spend in overcoming your own resistance (or that of your head office) to the study of the Japanese language is bound to prove a very worthwhile investment.

Lesson

5

Visiting I

OBJECTIVES

1   to indicate where you are going.

2   to indicate by what means you are going there.

3   to indicate how long it takes to get there.

4   to discuss how long you'll be in a certain place.

5   to learn the days of the week.

Lesson 5

TARGET EXPRESSIONS AND PATTERNS

1 I'm going to «place X».   **Watakushi wa «X» e ikimasu.**

2 (I)'ll go on «day X».   **«X»-yoobi ni ikimasu.**

3 (I)'ll go at «time X» o'clock.   **«X»-ji ni ikimasu.**

4 (I)'ll go by «transportaion X».   **«X» de ikimasu.**

5 from «place X» to «place Y».   **«X» kara «Y» made.**

6 It takes about «length of time X». **«X»-jikan gurai kakarimasu.**

SITUATION

At Mr. Brown's office, Mr. Brown tells Ms. Yamada he'll visit Nikkeiren (Japan Federation of Employers' Associations) next Monday. They discuss how he is going there, how long it takes to get there from Mr. Brown's house and how long he'll be there.

DIALOGUE

	Monday	getsuyoobi
	to (someplace)	e
	Nikkeiren	Nikkeeren
	to go	ikimasu
	noon	hiru
	here	koko
Brown	to come	kimasu

1	(I)'ll go to Nikkeiren Monday morning, so (I)'ll come here at about noon.	**Getsuyoobi no asa, Nikkeeren e ikimasu kara, hirugoro koko e kimasu.**

	car	kuruma
	by	de
Yamada	to go	irasshaimasu (respectful)

2	Are (you) going by car?	**Kuruma de irasshaimasu ka.**

— 52 —

Lesson 5

	taxi	**takushii**
	about how long?	**donogurai**
Brown	to take (in time)	**kakarimasu**

3 (I)'ll go by taxi, but about how long does it take (to go there)?

Takushii de ikimasu ga, donogurai kakarimasu ka.

	a place name in Tokyo	**Aoyama**
	from	**kara**
Yamada	to	**made**

4 (You) go from Aoyama to Maruno-uchi, so it takes about 20 minutes.

Aoyama kara Marunouchi made desu kara, nijup-pun gurai kakari-masu.

	at	**ni**
Yamada	(at) what time?	**nan-ji ni**

5 What time are (you) going there?

Nan-ji ni irasshaimasu ka.

Brown	at 9:30	**ku-ji han ni**

6 (I)'ll go at 9:30.

Ku-ji han ni ikimasu.

Yamada	to be, stay	**irasshaimasu** (respectful)

7 About how long are (you) going to stay there?

Donogurai achira ni irasshaimasu ka.

Brown

8 (I'll be there) for about 2 hours.

Ni-jikan gurai desu yo.

Yamada

9 (I) understand.

Wakarimashita.

— 53 —

Lesson 5

JAPANESE WRITING

1 ブラウン： 月曜日の朝、日経連へ行きますから、昼ごろここへ来ます。
2 山　　田： 車でいらっしゃいますか。
3 ブラウン： タクシーで行きますが、どのぐらいかかりますか。
4 山　　田： 青山から丸の内までですから、二十分ぐらいかかります。
5 山　　田： 何時にいらっしゃいますか。
6 ブラウン： 九時半に行きます。
7 山　　田： どのぐらいあちらにいらっしゃいますか。
8 ブラウン： 二時間ぐらいですよ。
9 山　　田： わかりました。

READING

1 **Brown:** **Getsuyoobi no asa, Nikkeeren e ikimasu kara, hirugoro koko e kimasu.**
2 **Yamada:** **Kuruma de irasshaimasu ka.**
3 **Brown:** **Takushii de ikimasu ga, donogurai kakarimasu ka.**
4 **Yamada:** **Aoyama kara Marunouchi made desu kara, nijup-pun gurai kakarimasu.**
5 **Yamada:** **Nan-ji ni irasshaimasu ka.**
6 **Brown:** **Ku-ji han ni ikimasu.**
7 **Yamada:** **Donogurai achira ni irasshaimasu ka.**
8 **Brown:** **Ni-jikan gurai desu yo.**
9 **Yamada:** **Wakarimashita.**

ADDITIONAL USEFUL EXPRESSIONS

1　　　　　　　　　　day before yesterday　　**ototoi**

A: (I) went to JETRO the day before yesterday.	**Ototoi Jetoro e ikimashita yo.**

　　　　　　　　　　by means of what?　　**nan de**

B: How [lit. By means of what] did (you) go?	**Nan de irasshaimashita ka.**

Lesson 5

	subway	**chikatetsu**

A:	(I) went by subway.	**Chikatetsu de ikimashita.**

2

	this week	**konshuu**
	Sunday	**nichiyoobi**
	on Sunday	**nichiyoobi ni**

A:	(I)'ll go to Osaka this Sunday [lit. on Sunday of this week].	**Konshuu no nichiyoobi ni Oosaka e ikimasu.**

	day after tomorrow	**asatte**
	airplane	**hikooki**

B:	It's the day after tomorrow, isn't it? Are (you) going by plane?	**Asatte desu ne.** **Hikooki de ikimasu ka.**

Shinkansen (Super-Express/Bullet Train)	**shinkansen**

A:	No. (I)'ll go by Shinkansen.	**Iie, Shinkansen de ikimasu.**

3

	when?	**itsu**

A:	When did Mr. Brown come here?	**Buraun-san wa itsu koko e kimashita ka.**

	last week	**senshuu**
	Saturday	**doyoobi**
	to come	**irasshaimasu** (respectful)

B:	(He) came last Saturday [lit. on Saturday of last week].	**Senshuu no doyoobi ni irasshaimashita.**

4

	next week	**raishuu**
	Tuesday	**kayoobi**
	to go back, return	**kaerimasu**

A:	I'll go back to Detroit Tuesday next week.	**Watakushi wa raishuu no kayoobi ni Detoroito e kaerimasu.**
B:	By what means will (you) go?	**Nan de irasshaimasu ka.**

Lesson 5

ship	**hune**
there, that place	**soko**
bus	**basu**
local train	**densha**
train (for long distance)	**kisha**

A:	(I)'ll go from Yokohama to San Francisco by ship, but from there (I)'ll go by bus/local train/train.	**Yokohama kara Sanhuranshisuko made hune de ikimasu ga, soko kara basu/densha/kisha de ikimasu.**

5

from what time?	**nan-ji kara**
till what time?	**nan-ji made**

A:	How long [lit. from what time till what time] are (you) in (your) office?	**Nan-ji kara nan-ji made jimusho ni irasshaimasu ka.**
B:	(I)'m (there) from 9:00 till 5:00.	**Ku-ji kara go-ji made imasu.**

6

A:	Is Mr. Brown in?	**Buraun-san wa imasu ka.**

by 2:30	**ni-ji han made ni**

B:	(He) isn't but (he)'ll come by 2:30.	**Imasen ga, ni-ji han made ni kimasu.**

7

what day of the week?	**nan-yoobi**

A:	What day of the week is it today?	**Kyoo wa nan-yoobi desu ka.**

Wednesday	**suiyoobi**

B:	It is Wednesday.	**Suiyoobi desu yo.**

Thursday	**mokuyoobi**

C:	It is Thursday.	**Mokuyoobi desu yo.**

Friday	**kin'yoobi**

D:	It is Friday.	**Kin'yoobi desu yo.**

Lesson 5

NOTES

1 Particles: **e** 'to,' **kara** 'from,' **made** 'as far as, until,' **ni** 'at, on, in,' **made ni** 'by' and **de** 'by means of'

A) Particle **e** denotes direction and is equivalent to the English 'to,' as in 'to (a place).'

(Subject) **wa**	(Place) **e**	(verb)
Buraun-san wa	**Oosaka e**	**ikimasu.**
Mr. Brown is going to Osaka.		

Examples:
 a) **Sumisu-san wa raishuu Tookyoo *e* ikimasu.**
   "Mr. Smith will go to Tokyo next week."
 b) **Kare wa asatte Igirisu *e* kaerimasu.**
   "He'll go back to England the day after tomorrow."
 c) **Itsu Nihon *e* irasshaimashita ka.**
   "When did (you) come to Japan?"

B) Particle **kara** following a noun means 'from' and is used to refer to a starting point or a starting time.

Examples:
 a) **Ano hito wa Shikago *kara* kimashita.**
   "(He) came from Chicago."
 b) **Gogo ichi-ji *kara* koko ni imasu.**
   "(I)'ll be here from 1:00 p.m. (on)."
 c) **Doko *kara* irasshaimashita ka.**
   "Where did (you) come from?"

C) Particle **made** means 'as far as (a place)' or 'up to and including (a place or time).'

Examples:
 a) **Ashita Kyooto *made* ikimasu.**
   "(I)'ll go as far as Kyoto tomorrow."
 b) **Kinoo hiru *made* kaisha ni imashita.**
   "Yesterday (I) was in the company until noon."
 c) **Aoyama kara Marunouchi *made* takushii de donogurai kakari-masu ka.**
   "About how long does it take (to go) from Aoyama to Marunouchi by taxi?"

D) Particle **ni** following time expressions is used to indicate the time when something happens.

Examples:
 a) **Yamamoto-san wa kyoo ku-ji *ni* koko e kimasu.**
   "Mr. Yamamoto will come here at 9:00 today."
 b) **Jakku wa raishuu no kayoobi *ni* Nihon e kimasu.**
   "Jack will come to Japan Tuesday next week."
 c) **Konban juu-ji ni Detoroito no shachoo ni denwa o kakemasu.**
   "(I)'ll phone the president in Detroit at 10:00 tonight."

— 57 —

Lesson 5

A time expression followed by **goro** 'about' occurs with or without **ni**. Thus, **Kare wa ni-ji goro (ni) kimasu yo.** "He'll come (at) about 2:00." Note that the following time expressions are always used without **ni:**

ima	now	**kyoo**	today
kesa	this morning	**kinoo**	yesterday
konban	this evening	**ashita**	tomorrow
mainichi	everyday	**konshuu**	this week

These words listed above are called 'time words'; they can occur independently (without particle **ni**) as adverbial expressions.

E) Particle **made ni** means 'by «a certain time»'

Examples: a) **Ashita go-ji *made ni* denwa-shimasu.**
　　　　　　　"(I)'ll call (you) tomorrow by 5:00."
　　　　　b) **Hiru goro *made ni* Nikkeeren e ikimasu.**
　　　　　　　"(I)'ll go to Nikkeiren by around noon."
　　　　　c) **Shachoo wa Detoroito kara kin'yoobi *made ni* kimasu.**
　　　　　　　"The president will come from Detroit by Friday."

F) Particle **de** 'by means of' is used to indicate the means by which an action is accomplished. In this lesson, **de** refers only to the means of transportation, but other cases will be introduced later.

Examples: a) **Takada-san wa mainichi kuruma *de* jimusho e kimasu.**
　　　　　　　"Mr. Takada comes to (his) office by car everyday."
　　　　　b) **Koko kara Toranomon made nan *de* irasshaimasu ka.**
　　　　　　　"How will (you) go to Toranomon from here?"
　　　　　c) **Watakushi wa Oosaka e shinkansen *de* ikimasu ga, hikooki *de* kaerimasu.**
　　　　　　　"(I)'ll go to Osaka by Shinkansen, but (I)'ll come back by plane."

2 Polite Expression: **irasshaimasu**

Irasshaimasu is a polite form used to exalt the position of the sentence subject. It can mean (a) 'is/are/will be' (b) 'go(es)/will go' and (c) 'come(s)/will come.' In other words, it is a polite equivalent of **imasu, ikimasu** and **kimasu.**

Examples: a) **Shachoo wa ima jimusho ni *irasshaimasu.* (=imasu)**
　　　　　　　"The president is now in his office."
　　　　　b) **Itsu Kyooto e *irasshaimashita* ka. (=ikimashita)**
　　　　　　　"When did (you) go to Kyoto?"
　　　　　c) **Buchoo wa ashita kaisha e *irasshaimasen* yo. (=kimasen)**
　　　　　　　"The general manager will not come to the company tomorrow."
　　　　　Note that: **irasshaimasu** CANNOT BE USED TO REFER TO ONESELF!

— 58 —

Lesson 5

3 Sentence Particle **ne**

Ne occurs at the end of the sentence and is used to invite the listener's agreement or acknowledgment, meaning "Do you agree with me?" or "Isn't that right?"

PRACTICE

1 Response Practice

Example:	Teacher:	**Doko e ikimasu ka. /Marunouchi/**
		"Where are (you) going?" /Marunouchi/
	Student:	**Marunouchi e ikimasu.**
		"(I)'m going to Marunouchi."

a) Doko e ikimasu ka. /Keedanren/   Keedanren e ikimasu.
b) Doko e ikimasu ka. /Detoroito/   Detoroito e ikimasu.
c) Doko e ikimasu ka. /honsha/   Honsha e ikimasu.
d) Doko e ikimashita ka.   Takada-san no otaku e ikimashita.
   /Takada-san no otaku/
e) Doko e ikimashita ka.   Oosaka no shisha e ikimashita.
   /Oosaka no shisha/

2 Response Practice

Example:	Teacher:	**Nikkeeren e nan de ikimasu ka. /chikatetsu/**
		"By what means are you going to Nikkeiren?" /subway/
	Student:	**Chikatetsu de ikimasu.**
		"(I)'m going (there) by subway."

a) Jimusho e nan de ikimasu ka.   Kuruma de ikimasu.
   /kuruma/
b) Nyuuyooku e nan de ikimasu ka.   Hikooki de ikimasu.
   /hikooki/
c) Kyooto e nan de ikimashita ka.   Shinkansen de ikimashita.
   /shinkansen/
d) Sanhuranshisuko e nan de   Hune de ikimashita.
   ikimashita ka. /hune/
e) Toranomon e nan de ikimasu ka.   Basu de ikimasu.
   /basu/
f) Shikago e nan de ikimasu ka.   Kisha de ikimasu.
   /kisha/
g) Yokohama e nan de ikimasu ka.   Densha de ikimasu.
   /densha/

— 59 —

Lesson 5

3 Response Practice

Example: Teacher: **Itsu Oosaka e ikimasu ka. /asatte/**
                "When are (you) going to Osaka?" /day after tomorrow/
         Student: **Asatte Oosaka e ikimasu.**
                "(I)'m going to Osaka the day after tomorrow."

a) **Itsu Amerika e kaerimasu ka. /raishuu no doyoobi ni/**
   Raishuu no doyoobi ni Amerika e kaerimasu.

b) **Itsu Jetoro e ikimasu ka. /konban/**
   Konban Jetoro e ikimasu.

c) **Itsu Jakku wa Nihon e kimasu ka. /ashita no asa/**
   Ashita no asa (Jakku wa) Nihon e kimasu.

d) **Itsu Keedanren e ikimashita ka. /senshuu no getsuyoobi ni/**
   Senshuu no getsuyoobi ni Keedanren e ikimashita.

e) **Itsu Yamamoto-san wa kimasu ka. /kyoo no hiru goro/**
   (Yamamoto-san wa) Kyoo no hiru goro kimasu.

f) **Nan-ji ni Tanaka-san wa kaerimasu ka. /go-ji ni/**
   (Tanaka-san wa) Go-ji ni kaerimasu.

g) **Nan-ji ni jimusho e kimasu ka. /taitee hachi-ji goro/**
   Taitee hachi-ji goro jimusho e kimasu.

h) **Nan-ji ni Detoroito e denwa o kakemasu ka. /juuichi-ji ni/**
   Juuichi-ji ni Detoroito e denwa o kakemasu.

i) **Kinoo nan-ji ni otaku e kaerimashita ka. /ni-ji goro/**
   Kinoo ni-ji goro uchi e kaerimashita.

j) **Kesa nan-ji ni kaisha e kimashita ka. /ku-ji han goro/**
   Kesa ku-ji han goro kaisha e kimashita.

4 Response Practice

Example: Teacher: **Otaku kara jimusho made donogurai kakarimasu ka. /sanjup-pun gurai/**
                "About how long does it take from your house to the office?"
         Student: **Sanjup-pun gurai kakarimasu.**
                "It takes about 30 minutes."

a) **Tookyoo kara Oosaka made donogurai kakarimasu ka. /shinkansen de san-jikan gurai/**
   Shinkansen de san-jikan gurai kakarimasu.

b) **Nyuuyooku kara Shikago made hikooki de dono gurai kakarimashita ka. /ni-jikan/**
   Ni-jikan gurai kakarimashita.

Lesson 5

5 Level Practice

Directions: Express the following sentences in a more polite form.

Example: Teacher: **Tanaka-san wa ashita kimasu.**
"Mr. Tanaka will come tomorrow."
Student: **Tanaka-san wa ashita irasshaimasu.**

a) **Takada-buchoo wa imasu ka.**   **Takada-buchoo wa irasshaimasu ka.**
b) **Itsu Amerika e ikimasu ka.**   **Itsu Amerika e irasshaimasu ka.**
c) **Ashita kaisha e kimasu ka.**   **Ashita kaisha e irasshaimasu ka.**
d) **Senshuu Kyooto e ikimashita ka.**   **Senshuu Kyooto e irasshaimashita ka.**
e) **Buraun-san wa san-ji made koko**   **Buraun-san wa san-ji made koko ni**
ni imashita.   **irasshaimashita.**

6 Communication Practice

Directions: Practice saying the days of the week, using the following patterns.

a) **Kyoo wa** ☐ **yoobi desu.**
b) **Ashita wa** ☐ **yoobi desu.**
c) **Asatte wa** ☐ **yoobi desu.**
d) **Kinoo wa** ☐ **yoobi deshita.**
e) **Ototoi wa** ☐ **yoobi deshita.**

7 Communication Practice

Directions: Tell the teacher where you are going or where you went.

Examples:
a) **Kyoo watakushi wa «place» e ikimasu.**
b) **Kinoo watakushi wa «place» e ikimashita.**
c) **Ashita watakushi wa «place» e ikimasu.**
d) **Senshuu no nichiyoobi watakushi wa «means» de «place» e ikimashita.**
e) **Raishuu no doyoobi watakushi wa «means» de «place» e ikimasu.**

8 Communication Practice

Directions: Teacher asks you at what time and how you came here and how long it took you.

Example: Teacher: **Kyoo nan-ji ni koko e kimashita ka.**
Student: **«time» ni kimashita.**
Teacher: **Nan de kimashita ka.**
Student: **«means» de kimashita.**
Teacher: **Koko made donogurai kakarimashita ka.**
Student: **«place» kara koko made «time» gurai kakarimashita.**

— 61 —

Lesson 5

EXERCISES

Give the teacher the following information.
1 Manager Smith will come to Japan next Tuesday.
2 Ms. Yamada is in the office from about 8:30 until about 5:00.
3 You'll go to Osaka the day after tomorrow by plane.
4 It takes 3 hours from Tokyo to Kyoto by the Shinkansen.
5 Mr. Yamamoto will come to your house this evening.
6 Yesterday wasn't Wednesday. It was Thursday.
7 It takes about 40 minutes from your house to Marunouchi by bus, but it takes about 15 minutes by car.
8 Mr. Brown is going back to America next Sunday by ship.

Model Answers:

1 **Sumisu-kachoo wa raishuu no kayoobi ni Nihon e kimasu.**
2 **Yamada-san wa hachi-ji han kara go-ji made jimusho ni imasu.**
3 **Asatte hikooki de Oosaka e ikimasu.**
4 **Shinkansen de Tookyoo kara Kyooto made san-jikan kakarimasu.**
5 **Yamamoto-san wa konban uchi e kimasu.**
6 **Kinoo wa suiyoobi ja arimasen deshita. Mokuyoobi deshita.**
7 **Uchi kara Marunouchi made basu de yonjup-pun gurai kakarimasu ga, kuruma de (wa) juugo-hun gurai kakarimasu.**
8 **Buraun-san wa raishuu no nichiyoobi ni Amerika e hune de kaerimasu.**

Lesson 5

BUSINESS INFORMATION

Visiting

1   Prior to the Visit: Since surprise visits in Japan are seldom considered pleasant, you should always give advance warning to clients and associates if you plan on visiting them. In addition, if you are a first-time visitor, you should acquire some sort of introduction (紹介 **shookai**) before calling, even if it is from the International Department of the very firm you wish to visit. Direct dialing without prior introduction is seen as presumptuous in Japan and will most likely *not* lead to the direct results you may have come to expect in other countries.

2   Upon Arrival: Like everywhere else in the world, large organizations in Japan always have a central reception area to assist visitors. The department you wish to visit, however, will probably be unfamiliar ground. Unlike offices in Europe and the U.S., few Japanese companies provide separate compartments or neatly labeled private offices for their staff. Instead, most firms here adhere to the open space system (大部屋制度 **oobeya seedo**), which means that all members of a certain department—from the **buchoo** to the clerical staff—share one large open space (**oobeya**). This space can be as small as a modest living room or large enough to occupy the entire floor of a building. To ensure a smooth visit to such an **oobeya,** you should note the following points:

Visiting etiquette:

1) Remove coats and hats prior to entering the department.
2) Do not call out to the person you wish to speak to or charge up to his desk. Instead, wait discreetly near the entrance until someone (usually one of the clerical staff) attends to you. He or she will then notify your client of your presence, or show you to a waiting area.

Seating arrangements:

1) Senior personnel are seated nearest the window, at desks which usually face the rest of the staff.
2) Desks are arranged in rows which usually make up individual groups in a section (課 **ka**). A group chief (係長 **kakarichoo**) sits at the head of each row and reports in turn to the section manager (課長 **kachoo**).
3) Clerical staff sit near the entrance. Generally called the supporting staff (庶務係 **shomu-gakari**), they perform such "support" tasks (庶務 **shomu**) as providing supplies, preparing meeting rooms and coordinating inter-department communications.

On the following page is a layout of a typical **oobeya.** In this instance, Department A has 46 members, including a **buchoo,** a **jichoo,** 4 **kachoo** (including 1 **buchoo dairi**), 4 **kakarichoo** and 14 female **shomu-gakari** whose desks are marked with a "doughnut."

— 63 —

Lesson 5

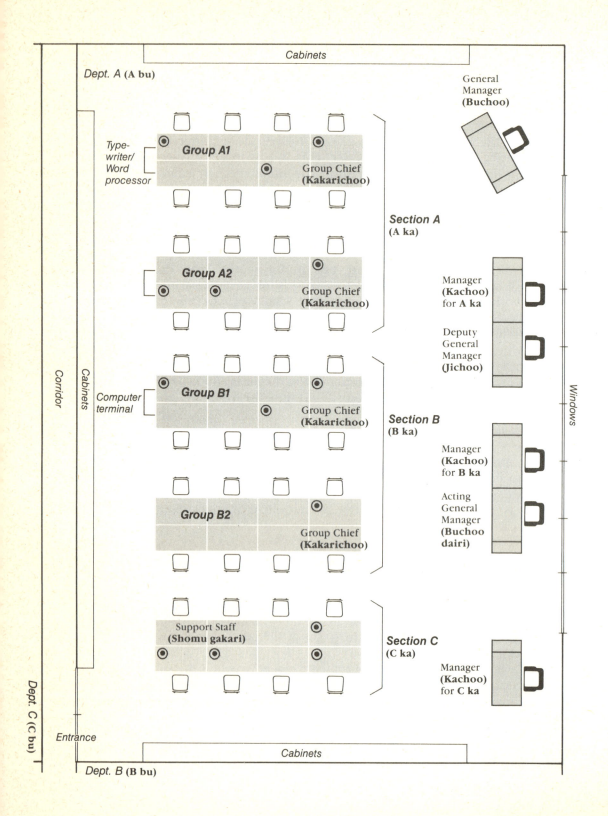

Lesson 6

Visiting II

OBJECTIVES

1 to give directions to taxi drivers.

2 to inquire about the price.

3 to talk with a receptionist.

4 to serve or receive a cup of tea.

5 to give the date.

Lesson 6

TARGET EXPRESSIONS AND PATTERNS

1   Please take (me) to «place X».   **«X» made onegai-shimasu.**

2   How much is (it)?   **Ikura desu ka.**

3   (I) have an appointment with Mr./Ms.   **«X» -san to yakusoku ga arimasu.**
    «name X».

4   (I) came on «day X» in «month Y».   **«Y» -gatsu «X» -ka/-nichi ni mairi-
                                              mashita.**

SITUATION

Mr. Brown goes to Nikkeiren by taxi to see Mr. Ohta of the International Division, to whom he had been introduced by Mr. Yamamoto at a party. Mr. Brown had made an appointment with Mr. Ohta at that time. Mr. Brown informs the receptionist of the purpose of his visit and is shown into the reception room.

DIALOGUE

Brown   (Mr. Brown gets into a taxi, and speaks to the driver.)

| **1** | Please take (me) to Marunouchi. | **Marunouchi made onegai-shimasu.** |

Driver   Tokyo Station   **Tookyoo-eki**

| **2** | (You) mean Tokyo Station? | **Tookyoo-eki desu ka.** |

Brown

| **3** | No. (I)'m going to Nikkeiren. | **Iie. Nikkeeren e ikimasu.** |

(The taxi arrives at Marunouchi.)

Driver   that (one) over there   **ano**
                          building   **biru**

| **4** | (Here) is Marunouchi. Nikkeiren is in that building over there. | **Marunouchi desu yo. Nikkeeren wa ano biru desu.** |

Brown   how much?   **ikura**

| **5** | How much is (it)? | **Ikura desu ka.** |

— 66 —

Lesson 6

Driver		950 yen	**kyuuhyaku-gojuu-en**

6	Well, (it)'s 950 yen.	**Eeto, kyuuhyaku-gojuu-en desu.**

Brown		1,000 yen	**sen-en**

7	Here [lit. Yes], please (let me pay) with 1,000 yen.	**Hai, sen-en de onegai-shimasu.**

Driver	50 yen change	**gojuu-en** **tsuri, otsuri** (polite)

8	50 yen is your change.	**Gojuu-en otsuri desu.**

Brown

9	Thanks.	**Doomo.**

(Mr. Brown comes to the reception desk of Nikkeiren.)

Brown	International Division Mr. Ohta with appointment to have	**kokusai-bu** **Oota-san** **to** **yakusoku** **arimasu**

10	I'm Brown from P & C (Ltd). (I)'ve an appointment with Mr. Ohta of the International Division.	**Watakushi Pii-ando-shii no Buraun desu. Kokusai-bu no Oota-san to yakusoku ga arimasu.**

Receptionist

11	Please wait a while.	**Shooshoo omachi-kudasai.**

(The receptionist calls Mr. Ohta.)

Receptionist	soon to come	**sugu** **mairimasu** (modest)

12	He will be (with you) in a minute. [lit. Ohta will come soon.]	**Oota wa sugu mairimasu.**

Lesson 6

(Mr. Ohta arrives.)

Ohta welcome! — **yoku irasshaimashita**
this way — **kochira**

13 Mr. Brown, welcome! Please come this way.	**Buraun-san, yoku irasshaimashita. Doozo kochira e.**

Brown thank you — **osoreirimasu** (modest)
[lit. (I)'m much obliged]

14 Thank you.	**Osoreirimasu.**

(Mr. Ohta guides Mr. Brown to the reception room, and as they sit down, an employee brings two cups of tea.)

Ohta tea — **ocha** (polite)

15 Please (have) some tea.	**Ocha doozo.**

Brown to receive, accept — **itadakimasu** (modest)

16 Thank you. [lit. (I)'ll drink (it).]	**Itadakimasu.**

Ohta

17 When did (you) come to Japan, Mr. Brown?	**Buraun-san wa itsu Nihon e irasshai-mashita ka.**

Brown May [lit. fifth month] — **go-gatsu**
the second day of the month — **hutsu-ka**

18 (I) came (to Japan) May 2nd.	**Go-gatsu hutsu-ka ni mairimashita.**

Ohta one month — **ik-kagetsu**
one month ago — **ik-kagetsu mae**

19 It was about one month ago, wasn't it?	**Ik-kagetsu gurai mae desu ne.**

Brown

20 Yes, that's right. [lit. it is so.]	**Ee, soo desu.**

Lesson 6

JAPANESE WRITING

1　ブラウン：　丸の内までお願いします。

2　ドライバー：　東京駅ですか。

3　ブラウン：　いいえ。日経連へ行きます。

4　ドライバー：　丸の内ですよ。日経連はあのビルです。

5　ブラウン：　いくらですか。

6　ドライバー：　ええと、九百五十円です。

7　ブラウン：　はい、千円でお願いします。

8　ドライバー：　五十円、おつりです。

9　ブラウン：　どうも。

10　ブラウン：　私、ピー・アンド・シーのブラウンです。
国際部の太田さんと約束があります。

11　レセプショニスト：　少々お待ちください。

12　レセプショニスト：　太田はすぐまいります。

13　太　　田：　ブラウンさん、よくいらっしゃいました。どうぞこちらへ。

14　ブラウン：　恐れ入ります。

15　太　　田：　お茶どうぞ。

16　ブラウン：　いただきます。

17　山　　田：　ブラウンさんはいつ日本へいらっしゃいましたか。

18　ブラウン：　五月二日にまいりました。

19　太　　田：　一か月ぐらいまえですね。

20　ブラウン：　ええ、そうです。

READING

1	Brown:	Marunouchi made onegai-shimasu.
2	Driver:	Tookyoo-eki desu ka.
3	Brown:	Iie. Nikkeeren e ikimasu.
4	Driver:	Marunouchi desu yo. Nikkeeren wa ano biru desu.
5	Brown:	Ikura desu ka.
6	Driver:	Eeto, kyuuhyaku-gojuu-en desu.
7	Brown:	Hai, sen-en de onegai-shimasu.
8	Driver:	Gojuu-en otsuri desu.
9	Brown:	Doomo.
10	Brown:	Watakushi Pii-ando-shii no Buraun desu. Kokusai-bu no Oota-san to yakusoku ga arimasu.
11	Receptionist:	Shooshoo omachi-kudasai.
12	Receptionist:	Oota wa sugu mairimasu.
13	Ohta:	Buraun-san, yoku irasshaimashita. Doozo kochira e.
14	Brown:	Osoreirimasu.
15	Ohta:	Ocha doozo.
16	Brown:	Itadakimasu.
17	Ohta:	Buraun-san wa itsu Nihon e irasshaimashita ka.
18	Brown:	Go-gatsu hutsu-ka ni mairimashita.
19	Ohta:	Ik-kagetsu gurai mae desu ne.
20	Brown:	Ee, soo desu.

Lesson 6

ADDITIONAL USEFUL EXPRESSIONS

1 On the phone

A: Is Mr. Ohta in?	**Oota-san, irasshaimasu ka.**

	to be	**orimasu** (modest)

B: Yes, (he) is. Just a moment, please. [lit. Please wait a while.]	**Hai, orimasu. Shooshoo omachi-kudasai.**

2 At the parking place

	this (one)	**kono**
	this car	**kono kuruma**

A: Is this car Mr. Tanaka's car?	**Kono kuruma wa Tanaka-san no kuruma desu ka.**

	that (one)	**sono**
	that car	**sono kuruma**

B: No, that's wrong. (His car) is that car.	**Iie, chigaimasu yo. Sono kuruma desu yo.**

3 In the reception room

	coffee	**koohii**
	would you care for?	**ikaga desu ka**

A: Would you care for some coffee?	**Koohii wa ikaga desu ka.**

	don't bother	**okamai naku**

B: Please don't bother.	**Doozo okamainaku.**

	cigarette, tobacco	**tabako**

A: Please have a cigarette.	**Tabako doozo.**

	to be fine	**kekkoo desu**

B: No, thank you. [lit. (I)'m fine (as I am).]	**Iie, kekko desu.**

— 70 —

Lesson 6

4 At the office

	until when?	**itsu made**

A:	How long will (you) be in Japan? [lit. Until about when will (you) be in Japan?]	**Itsu goro made Nihon ni irasshai-masu ka.**

	the year 1990	**Sen-kyuuhyaku-kyuujuu-nen**
	September	**ku-gatsu**

B:	(I)'ll be (here) till September, 1990.	**Sen-kyuuhyaku-kyuujuu-nen no ku-gatsu made orimasu.**

	three years	**san-nen**
	from now, future	**saki**

A:	It is three years from now, isn't it?	**San-nen saki desu ne.**
B:	Yes, that's right.	**Ee, soo desu.**

5 At the reception desk

A:	Is Mr. Takada of the International Communication Department in?	**Kokusai-kooryuu-bu no Takada-san irasshaimasu ka.**

	appointment	**oyakusoku** (respectful)

B:	Do (you) have an appointment?	**Oyakusoku desu ka.**
A:	No, (I) don't have an appointment.	**Iie, yakusoku wa arimasen.**
B:	Please wait a while.	**Shooshoo omachi-kudasai.**

6 what date?/how many days? **nan-nichi**

A:	What date is it today?	**Kyoo wa nan-nichi desu ka.**
B:	It [lit. Today] is the 2nd.	**Kyoo wa hutsu-ka desu yo.**

Lesson 6

7

	this year	**kotoshi**
	last year	**kyonen***
	next year	**rainen***
	what year?/how many years?	**nan-nen**
	what year in the Showa Era?	**Shoowa nan-nen**

A:	What year in the Showa Era is this year?	**Kotoshi wa Shoowa nan-nen desu ka.**
B:	This [lit. This year] is Showa 62.	**Kotoshi wa Shoowa rokujuuni-nen desu.**

Does not appear in sample dialogue. Introduced for reference only.

REFERENCE

1 Months of the year **(-gatsu)**

ichi-gatsu	January	**shichi-gatsu**	July
ni-gatsu	February	**hachi-gatsu**	August
san-gatsu	March	**ku-gatsu**	September
shi-gatsu	April	**juu-gatsu**	October
go-gatsu	May	**juuichi-gatsu**	November
roku-gatsu	June	**juuni-gatsu**	December

2 Number of months **(-kagetsu)**

ik-kagetsu	1 month	**rok-kagetsu**	6 months
ni-kagetsu	2 months	**juk-kagetsu**	10 months
san-kagetsu	3 months	**nijuuyon-kagetsu**	24 months

3 The dates and the number of days **(-ka/-nichi)**

tsuitachi	the first day of the month
ichi-nichi	one day
hutsu-ka	the 2nd, or 2 days
mik-ka	the 3rd, or 3 days
yok-ka	the 4th, or 4 days
itsu-ka	the 5th, or 5 days
mui-ka	the 6th, or 6 days
nano-ka	the 7th, or 7 days
yoo-ka	the 8th, or 8 days
kokono-ka	the 9th, or 9 days
too-ka	the 10th, or 10 days
juuichi-nichi	the 11th, or 11 days
juuni-nichi	the 12th, or 12 days
juusan-nichi	the 13th, or 13 days
juuyok-ka	the 14th, or 14 days
juugo-nichi	the 15th, or 15 days
juuroku-nichi	the 16th, or 16 days

— 72 —

Lesson 6

juushichi-nichi	the 17th, or 17 days
juuhachi-nichi	the 18th, or 18 days
juuku-nichi	the 19th, or 19 days
hatsu-ka	the 20th, or 20 days
nijuuichi-nichi	the 21st, or 21 days
nijuuni-nichi	the 22nd, or 22 days
nijuusan-nichi	the 23rd, or 23 days
nijuuyok-ka	the 24th, or 24 days
nijuugo-nichi	the 25th, or 25 days
nijuuroku-nichi	the 26th, or 26 days
nijuushichi-nichi	the 27th, or 27 days
nijuuhachi-nichi	the 28th, or 28 days
nijuuku-nichi	the 29th, or 29 days
sanjuu-nichi	the 30th, or 30 days
sanjuuichi-nichi	the 31st, or 31 days

4 The years and the number of years (-nen)

ichi-nen	1 year
gan-nen	the year 1
ni-nen	the year 2, or 2 years
san-nen	the year 3, or 3 years
go-nen	the year 5, or 5 years
juu-nen	the year 10, or 10 years
hyaku-nen	the year 100, or 100 years
sen-nen	the year 1000, or 1000 years
Sen-kyuuhyaku-hachijuuyo-nen	the year 1984, or 1984 years.

NOTES

1 Subject Particle **ga**

Ga is a particle indicating the subject of the sentence. Please note, however, that the subject of the Japanese sentence does not always coincide with the subject of the English sentence. In the sentence **Kokusai-bu no Oota-san to yakusoku ga arimasu** (Sentence 10, in the DIALOGUE of this lesson), **arimasu** is translated as '(I) have.' The literal meaning of **arimasu** is '(something) exists,' and the more literal English equivalent would be: "There is an appointment with Mr. Ohta of the International Division." Accordingly, the particle **ga** is used after **yakusoku** to indicate it is the subject of the sentence.

As you have learned, the particle **wa** also indicates the subject of the sentence. Unlike **ga,** however, **wa** refers to the general topic of the sentence and means 'as for.'

Compare: **Tanaka-san *ga* kimashita.**   "Mr. Tanaka came."
                                              and
            Tanaka-san *wa* kimashita.   "As for Mr. Tanaka, he came."

Generally speaking, **ga** is used to stress the subject and **wa** is used rather to emphasize the predicate.

— 73 —

Lesson 6

Compare: **a) Sumisu-san *ga* shachoo desu.**
"MR. SMITH is the president." (It tells us who the president is.)
and
b) Sumisu-san *wa* shachoo desu.
"Mr. Smith is THE PRESIDENT." (It tells us what title he has.)

In negative sentences, more important information is in the predicate part, so **wa** is usually used to indicate the subject of the sentence.

Compare: **Yamada-san *ga* ikimasu.**   "MS. YAMADA will go."
and
Yamada-san *wa* ikimasen.   "Ms. Yamada will NOT GO."

Arimasu always refers to the existence of something inanimate, while **imasu** is used to indicate the existence of something animate.

Examples: **a) Kuruma ga *arimasu* ka.**
"Do you have a car? [lit. Is there a car?]"
b) Nikkeeren wa Marunouchi ni *arimasu*.
"Nikkeiren is in Marunouchi."
c) Buraun-san wa ima Tookyoo-eki ni *imasu*.
"Mr. Brown is in Tokyo Station now."
d) Yamamoto-san wa uchi ni *imasu* ka.
"Is Mr. Yamamoto in?"

2 Kono/sono/ano

Kono/sono/ano are "restricted" words and cannot be used by themselves. They always modify the noun that directly follows.
Kono refers to an object/person located near the speaker. **Sono** refers to an object/person located near the person addressed. **Ano,** already introduced in Lesson 2 (i.e. **ano hito** 'that person' or 'he/she') refers to an object/person located at some distance from both the speaker and the person addressed.

3 Polite Expressions: **mairimasu** and **orimasu**

In polite speech, a modest verb **mairimasu,** usually refers to the speaker himself or to members of the speaker's group. It has two meanings: 'to come' and 'to go.' **Orimasu** is also a modest verb, meaning 'to be (located).'
Please study the following chart carefully:

Meaning	Formal Plain	Formal Polite	
		Respectful	Modest
be/will be, stay(s)/will stay	**imasu**	**irasshaimasu**	**orimasu**
go(es)/will go	**ikimasu**	**irasshaimasu**	**mairimasu**
come(s)/will come	**kimasu**	**irasshaimasu**	**mairimasu**

4 Time Counters: **-ka/-nichi, -getsu, -kagetsu** and **-nen**

By using **-ka/-nichi,** the Japanese name the days of the month and count the number of

— 74 —

Lesson 6

days. It is combined with all Japanese origin numerals (2 through 10, and 20). The first day of the month is an exception for which the term **tsuitachi** is used.

Japanese origin numerals		The day of the month/days
hito	(1)	**(tsuitachi)**
huta	(2)	**hutsu-ka**
mi	(3)	**mik-ka**
yo	(4)	**yok-ka**
itsu	(5)	**itsu-ka**
mu	(6)	**mui-ka**
nana	(7)	**nano-ka**
ya	(8)	**yoo-ka**
kokono	(9)	**kokono-ka**
too	(10)	**too-ka**
hata	(20)	**hatsu-ka**

Note: Just memorize the days of the month.
-**gatsu** combined with numerals shows the calendar months.
-**kagetsu** following numerals counts the number of months.
-**nen** combined with numerals names the years and counts the number of the years.

5 Idiomatic Expressions
a) **Osoreirimasu** literally means '(I)'m much obliged,' but it is usually used as an extremely polite and formal way to express one's gratitude.
In another context, it is used to mean "I'm sorry" or "Excuse me." Thus, **Osoreirimasu ga, onamae wa?** "Excuse (me), but what is (your) name?"
b) **Itadakimasu** is commonly used by a guest when he begins to drink or eat.
c) **Doozo okamainaku** is an idiomatic expression used by a guest when he is served something (for example, tea, coffee, etc.) by the host; it means "Please don't bother," or "Don't go to any trouble."

6 The Years According to the Traditional Japanese System
Shoowa refers to the period of the present emperor's reign which started in 1926.
Shoowa 59 refers to the 59th year of the present emperor's reign.
The Japanese customarily refer to the reigning periods of the emperors when naming a certain year or a span of years. Historically, an emperor's reign had many era names, but in modern times emperors use only one era name for their period of reign. When a new emperor succeeds to the throne, a new era begins. If an emperor passes away within a certain year, the new emperor's reign begins in that same year as well. Thus the end of the Taisho Era **(Taishoo 15)** became **Shoowa 1.** (Note: Emperor Taisho passed away in 1926 and the present emperor ascended the throne in the same year.) To figure out the year in Showa terms, substract 25 from the Western calendar year.

Reference: Meiji Era 1868—1912
Taisho Era 1912—1926
Showa Era 1926—

— 75 —

Lesson 6

PRACTICE

1 Days of the month

Directions: Please fill in the blanks and, to practice pronunciation, repeat after the teacher.

1st:	**tsuitachi**	11th:	**juuichi-nichi**	21st:	**nijuuichi-nichi**
2nd:	_____	12th:	_____	22nd:	_____
3rd:	**mik-ka**	13th:	_____	23rd:	_____
4th:	**yok-ka**	14th:	**juuyok-ka**	24th:	**nijuuyok-ka**
5th:	_____	15th:	_____	25th:	_____
6th:	**mui-ka**	16th:	_____	26th:	_____
7th:	**nano-ka**	17th:	**juushichi-nichi**	27th:	_____
8th:	**yoo-ka**	18th:	_____	28th:	_____
9th:	**kokono-ka**	19th:	_____	29th:	_____
10th:	**too-ka**	20th:	**hatsu-ka**	30th:	_____
				31st:	_____

2 Communication Practice

Directions: Give the exact date for each of the following, using a calendar if necessary.

Example: **Konshuu no kin'yoobi wa nano-ka desu.**
"This Friday is the 7th."

a) today
b) Tuesday last week
c) this Wednesday
d) tomorrow
e) Saturday next week
f) yesterday
g) Sunday last week
h) day after tomorrow
i) Monday next week
j) day before yesterday
k) this Thursday
l) Friday last week

3 Communication Practice

Directions: Teacher asks what date it is and you provide the answers listed below:

Example: Teacher: **Sore wa itsu deshita ka.** "When was it?"
Student: **Ni-gatsu mik-ka deshita.** "It was February 3rd."

a) September 9, last year
b) March 3, 1980
c) January 10, this year
d) August 14, Showa 20
e) July 4, 1776
f) June 20, 1935

4 Response Practice

Example: Teacher: **Kyoo yakusoku ga arimasu ka. /Yamamoto-san/**
"Do (you) have any appointment today?" /Mr. Yamamoto/

Student: **Ee, kyoo Yamamoto-san to yakusoku ga arimasu.**
"Yes, (I)'ve an appointment with Mr. Yamamoto."

— 76 —

Lesson 6

a) Konban yakusoku ga arimasu ka. /Nikkeeren no Oota-san/ — Ee, Nikkeeren no Oota-san to yakusoku ga arimasu.

b) Ashita yakusoku ga arimasu ka. /Sumisu-shachoo/ — Ee, Sumisu-shachoo to yakusoku ga arimasu.

c) Kyoo yakusoku ga arimasu ka. /Jetoro no Takada-san/ — Ee, Jetoro no Takada-san to yakusoku ga arimasu.

d) Konshuu no kinyoobi ni yakusoku ga arimasu ka. /Yamada-san/ — Ee, Yamada-san to yakusoku ga arimasu.

e) Assatte yakusoku ga arimasu ka. /honsha no Buraun-san/ — Ee, honsha no Buraun-san to yakusoku ga arimasu.

5 Level Practice

Directions: Change the teacher's sentences (Formal Plain) into "Formal Polite" sentences.

Examples: Teacher: **Tanaka-san wa san-ji ni kimasu.** (Formal Plain)
"Mr. Tanaka will come at 3."
Student: **Tanaka-san wa san-ji ni irasshaimasu.** (Formal Polite)

a) Buraun-san wa ashita Oosaka e ikimasu. — Buraun-san wa ashita Oosaka e irasshaimasu.

b) Nan-ji made koko ni imasu ka. — Nan-ji made koko ni irasshaimasu ka.

c) Kyoo Takada-san wa jimusho ni imasu ka. — Kyoo Takada-san wa jimusho ni irasshaimasu ka.

d) Watakushi wa asatte Keedanren e ikimasu. — Watakushi wa asatte Keedanren e mairimasu.

e) Shachoo, Yamamoto-san ga kimashita. — Shachoo, Yamamoto-san ga irasshaimashita.

f) Kinoo Buraun-san wa kaisha ni imasen deshita. — Kinoo Buraun-san wa kaisha ni irasshaimasen deshita.

g) Sengetsu Nihon e kimashita. — Sengetsu Nihon e mairimashita.

h) Kesa Tanaka-san wa koko e kimasen deshita. — Kesa Tanaka-san wa koko e irasshaimasen deshita.

6 Response Practice

Example: Teacher: **Itsu Nihon e irasshaimashita ka.** /kyonen no juu-gatsu/
"When did (you) come to Japan? /last October/"

Student: **Kyonen no juu-gatsu ni mairimashita.**
"(I) came (here) October last year."

a) Itsu Oosaka e irasshaimasu ka. /raishuu no kayoobi/ — Raishuu no kayoobi ni mairimasu.

b) Itsu Amerika e irasshaimashita ka. /sen-kyuuhyaku-rokujuuroku-nen/ — Sen-kyuuhyaku-rokujuuroku-nen ni mairimashita.

c) Itsu Tookyoo-eki e irasshaimasu ka. /sugu/ — Sugu mairimasu.

— 77 —

Lesson 6

d) Itsu Nikkeeren e irasshaimasu ka.
   /raigetsu no tsuitachi/

Raigetsu no tsuitachi ni mairimasu.

e) Itsu Jetoro e irasshaimashita ka.
   /ichi-gatsu too-ka/

Ichi-gatsu too-ka ni mairimashita.

EXERCISES

a) Find the appropriate Japanese expression for when you want to:

As a host:
1. Welcome Mr. Yamamoto to your house.
2. Tell him to come this way.
3. Ask if he would like to smoke.
4. Offer him tea.

As a guest:
1. Thank him (politely).
2. Thank him (casually).
3. Refuse a cigarette.
4. Tell your host not to go to any trouble (to offer tea).

b) Give the teacher the following information:
1. Mr. Ohta is a person of the International Division of Nikkeiren.
2. Keidanren is that building over there.
3. Mr. Brown came to Japan on the 2nd of this May.
4. Mr. Smith [lit. Manager Smith] came to Japan in November, 1983.
5. Ms. Yamada has an appointment with Mr. Takada this evening.
6. 1960 was Showa 35.
7. This car is Mr. Brown's car, but that car is your car.
8. Next Sunday is June 20.

Model Answers:

a)
1. Yoku irasshaimashita.
2. Doozo kochira e.
3. Tabako wa ikaga desu ka.
4. Ocha o doozo.

1. Arigatoo gozaimasu.
2. Doomo.
3. Kekkoo desu.
4. Doozo okamainaku.

b)
1. Oota-san wa Nikkeeren no Kokusai-bu no hito desu.
2. Keedanren wa ano biru desu.
3. Buraun-san wa kotoshi go-gatsu hutsu-ka ni Nihon e kimashita/irasshaimashita.
4. Sumisu-kachoo wa sen-kyuuhyaku-hachijuusan-nen juuichi-gatsu ni Nihon e/ni kimashita/irasshaimashita.
5. Yamada-san wa konban Takada-san to yakusoku ga arimasu.
6. Sen-kyuuhyaku-rokujuu-nen wa Shoowa sanjuugo-nen deshita.
7. Kono kuruma wa Buraun-san no kuruma desu ga, ano kuruma wa watakushi no kuruma desu.
8. Tsugi no nichiyoobi wa roku-gatsu hatsu-ka desu.

Lesson 6

BUSINESS INFORMATION

Polite Expressions (keigo)

As briefly mentioned in Lesson 2, the hierarchic nature of Japanese society is reflected in its language, which incorporates several different levels of speech or conversation. Each level is suitable for use in different social situations, as follows:

1) Informal Speech is used with those who are younger than you are, or in a more subordinate position. Although the informal level of speech occasionally appears in this text to create realistic dialogue, you should play it safe and avoid this level in polite circles so as not to accidentally offend others.

2) Formal Plain Speech is used with unfamiliar persons in everyday situations, or with familiar persons in formal situations. This is the predominant level of speech in Japanese society and the one most appropriate for normal business conversations.

3) Formal Polite Speech is used in formal situations, and the vocabulary and expressions of this level are referred to as keigo (敬語). There are two divisions of keigo:

a. **A respectful level,** used when addressing elders, high-ranking persons, or customers whom you wish to show respect to by elevating their status above your own.

b. **A modest level,** used to refer to yourself, or to members of your "group" (family, company, etc.), when speaking with others *not* included in the group. It is a humbling form of speech, i.e. a polite lowering of your own status in relation to that of the listener.

The modest level of polite speech is probably the most alien to overseas visitors, many of whom are accustomed to talking openly about their family or company, and are indeed expected to project self-confidence about their own achievements. However, in Japan, the etiquette-conscious individual is careful to behave in exactly the opposite manner. In the DIALOGUE, for example, the receptionist at Nikkeiren omits Mr. Ohta's title when speaking of him, and refers to him simply as "Ohta". She also uses the modest verb **"mairimasu"** to indicate that he will be coming shortly. This is because the receptionist and Mr. Ohta belong to the same group, i.e. Nikkeiren, whereas Mr. Brown is an "outsider." It is also not uncommon for a Japanese to introduce his younger brother to an important colleague by saying, **"Kore wa gutee** (愚弟) **desu,"** which literally means, "This is my stupid younger brother." Similarly, a polite Japanese businessman could refer to his own wife as **gusai** (愚妻) "my stupid, worthless wife"; to his house as **settaku** (拙宅) "my poor house"; and his company as **heesha** (弊社) "my humble company." Still, there are limits to one's modesty, and times when respect for superiors has to take precedence over humility before strangers. No matter what the circumstances, there is no term in Japanese that will permit you to ever refer to your own employer as "my stupid boss."

— 79 —

Lesson 6

The foreign businessman is encouraged to learn keigo as much as he can in order to ensure smooth relations with his Japanese counterparts. Faced with the prospect of having to master several levels of vocabulary and expression, in *addition* to memorizing titles and positions, you may at this point be ready to throw in the towel altogether. You should keep in mind, however, that the mastery of keigo is by no means an easy task even for the Japanese themselves. Most companies in fact provide their staff with a full training course in the use of keigo, complete with books which give detailed, case-by-case explanations about the keigo to use in different business situations.

The best advice, therefore, is not to despair. Review the chart provided below and do not hesitate to practice your Japanese whenever the occasion permits. Every attempt at the proper use of keigo will no doubt be recognized and appreciated by your Japanese colleagues who have struggled themselves to master it.

VERB (MEANING)	FORMAL POLITE		FORMAL PLAIN
	Used when addressing/speaking of respected elders, business customers		Used when speaking with persons you don't know well, or when conversing with familiar persons in formal situations (Predominant level of speech in everyday conversation).
	RESPECTFUL	MODEST	
suru (do)	**nasaimasu**	**itashimasu**	**shimasu**
iku (go)	**irasshaimasu**	**mairimasu/ ukagaimasu**	**ikimasu**
kuru (come)	**irasshaimasu/ oide-ni-narimasu**	**mairimasu**	**kimasu**
au (meet)	**oai-ni-narimasu**	**omeni-kakarimasu**	**aimasu**
matsu (wait)	**omachi-ni-narimasu**	**omachi-itashimasu**	**machimasu**
iru (am/is/are)	**irasshaimasu**	**orimasu**	**imasu**

Lesson 7

At the Office

OBJECTIVES

1   to ask or indicate where something is.

2   to describe the age, size, price etc. of an item.

3   to ask whether or not you should do something.

4   to ask someone to do something with you.

Lesson 7

TARGET EXPRESSIONS AND PATTERNS

1 Where is «item X»? **«X» wa doko ni arimasu ka.**

2 «person/item X» is | in / inside / on / under | «place Y». **«X» wa «Y»** | ni / no naka ni / no ue ni / no shita ni | **arimasu.**

3 This is «adjective». **Kore wa «adjective» desu.**

4 «adjective» + «noun». «adjective» + «noun».

5 Shall (I) do...? **(Watakushi ga)...shimashoo ka.**

6 Let's do... **...shimashoo.**

SITUATION

Mr. Brown decides to install a Japanese word processor in his office. To find out where a showroom is, Mr. Brown asks Ms. Yamada for an English telephone book and a map of Tokyo. Both are in his office, but the English telephone book is old and the map is too bulky. Mr. Brown decides to buy new ones on his way to MITI.

DIALOGUE

word processor	**waapuro**
showroom	**shooruumu**
to need	**irimasu**
Brown telephone book	**denwa-choo**

1	Ms. Yamada, (we) need a word processor in this office, don't we? (I)'m going to call the showroom, but where is the telephone book?	**Yamada-san, kono jimusho ni waapuro ga irimasu nee. Shooruumu e denwa-shimasu ga, denwa-choo wa doko ni arimasu ka.**

Japanese (language)	**nihongo**
English (language)	**eego**
English one	**eego no**
Yamada bookshelf	**hondana**

2	The Japanese telephone book is here, but the English one is on that bookshelf over there.	**Nihongo no denwa-choo wa koko ni arimasu ga, eego no wa ano hondana ni arimasu.**

Lesson 7

(Mr. Brown takes the English phone book from the bookshelf.)

	a little	chotto
	(is) old	hurui
	(is) new	atarashii
Brown	new one	atarashii no

3 | This is a little old, isn't it? (We) need a new one, don't we? | **Kore wa chotto hurui desu nee. Atarashii no ga irimasu ne.**

Yamada	to buy	kaimasu

4 | Well, (I)'ll buy (it) tomorrow. | **Jaa, ashita kaimasu.**

	and then	sore kara
Brown	map	chizu

5 | And then, do (you) have a map of Tokyo? | **Sore kara, Tookyoo no chizu wa arimasu ka.**

	cabinet	kyabinetto
Yamada	inside	naka

6 | The map is inside that cabinet. | **Chizu wa sono kyabinetto no naka ni arimasu.**

	(is) big	ookii
Brown	inconvenient	huben

7 | Oh, this is a big map, isn't it? (This) is a little inconvenient. | **Aa, kore wa ookii chizu desu nee. Chotto huben desu yo.**

	also	mo
Yamada	shall (I/we) buy?	kaimashoo ka

8 | Well, shall (I) buy a map, too? | **Jaa, chizu mo kaimashoo ka.**

	more	motto
	(is) small	chiisai
	smaller one	motto chiisai no
Brown	(is) good	ii

9 | Yes. A smaller one would be good. | **Ee, motto chiisai no ga ii desu yo.**

— 83 —

Lesson 7

Yamada

| **10** | (I) see. [lit. (I) understood.] | **Wakarimashita.** |

	MITI	**Tsuusan-shoo**
	I	**boku** (male only)
Brown	and	**to**

| **11** | Oh, (I)'ll go to MITI this afternoon, so I'll buy a phone book and a map. | **Aa, gogo Tsuusan-shoo e ikimasu kara, boku ga denwa-choo to chizu o kaimasu yo.** |

	please do so [lit. (I) request]	**onegai-shimasu**
	Chinese character	**kanji**
Yamada	convenience	**benri**

| **12** | Is that so? Then, please do so. You [lit. Mr. Brown] understand kanji too, so it is really convenient, isn't it? | **Soo desu ka. Jaa, onegai-shimasu. Buraun-san wa kanji mo wakarimasu kara, hontoo ni benri desu nee.** |

JAPANESE WRITING

1　ブラウン：　山田さん、この事務所にワープロがいりますねえ。ショールームへ電話しますが、
　　　　　　　電話帳はどこにありますか。
2　山　田：　日本語の電話帳はここにありますが、英語のはあの本棚にあります。
3　ブラウン：　これはちょっと古いですねえ。新しいのがいりますね。
4　山　田：　じゃあ、あした買います。
5　ブラウン：　それから、東京の地図はありますか。
6　山　田：　地図はそのキャビネットの中にあります。
7　ブラウン：　ああ、これは大きい地図ですねえ。ちょっと不便ですよ。
8　山　田：　じゃあ、地図も買いましょうか。
9　ブラウン：　ええ、もっと小さいのがいいですよ。
10　山　田：　わかりました。
11　ブラウン：　ああ、午後通産省へ行きますから、ぼくが電話帳と地図を買いますよ。
12　山　田：　そうですか。じゃあ、お願いします。ブラウンさんは漢字もわかりますから、
　　　　　　　本当に便利ですねえ。

READING

1　Brown:　Yamada-san, kono jimusho ni waapuro ga irimasu nee. Shoo-ruumu e denwa-shimasu ga, denwa-choo wa doko ni arimasu ka.
2　Yamada:　Nihongo no denwa-choo wa koko ni arimasu ga, eego no wa ano hondana ni arimasu.
3　Brown:　Kore wa chotto hurui desu nee. Atarashii no ga irimasu ne.
4　Yamada:　Jaa, ashita kaimasu.

— 84 —

Lesson 7

5 Brown: Sore kara, Tookyoo no chizu wa arimasu ka.
6 Yamada: Chizu wa sono kyabinetto no naka ni arimasu.
7 Brown: Aa, kore wa ookii chizu desu nee. Chotto huben desu yo.
8 Yamada: Jaa, chizu mo kaimashoo ka.
9 Brown: Ee, motto chiisai no ga ii desu yo.
10 Yamada: Wakarimashita.
11 Brown: Aa, gogo Tsuusan-shoo e ikimasu kara, boku ga denwa-choo to chizu o kaimasu yo.
12 Yamada: Soo desu ka. Jaa, onegai-shimasu. Buraun-san wa kanji mo wakari-masu kara, hontoo ni benri desu nee.

ADDITIONAL USEFUL EXPRESSIONS

1 At the office

| | newspaper | **shinbun** |

| A: | Where is today's newspaper? | **Kyoo no shinbun wa doko ni arimasu ka.** |

	desk	**tsukue**
	on	**ue**
	on the desk	**tsukue no ue**

| B: | It's on Ms. Yamada's desk. | **Yamada-san no tsukue no ue ni arimasu.** |

2 At the office

| | dictionary | **jisho** |

| A: | Where is the English dictionary? | **Eego no jisho wa doko desu ka.** |

	magazine	**zasshi**
	under	**shita**
	under the magazine	**zasshi no shita**

| B: | It's under that magazine. | **Sono zasshi no shita desu.** |

3 At the showroom

| A: | Is this word processor good? | **Kono waapuro wa ii desu ka.** |
| B: | Yes, (it)'s very convenient. | **Ee, totemo benri desu yo.** |

— 85 —

Lesson 7

4 At the office

	shall (I/we) go?	**ikimashoo ka**

A:	When shall (I/we) go to MITI?	**Itsu Tsuusan-shoo e ikimashoo ka.**

	let's go	**ikimashoo**

B:	Let's go now.	**Ima ikimashoo.**

5 At the school

	what language?	**nani-go**
	book	**hon**

A:	In what language is the book (written)?	**Nani-go no hon desu ka.**

	French	**huransugo**
	German	**doitsugo***
	Italian	**itariago***
	Spanish	**supeingo***
	Russian	**roshiago***
	Chinese	**chuugokugo***

B:	This is a French book.	**Huransugo no hon desu yo.**

Does not appear in sample dialogue. Introduced for reference only.

	(is) difficult	**muzukashii**

A:	Is French difficult?	**Huransugo wa muzukashii desu ka.**

	(is) easy	**yasashii**

B:	No, (it) isn't difficult. (It)'s easy.	**Iie, muzukashiku arimasen yo. Yasashii desu yo.**

REFERENCE

taipuraitaa	typewriter	**hasami**	scissors
pen	pen	**joogi**	ruler
boorupen	ball-point pen	**keshigomu**	eraser
enpitsu	pencil	**seroteepu**	Scotch tape
shaapupen	mechanical pencil	**huutoo**	envelope
shin	lead	**memo-choo**	memo pad
kami	paper	**nori**	glue, paste
hotchikisu	stapler	**dentaku**	electric calculator
kurippu	clip		

Lesson 7

NOTES

1 Adjectives

Hurui is an adjective, meaning '(is) old.' All adjectives in Japanese end in a vowel + **i**. However, all words which end in vowel + **i** are not necessarily adjectives.

Not all adjectives in English have equivalent forms in Japanese, and not all Japanese adjectives translate directly into English.

Japanese adjectives, like verbs, are inflected as follows:

Present Affirmative	**hurui *desu***	(is) old
Present Negative	**huru*ku arimasen***	(is not) old
Past Affirmative	**(huru*katta desu*)*** **hurui *deshita***	(was) old
Past Negative	**huru*ku arimasen deshita***	(was not) old

*This inflected form will be discussed later.

Inflections of Japanese adjectives resemble Japanese copula inflections. Note that the negative of all adjectives is formed by removing the final vowel **i** of the adjective and replacing it with **ku**. Note that there are two forms of the adjective 'good': **ii** and **yoi.** Although **ii** is more common as an affirmative form, the negative **yoku arimasen** is formed from the alternative **yoi.** Adjectives in Japanese are used both as sentence predicates and as noun modifiers. Therefore, English equivalents are indicated with (is) i.e. **hurui** '(is) old.' Japanese adjectives are sometimes used without copula in informal speech, functioning as the predicate.

Compare: **Kono hon wa *atarashii* desu.** "This book *is new.*" (sentence predicate)

and

Kore wa *atarashii* hon desu. "This is a *new* book." (noun modifier)

2 Particle **nee**

Nee is similar to **ne** in that it sometimes invites the listener's agreement, but more often this longer form expresses that the speaker is deep in thought or troubled.

Example: **Kono taipuraitaa wa chotto hurui desu nee.**
"This typewriter is a little old, isn't it? [imp. What shall we do about it?]"

3 **No** 'the one(s)'

The **no** introduced in this lesson (i.e. **eego no,** in DIALOGUE **2**) is a noun meaning 'the one(s).' It usually refers to something or someone whose specific identity is understood from the context.

4 Particles: **o, to** and **mo**

A) The particle **o** indicates that the preceding noun is the direct object of the following verb.

Example: **Watakushi wa atarashii kuruma *o* kaimasu.**
"I'll buy a new car."

— 87 —

Lesson 7

B) The particle **to** 'and' always joins nouns but cannot join verbs or adjectives.

Examples: a) **Ashita Keedanren *to* Jetoro e ikimasu.**
"(I)'ll go to Keidanren and JETRO tomorrow."

        b) **Konban Buraun-san *to* Yamada-san *to* Takada-san ga uchi e kimasu.***
"This evening Mr. Brown, Ms. Yamada and Mr. Takada will come to my home."
*Unlike the English 'and,' **to** can occur after each noun in a series except the last.

C) The particle **mo** following a noun means 'also, too.'

Examples: a) **Jakku *mo* Nihon e kimasu.**
"Jack also will come to Japan."

        b) **Yamada-san wa kuruma *mo* kaimashita.**
"Ms. Yamada bought a car, too."

5 Tentative form **-mashoo**

The tentative form of a verb is made by replacing the **-masu** with **-mashoo**. It means "let's do such-and-such," but in a question it means "shall I do such-and-such?" or "shall we do such-and-such?"

Examples: a) **Kyooto e iki*mashoo*.**
"Let's go to Kyoto."

        b) **Watakushi ga Jetoro ni denwa-shi*mashoo ka*.**
"Shall I phone JETRO?"

        c) **Chikatetsu de iki*mashoo ka*.**
"Shall (we) go by subway?"

6 Verb **irimasu**

The verb **irimasu** is an intransitive verb and means 'to be necessary.' It is often used in the sense of 'to need (something)' as in the following pattern:

someone (or something) who is in need	object that is needed	need(s)/ will need
Watakushi wa	**atarashii kuruma ga**	***irimasu.***
I need a new car.		

7 Pronoun **boku**

Boku is an informal term used only by males. It is recommended that the businessman use the formal term, **watakushi,** when introducing himself. Females can also use this expression.

PRACTICE

1 Response Practice

Example: Teacher: **Denwa-choo wa doko ni arimasu ka. /sono hondana/**
"Where is the phone book?" /that bookshelf/

— 88 —

Lesson 7

Student: **Denwa-choo wa sono hondana ni arimasu.**
"The phone book is on that bookshelf."

a) **Kyoo no shinbun wa doko ni arimasu ka. /ano teeburu no ue/**

Kyoo no shinbun wa ano teeburu no ue ni arimasu.

b) **Takada-san no meeshi wa doko ni arimasu ka. /koko/**

Takada-san no meeshi wa koko ni arimasu.

c) **Yamamoto-san no shookaijoo wa doko ni arimasu ka. /ano kyabinetto no naka/**

Yamamoto-san no shookaijoo wa ano kyabinetto no naka ni arimasu.

d) **Anata no jimusho wa doko ni arimasu ka. /Marunouchi/**

Watakushi no jimusho wa Marunouchi ni arimasu.

2 Transformation Practice

Example: Teacher: **Kono hon wa hurui desu.** "This book is old."
Student: **Kore wa hurui hon desu.** "This is an old book."

a) **Sono kuruma wa atarashii desu.** **Sore wa atarashii kuruma desu.**
b) **Ano jisho wa ii desu.** **Are wa ii jisho desu.**
c) **Sono zasshi wa hurui desu.** **Sore wa hurui zasshi desu.**
d) **Kono hon wa yasashii desu.** **Kore wa yasashii hon desu.**

3 Response Practice

Example: Teacher: **Sono zasshi wa atarashii desu ka.**
"Is that magazine new?"
Student: **Iie, atarashiku arimasen.**
"No, (it) isn't new."

a) **Nihongo wa muzukashii desu ka.** **Iie, muzukashiku arimasen.**
b) **Sono jisho wa ii desu ka.** **Iie, yoku arimasen.**
c) **Anata no kuruma wa ookii desu ka.** **Iie, ookiku arimasen.**
d) **Ano kaisha wa chiisai desu ka.** **Iie, chiisaku arimasen.**

4 Response Practice

Example: Teacher: **Ikimashoo ka.** "Shall (we) go?"
Student: **Ee, ikimashoo.** "Yes, let's go."

a) **Are o kaimashoo ka.** **Ee, kaimashoo.**
b) **Buraun-san ni denwa-shimashoo ka.** **Ee, denwa-shimashoo.**
c) **Ima kaerimashoo ka.** **Ee, kaerimashoo.**
d) **Koko ni imashoo ka.** **Ee, imashoo.**

5 Transformation Practice

Example: Teacher: **Kyooto e ikimasu ka.**
"Do (you) go to Kyoto?"

— 89 —

Lesson 7

Student: **Kyooto e ikimashoo ka.**
"Shall (I/we) go to Kyoto?"

a) Shachoo ni denwa o kakemasu ka.   Shachoo ni denwa o kakemashoo ka.
b) Ashita hachi-ji ni kimasu ka.   Ashita hachi-ji ni kimashoo ka.
c) Takushii de ikimasu ka.   Takushii de ikimashoo ka.
d Kyoo koko ni imasu ka.   Kyoo koko ni imashoo ka.
e) Konban denwa-shimasu ka.   Konban denwa-shimashoo ka.

6 Expansion Practice

Example: Teacher: **Zasshi o kaimashita. /shinbun/**
"(I) bought a magazine." /newspaper/
Student: **Zasshi to shinbun o kaimashita.**
"(I) bought a magazine and a newspaper."

a) **Pen ga irimasu. /kami/**   **Pen to kami ga irimasu.**
b) **Waapuro ga arimasu. /taipuraitaa/**   **Waapuro to taipuraitaa ga arimasu.**
c) **Yamamoto-san ga irasshaimasu.**   **Yamamoto-san to Takada-san ga**
    /Takada-san/   **irasshaimasu.**
d) **Oosaka e denwa-shimashita.**   **Oosaka to Yokohama e denwa-**
    /Yokohama/   **shimashita.**

7 Transformation Practice

Example: Teacher: **Atarashii jisho ga arimasu.**
"There is a new dictionary."
Student: **Atarashii no ga arimasu.**
"There is a new one."

a) **Hurui kuruma o kaimashita.**   **Hurui no o kaimashita.**
b) **Yasashii hon ga arimasu ka.**   **Yasashii no ga arimasu ka.**
c) **Ii chizu o kaimashoo.**   **Ii no o kaimashoo.**
d) **Chiisai dentaku wa huben desu.**   **Chiisai no wa huben desu.**

8 Communication Practice

Directions: Using the following patterns, tell the teacher where a certain thing is in your office or study.

Examples: «item X» **wa** «place Y» **ni arimasu.**   "«X» is in «Y»."
    «item X» **wa** «place Y» **no ue ni arimasu.**   "«X» is on «Y»."
    «item X» **wa** «place Y» **no naka ni arimasu.**   "«X» is in/inside «Y»."
    «item X» **wa** «place Y» **no shita ni arimasu.**   "«X» is under «Y»."

9 Communication Practice

Directions: Tell the teacher what you need now, using the following pattern. If you don't know how you refer to it, ask the teacher what it's called.

Lesson 7

Example: **(Watakushi wa) ima «item X» ga irimasu.**
"Now I need «X»."

EXERCISES

a) Give the teacher the following information:
1 English (language) magazines are on that table over there.
2 The Japanese phone book is on Mr. Tanaka's desk.
3 Mr. Yamamoto will buy a new car next Saturday.
4 This small dictionary isn't good. You need a larger one.
5 That word processor is very convenient.
6 The Japanese (language) isn't difficult.
7 This book is (written in) French, but that one is in German.
8 You need a pencil and some paper.
9 Jack's letter of introduction is in your cabinet.
10 Yesterday, Ms. Yamada bought a map of Tokyo and a Spanish dictionary.

b) Translate the following conversations into Japanese:

	Questions	Answers
1	Shall I come to the office next Sunday?	Yes, please do so.
2	Shall I phone Mr. Takada?	No, I'll call him tonight.
3	Shall we go to MITI today?	Yes, let's go.
4	Shall I stay here until 7:00?	Yes, please do so.
5	Shall I buy some cigarettes?	No, thank you.

Model Answers:

a)
1 **Eego no zasshi wa ano teeburu no ue ni arimasu.**
2 **Nihongo no denwa-choo wa Tanaka-san no tsukue no ue ni arimasu.**
3 **Yamamoto-san wa tsugi no doyoobi ni atarashii kuruma o kaimasu.**
4 **Kono chiisai jisho wa yoku arimasen. Motto ookii no ga irimasu.**
5 **Ano waapuro wa totemo benri desu.**
6 **Nihongo wa muzukashiku arimasen.**
7 **Kono hon wa huransugo desu ga, are wa doitsugo no desu.**
8 **Enpitsu to kami ga irimasu.**
9 **Jakku no shookaijoo wa watakushi no kyabinetto no naka ni arimasu.**
10 **Kinoo Yamada-san wa Tookyoo no chizu to Supeingo no jisho o kaimashita.**

b)
1 **Tsugi no nichiyoobi jimusho e kimashoo ka.** — **Ee, onegai-shimasu.**
2 **Takada-san ni denwa-shimashoo ka.** — **Iie, konban denwa-shimasu.**
3 **Kyoo Tsuusan-shoo e ikimashoo ka.** — **Ee, ikimashoo.**
4 **Shichi-ji made koko ni imashoo ka.** — **Ee, onegai-shimasu.**
5 **Tabako o kaimashoo ka.** — **Iie, kekko desu.**

— 91 —

Lesson 7

BUSINESS INFORMATION

The Japanese Writing System

Japanese is written with **kanji** (漢字, characters of Chinese origin) and two sets of phonetic symbols called **kana: hiragana** (ひらがな) and **katakana** (カタカナ). Like the Egyptian hieroglyphics, **kanji** are derived from symbols and pictures that in ancient times represented the sun, moon, rice fields and other phenomena, and are consequently sometimes also referred to as pictographs. A single **kanji** may be composed of one symbol or several symbols; it may also be read in different ways, depending on the words and other **kanji** it appears with; but it usually contains only one basic meaning.

Examples of **kanji** and their pictorial origins*:

月 = **tsuki; getsu/gatsu**
meaning: MOON/MONTH

火 = **hi; ka**
meaning: FIRE

山 = **yama; san**
meaning: MOUNTAIN

雨 = **ame/ama; u**
meaning: RAIN

魚 = **sakana/uo; gyo**
meaning: FISH

木 = **ki; boku, moku; ko**
meaning: TREE

森 = **mori; shin**
meaning: FOREST

人 = **hito; jin, nin**
meaning: HUMAN BEING

川 = **kawa; sen**
meaning: RIVER

馬 = **uma; ma, ba**
meaning: HORSE

A New Dictionary of Kanji Usage, publ. by Gakken, 1982; Kadokawa Jigen Jiten, publ. by Kadokawa Shoten, 1972.

Hiragana and **katakana** were originally developed by isolating parts of, or abbreviating, **kanji** to form individual syllables. Unlike **kanji, kana** have no intrinsic meaning unless combined with other **kana** or **kanji** to form words. In Japanese writing, therefore, one or more **kanji** will form the core of a word, i.e. the part that contains the meaning, and **hiragana** will be used for its inflected ending, if any, e.g. *ikimasu* (行きます, I will go); *ikimashita* (行きました, I went). **Hiragana** are also used for particles, suffixes and prefixes.

The following chart shows various **hiragana** and **katakana** symbols together with the **kanji** from which they are derived. At a time when the Japanese had no written language of their own, these Chinese characters were used to represent phonetically-similar Japanese syllables, without regard for the meaning of the original characters. A glance at

— 92 —

Lesson 7

the complexity of some of these **kanji** will indicate why drastic simplification was in order.*

Hiragana	Original **Kanji**	**Katakana**	Original **Kanji**	Pronunciation
あ	安	ア	阿	= a
い	以	イ	伊	= i
う	宇	ウ	宇	= u
え	衣	エ	江	= e
お	於	オ	於	= o
か	加	カ	加	= ka
き	幾	キ	幾	= ki
な	奈	ナ	奈	= na
は	波	ハ	八	= ha
ほ	保	ホ	保	= ho
み	美	ミ	三	= mi
ゆ	由	ユ	由	= yu
れ	礼	レ	礼	= re
の	乃	ノ	乃	= no
そ	曽	ソ	曽	= so

*W. Hadamitzky and M. Spahn, **Kanji & Kana**, publ. by Charles E. Tuttle, 1981, p.p. 18-21.*

There appear to have been no hard and fast rules for converting **kanji** into **kana.** In some cases, both **hiragana** and **katakana** are derived from the same **kanji,** while in other cases they are based on different characters. Note also that most **hiragana** are stylized, esthetic contractions of **kanji.** These flowing, graceful symbols have traditionally been considered more appropriate for poetic and literary expression; even today, many trendy advertisers favor short, **hiragana**-only messages for a more informal and stylish "look". **Katakana,** on the other hand, were mostly formed by isolating parts of **kanji.** It has been suggested that these symbols were developed as a form of shorthand by students of Buddhist scripture who wrote the meanings and pronunciations of unfamiliar characters in the margins of their texts.** In contrast to **hiragana, katakana** have a distinctive, angular appearance and are used mainly for terms borrowed from foreign (non-Chinese) languages [See Lesson 8].

**W. Hadamitzky and M. Spahn, op. cit., p. 19.*

To read a normal Japanese newspaper, you will have to learn both sets of **kana** (46 symbols each) and about 2,000 **kanji**—approximately the number Japanese students know by the time they graduate from high school. This is a daunting prospect for foreign businessmen. Indeed, many recoil at the mere sight of **kanji**-filled documents and immediately go off in search of translations, confident that anything vitally important will be available in their native tongue anyway.

If you are suffering from such "kanji allergy," it would be useful to remember that, for one thing, the number of Japanese titles currently available in other languages is still very limited. Although most government agencies and industrial associations do try to accommodate foreign visitors, and there are now various Japanese-to-English information services catering to industries like finance and electronics, there remains a considerable imbalance in the trade of information between East and West. Also, getting translations in Japan costs time and money, so the translated material could even become obsolete by

— 93 —

Lesson 7

the time you finally get to read it. Moreover, published translations are often incomplete. Whether for reasons of space, time or funds, many omit valuable information, including graphs and charts. You could end up with a version so abbreviated or generalized that it hardly serves your specific business needs. Last but not least, foreign-language materials are of course more costly than Japanese publications; and foreign bookstores in Japan are few and far between.

Throughout this text, Japanese writing is provided for your reference. If you start by *recognizing* **kanji** and associating them with their meanings, even without knowing how to pronounce them, you will still be far better off than not knowing anything at all.

The following is a list of **kanji** that you are bound to encounter frequently during your stay in Japan:

Kanji	Pronunciation	Breakdown of Characters	Meaning
非常口	**Hi-joo-guchi**	(not) + (normal) + (mouth)	EMERGENCY EXIT
営業中	**Ee-gyo-chuu**	(operation) + (business) + (middle)	OPEN FOR BUSINESS
禁煙	**Kin'-en**	(prohibition) + (smoke)	NO SMOKING
注意	**Chuu-i**	(concentration) + (mind)	CAUTION
化粧室	**Ke-shoo-shitsu**	(disguise) + (ornament) + (room)	RESTROOM
両替	**Ryoo-gae**	(currency [ancient]) + (exchange)	MONEY EXCHANGE
入口	**Iri-guchi**	(enter) + (mouth)	ENTRANCE
出口	**De-guchi**	(go out) + (mouth)	EXIT
地下鉄	**Chi-ka-tetsu**	(ground) + (under) + (iron)	SUBWAY
渋滞	**Juu-tai**	(stagnant) + (stay)	TRAFFIC JAM
六本木	**Rop-pon-gi**	(six) + (long units) + (trees)	Place name in Tokyo
虎の門	**Tora-no-mon**	(tiger) + ('s) + (gate)	Place name in Tokyo

— 94 —

Lesson 8

At the Store

OBJECTIVES

1 to buy something at a Japanese store.

2 to ask someone to give you something.

3 to ask someone to do something for you.

4 to ask a clerk to write a receipt.

5 to describe colors.

Lesson 8

TARGET EXPRESSIONS AND PATTERNS

1 Please give me «item X».   «X» o kudasai.

2 Please do... for me.   ...shite kudasai.

3 Would (you) like/how about «item X»?   «X» wa ikaga desu ka.

4 The one(s) belonging to «person/item   «X» no.
   X».

5 Polite form of 'to have.'   Gozaimasu.

SITUATION

Mr. Brown goes to a bookstore and buys a map of Tokyo and an English telephone book.
Mr. Brown asks the clerk to address the receipt to his company, P & C, Ltd.

DIALOGUE

Clerk

1	Welcome!	Irasshaimase.

		to show	misemasu
		showing	misete
Brown		please show (me)	misete kudasai

2	Please show (me) that map.	Sono chizu o misete kudasai.

Clerk   which one?   dore

3	Which one is (it)?	Dore desu ka.

Brown   (is) white   shiroi

4	(It) is that white one.	Sono shiroi no desu yo.

Clerk

5	Is (it) this one? Please.	Kore desu ka. Doozo.

— 96 —

Lesson 8

(Mr. Brown looks over the map)

Brown

not so much — **amari** /+ negative/
(is) detailed — **kuwashii**

| 6 | This is not so detailed. Don't (you) have a more detailed one? | **Kore wa amari kuwashiku arimasen nee. Motto kuwashii no wa arimasen ka.** |

Clerk

to have — **gozaimasu** (polite)
that one over there — **are**
would you like?/how about? — **ikaga desu ka**

| 7 | (We) have (one). How about that one over there? | **Gozaimasu. Are wa ikaga desu ka.** |

(Clerk gets that map and hands it over to Mr. Brown.)

Brown

just, exactly — **choodo**
please give (me) this — **kore o kudasai**

| 8 | Oh, this is just right. Please give (me) this one. | **Aa, kore wa choodo ii desu nee. Kore o kudasai.** |

Clerk

| 9 | Thank you very much. | **Arigatoo gozaimasu.** |

Brown

| 10 | And do (you) have an English telephone book? | **Sore kara, eego no denwa-choo wa arimasu ka.** |

Clerk

| 11 | Yes, (we) do. (It) is this one. | **Hai, gozaimasu. Kore desu.** |

Brown

| 12 | Oh, this is fine. [lit. this is fine, isn't it?] Please give (me) this one, too. How much are (these)? | **Aa, kore wa ii desu ne. Kore mo kudasai. Ikura desu ka.** |

— 97 —

Lesson 8

	a 1,500 yen map	**sen-gohyaku-en no chizu**
	a 2,000 yen phone book	**nisen-en no denwa-choo**
Clerk	total	**gookee**

13 (Those) are a 1,500 yen map and a 2,000 yen phone book, so the total is 3,500 yen.

Sen-gohyaku-en no chizu to nisen-en no denwa-choo desu kara, gookee (wa) sanzen-gohyaku-en desu.

(Mr. Brown hands over the money)

	company's	**kaisha no**
	a receipt	**ryooshuusho**
	to write	**kakimasu**
	writing	**kaite**
Brown	please write	**kaite kudasai**

14 Please write a receipt because these are for my company.

Ryooshuusho o kaite kudasai, kore wa kaisha no desu kara.

Clerk	name	**namae, onamae** (respectful)

15 (What is) your company's name?

Kaisha no onamae wa.

	corporation, Ltd.	**kabushikigaisha**
Brown	P & C, Ltd.	**Pii-ando-shii-kabushikigaisha**

16 (It) is P & C, Ltd.

Pii-ando-shii-kabushikigaisha desu.

Clerk

17 Please wait a while.

Shooshoo omachi-kudasai.

(Clerk hands over the receipt)

	every time	**maido**
Clerk	again	**mata**

18 Thank you very much for your continued patronage [lit. for coming here every time]. Please (come) again.

Maido arigatoo gozaimasu. Mata doozo.

— 98 —

Lesson 8

JAPANESE WRITING

1 **クラーク**： いらっしゃいませ。
2 **ブラウン**： その地図を見せてください。
3 **クラーク**： どれですか。
4 **ブラウン**： その白いのですよ。
5 **クラーク**： これですか。どうぞ。
6 **ブラウン**： これはあまり詳しくありませんねえ。もっと詳しいのはありませんか。
7 **クラーク**： ございます。あれはいかがですか。
8 **ブラウン**： ああ、これはちょうどいいですねえ。これをください。
9 **クラーク**： ありがとうございます。
10 **ブラウン**： それから、英語の電話帳はありますか。
11 **クラーク**： はい、ございます。これです。
12 **ブラウン**： ああ、これはいいですね。これもください。いくらですか。
13 **クラーク**： 千五百円の地図と二千円の電話帳ですから、合計は三千五百円です。
14 **ブラウン**： 領収書を書いてください、これは会社のですから。
15 **クラーク**： 会社のお名前は。
16 **ブラウン**： ピー・アンド・シー株式会社です。
17 **クラーク**： 少々、お待ちください。
18 **クラーク**： 毎度ありがとうございます。又どうぞ。

READING

1 Clerk: **Irasshaimase.**
2 Brown: **Sono chizu o misete kudasai.**
3 Clerk: **Dore desu ka.**
4 Brown: **Sono shiroi no desu yo.**
5 Clerk: **Kore desu ka. Doozo.**
6 Brown: **Kore wa amari kuwashiku arimasen nee. Motto kuwashii no wa arimasen ka.**
7 Clerk: **Gozaimasu. Are wa ikaga desu ka.**
8 Brown: **Aa, kore wa choodo ii desu nee. Kore o kudasai.**
9 Clerk: **Arigatoo gozaimasu.**
10 Brown: **Sore kara, eego no denwa-choo wa arimasu ka.**
11 Clerk: **Hai, gozaimasu. Kore desu.**
12 Brown: **Aa, kore wa ii desu ne. Kore mo kudasai. Ikura desu ka.**
13 Clerk: **Sen-gohyaku-en no chizu to nisen-en no denwa-choo desu kara, gookee (wa) sanzen-gohyaku-en desu.**
14 Brown: **Ryooshuusho o kaite kudasai, kore wa kaisha no desu kara.**
15 Clerk: **Kaisha no onamae wa.**
16 Brown: **Pii-ando-shii-kabushikigaisha desu.**
17 Clerk: **Shooshoo omachi-kudasai.**
18 Clerk: **Maido arigatoo gozaimasu. Mata doozo.**

Lesson 8

ADDITIONAL USEFUL EXPRESSIONS

1 At the office

A: Do (you) have some clips?	**Kurippu, arimasu ka.**

how many? [lit. how many units?]	**ikutsu**

B: Yes, (I) have both large ones and small ones. How many units do (you) need?	**Ee, ookii no mo chiisai no mo arimasu yo. Ikutsu irimasu ka.**

one unit	**hito-tsu** *
two units	**huta-tsu** *
three units	**mit-tsu** *
four units	**yot-tsu** *
five units	**itsu-tsu**
six units	**mut-tsu** *
seven units	**nana-tsu** *
eight units	**yat-tsu** *
nine units	**kokono-tsu** *
ten units	**too** *

A: Please give (me) five large ones.	**Ookii no o itsu-tsu kudasai.**

Does not appear in sample dialogue. Introduced for reference only.

2 At the store

(is) red	**akai** *
(is) black	**kuroi**
(is) blue	**aoi** *
(is) yellow	**kiiroi** *
(is) brown	**chairoi** *
ashtray	**haizara**

A: How much is that black ashtray?	**Sono kuroi haizara wa ikura desu ka.**
B: (It) is 700 yen for one.	**Hito-tsu nanahyaku-en desu.**
A: How many units do (you) have?	**Ikutsu arimasu ka.**

Does not appear in sample dialogue. Introduced for reference only.

Lesson 8

	many	**takusan**

B:	(I) have a lot of those.	**Sore wa takusan gozaimasu.**
A:	Well, please give (me) six.	**Jaa, mut-tsu kudasai.**

3 At the store

	check	**kogitte**
	with/by	**de**
	is it all right?	**ii desu ka**

A:	Is (it) all right (to pay) with a check?	**Kogitte de ii desu ka**

	to be troubled	**komarimasu**

B:	(I)'m sorry, but (we) can't accept a check. [lit. we are troubled a little with a check.]	**Sumimasen ga, kogitte wa chotto komarimasu.**

	credit card	**kurejitto-kaado**

A:	Well, how about a credit card?	**Jaa, kurejitto-kaado wa.**
B:	Credit cards are fine.	**Kurejitto-kaado wa kekkoo desu.**

4 At the store

	10,000 yen note	**ichiman-en-satsu**

A:	Is it all right (to pay) with a 10,000 yen note?	**Ichiman-en-satsu de ii desu ka.**
B:	Yes, (it)'s fine.	**Hai, kekkoo desu.**

NOTES

1 Gerund Form + **kudasai**

When **kudasai** is preceded by a noun + particle **o,** this structure means "Please give (me)...." **Kore o kudasai** "Please give (me) this one" or **Sore o kudasai** "Please give (me) that one" are extremely useful ways of asking for things when you don't know what they are called. In a restaurant, you can point to a plastic food model or to the menu while saying **"Kore o kudasai."**

On the other hand, when **kudasai** is preceded by a verb gerund form,* it means "Please do such-and-such (for me)."

*Japanese verbs have a form ending in **-te** (or **-de),** which is called the GERUND or, sometimes, the **-te** form.

—101—

Lesson 8

Meanings	Formal Non-past	Gerund
to be, to have	**arimasu**	atte
to be, to stay	**imasu**	ite
to go	**ikimasu**	itte
to return	**kaerimasu**	kaette
to buy	**kaimasu**	katte
to telephone	**(denwa o) kakemasu**	(denwa o) kakete
to come	**kimasu**	kite
to be troubled	**komarimasu**	komatte
to show	**misemasu**	misete
to do	**shimasu***	shite
to understand	**wakarimasu**	wakatte

***shimasu** in **denwa-shimasu** 'to make a telephone call' (in Lesson 4), independently means 'to do.'

Examples: **a) Ashita Oosaka e it*te kudasai*.**
"Please go to Osaka tomorrow."
b) Boku no kuruma o kat*te kudasai*.
"Please buy my car."
c) Kyoo Takada-san ni denwa-shit*e kudasai*.
"Please call Mr. Takada today."
d) San-ji made koko ni it*e kudasai*.
"Please stay here till three."

Omachi-kudasai (in Lesson 3 and in ADDITIONAL USEFUL EXPRESSIONS of this lesson), a more polite expression using **kudasai,** will be discussed in a later lesson.

2 Kore/sore/are/dore

Like **kono/sono/ano** introduced in Lesson 6, **kore/sore/are** are used depending upon the distance between speaker and the listener, as follows:

item(s) close to the speaker	item(s) removed from the speaker, but close to the listener	item(s) removed from both the speaker and the listener	question word
kono (hon) 'this (book)'	**sono (hon)** 'that (book)'	**ano (hon)** 'that (book) over there'	**dono (hon)** 'which (book)?'
kore** 'this one'	**sore** 'that one'	**are** 'that one over there'	**dore** 'which?'

****Kore** is also acceptable when introducing someone in the same group as oneself, but of a lower position. The most frequent use is to introduce one's own family.

Examples: **a) *Kore* wa Takada-san no zasshi desu.**
"This is Mr. Takada's magazine."
b) *Kore* wa watakushi no musume desu.
"This is my daughter."
c) *Sore* wa anata no kogitte desu ka.
"Is that your check?"
d) *Are* wa Yamada-san no otaku desu.
"That house over there is Ms. Yamada's."

—102—

Lesson 8

   e) *Dore* ga ii jisho desu ka.
      "Which one is a good dictionary?"

3 Gozaimasu

Gozaimasu is a polite equivalent of **arimasu** and means 'is located in' or 'have.'

Examples: a) **Honsha wa Detoroito ni gozaimasu.**
                "Our head office is in Detroit."
            b) **Tookyoo no chizu wa gozaimasu ga, Yokohama no wa gozaima-
                sen.**
                "(I) have a map of Tokyo, but not of Yokohama."

Note that **gozaimasu** in **arigatoo gozaimasu** or **ohayoo gozaimasu** is added to merely express a more polite/formal attitude. In such cases, it is not a corresponding form of **arimasu.**

4 Counter -tsu 'unit'

Counter **-tsu** always occurs with some Japanese origin numerals (introduced in Lesson 6 Note 4) and is used to count unit objects which are inanimate. As you see in ADDITIONAL USEFUL EXPRESSIONS of this lesson, **-tsu** occurs with 1 through 9. To count the number of units beyond 10, the Chinese origin numerals are used independently (without counter **-tsu**).
Note that in Japanese, these combinations (numeral + counter) are often used adverbially, so they usually occur without any following particles.

Examples: a) **Kurippu wa *mit-tsu* arimasu.**   "There are three clips."
            b) **Haizara o *yot-tsu* kudasai.**   "Please give (me) four ashtrays."
            c) **Isu ga *itsu-tsu* irimasu.**   "(We) need five chairs."

5 More about **no** 'the one(s)'

When particle **no** is immediately followed by the noun **no** 'the one(s)' introduced in Lesson 7, these two **no** are contracted to a single **no.** Then, **kaisha no kuruma** 'a company's car' will become **kaisha no** 'a company's one.'

Compare: **Kono zasshi wa Tanaka-san *no* zasshi desu.**
           "This magazine is Mr. Tanaka's magazine."
           Kono zasshi wa Tanaka-san *no no* desu. [erroneous]
           "This magazine is Mr. Tanaka's one."
           Kono zasshi wa Tanaka-san *no* desu. [correct, contracted form of above]
           "This magazine is Mr. Tanaka's."

6 Clerk's Expressions

Irasshaimase commonly used by the clerk for greeting a customer entering a store, means 'welcome.' **Ikaga desu ka** is often used in making a suggestion or in inquiring how something is. «Item» **wa ikaga desu ka** means "how about «item»?" or "would you like «item»?" **Maido arigatoo gozaimasu,** an idiomatic expression used by clerks, literally means "Thank you very much every time", but this is commonly used whenever any customer leaves the store. **Mata doozo,** literally meaning "please again," is used to mean "please come again."

—103—

Lesson 8

PRACTICE

1 Communication Practice

Directions: Teacher prepares the following articles with prices beforehand. You pick up one of them and ask the teacher its price and decide whether or not to buy it.
Articles to be prepared: Various maps, books, large dictionary, small dictionary, newspapers, various kinds of pens and pencils.

Example: Student: **Sono «article» wa ikura desu ka.**
"How much is that «article»?"
Teacher: **Kore wa «price» -en desu yo. Doozo.**
"This is «price» yen. Please."
Student: **Kore wa ii desu nee. Kono «article» o kudasai.**
"This is good, isn't it? Please give (me) this «article»."
or
Amari yoku arimasen nee. Kore wa kekkoo desu.
"(This) is not so good, is it? (I) don't want to take it."

2 Response Practice

Example: Teacher: **Kore o misemashoo ka.**
"Shall (I) show (you) this one?"
Student: **Ee, misete kudasai.**
"Yes, please show (me that one)."

a) **Ima Jetoro e ikimashoo ka.** **Ee, itte kudasai.**
b) **Ashita chizu o kaimashoo ka.** **Ee, katte kudasai.**
c) **Roku-ji made koko ni imashoo ka.** **Ee, ite kudasai.**
d) **Takada-san ni denwa-shimashoo ka.** **Ee, (denwa)-shite kudasai.**
e) **Ryooshuusho o kakimashoo ka.** **Ee, kaite kudasai.**
f) **Jimusho e kaerimashoo ka.** **Ee, kaette kudasai.**

3 Response Practice

Example: Teacher: **Nihongo wa muzukashii desu ka.**
"Is Japanese difficult (to learn)?"
Student: **Iie, amari muzukashiku arimasen.**
"No, it is not so difficult."

a) **Sono jisho wa kuwashii desu ka.** **Iie, amari kuwashiku arimasen.**
b) **Anata no kuruma wa ookii desu ka.** **Iie, amari ookiku arimasen.**
c) **Doitsugo wa yasashii desu ka.** **Iie, amari yasashiku arimasen.**
d) **Sono hon wa ii desu ka.** **Iie, amari yoku arimasen.**

4 Response Practice

Example: Teacher: **Kore wa kaisha no kuruma desu ka.**
"Is this your company's car?"

—104—

Lesson 8

Student: **Ee, kaisha no desu.**
"Yes, (this) is my company's."

a) **Sore wa Nihon no chizu desu ka.**   **Ee, Nihon no desu.**
b) **Kore wa Tanaka-san no pen desu**   **Ee, Tanaka-san no desu.**
  ka.
c) **Sore wa anata no meeshi desu ka.**   **Ee, watakushi no desu.**

5 Communication Practice

Directions: Give real information to the teacher in answering the following questions.

Example: Teacher: **Kurippu wa ikutsu arimasu ka.**
                    "How many clips are there?"
                Student: **Kurippu wa huta-tsu arimasu.**
                    "There are two clips."

a) **Otaku ni teeburu wa ikutsu arimasu ka.**
b) **Jimusho ni denwa wa ikutsu arimasu ka.**
c) **Kaisha ni waapuro wa ikutsu arimasu ka.**
d) **Otaku ni hondana wa ikutsu arimasu ka.**
e) **Jimusho ni kyabinetto wa ikutsu arimasu ka.**

6 Communication Practice

Directions: Practice correctly saying company names in Japanese, using names of companies which really exist.

Examples: a) **Watakushi no kaisha wa «company» (kabushikigaisha) desu.**
                b) **«acquaintance» -san no kaisha wa «company» (kabushikigaisha) desu.**

EXERCISES

a) Ask the clerk:
    1   to show you a map of Yokohama.
    2   if he has an English newspaper.
    3   how much that red pen over there is.
    4   to show you a good French dictionary.
    5   if he has a new magazine.
    6   how much this black pencil is.
    7   to show you that yellow ashtray over there.
    8   if he has smaller cabinets.
    9   how much that old typewriter is.

b) Prepare a dialogue in Japanese for the following situation:
    (Mr. Brown enters a bookstore.)
    1   The clerk greets Mr. Brown.
    2   Mr. Brown asks if they have any German dictionaries.

Lesson 8

3   The clerk answers that they do.
4   Mr. Brown asks the clerk to show him a new one.
5   The clerk shows him a dictionary and says it's a good dictionary.
6   Mr. Brown asks the price.
7   The clerk answers that it's 3,800 yen.
8   Mr. Brown asks if they have any more detailed ones.
9   The clerk answers that they have some, but they are old.
10   Mr. Brown decides to buy a new one and asks if he can pay with his check.
11   The clerk answers that they will be troubled with the check.
12   Mr. Brown asks the clerk if a 5,000 yen note is acceptable.
13   The clerk asks him to wait a moment. When the clerk returns, he gives Mr. Brown 1,200 yen change.
14   Mr. Brown asks the clerk to make out a receipt for it.
15   The clerk hands it over to Mr. Brown, thanks him, and asks him to come again.

Model Answers:

a)   1   **Yokohama no chizu o misete kudasai.**
     2   **Eego no shinbun wa arimasu ka.**
     3   **Ano akai pen wa ikura desu ka.**
     4   **Ii huransugo no jisho o misete kudasai.**
     5   **Atarashii zasshi wa arimasu ka.**
     6   **Kono kuroi enpitsu wa ikura desu ka.**
     7   **Ano kiiroi haizara o misete kudasai.**
     8   **Motto chiisai kyabinetto wa arimasu ka.**
     9   **Ano hurui taipuraitaa wa ikura desu ka.**

b)   1   **Irrasshaimase.**
     2   **Doitsugo no jisho wa arimasu ka.**
     3   **Hai, gozaimasu.**
     4   **Atarashii no o misete kudasai.**
     5   **Kore desu. Ii jisho desu yo.**
     6   **Ikura desu ka.**
     7   **Sanzen-happyaku-en desu.**
     8   **Motto kuwashii no wa arimasu ka.**
     9   **Hai, gozaimasu ga, hurui desu.**
   10   **Atarashii no o kudasai. Kogitte de ii desu ka.**
   11   **Kogitte wa komarimasu.**
   12   **Gosen-en-satsu de ii desu ka.**
   13   **Shooshoo omachi-kudasai. Sen-nihyaku-en otsuri desu.**
   14   **Ryooshuusho o kaite kudasai.**
   15   **Ryooshuusho desu, doozo. Maido arigatoo gozaimasu. Mata doozo.**

Lesson 8

BUSINESS INFORMATION

Borrowed Words

Like most other languages, Japanese incorporates many foreign elements. Some of these, like the Chinese and Korean elements, have been an integral part of the native language for thousands of years. Certain Dutch and Portuguese terms, which were introduced just a few hundred years ago when Japan first came into contact with the West, have also been accepted into the indigenous vocabulary. **Pan** (パン, bread), for example, is derived from the Portuguese term, *pão*. However, most of the foreign-based terms introduced so far in this text date from after the Meiji Restoration (1868) and even after World War II— a fact that attests to both the eagerness with which Japanese adopted European culture in the 19th century and the overwhelming influence of the United States in the 20th. Today, "borrowed" words—written in **katakana**—are used extensively in all walks of life and in virtually all businesses, to the extent that many borrowed terms have become more familiar than their Japanese equivalents, e.g. **konpyuuta** (コンピュータ, computer) would be far more easily understood than the original **denshi keesan-ki** (電子計算機); and **kitchin** (キッチン , kitchen) is widely used instead of **daidokoro** (台所).

The phenomenon of borrowed words is a subject of heated debate in Japan. Some language authorities have suggested the brisk pace of technological progress as one reason for the proliferation of foreign terms in the Japanese vocabulary. Back in the Meiji Era, Japanese had more time to digest new concepts little by little and to coin appropriate Japanese words for them. But the speed at which products are now being invented prevents this gradual "Japanizing" process, and foreign words have had to be taken over lock, stock and barrel. The accelerated internationalization of Japanese society has of course also contributed to the surging popularity of foreign terms. In addition, foreign terms are generally thought to sound sophisticated. Some Japanese use borrowed terms in everyday conversation in the hope of appearing more authoritative or simply more fashionable. Likewise, foreign words and slogans appear in everything from names of restaurants to advertisements to T-shirts, just to provide that extra note of chic, that "foreign flair." Often, the terms are used with no concern for their actual meaning—to the endless amusement of the foreign visitor.

You will of course find borrowed terms a very useful and easy way of expanding your basic Japanese vocabulary. However, you should take care to pronounce them as the Japanese do, usually by adding an extra syllable after every consonant, e.g. **basu,** for "bus"; **biiru,** for "beer". Unless you "distort" these words in the Japanese manner, you may not be understood at all. Also, you should note that while many foreign-based terms are abbreviations of the original, and others are just pronounced differently, some have meanings that are entirely different from those of their foreign sources. For example, **hotto** (ホット , "hot") means a cup of hot coffee, and is hardly ever used to describe the temperature; **handoru** (ハンドル , "handle") is a steering wheel in a car. One final word of caution is that too many borrowed words in a conversation may sound pretentious or clumsy to the Japanese listener or, if his English level is not so advanced, just plain unintelligible. Also, of course, overuse of borrowed words will slow down your own mastery of *authentic* Japanese terms.

—107—

Lesson 8

Below is a sampling of business-related borrowed terms, grouped roughly according to the pronunciation of the final syllable. When the original Japanese term appears alongside the borrowed one, this indicates both are used interchangeably.

Additional useful borrowed terms.

Maaketto (マーケット , market; 市場 **shijoo**)
Meritto (メリット , merit)
Demeritto (デメリット , demerit)
Risuto (リスト , list)
Repooto (レポート , report; 報告書 **hookokusho**)
Patento (パテント , patent; 特許 **tokkyo**)
Konseputo (コンセプト , concept; 概念 **gainen**)
Kosuto (コスト , cost; 原価 **genka**)
Purojekuto (プロジェクト , project)
Ahutaa Saabisu (アフターサービス , after-sales service)
Konsensasu (コンセンサス , concensus)
Bijinesu (ビジネス , business)
Sutaffu (スタッフ , staff)
Reberu (レベル , level)
Gureedo-appu (グレードアップ , up-grade)
Maaketingu (マーケティング , marketing)
Puranningu (プランニング , planning)
Chiimu (チーム , team)
Sutoratejii (ストラテジー , strategy; 戦略 **senryaku**)
Purezenteeshyon (プレゼンテーション , presentation)
Sekushyon (セクション , section)
Dishijon (ディシジョン , decision; 決定 **kettei**)
Aidea (アイデア , idea)

Contractions:

Sarariiman (サラリーマン , salaried worker [lit. man])
Masukomi (マスコミ , mass communication)
Pasokon (パソコン , personal computer)
O-Eru (オーエル, "O.L." or office lady, i.e. female clerk)
Shii-Effu (シーエフ, "C.F." or commercial film, i.e. TV commercial)

Caution:

Saabisu (サービス , service): Frequently also used to indicate something is free of charge.
Tsuuru (ツール , tool): Used primarily in reference to sales (セールスツール **seerusu tsuuru**) or marketing (マーケティングツール **maaketingu tsuuru**), not to crafts or engineering.
Taitoru (タイトル , title): Refers to headings or cover pages of reports and publications, as well as to film titles, but not to a person's rank or position.
Puromooto/Puromooshyon (プロモート/プロモーション , to promote/promotion): Refers to publicity and advertising only, not to one's rise up the corporate ladder.

—108—

Lesson 9

Making Appointments

OBJECTIVES

1 to make an appointment for lunch.

2 to tell someone where you'll meet him/her.

3 to say what you like to do.

4 to say you like or don't like something.

5 to indicate general topics by using the particle *wa*.

Lesson 9

TARGET EXPRESSIONS AND PATTERNS

1 How about having lunch together with (me)?

Ohiru o goissho ni ikaga desu ka.

2 (I)'d like to talk with (you).

Ohanashi-shitai (n*) desu.

3 How about Italian cuisine?

Itaria-ryoori wa ikaga desu ka.

4 I like Italian cuisine.

Watakushi wa itaria-ryoori ga suki desu.

5 (I) work till noon on Saturdays. [lit. As for Saturdays, (I) work till noon.]

Doyoobi wa hiru made hatarakimasu.

***n** is the contraction of **no,** which is more formal.

SITUATION

Mr. Brown calls Mr. Kawamoto of Japan Automobile Manufacturers Association Inc. **(Nihon-Jidoosha-Koogyookai** 日本自動車工業会 **),** who was introduced to him by Mr. Takada from JETRO. After talking with Mr. Kawamoto on the phone, Mr. Brown invites him to lunch. They are already on familiar terms.

DIALOGUE

		Mr. Kawamoto	Kawamoto-san
Brown		work, job	shigoto

1	By the way, Mr. Kawamoto, do (you) work on Saturdays too? [lit. Do (you) have work on Saturdays, too?]	Tokoro de, Kawamoto-san, doyoobi mo shigoto ga arimasu ka.

Kawamoto	to work	hatarakimasu

2	Yes, (I) work until noon.	Ee, hiru made hatarakimasu.

		next	tsugi no
		lunch	chuushoku
		already	moo
Brown		plan, schedule	yotee

3	Do (you) have any plans for lunch next Saturday? [lit. As for next Saturday, do (you) already have any plans for lunch?]	Tsugi no doyoobi wa, moo chuu-shoku no yotee ga arimasu ka.

—110—

Lesson 9

Kawamoto

4	No, (I) don't.	**Iie, arimasen.**

lunch [lit. noon]	**ohiru**
together with	**issho ni, goissho ni** (polite)
various	**iroiro**
talk, conversation	**hanashi, ohanashi** (polite)
to talk, speak	**hanashimasu**
to talk	**ohanashi-shimasu** (polite)
to want to talk	**ohanashi-shitai (n) desu** (polite)

Brown

5	Well then, how about (having) lunch together with (me)? (I)'d like to talk (with you about) various (things), so [imp. can you come?]	**Jaa, ohiru o goissho ni ikaga desu ka. Iroiro ohanashi-shitai desu kara…**

Kawamoto   to meet   **aimasu**

6	That's fine. Where shall (we) meet?	**Sore wa kekkoo desu nee. Doko de aimashoo ka.**

Brown   to visit, call   **ukagaimasu** (modest)

7	I'll go to your [lit. Mr. Kawamoto's] office at about 12:30.	**Watakushi ga juuni-ji han goro Kawamoto-san no jimusho e ukagai-masu.**

our company	**uchi no kaisha, toosha**
near	**chikaku ni**
fairly	**nakanaka**
restaurant	**resutoran, ryooriya**
cooking, cuisine	**ryoori**

Brown

8	There is a fairly good Italian restaurant near our company. How about Italian cuisine?	**Uchi no kaisha no chikaku ni naka-naka ii itaria-resutoran ga arimasu ga, itaria-ryoori wa ikaga desu ka.**

Kawamoto   to like   **suki desu**

9	Italian cuisine? (I) like (it) very much.	**Itaria-ryoori desu ka. Totemo suki desu yo.**

Lesson 9

| Brown | to invite | **shootai-suru** |

| **10** | Oh, is that right? Then let's do so. And (I)'d like to invite Mr. Takada of JETRO also, but [imp. is that OK?] | **Aa, soo desu ka. Jaa soo shimashoo. Sore kara, Jetoro no Takada-san mo shootai-shitai n desu ga…** |

| Kawamoto | (is) happy, gay | **tanoshii** |

| **11** | That'll be nice. [lit. That'll be a happy (occasion)] | **Sore wa tanoshii desu nee.** |

| Brown | well then to meet | **de wa** / **ome ni kakarimasu** (polite) |

| **12** | Well then, (I)'ll see (you) on Saturday. [lit. let (me) impose myself on (your) sight.] | **De wa, doyoobi ni ome ni kakarimashoo.** |

| Kawamoto | | |

| **13** | Well then, (I'll see you) again. Good-bye. | **De wa mata. Sayoonara.** |

| Brown | excuse me | **gomen-kudasai** |

| **14** | Good-bye. Excuse me. [imp. but I'll leave now.] | **Shitsuree-shimasu. Gomen-kudasai.** |

JAPANESE WRITING

1 ブラウン： ところで、川本さん、土曜日も仕事がありますか。
2 川　本： ええ、昼まで働きます。
3 ブラウン： 次の土曜日は、もう昼食の予定がありますか。
4 川　本： いいえ、ありません。
5 ブラウン： じゃあ、お昼をご一緒にいかがですか。いろいろお話したいですから…
6 川　本： それは結構ですねえ。どこで会いましょうか。
7 ブラウン： 私が十二時半ごろ川本さんの事務所へ伺います。
8 ブラウン： うちの会社の近くになかなかいいイタリアレストランがありますが、イタリア料理はいかがですか。
9 川　本： イタリア料理ですか。とても好きですよ。

Lesson 9

10　**ブラウン**：　ああ、そうですか。じゃあそうしましょう。それから、ジェトロの高田さんも招待したい
　　　　　　　　んですが…
11　**川　本**：　それは楽しいですねえ。
12　**ブラウン**：　では、土曜日にお目にかかりましょう。
13　**川　本**：　では、又。さようなら。
14　**ブラウン**：　失礼します。ごめんください。

READING

1　**Brown:**　　Tokoro de, Kawamoto-san, doyoobi mo shigoto ga arimasu ka.
2　**Kawamoto:**　Ee, hiru made hatarakimasu.
3　**Brown:**　　Tsugi no doyoobi wa, moo chuushoku no yotee ga arimasu ka.
4　**Kawamoto:**　Iie, arimasen.
5　**Brown:**　　Jaa, ohiru o goissho ni ikaga desu ka. Iroiro ohanashi-shitai
　　　　　　　　desu kara…
6　**Kawamoto:**　Sore wa kekkoo desu nee. Doko de aimashoo ka.
7　**Brown:**　　Watakushi ga juuni-ji han goro Kawamoto-san no jimusho e
　　　　　　　　ukagaimasu.
8　**Brown:**　　Uchi no kaisha no chikaku ni nakanaka ii itaria-resutoran ga
　　　　　　　　arimasu ga, itaria-ryoori wa ikaga desu ka.
9　**Kawamoto:**　Itaria-ryoori desu ka. Totemo suki desu yo.
10　**Brown:**　　Aa, soo desu ka. Jaa soo shimashoo. Sore kara, Jetoro no
　　　　　　　　Takada-san mo shootai-shitai (n) desu ga…
11　**Kawamoto:**　Sore wa tanoshii desu nee.
12　**Brown:**　　De wa, doyoobi ni ome ni kakarimashoo.
13　**Kawamoto:**　De wa mata. Sayoonara.
14　**Brown:**　　Shitsuree-shimasu. Gomen-kudasai.

ADDITIONAL USEFUL EXPRESSIONS

1 On the phone

free time, leisure	**hima**
free time	**ohima** (polite)

A:	Mr. Tanaka, are (you) free tonight? [lit. is tonight free time?]	**Tanaka-san, konban ohima desu ka.**
B:	(I)'ve already plans for tonight, but [imp. I wish I could come.]	**Konban wa moo yotee ga arimasu ga…**
A:	Is that so? How about tomorrow night?	**Soo desu ka. Ashita no ban wa ikaga desu ka.**

—113—

Lesson 9

in particular	**betsu ni**

B: I've no appointment in particular.	**Betsu ni yakusoku wa arimasen.**

your wife	**okusan/okusama** (respectful)
with your wife	**okusama to issho ni**
dinner	**yuushoku**
breakfast	**chooshoku***
for dinner	**yuushoku ni**

A: Then, please come with your wife to (my) house for dinner.	**Jaa, okusama to issho ni uchi e yuushoku ni irasshatte kudasai.**

Does not appear in sample dialogue. Introduced for reference only.

my wife	**kanai** (modest)

B: Thank you very much. (I)'ll go (to your house) with my wife.	**Arigatoo gozaimasu. Kanai to issho ni ukagaimasu.**

2 At the office

A: Did (you) already meet Mr. Takada?	**Moo Takada-san ni aimashita ka.**

not yet	**mada** /+negative/

B: No, (I) haven't seen (him) yet.	**Iie, mada ome ni kakarimasen.**

3 On the phone

within the near future	**chikai uchi ni**
by all means	**zehi**

A: By all means, please come to Osaka in the near future.	**Chikai uchi ni zehi Oosaka e irasshatte kudasai.**
B: Yes, I also want to go.	**Ee, watakushi mo ukagaitai (n) desu.**

4 At the office

Japanese cooking/cuisine	**nihon-ryoori**

A: Do (you) like Japanese cuisine?	**Nihon-ryoori ga suki desu ka.**

—114—

Lesson 9

| | a great liking | **daisuki** |
| | to eat | **tabemasu** |

| B: | Yes, I like Japanese cuisine very much. (I) ate (it) in America too. | **Ee, boku wa nihon-ryoori ga daisuki desu. Amerika de mo tabemashita yo.** |
| A: | How about your wife? | **Okusan wa.** |

| | dislike | **kirai** |

| B: | My wife dislikes Japanese cuisine. | **Kanai wa nihon-ryoori ga kirai desu.** |

REFERENCE

1 Family Terms

	speaker's family (Plain or Modest)	another's household (Respectful)
family	**kazoku**	**gokazoku**
husband	**shujin**	**goshujin**
father	**chichi**	**otoosan, otoosama**
mother	**haha**	**okaasan, okaasama**
parents	**ryooshin**	**goryooshin**
child	**kodomo**	**okosan**
son	**musuko**	**musukosan, botchan***
daughter	**musume**	**musumesan, ojoosan***
brother, sister	**kyoodai****	**gokyoodai****
older brother	**ani**	**oniisan, oniisama**
older sister	**ane**	**oneesan, oneesama**
younger brother	**otooto**	**otootosan**
younger sister	**imooto**	**imootosan**
grandfather	**sohu**	**ojiisan, ojiisama**
grandmother	**sobo**	**obaasan, obaasama**
grandchild	**mago**	**omagosan**
uncle	**oji**	**ojisan,***** **ojisama**
aunt	**oba**	**obasan,***** **obasama**
cousin	**itoko**	**oitokosan**
nephew	**oi**	**oigosan**
niece	**mee**	**meegosan**

* Both **botchan** 'another's son' and **ojoosan** 'another's daughter' are usually used for young children.
** **Kyoodai** can indicate both brothers and/or sisters.
*** **Ojiisan** and **ojisan** are quite similar in pronunciation, but note the difference between double **i** and single **i**. The same holds true for **obaasan and obasan.**

—115—

Lesson 9

2 Food

washoku, nihon-ryoori	Japanese cuisine
yooshoku, seeyoo-ryoori	Western cuisine
chuuka-ryoori	Chinese cuisine
huransu-ryoori	French cuisine
«country»-ryoori	«country's» cuisine
gohan	food, meal
asa-gohan	breakfast
hiru-gohan	lunch
ban-gohan	supper

NOTES

1 -**tai** form 'want to (do)'
Ohanashi-shitai 'to want to talk' is composed of **(ohanashi)**, **-shi,** the stem of the verb **shimasu,** and **-tai** 'to want to' or 'would like to.' You may make this form with most verbs by replacing **-masu** with **-tai.**

Examples:	a)	**ikimasu**	'(I) go'	→	**iki*tai* (n) desu**	"(I) want to go."
	b)	**kaimasu**	'(I) buy'	→	**kai*tai* (n) desu**	"(I) want to buy."
	c)	**kakimasu**	'(I) write'	→	**kaki*tai* (n) desu**	"(I) want to write."
	d)	**misemasu**	'(I) show'	→	**mise*tai* (n) desu**	"(I) want to show."
	e)	**tabemasu**	'(I) eat'	→	**tabe*tai* (n) desu**	"(I) want to eat."

This **-tai** form is a kind of adjective; the **-tai** form alone is informal. In ordinary conversations, **-tai** form is followed by **desu/n desu** in the case of the formal affirmative as in the above examples. The formal negative is its **-ku** form plus **arimasen,** as in **ikitaku arimasen** "(I) don't want to go." N in **-tai n desu** is a noun meaning 'fact' or 'matter,' so the verb stem + **-tai** + **n desu** literally translates into a phrase beginning with "it is the fact that..." **Ikitai n desu,** for example, means " It is the fact that I want to go." It is usually used only to soften the directness of the statement. Therefore, there is no difference in meaning between **-tai desu** and **-tai n desu.** The **-tai** form of a verb used without the **(n) desu** is the more informal expression. (Informal forms of verbs and adjectives will be discussed later.)
When a transitive verb is used in this **-tai** form, its object (what you want to do) is commonly indicated by the particle **ga.**

Compare:	**Chizu *o* kaimasu.**	"(I)'ll buy a map."
	and	
	Chizu *ga* kaitai (n) desu.	"(I) want to buy a map."

Note that particle **o** can also be used: **chizu *o* kaitai (n) desu.**
In this -tai sentence, the one who desires to do something is usually indicated by the particle **wa.** Thus,

—116—

Lesson 9

Person who wants to do something	What he wants to do	-tai (want)
Watakushi wa	**atarashii kuruma ga kai**	**-tai (n) desu.**
I want to buy a new car.		

Examples:
  a) **Ashita Kyooto e iki*tai (n) desu* ga* ...**
      "(I)'d like to go to Kyoto tomorrow, but [imp. may I do so?]"
  b) **Nichiyoobi wa hataraki*taku arimasen*.**
      "(I) don't want to work on Sundays."
  c) **Boku wa kyoo doitsugo no jisho ga kai*tai (n) desu*.**
      "I'd like to buy a German dictionary today."

*The particle **ga** following a -**tai** sentence is used to indicate doubt as to the fulfillment of the wish, or to ask the listener for his opinion or permission regarding the wish.

2 Particle wa

Particle **wa** is used to indicate not only the subject of a sentence, but also the topic of a sentence (See this lesson's DIALOGUE 3).

Compare:
  Tsugi no doyoobi *wa* Tanaka-san ga uchi e kimasu. (Topic)
  "As for next Saturday, Mr. Tanaka will come to my house."
  and
  Tanaka-san *wa* tsugi no doyoobi ni uchi e kimasu. (Subject)
  "Mr. Tanaka will come to my house next Saturday."

Generally speaking, in Japanese any noun becomes the topic of a sentence when it is followed by **wa** and occurs at the beginning of the sentence. Thus, in this case, particle **wa** is often translated (literally), 'as for.'

Examples:
  a) **Oosaka *wa* shachoo ga raishuu ikimasu.**
      "As for Osaka, the president will go (there) next week."
  b) **Chizu *wa* boku ga kaimashita.**
      "As for the map, I bought (it)."
  c) **Ashita *wa* jimusho e irasshaimasu ka.**
      "As for tomorrow, are (you) coming to the office?"
  d) **Doitsu-ryoori *wa* kanai ga suki desu.**
      "As for German food, my wife likes it."

3 Suki and Kirai

Both **suki** and **kirai** are nouns, but when they are directly followed by the copula **desu**, they are used as predicate adjectives: **suki desu** means '(is) pleasing' or 'to like' and **kirai desu** '(is) displeasing' or 'to dislike.' As with the -**tai** form, in a sentence with **suki desu** or **kirai desu,** the thing which is liked or disliked is followed by the particle **ga.**

Examples:
  a) **Watakushi *wa* nihon-ryoori *ga* suki desu.**
      "I like Japanese cuisine."
  b) **Yamada-san *wa* koohii *ga* kirai desu.**
      "Ms. Yamada dislikes coffee."

—117—

Lesson 9

4 **Moo/Mada**

Moo + an affirmative means 'already' or 'yet,' while **mada** + negative means 'not yet.' **Mada** often occurs in replying with the negative to a question with **moo,** while **moo** occurs in replying with the affirmative to a question with **mada.**

Examples: **a)** *Moo* **chizu o kaimashita ka.**
        "Have (you) bought a map already?"
        Ee, *moo* **kaimashita.**
        "Yes, (I) have already bought (it)." (**moo** + past)
        Iie, *mada* **kaimasen.**
        "No, (I) haven't bought (it) yet." (**mada** + non-past)

    b) *Mada* **Tanaka-san ni aimasen ka.**
        "Haven't (you) met Mr. Tanaka yet?"
        Hai*, *mada* **aimasen.**
        "That's right. (I) haven't met (him) yet." (**mada** + non-past)
        Iie*, *moo* **aimashita.**
        "That's wrong. (I) have already met (him)." (**moo** + past)

***Hai/ee** literally means "that's right" or "you're right," and **iie** means "that's wrong" or "you're wrong." **Hai/ee** confirms a statement, whether affirmative or negative, and **iie** denies a statement, whether affirmative or negative. Therefore, use of **hai/ee** and **iie** is different from that of the English 'yes' and 'no,' since 'yes' is always affirmative, and 'no' always negative. Carefully note the above examples.

5 Special Use of Particle **ni**

Particle **ni** in the sentence **Tanaka-san ni aimashita ka** "Did you meet Mr. Tanaka?" (in the ADDITIONAL USEFUL EXPRESSIONS of this lesson) basically means 'to.' But in Japanese, the verb **aimasu** 'to meet' is always preceded by **ni** when the object of the meeting is mentioned.

Example: **Buraun-san wa Kawamoto-san** *ni* **aimashita.**
        "Mr. Brown met Mr. Kawamoto. [lit. Mr. Brown met to Mr. Kawamoto.]"

6 Polite Expressions

Ukagaimasu, a modest verb meaning 'to visit,' is used when referring to the speaker himself or to members of the speaker's group.

Ome ni kakarimasu is usually used by the speaker when he talks of meeting people he should respect, never in reference to someone else who will meet the speaker.

Gomen-kudasai, in this lesson, means "Excuse me, [imp. but I'll be leaving now]" but it is also used when entering a house or a company to call attention to yourself.

—118—

Lesson 9

PRACTICE

1 Transformation Practice

Example: Teacher: **Ohanashi-shimasu.** "(I)'ll talk (with you)."
Student: **Ohanashi-shitai (n) desu.** "(I) want to talk (with you)."

a) **Ashita Buraun-san ni aimasu.**   **Ashita Buraun-san ni aitai (n) desu.**
b) **Ima uchi e denwa o kakemasu.**   **Ima uchi e denwa ga kaketai (n) desu.**
c) **Konban otaku e ukagaimasu.**   **Konban otaku e ukagaitai (n) desu.**
d) **Raishuu Kyooto e ikimasu.**   **Raishuu Kyooto e ikitai (n) desu.**
e) **Amerika e kaerimasu.**   **Amerika e kaeritai (n) desu.**
f) **Nihon-ryoori o tabemasu.**   **Nihon-ryoori ga tabetai (n) desu.**
g) **Ii hon o kakimasu.**   **Ii hon ga kakitai (n) desu.**

2 Response Practice

Example: Teacher: **Detoroito e kaeritai (n) desu ka.**
"Do (you) want to go back to Detroit?"
Student: **Iie, kaeritaku arimasen.**
"No, (I) don't want to go back (to Detroit)."

a) **Atarashii pen ga kaitai (n) desu ka.**   **Iie, kaitaku arimasen.**
b) **Sumisu-san ni aitai (n) desu ka.**   **Iie, aitaku arimasen.**
c) **Honsha ni denwa-shitai (n) desu ka.**   **Iie, (denwa)-shitaku arimasen.**
d) **Nichiyoobi mo hatarakitai (n) desu ka.**   **Iie, hatarakitaku arimasen.**

3 Communication Practice

Directions: Tell the teacher what you want to do now, using the following patterns.

a) **Ima «item» ga kaitai (n) desu.** "Now (I) want to buy «item»."
b) **Ima «place» e ikitai (n) desu.** "Now (I) want to go to «place»."
c) **Ima «name»-san ni denwa-shitai (n) desu.** "Now (I) want to call Mr./Ms. «name»."
d) **Ima «name»-san ni ome ni kakaritai (n) desu.** "Now (I) want to see Mr./Ms. «name»."
e) **Ima «item» ga tabetai (n) desu.** "Now (I) want to eat «item»."

Lesson 9

4 Transformation Practice

Directions: Rephrase each of the following, using the cue given as the main topic.

Example: Teacher: **Yamada-san ga ashita uchi e kimasu. /ashita/**
"Ms. Yamada will come to (my) house tomorrow." /tomorrow/
Student: **Ashita wa Yamada-san ga uchi e kimasu.**
"(As for) tomorrow, Ms. Yamada will come to (my) house."

a) **Tanaka-san ga kono kogitte o kakimashita. /kono kogitte/** **Kono kogitte wa Tanaka-san ga kakimashita.**
b) **Shachoo ga kayoobi ni Oosaka e ikimasu. /kayoobi/** **Kayoobi wa shachoo ga Oosaka e ikimasu.**
c) **Takada-san ga denwa o kakema-shita. /denwa/** **Denwa wa Takada-san ga kakemashita.**
d) **Buraun-san ga kono kuruma o kaimashita. /kono kuruma/** **Kono kuruma wa Buraun-san ga kaimashita.**

5 Response Practice

Directions: Answer the teacher's questions with particular attention to the use of the Japanese **hai/iie.**

Example: Teacher: **Tanaka-san wa imasen ka. /ee/**
"Isn't Mr. Tanaka in?" /right/
Student: **Ee, imasen.**
"You're right. (He) isn't in."

a) **Anata wa Buraun-san ja arimasen ka. /ee/** **Ee, Buraun(-san) ja arimasen.**
b) **Kyoo kuruma de kimasen deshita ka. /iie/** **Iie, kuruma de kimashita.**
c) **Chuushoku no yotee wa arimasen ka. /ee/** **Ee, (yotee wa) arimasen.**
d) **Sumisu-san ni aimasen deshita ka. /iie./** **Iie, aimashita.**
e) **Nihon-ryoori o tabemasen deshita ka. /ee/** **Ee, tabemasen deshita.**

—120—

Lesson 9

6 Response Practice

Example: Teacher: **Moo aimashita ka. /iie/**
              "Have (you) already met (him)?" /no/
              Student: **Iie, mada aimasen.**
              "No, (I) haven't met (him) yet."

a) **Mada kaimasen ka. /ee/**   **Ee, mada kaimasen.**
b) **Moo denwa-shimashita ka. /iie/**   **Iie, mada denwa-shimasen.**
c) **Moo misemashita ka. /ee/**   **Ee, moo misemashita.**
d) **Mada kimasen ka. /iie/**   **Iie, moo kimashita.**
e) **Moo kaerimashita ka. /iie/**   **Iie, mada kaerimasen.**
f) **Mada kakimasen deshita ka. /iie/**   **Iie, moo kakimashita.**
g) **Mada ikitai desu ka. /ee/**   **Ee, mada ikitai desu.**
h) **Moo wakarimashita ka. /iie/**   **Iie, mada wakarimasen.**
i) **Mada suki desu ka. /iie/**   **Iie, moo suki ja arimasen.**
j) **Moo kirai desu ka. /ee/**   **Ee, moo kirai desu.**

Note to the teacher: When the above practice is completed, please repeat it using different cues, i.e. **ee** for **iie** and vice versa.

EXERCISES

a) Ask the teacher the following, using polite Japanese.
1   Does the teacher already have an appointment for lunch tomorrow?
2   Is the teacher going to work next Saturday too?
3   You want to see the teacher next Friday night, but is he/she free?
4   Will the teacher please come to have lunch at your house next Sunday?
5   Has the teacher already been to America?
6   Does the teacher like Chinese cuisine?
7   Has the teacher eaten German cuisine yet?
8   Is the teacher happy every day?

b) Please inform the teacher in Japanese that:
1   Mr. Brown works from 8:30 to 5:30 every day.
2   You want to buy a smaller car in the near future.
3   Mr. Kawamoto will be free tonight.
4   You have already invited Mr. Yamamoto for lunch.
5   Yesterday, you and Ms. Yamada ate Chinese cuisine for dinner.
6   Your wife wants to see the teacher's wife.
7   The president of your company doesn't want to go to Japanese restaurants.
8   You want to show your office to the teacher, by all means.
9   Mr. Tanaka's dictionary is fairly good.

—121—

Lesson 9

Model Answers:

a) 1 Ashita wa moo chuushoku no yotee ga arimasu ka.
2 Tsugi no doyoobi mo hatarakimasu ka.
3 Tsugi no kin'yoobi no yoru ome ni kakaritai n desu ga, ohima desu ka.
4 Tsugi no nichiyoobi uchi e chuushoku ni irasshatte kudasai.
5 Moo Amerika e irasshaimashita ka.
6 Chuuka-ryoori wa suki desu ka.
7 Doitsu-ryoori wa moo tabemashita ka.
8 Mainichi tanoshii desu ka.

b) 1 Buraun-san wa mainichi hachi-ji han kara go-ji han made hatarakimasu.
2 Chikai uchi ni motto chiisai kuruma ga kaitai n desu.
3 Kawamoto-san wa konban ohima desu.
4 Moo Yamamoto-san o chuushoku ni shootai-shimashita.
5 Kinoo Yamada-san to issho ni yuushoku ni chuuka-ryoori o tabemashita.
6 Kanai wa okusama ni oai-shitai n desu.
7 Shachoo wa nihon-ryooriya e ikitaku arimasen.
8 Zehi jimusho o omise-shitai n desu.
9 Tanaka-san no jisho wa nakanaka ii desu.

Lesson 9

BUSINESS INFORMATION

The Business Luncheon I

One-to-one discussions in a relaxed drinking spot after working hours are traditionally the most effective means of cultivating business relationships in Japan. The business luncheon, however, is fast gaining popularity and is a good alternative if your personal schedule does not allow for leisurely after-hours socializing. There is usually a purpose behind every invitation in Japan; so it may be advisable to ask your client out to lunch only when you have a specific deal or request in mind, or when you wish to express your appreciation for your client's patronage, or just for the time he may have taken to discuss business with you.

To make sure that your business lunches go smoothly, you should note the following:

1 Whom to Invite, and How Many: As with all other business situations in Japan, it is important to consider the professional positions of the persons you wish to invite. If you overlook significant members of a group or company, you may ruffle their feathers and perhaps cause considerable damage to your budding business relationship. To play it safe, you should make a preliminary call to an acquaintance within the company itself to confirm that the parties you intend to invite are in fact the ones you should. Also, it is best to proceed with caution when inviting third (or more) parties. Once you have decided on your main guest, you should invite others only if their presence will benefit him or her. Japanese businessmen tend to be on the shy side and may regard unfamiliar persons as less of a business opportunity than as a nuisance. In no case should you ask a visiting relative or personal acquaintance along for the ride, as this would be considered an impertinence. Spouses, too, are seldom included in business lunches unless both parties are on very friendly terms, and even then only after a major transaction has been concluded. In short, the key rule for group participation is, "The fewer the better." And once the guest list has been drawn up, it is of course courteous to let your target guest know who will be coming, as Mr. Brown does in the DIALOGUE.

2 When and Where to Go: The standard time for lunch in Japan is 12:00 to 13:00 on weekdays. You should try to fit your business lunch into this one hour out of consideration for your counterpart's busy schedule. In contrast to some countries, the long, leisurely midday meal is not so appealing in Japan.

The standard choice for business lunches is a conveniently located, cozy restaurant. Many foreign businessmen find that ethnic restaurants, preferably those serving their native cuisine, are highly appreciated by Japanese clients; besides, the food and decor can help generate small talk during awkward lulls in the conversation. Frequent restaurant-going is bound to be expensive, of course, but like in many other countries, business lunches are tax-deductible in Japan—another reason for their growing popularity.

Lesson 9

3 The Bill, and other Minor Details: "Going Dutch" at business lunches is unheard of in Japan. When you propose a lunch, you should be prepared to pay. Also, you should note that it is customary to provide transportation for your guest when you are inviting, particularly if he is a high-ranking person. Whether you choose to drive yourself, hire a chauffeur, or send a staff member as escort, you should at least offer some form of transport even though, in most cases, your guest will politely decline your offer.

A final word of advice is that you should not overdo the business lunch. It is important to be patient and to take things one step at a time, as too-much-too-soon is likely to impose unwelcome pressure on your counterpart and so lead to unwelcome results. A simple meal in a medium-priced restaurant is an appropriate start, and menu and restaurant can be upgraded gradually as your negotiations and business take shape. The four-star restaurant with the lavish multi-course meal should be reserved only after your business deal has gone through.

Lesson 10

Business Luncheons

OBJECTIVES

1 to order food and drink at a restaurant.

2 to ask someone what he likes.

3 to say which one is better or the best for you.

4 to ask for someone's cooperation.

5 to count various items.

Lesson 10

TARGET EXPRESSIONS AND PATTERNS

1 Which do (you) like, «item X» or «item Y»?

   «X» to «Y» to dochira ga suki desu ka.

2 (I) prefer «item X».

   «X» no hoo ga suki desu.

3 Which do (you) like best, «item X», «item Y» or «item Z»?

   «X» to «Y» to «Z» no uchi de dore ga ichi-ban suki desu ka.

4 (I) like «item X» best.

   «X» ga ichi-ban suki desu.

5 (We) look forward to (your) continued support/cooperation. [lit. please continue (your) good favors towards (us).]

   Kongo tomo yoroshiku onegai-shimasu.

SITUATION

Mr. Brown goes to Japan Automobile Manufacturers Association Inc., to meet Mr. Kawamoto. Mr. Brown takes him to an Italian restaurant.

DIALOGUE

drink(s)	nomimono
what	nani
do you like?	osuki desu ka (respectful)
store	mise
Italian wine	itaria-wain

Brown

1	As for drinks, what do (you) like? This restaurant [lit. store] has good Italian wine, but (do you care for it?)	Nomimono wa nani ga osuki desu ka. Kono mise ni wa, itaria-wain no ii no ga arimasu ga...

Kawamoto

2	Well then, (I) will take wine.	Jaa, wain o itadakimasu.

white	shiro (noun)
red	aka (noun)
white or red	shiro to aka to
which?	dochira

Brown

3	As for wine, which do (you) like, white or red?	Wain wa, shiro to aka to dochira ga ii desu ka.

—126—

Lesson 10

Kawamoto	the red one [lit. the alternative of the red one.]	**aka no hoo**

| 4 | I like the red one better, but... | **Watakushi wa aka no hoo ga suki desu ga...** |

Brown	to order	**chuumon-shimasu**

| 5 | Well then, let's order red. | **Jaa, aka o chuumon-shimashoo.** |

(Mr. Brown calls a waiter, and looks over the wine list)

	one bottle	**ip-pon**
	something	**nani ka**
Brown	snack (to go with drinks)	**tsumami, otsumami** (polite)

| 6 | One bottle of this red wine and something as a snack, please. | **Kono aka-wain ip-pon to nani ka otsumami o onegai-shimasu.** |

	certainly [lit. (I) have respectfully obeyed.]	**kashikomarimashita**
	hors d'oeuvres	**oodoburu**
	ham	**hamu**
Waiter	cheese	**chiizu**

| 7 | Certainly, (sir). (We) have ham and cheese as hors d'oeuvres. | **Kashikomarimashita. Oodoburu wa hamu to chiizu desu ga...** |

	one more person	**moo hitori**
	guest, customer	**kyaku, okyakusama** (respectful)
	after arriving	**irasshatte kara** (respectful)
Brown	to ask, order	**tanomimasu**

| 8 | That's fine. And, as for dishes, (I)'ll order them after one more guest arrives, so (please wait). | **Kekkoo desu. Sore kara, ryoori wa moo hitori okyakusama ga irasshatte kara, tanomimasu kara...** |

Waiter	to have, bring	**mochimasu, omochi-shimasu** (respectful)

| 9 | Well then, (I)'ll bring the wine and hors d'oeuvres soon. | **De wa, sugu wain to oodoburu o omochi-shimasu.** |

—127—

Lesson 10

	Mr. Takada	Takada-kun
Kawamoto	(is) late	osoi

10 | Mr. Takada is late, isn't he? | **Takada-kun wa osoi desu nee.**

	meeting	kaigi
	to finish	owarimasu
Brown	after finishing	owatte kara

11 | Oh, (it)'s because Mr. Takada will come after the meeting finishes. | **Aa, Takada-san wa kaigi ga owatte kara, irasshaimasu kara...**

Kawamoto	the most, the best	**ichiban**

12 | Is that so? By the way, as for drinks, what do (you) [lit. does Mr. Brown] like best? | **Soo desu ka. Tokorode, Buraun-san wa nomimono wa nani ga ichiban suki desu ka.**

	whisky	uisukii
	recently	kono goro
	Japanese *sake*	sake, osake (polite)
	frequently, often	yoku
Brown	to drink	nomimasu

13 | I like whisky best, but recently (I) often drink *sake*, too. | **Boku wa uisukii ga ichiban suki desu ga, kono goro osake mo yoku nomimasu yo.**

(The waiter brings a bottle of wine and hors d'oeuvres.)

Waiter	thank you for waiting [lit. (I) have caused (you) to wait.]	**omatase-shimashita**

14 | Thank you for waiting. Please. | **Omatase-shimashita. Doozo.**

	to start	hajimemasu
	from now on	kongo
	also from now on	kongo tomo
Brown	your good-will, please	yoroshiku onegai-shimasu

15 | Well, Mr. Takada has not arrived yet, but shall (we) start? Mr. Kawamoto, (I) look forward to your continued cooperation. | **Jaa, Takada-san wa mada desu ga, hajimemashoo ka. Kawamoto-san, kongo tomo yoroshiku onegai-shimasu.**

—128—

Lesson 10

	it is I/we (who should say so)	kochira koso
Kawamoto	toast, cheers	kanpai

16 It is we who will be looking forward to your cooperation. Well then, cheers! — **Kochira koso yoroshiku onegai-shimasu. De wa, kanpai.**

Brown

17 Cheers! — **Kanpai.**

JAPANESE WRITING

1　ブラウン：　飲み物は何がお好きですか。この店には、イタリアワインのいいのがありますが…

2　川　本：　じゃあ、ワインをいただきます。

3　ブラウン：　ワインは、白と赤とどちらがいいですか。

4　川　本：　私は赤の方が好きですが…

5　ブラウン：　じゃあ、赤を注文しましょう。

6　ブラウン：　この赤ワイン一本と、何かおつまみをお願いします。

7　ウエイター：　かしこまりました。オードブルはハムとチーズですが…

8　ブラウン：　結構です。それから、料理はもう一人お客さまがいらっしゃってから頼みますから…

9　ウエイター：　では、すぐワインとオードブルをお持ちします。

10　川　本：　高田君は遅いですねえ。

11　ブラウン：　ああ、高田さんは会議が終ってからいらっしゃいますから…

12　川　本：　そうですか。ところで、ブラウンさんは飲み物は何が一番好きですか。

13　ブラウン：　ぼくはウイスキーが一番好きですが、この頃お酒もよく飲みますよ。

14　ウエイター：　お待たせしました。どうぞ。

15　ブラウン：　じゃあ、高田さんはまだですが、始めましょうか。川本さん、今後ともよろしくお願いします。

16　川　本：　こちらこそよろしくお願いします。 では、 乾杯。

17　ブラウン：　乾杯。

READING

1　Brown:　Nomimono wa nani ga osuki desu ka. Kono mise ni wa, itaria-wain no ii no ga arimasu ga…

2　Kawamoto: Jaa, wain o itadakimasu.

3　Brown:　Wain wa, shiro to aka to dochira ga ii desu ka.

4　Kawamoto: Watakushi wa aka no hoo ga suki desu ga…

5　Brown:　Jaa, aka o chuumon-shimashoo.

6　Brown:　Kono aka-wain ip-pon to nani ka otsumami o onegai-shimasu.

7　Waiter:　Kashikomarimashita. Oodoburu wa hamu to chiizu desu ga…

8　Brown:　Kekkoo desu. Sore kara, ryoori wa moo hitori okyakusama ga irasshatte kara, tanomimasu kara…

—129—

Lesson 10

9	Waiter:	De wa, sugu wain to oodoburu o omochi-shimasu.
10	Kawamoto:	Takada-kun wa osoi desu nee.
11	Brown:	Aa, Takada-san wa kaigi ga owatte kara, irasshaimasu kara...
12	Kawamoto:	Soo desu ka. Tokorode, Buraun-san wa nomimono wa nani ga ichiban suki desu ka.
13	Brown:	Boku wa uisukii ga ichiban suki desu ga, kono goro osake mo yoku nomimasu yo.
14	Waiter:	Omatase-shimashita. Doozo.
15	Brown:	Jaa, Takada-san wa mada desu ga, hajimemashoo ka. Kawamoto-san, kongo tomo yoroshiku onegai-shimasu.
16	Kawamoto:	Kochira koso yoroshiku onegai-shimasu. De wa, kanpai.
17	Brown:	Kanpai.

ADDITIONAL USEFUL EXPRESSIONS

1   After the meal

(is) delicious	**oishii**
it was a feast	**gochisoosama (deshita)**

A: (That) was delicious cuisine! Thank you. [lit. It was a feast.]	**Oishii ryoori deshita nee. Gochisoo-sama deshita.**

one glassful/cupful	**ip-pai**
one more glassful/cupful	**moo ip-pai**

B: How about another glass of wine?	**Wain o moo ip-pai ikaga desu ka.**

enough, fully	**juubun**

A: No, thank you. (I)'ve already had enough.	**Iie, kekkoo desu. Moo juubun itada-kimashita.**

2   While drinking coffee after the meal

meat	**niku**
fish	**sakana**
vegetable	**yasai**
among (X and Y and Z)	**uchi de**

A: Which do (you) like best, meat, fish or vegetables?	**Niku to sakana to yasai no uchi de, dore ga ichiban suki desu ka.**

of course	**mochiron**

B: Of course, (I) like meat best.	**Mochiron, niku ga ichiban suki desu.**

—130—

Lesson 10

more than meat	**niku yori**
especially	**toku ni**
sashimi, raw fish	**sashimi**

A: I like fish more than meat. (I) especially like *sashimi*.	**Boku wa niku yori sakana no hoo ga suki desu. Toku ni sashimi ga suki desu yo.**

3 At a Japanese restaurant with a close friend

A: What would (you) like to (have)? [lit. What is good (for you)?]	**Nani ga ii desu ka.**

tempura, a Japanese deep fried dish	**tenpura**

B: I'll (have) tempura. [lit. As for me,...]	**Boku wa tenpura.**

pork cutlet	**tonkatsu**

C: I'd like a pork cutlet.	**Boku wa tonkatsu.**
A: How about drinks?	**Nomimono wa.**
B: (I'd like) beer.	**Biiru.**
C: Me, too.	**Boku mo.**

one portion	**ichi-ninmae**
two portions	**ni-ninmae**

A: (We)'d like one portion of *tempura*, two portions of pork cutlet, and then three bottles of beer.	**Tenpura ichi-ninmae, tonkatsu ni-ninmae, sore kara biiru san-bon onegai-shimasu.**

(After the meal)

bill, check	**kaikee, oaiso**

A: Check, please.	**Kaikee onegai-shimasu.**
Waitress: Thank you very much. It's 6,000 yen.	**Arigatoo gozaimasu. Rokusen-en desu.**

—131—

Lesson 10

REFERENCE

shokudoo	dining room	**mizu**	cold water
sushiya	*sushi* shop	**oyu**	hot water
tenpuraya	*tempura* shop	**koocha**	black tea
sobaya	*soba* shop	**miruku, gyuunyuu**	milk
kissaten	tea room, coffee shop	**sukiyaki**	*sukiyaki*
gohan	cooked rice	**soba/udon**	noodles
pan	bread	**yakitori**	*yakitori*
kudamono	fruit	**tamago**	egg
okashi	cake, sweets	**gyuuniku**	beef
		butaniku	pork
		toriniku	fowl, chicken

NOTES

1 **Yori and Hoo**

X yori Y no hoo ga suki desu means "I like Y better than X." This pattern is used to express a preference for one of two alternatives. Note that the preferred alternative is usually followed by **no hoo ga** and sometimes by **ga** alone. As predicates, adjectives also occur in this pattern, as in Examples **b)** and **c)** below.

Examples:
    a) **Boku wa Tookyoo yori Kyooto *(no hoo) ga* suki desu.**
        "I like Kyoto better than Tokyo."
    b) **Tanaka-san no kaisha yori uchi no kaisha *(no hoo) ga* ookii desu.**
        "Our company is larger than Mr. Tanaka's."
    c) **Kono biru yori ano biru *(no hoo) ga* hurui n desu ka.**
        "Is that building over there older than this building?"
    d) **Wain yori biiru *(no hoo) ga* nomitai n desu.**
        "(I) want to drink beer more than wine."

Dochira 'which one?' is used when asking someone to choose between two items as in the following pattern: **X to Y to, dochira (no hoo) ga...** 'of X and Y, which is more...'

Examples:
    a) **Yokohama *to* Koobe *to, dochira (no hoo) ga* suki desu ka.**
        "Which do (you) like, Yokohama or Kobe?"
    b) **Kono hon *to* ano hon *to, dochira (no hoo) ga* atarashii desu ka.**
        "Which is newer, this book or that book?"

In answering the above questions, the alternative which isn't chosen may be omitted.

Example: **Yokohama *(no hoo) ga* suki desu.** "(I) like Yokohama better."

2 **Ichiban**

Ichiban meaning 'the first,' 'the best,' 'the greatest' or 'the most' is used in designating one's choice among three or more alternatives.

—132—

Lesson 10

Example: **Nomimono wa biiru ga *ichiban* suki desu.**
"As for drinks, (I) like beer best."

In order to ask about a choice among three or more alternatives, the pattern **X to Y to Z no uchi de, dore ga ichiban...** "which is the best/most...among X, Y and Z?" is used.

Example: **Nihongo *to* chuugokugo *to* roshiago *no uchi de, dore ga ichiban* muzukashii desu ka.**
"Which is the most difficult, Japanese, Chinese or Russian?"

3 **-te kara** 'after doing'
Verb gerund + **kara** means 'after doing such-and-such.'

Examples: a) **Wain o non*de kara*, ikimashoo.**
"After drinking wine, let's go."
b) **Nihon e/ni ki*te kara*, Yamada-san ni aimashita.**
"After coming to Japan, (I) met Ms. Yamada."

Don't confuse this pattern with a verb + **kara** meaning 'so.'

Compare: **Takada-san ga ki*te kara*, ryoori o chuumon-shimasu.**
"After Mr. Takada has arrived, (I)'ll order food."
and
Takada-san ga ki*ta kara*, ryoori o chuumon-shimashita.
"Mr. Takada arrived, so (I) ordered dishes."

4 Counters: **-pon** (or **-hon** or **-bon**), **-ri** (or **-nin**), **-pai** (or **-hai**) and **-ninmae**
A) **-pon** is used to count long and cylindrical objects such as bottles, pens, trees, legs, etc. This counter combines with Chinese-origin numerals and may change in pronunciation depending upon the preceding numeral. Thus, **ip-pon, ni-hon, san-bon, yon-hon, go-hon, rop-pon, nana-hon, hap-pon, kyuu-hon, jup-pon,** 'one bottle, two bottles...ten bottles (or trees, etc.).' Note that in questions, **nan-bon** is used, meaning 'how many (long and cylindrical) objects?'

B) **-ri** and **-nin** are used to count people. **-ri** is used only to count one or two persons and is combined with numerical expressions of Japanese origin, **hito** 'one' and **huta** 'two' (Lesson 6, Note 4). **-nin** is used to indicate three or more persons, and is combined with numerical expressions of Chinese origin (Lesson 3). Thus, **hito-ri, huta-ri, san-nin, yo-nin, go-nin, roku-nin, shichi-nin, hachi-nin, kyuu-nin, juu-nin.** In questions, **nan-nin** is used, meaning 'how many people?'

C) **-pai** is used to count glassfuls or cupfuls, and combines with Chinese-origin numerals. Numbers from one to ten are as follows:
ip-pai, ni-hai, san-bai, yon-hai, go-hai, rop-pai, nana-hai, hap-pai, kyuu-hai, jup-pai. In questions, **nan-bai** 'how many glasses/cups?' is used.

—133—

Lesson 10

D) **-ninmae** is used to count portions of food and combines with Chinese-origin numerals. **ichi-ninmae, ni-ninmae, san-ninmae, yo-ninmae, go-ninmae, roku-ninmae, nana-ninmae, hachi-ninmae, kyuu-ninmae, juu-ninmae** 'one portion...ten portions.' In questions, **nan-ninmae** is used, meaning 'how many portions?'

5 Words for Colors
Shiroi '(is) white' and **akai** '(is) red' are adjectives, while **shiro** 'the color white' and **aka** 'the color red' are nouns. Most color adjectives become nouns when the final **i** is omitted.

6 Koso
Koso is an emphatic particle meaning 'none other than.' **Kochira koso** in the DIALOGUE of this lesson is used to emphasize that "the person who should ask for your good-will is I [lit. this side]."

7 **-kun** is frequently used instead of **-san** to refer to someone younger or of a lower position than the speaker, and is usually used to address a male person, e.g. **Takada-kun.**

PRACTICE

1 Response Practice

Example:	Teacher:	**Shiro to aka to, dochira ga suki desu ka. /aka/**
		"Which do (you) like, the white one or the red one?" /red one/
	Student:	**Aka no hoo ga suki desu.**
		"(I) like the red one better."

a) **Osake to biiru to, dochira ga suki desu ka. /biiru/**   Biiru no hoo ga suki desu.

b) **Yokohama to Nagoya to, dochira ga ookii desu ka. /Yokohama/**   Yokohama no hoo ga ookii desu.

c) **Nihongo to doitsugo to, dochira ga muzukashii desu ka. /Nihongo/**   Nihongo no hoo ga muzukashii desu.

d) **Tenpura to tonkatsu to, dochira ga tabetai desu ka. /tenpura/**   Tenpura no hoo ga tabetai desu.

e) **Kono chizu to ano chizu to, dochira ga ii desu ka. /ano chizu/**   Ano chizu no hoo ga ii desu.

2 Response Practice

Example:	Teacher:	**Niku to sakana to yasai no uchi de, nani ga ichiban suki desu ka. /yasai/**
		"Which do (you) like best, meat, fish or vegetables?"
	Student:	**Yasai ga ichiban suki desu.**
		"(I) like vegetables best."

a) **Tenpura to tonkatsu to sukiyaki no uchi de, dore ga ichiban suki desu ka. /tonkatsu/**   Tonkatsu ga ichiban suki desu.

—134—

Lesson 10

b) Gyuuniku to butaniku to toriniku no uchi de, dore ga ichiban oishii desu ka. /gyuuniku/   Gyuuniku ga ichiban oishii desu.

c) Osake to biiru to uisukii no uchi de, dore ga ichiban nomitai desu ka. /osake/   Osake ga ichiban nomitai desu.

d) Kore to sore to are no uchi de, dore ga ichiban yasui desu ka. /are/   Are ga ichiban yasui desu.

3 Transformation Practice

Example: Teacher: **Okyakusama ga kimasu. Ryoori o chuumon-shimasu.**
"The guest comes. (I)'ll order dishes."
         Student: **Okyakusama ga kite kara, ryoori o chuumon-shimasu.**
"After the guest comes, (I)'ll order dishes."

a) **Kaigi ga owarimasu. Uchi e/ni kaerimasu.**   **Kaigi ga owatte kara, uchi e/ni kaerimasu.**

b) **Nihon e/ni kimashita. Takada-san ni aimashita.**   **Nihon e/ni kite kara, Takada-san ni aimashita.**

c) **Yuushoku ga owarimasu. Takada-san ni denwa-shimasu.**   **Yuushoku ga owatte kara, Takada-san ni denwa-shimasu.**

d) **Wain o kaimasu. Yamamoto-san no otaku e/ni ikimasu.**   **Wain o katte kara, Yamamoto-san no otaku e/ni ikimasu.**

e) **Hiru made hatarakimashita. Kyooto e/ni ikimashita.**   **Hiru made hataraite kara, Kyooto e/ni ikimashita.**

4 Response Practice

Example: Teacher: **Ima jimusho ni nan-nin imasu ka. /yo-nin/**
"How many people are in the office now?" /four people/
         Student: **Yo-nin imasu.**
"There are four people."

a) **Biiru o nan-bon tanomimasu ka. /ni-hon/**   **Ni-hon tanomimasu.**

b) **Wain o nan-bai nomimashita ka. /san-bai/**   **San-bai nomimashita.**

c) **Okyakusama wa nan-nin kimasu ka. /go-nin/**   **Go-nin kimasu.**

d) **Tenpura o nan-ninmae chuumon-shimasu ka. /roku-ninmae/**   **Roku-ninmae chuumon-shimasu.**

e) **Enpitsu wa nan-bon irimasu ka. /jup-pon/**   **Jup-pon irimasu.**

5 Communication Practice

Directions: Indicate to the teacher in Japanese which of the following items you prefer or like best. When completed repeat the entire exercise asking the teacher to indicate his/her preference(s).

—135—

Lesson 10

a) beer, wine or whisky
b) Western cuisine, Chinese cuisine or Japanese cuisine
c) coffee or tea
d) New York, Chicago or Hawaii
e) *sukiyaki* or *sashimi*
f) taxi or subway
g) beef, pork or fish

EXERCISES

a) Ask your guest: Reply as a guest:

1   Which (he) likes better, beer or *sake*.   (I) like beer better.
2   If (he)'ll have some cheese.   No, thank you.
3   If (he)'ll have some more beer.   Yes, please.
4   If (he)'ll have some tea.   (I) want to drink some water, please.
5   If (he) likes this type of food.   (I) like (it) very much.

b) Give the teacher the following information in Japanese:
1   Mr. Tanaka's car is bigger than mine.
2   Ms. Yamada dislikes *sake*.
3   The Chinese food in this restaurant is very delicious.
4   This word processor is the newest one.
5   Mr. Yamamoto has a meeting scheduled for this afternoon.
6   Mrs. Brown doesn't want to have *sashimi,* but Mr. Brown likes it very much.
7   After having dinner, let's have some fruit.
8   Mr. Takada will invite Mr. Brown to a very nice *sushi* shop before long.

Model Answers:

a) 1 **Biiru to osake to dochira ga suki desu ka.**   **Biiru no hoo ga suki desu.**
    2 **Chiizu wa ikaga desu ka.**   **Iie, kekkoo desu.**
    3 **Biiru o moo ip-pai ikaga desu ka.**   **Ee, onegai-shimasu.**
    4 **Ocha wa ikaga desu ka.**   **Omizu (o) onegai-shimasu.**
    5 **Kono ryoori wa osuki desu ka.**   **Totemo suki desu.**

b) 1 **Tanaka-san no kuruma wa watakushi no yori ookii desu.**
    2 **Yamada-san wa osake ga kirai desu.**
    3 **Kono resutoran no chuuka-ryoori wa totemo oishii desu.**
    4 **Kono waapuro wa ichiban atarashii desu.**
    5 **Yamamoto-san wa kyoo no gogo kaigi no yotee ga arimasu.**
    6 **Buraun-san no okusan wa sashimi ga/o tabetaku arimasen ga, Buraun-san
       wa totemo suki desu.**
    7 **Yuushoku o tabete kara, kudamono o tabemashoo.**
    8 **Takada-san wa chikai uchi ni Buraun-san o totemo ii sushiya ni shootai-
       shimasu.**

—136—

Lesson 10

BUSINESS INFORMATION

The Business Luncheon II

1 The Seating: Whether you are in a Western-style dining room, a Japanese restaurant or a reception lounge, the rule of thumb is that the guests sit on the far side of the room and the hosts sit on the side nearest the entrance. Also, the highest-ranking guest occupies the most central seat and, as much as possible, the highest-ranking host takes the seat directly opposite him. You should also note the following variations of the basic arrangement:
  1) In case there are only two places available, the senior official takes the one furthest from the door even if this may not be directly opposite that of his counterpart (Diagram #1).
  2) In the event there are three or more participants, you should follow the order illustrated in Diagram #2.

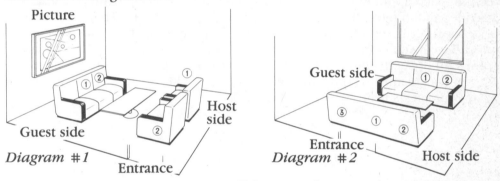

In many Japanese restaurants, your room will have a **tokonoma** (床の間, alcove) with **kakejiku** (掛軸, hanging scroll) and **ikebana** (生花, flower arrangement), as illustrated in Diagram #3. Overseas visitors occasionally feel that the choice seat in such a room would be the one facing the alcove, but in fact the main guest is always seated directly in front of the **tokonoma,** with his back to the **kakejiku** and **ikebana.** Some say that this particular arrangement has its roots in the medieval concern for personal security, since this seat faces the entrance and is the best one for observing all the comings and goings. It has also been suggested that, because the **tokonoma** was historically reserved for religious artifacts, it was therefore a very special and revered space in the room. Consequently, if you end up with your back to the **tokonoma,** you should hide your disappointment in not being able to enjoy the beautiful **kakejiku** and rest assured that you do have the best seat in the house.

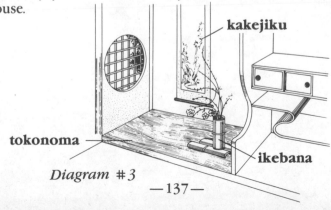

Lesson 10

2   The Conversation: Much more important than the seating arrangement, of course, is the topic of conversation. Although, as mentioned in the previous lesson, everyone attends a business lunch with business objectives in mind, there is no such thing in Japan as a real "working" lunch or dinner. Foreign visitors who attend lunches with high hopes of clinching a contract are invariably disappointed with what they consider their counterparts' evasiveness throughout the meal. In fact, the purpose of the business lunch in Japan is not to discuss problems or work out solutions. Rather, it is to enhance a sense of intimacy between business affiliates and provide a lubricant for present or future negotiations. If you are being invited to lunch, this does not necessarily mean that there are urgent business matters to be discussed, but that your prospective partner or client may simply want to check out your personality (人柄 **hitogara**) prior to engaging your services.

Consequently, all talk about schedules and other explicitly business-related topics should be left for a more formal opportunity. It is far more important during the lunch to show sensitivity toward your counterpart, e.g. by asking questions, listening to him, and trying to understand his needs and those of his company. Often a foreign businessman will see the lunch appointment as a prime public relations opportunity and launch into an extended monologue about his own firm and all its merits. There are few things more inappropriate in the mind of the Japanese businessman than this sort of sales pitch, which he considers a real impediment to genuine communication. You may feel pleased at the end of such a presentation that the prospective client now has a detailed knowledge of your company. Unfortunately, none of the information you gave may have been what your guests really wanted to hear.

Lesson 11

On the Way to the Showroom

OBJECTIVES

1   to ask or indicate how to get to train stations.

2   to ask or show the way to get to places.

3   to tell a taxi driver how to get to where you want to go.

Lesson 11

TARGET EXPRESSIONS AND PATTERNS

1 Excuse me, but... **Chotto ukagaimasu ga...**

2 (I)'d like to go to «place X», but please show (me) the way. **«X» e/ni ikitai n desu ga, michi o oshiete kudasai.**

3 Please go straight along this street, and turn to the right. **Kono michi o massugu itte, migi e/ni magatte kudasai.**

4 «item X» or «item Y» **«X» ka «Y».**

5 Please stop (the car) in front of «place X». **«X» no mae de tomete kudasai.**

6 «person/item X» is behind «person/item Y». **«X» wa «Y» no ura ni arimasu.**

SITUATION

Mr. Brown plans to buy a word processor to speed up his office work, and goes to a business machine showroom. However, he has never been there, so he asks various people how to get there.

DIALOGUE

(At the subway station)

	sorry to bother (you), but [lit. It is inexcusable, but...]	**sumimasen ga...**
Brown	a place name in Tokyo	**Ootemachi**

1	Sorry to bother (you), but (I)'d like to go to Otemachi, but [imp. would you tell me how to get there?]	**Sumimasen ga, Ootemachi e/ni ikitai n desu ga...**

a place name in Tokyo	**Asakusa**
Asakusa-bound	**Asakusa-iki**
to get on, take (a vehicle)	**norimasu**
a place name in Tokyo	**Nihonbashi**
at, in	**de**
Tozai Line	**Toozaisen**

—140—

Lesson 11

Station Employee	to transfer	norikaemasu

| **2** | Otemachi? Take (the train) bound for Asakusa to Nihonbashi and please transfer there to the Tozai Line. | **Ootemachi desu ka. Asakusa-iki ni notte, Nihonbashi made itte, soko de Toozaisen ni norikaete kudasai.** |

Brown	train for where	nani-iki

| **3** | To what train should (I) transfer? | **Nani-iki ni norikaemasu ka.** |

	a place name in Tokyo	Nakano
	or	ka
Station Employee	a place name in Tokyo	Mitaka

| **4** | To (the train) for Nakano or Mitaka. Otemachi is the next station, so... [imp. get off there.] | **Nakano-iki ka Mitaka-iki desu. Ootemachi wa tsugi no eki desu kara...** |

Brown

| **5** | Thank you very much. | **Doomo arigatoo.** |

(On the street at Otemachi)

	to ask, inquire	ukagaimasu (modest)
	Excuse me, but...	chotto ukagaimasu ga...
	[lit. I'm going to inquire a little...]	
	this area	kono hen
Brown	office machine	jimu-kiki

| **6** | Excuse me, but aren't there any showrooms for office machines in this area? | **Chotto ukagaimasu ga, kono hen ni jimu-kiki no shooruumu wa arimasen ka.** |

	police box	kooban
	policeman	keekan
Passer-by	to ask	kikimasu

| **7** | Well, (I) don't know. Please ask a policeman in that police box. | **Saa, wakarimasen. Soko no kooban de keekan ni kiite kudasai.** |

Lesson 11

(At the police box)

	Tokyo Machinery (Ltd.)	**Tookyoo-kiki**
	way, street, road	**michi, toori**
Brown	to teach	**oshiemasu**

8	(I)'d like to go to the Tokyo Machinery showroom. Would (you) please tell (me) how to get there?	**Tookyoo-kiki no shooruumu e/ni ikitai n desu ga, michi o oshiete kudasai.**

	straight	**massugu**
	the second	**ni-ban-me**
	intersection	**koosaten, yotsukado**
	right	**migi**
Policeman	to turn	**magarimasu**

9	Please go straight along this street and turn right at the second intersection.	**Kono michi o massugu itte, ni-ban-me no koosaten o migi e/ni magatte kudasai.**

Brown	corner	**kado**

10	At the second corner?	**Ni-ban-me no kado desu ne.**

	left	**hidari**
	left side	**hidari-gawa**
	post office	**yuubinkyoku**
Policeman	next door	**tonari**

11	Yes, that's right. And then, there is a post office on the left-hand side. The showroom is next door to it.	**Ee, soo desu. Sore kara, hidari-gawa ni yuubinkyoku ga arimasu. Shooruumu wa sono tonari desu.**

Brown

12	(I) understand. Thank you so much.	**Wakarimashita. Doomo arigatoo.**

—142—

Lesson 11

JAPANESE WRITING

1　ブラウン：　すみませんが、大手町へ行きたいんですが…
2　駅　　員＊：　大手町ですか。浅草行きに乗って、日本橋まで行って、そこで東西線に乗り換えてください。
3　ブラウン：　何行きに乗り換えますか。
4　駅　　員：　中野行きか三鷹行きです。大手町は次の駅ですから…
5　ブラウン：　どうもありがとう。
6　ブラウン：　ちょっと伺いますが、この辺に事務機器のショールームはありませんか。
7　通行人＊＊：　さあ、わかりません。そこの交番で警官に聞いてください。
8　ブラウン：　東京機器のショールームへ行きたいんですが、道を教えてください。
9　警　　官：　この道をまっすぐ行って、二番目の交差点を右へ曲がってください。
10　ブラウン：　二番目の角ですね。
11　警　　官：　ええ、そうです。それから、左側に郵便局があります。ショールームはその隣です。
12　ブラウン：　わかりました。どうもありがとう。

NOTE:　＊駅員（**ekiin**, station employee）,　＊＊通行人（**tsuukoonin**, passer-by）

READING

1　Brown:　**Sumimasen ga, Ootemachi e/ni ikitai n desu ga…**
2　Station Employee:　**Ootemachi desu ka. Asakusa-iki ni notte, Nihonbashi made itte, soko de Toozaisen ni norikaete kudasai.**
3　Brown:　**Nani-iki ni norikaemasu ka.**
4　Station Employee:　**Nakano-iki ka Mitaka-iki desu. Ootemachi wa tsugi no eki desu kara…**
5　Brown:　**Doomo arigatoo.**
6　Brown:　**Chotto ukagaimasu ga, kono hen ni jimu-kiki no shooruumu wa arimasen ka.**
7　Passer-by:　**Saa, wakarimasen. Soko no kooban de keekan ni kiite kudasai.**
8　Brown:　**Tookyoo-kiki no shooruumu e/ni ikitai n desu ga, michi o oshiete kudasai.**
9　Policeman:　**Kono michi o massugu itte, ni-ban-me no koosaten o migi e/ni magatte kudasai.**
10　Brown:　**Ni-ban-me no kado desu ne.**
11　Policeman:　**Ee, soo desu. Sore kara hidari-gawa ni yuubinkyoku ga arimasu. Shooruumu wa sono tonari desu.**
12　Brown:　**Wakarimashita. Doomo arigatoo.**

—143—

Lesson 11

ADDITIONAL USEFUL EXPRESSIONS

1 In the taxi

end (of a street)	**tsukiatari**

Passenger:	Please go straight along this street and turn left at the end.	**Kono michi o massugu itte, tsuki-atari o hidari e/ni magatte kudasai.**
Driver:	To the left at the end, right?	**Tsukiatari o hidari desu ne.**

front	**mae**
in front of the bank	**ginkoo no mae de**
to stop	**tomemasu**

Passenger:	Please stop (the car) in front of that bank.	**Sono ginkoo no mae de tomete kudasai.**

2 At the office

embassy	**taishikan**
British Embassy	**Igirisu-taishikan**

A:	(I)'d like to go to the British Embassy, but (I) don't know how to get there.	**Igirisu-taishikan e/ni ikitai n desu ga, michi ga wakarimasen.**

to draw, write	**kakimasu**

B:	Well then, shall (I) draw a map?	**De wa, chizu o kakimashoo ka.**
A:	Yes, please.	**Ee, onegai-shimasu.**

3 On the street

this way (near the speaker)	**kochira**
that way (near the listener)	**sochira***
that way (away from both)	**achira***
this way (direction)	**kochira no hoo**

A:	Is the British Embassy in this direction?	**Igirisu-taishikan wa kochira no hoo desu ka.**

*Does not appear in sample dialogue. Introduced for reference only.

—144—

Lesson 11

opposite	**hantai**
back side	**ura**

B:	No, it's the opposite (way). The British Embassy is on the other side of that building.	**Iie, hantai desu yo. Igirisu-taishikan wa ano biru no ura desu yo.**

4 At the office

apartment (usually a rather good one)	**manshon**
location, place	**tokoro**

A:	Your apartment is in a good location, isn't it?	**Otaku no manshon wa ii tokoro ni ari masu nee.**

park	**kooen**
back, rear, behind	**ushiro**
church	**kyookai**
quiet	**shizuka**

B:	Right. A park is in the front and a church is in the back, so it's very quiet.	**Ee, mae ga kooen de, ushiro ga kyookai desu kara, totemo shizuka desu yo.**

vicinity	**soba**
immediate vicinity	**sugu soba**
factory	**koojoo**
(is) noisy	**yakamashii**

A:	That's good. There is a factory in the immediate vicinity of my home, so it's very noisy.	**Ii desu nee. Uchi wa sugu soba ni koojoo ga arimasu kara, totemo yakamashii desu yo.**

REFERENCE

depaato	department store	**tera, otera**	temple
suupaa	super market	**jinja**	shrine
kusuriya	drugstore	**keesatsusho**	police station
nikuya	meat store	**shooboosho**	fire station
yaoya	vegetable store	**gakkoo**	school
sakanaya	fish store	**byooin**	hospital
hon'ya	bookstore	**shingoo**	signal
denkiya	electric appliance store	**koosoku-dooro**	highway
		intaa-chenji	interchange
otearai, benjo	toilet	**ryookinjo**	tollgate
basu-tee	bus stop		

—145—

Lesson 11

NOTES

1 More about the Gerund (-**te** form)

When two or more sentences are combined into one, all verbs except the final one in the sentence usually appear in the gerund form.

Asakusa-iki ni norimasu.	Nihonbashi made ikimasu.
(I)'ll get on (the train) for Asakusa.	(I)'ll go as far as Nihonbashi.
Asakusa-iki ni not*te*, Nihonbashi made ikimasu.	
(I)'ll get on (the train) for Asakusa and go as far as Nihonbashi.	

As shown in the DIALOGUE of this lesson, the gerund is also combined with **kudasai** 'please' to express a request.

Compare: **Kono michi o it*te* kudasai. Ni-ban-me no kado o migi e/ni magat*te* kudasai.**
"Please go along this street. Please turn right at the second corner."

and

Kono michi o it*te*, ni-ban-me no kado o migi e/ni magat*te* kudasai.
"Please go along this street and turn right at the second corner."

The gerund form of the copula **desu** 'to be' simply remains as **de.**

Example: **Mae ga kooen *de*, ushiro ga kyookai desu.**
"(In) the front is a park and (in) the back is a church."

Please note that the gerund form is also used when two or more sentences containing adjectives are combined, as follows:

        Tanaka-san no kuruma wa *ookikute*, boku no wa chiisai desu.
        "Mr. Tanaka's car is big, and mine is small."

To form adjective gerunds, drop the final **-i** of the adjective (i.e. **ookii − i = ooki**) and add **kute** (i.e. **ooki + kute = ookikute**). (Refer to Lesson 7, Notes **1**)

2 Particle **de** 'at, in'

De preceded by a place noun is used to indicate the place where something happens.

Examples:	a) **Ginkoo no mae *de* tomete kudasai.**	"Please stop (the car) in front of the bank."
	b) **Kooban *de* kikimasu.**	"(I)'ll ask at the police box."
	c) **Ano resutoran *de* tabema-shoo.**	"Let's eat at that restaurant."

Note that **de** is a 'location particle' only used with action verbs. Where no action takes place, another 'location particle' **ni** is normally used.

—146—

Lesson 11

Compare: **Mainichi ano jimusho *de* hata-rakimasu.**   "(I) work in that office every day."

and

Ano hon wa jimusho *ni* arimasu.   "That book is in the office."

3 Particle **o** 'through, along'
A noun of place + **o** indicates the place through which an action passes.

Examples:
a) **Kono michi *o* ikimasu.**   "(I)'ll go along this street."
b) **Sono kado *o* hidari e/ni magarimashoo.**   "Let's turn left at that corner."

4 Particle **ka** 'or'
Ka between nouns means 'or.'

Examples:
a) **Hon *ka* zasshi o kaimashoo.**   "Let's buy a book or a magazine."
b) **Amerika *ka* Igirisu e/ni ikitai n desu.**   "(I) want to go to America or England."
c) **Buraun-san *ka* Yamada-san ga kimasu.**   "Mr. Brown or Ms. Yamada will come."
d) **Kin'yoobi *ka* doyoobi ni denwa-shimasu.**   "(I)'ll call you on Friday or Saturday."

Please note: **Ka**, unlike **X to Y to, dochira** 'which, X or Y?' (Lesson 10), is normally used in direct statements rather than in questions regarding choice.

5 Ordinal Numbers
A cardinal number is changed to its ordinal form by adding the suffix **-me.**

Examples:
a) **ni-ban**   'number 2'   →   **ni-ban-*me***   'the second'
b) **san-kagetsu**   'three months'   →   **san-kagetsu-*me*** 'the third month'
c) **yot-tsu**   'four units'   →   **yot-tsu-*me***   'the fourth unit'

6 Ways to indicate location
There are two ways to express where something or someone is located: **X wa Y desu** and **X wa Y ni arimasu** (or **imasu**).

Compare: **Kuruma wa eki no mae desu.**
"The car is (in) front of the station."

and

Kuruma wa eki no mae ni arimasu.
"The car is in front of the station."

—147—

Lesson 11

PRACTICE

1 Transformation Practice

Example: Teacher: **Asakusa-iki ni notte kudasai. Nihonbashi made itte kudasai.**
"Please get on the train for Asakusa. Please go as far as Nihonbashi."
Student: **Asakusa-iki ni notte, Nihonbashi made itte kudasai.**
"Please get on the train for Asakusa and go as far as Nihonbashi."

a) **Kono michi o massugu itte kudasai. Yuubinkyoku no kado o migi e/ni magatte kudasai.**　**Kono michi o massugu itte, yuubinkyoku no kado o migi e/ni magatte kudasai.**
b) **Doyoobi ni jimusho e/ni kite kudasai. Hiru made hataraite kudasai.**　**Doyoobi ni jimusho e/ni kite, hiru made hataraite kudasai.**
c) **Sumisu-san ni denwa-shite kudasai. Iroiro hanashite kudasai.**　**Sumisu-san ni denwa-shite, iroiro hanashite kudasai.**

2 Transformation Practice

Example: Teacher: **Oosaka e/ni ikimasu. Tanaka-san ni aimasu.**
"(I)'ll go to Osaka. (I)'ll see Mr. Tanaka."
Student: **Oosaka e/ni itte, Tanaka-san ni aimasu.**
"(I)'ll go to Osaka and see Mr. Tanaka."

a) **Tanaka-san ni denwa-shimashita. Chuushoku ni shootai-shimashita.**　**Tanaka-san ni denwa-shite, chuushoku ni shootai-shimashita.**
b) **Uchi e/ni kaerimasu. Biiru o nomimasu.**　**Uchi e/ni kaette, biiru o nomimasu.**
c) **Kono hon wa Takada-san no desu. Ano hon wa boku no desu.**　**Kono hon wa Takada-san no de, ano hon wa boku no desu.**
d) **Sumisu-san wa shachoo desu. Nyuuyooku ni imasu.**　**Sumisu-san wa shachoo de, Nyuuyooku ni imasu.**

3 Communication Practice

Directions: Ask where the following are located.

Example: Teacher: **Ginkoo**
Student: **Chotto ukagaimasu ga, kono hen ni ginkoo wa arimasen ka.**
"Excuse me, but isn't there a bank around here?"

a) **yuubinkyoku**　　c) **otearai**　　e) **kooban**
b) **denwa**　　d) **byooin**　　f) **basu-tee**

—148—

Lesson 11

4 Communication Practice

Directions: For each of the following, explain in Japanese that you will be going to the place indicated, and transferring to the form of transportation indicated.

Example: Teacher: **Nihonbashi, Toozaisen**
Student: **Nihonbashi made itte, Toozaisen ni norikaemasu.**
"(I)'ll go as far as Nihonbashi and transfer to the Tozai Line."

a) **Toranomon, chikatetsu**
b) **Aoyama, basu**
c) **Shikago, hikooki**
d) **Nagoya, Shinkansen**

5 Communication Practice

Directions: Examine the map and complete the following sentences.

Church	School	Park

Bank	Station	
	Telephone	Department Store
Post Office		

Book Store	Fish Store	Restaurant	Meat Store	Drug Store	Vegetable Store

a) **Gakkoo wa [＿＿] no ura desu.**
b) **Kyookai no tonari wa [＿＿] desu.**
c) **Denwa wa [＿＿] no mae ni arimasu.**
d) **Yuubinkyoku wa [＿＿] no tonari desu.**
e) **Resutoran no mae wa [＿＿] desu.**
f) **Depaato no tonari ni [＿＿] ga arimasu.**
g) **Honya wa [＿＿] no tonari desu.**
h) **Yaoya no tonari wa [＿＿] desu.**
i) **Kusuriya wa nikuya no [＿＿] desu.**
j) **Sakanaya wa eki no [＿＿] ni arimasu.**

6 Expansion Practice

Example: Teacher: **Nakano-iki ni notte kudasai. /Mitaka-iki/**
"Please take (the train) for Nakano." /(the train) for Mitaka/
Student: **Nakano-iki ka Mitaka-iki ni notte kudasai.**
"Please take (the train) for Nakano or Mitaka."

Lesson 11

a) Biiru o nomimashoo ka. /wain/   Biiru ka wain o nomimashoo ka.
b) Yamada-san wa ginkoo e/ni   Yamada-san wa ginkoo ka yuubin-
    ikimashita. /yuubinkyoku/   kyoku e/ni ikimashita.
c) Waapuro ga irimasu. /taipuraitaa/   Waapuro ka taipuraitaa ga irimasu.

EXERCISES

a) Give the following instructions in Japanese to the taxi driver:
1 Turn to the left at the next corner.
2 Go along this street as far as the end of the street.
3 Stop in front of the American Embassy.
4 Turn to the right at the corner where the hospital is.

b) Express the following in Japanese to the station employee:

Express the following in Japanese to the station employee:	Reply in Japanese (as the station employee):
1 You'd like to go to Aoyama but...	Take this train and go as far as Shinbashi, and transfer to the Ginza Line.
2 What is the next station?	It's Ikebukuro.
3 Where is the toilet?	It's over there.
4 Where is the British Embassy?	There is a police box in front of the station, so please ask a policeman.
5 Does this train go to Nakano?	No, it doesn't go to Nakano. Get on the train for Asakusa and transfer at the next station to the Tozai Line.

Model Answers:

a) 1 Tsugi no kado o hidari e/ni magatte kudasai.
2 Kono michi o tsukiatari made itte kudasai.
3 Amerika taishikan no mae de tomete kudasai.
4 Byooin no kado o migi e/ni magatte kudasai.

b) 1 Aoyama e/ni ikitai n desu ga...   Kono densha ni notte, Shinbashi made itte, soko de Ginzasen ni norikaete kudasai.
2 Tsugi no eki wa doko desu ka.   Ikebukuro desu.
3 Otearai wa doko desu ka.   Achira desu.
4 Igirisu taishikan wa doko desu ka.   Eki no mae ni kooban ga arimasu kara, keekan ni kiite kudasai.
5 Kono densha wa Nakano e/ni ikimasu ka.   Iie, Nakano e/ni wa ikimasen. Asakusa-iki ni notte, tsugi no eki de Toozaisen ni norikaete kudasai.

—150—

Lesson 11

BUSINESS INFORMATION

Getting Around by Taxi

The public transportation system in Japan is frequently crowded, but extremely reliable and well-run. Detailed information about public transportation can be picked up at most hotels, tourist information centers and foreign bookstores. However, since businessmen often prefer the convenience and comfort of air-conditioned (and occasionally TV-equipped) taxis, the following information has been provided for your reference.

1) There are two types of taxis in Japan, company-owned and private. Private cabs have a lighted sign "個人" (**kojin,** private) on the roof and are usually more sedate in color. There is no real advantage in taking one over the other, except that private cabs tend to be more fancy inside and better maintained.

2) Standard-sized cars legally seat five adults, including the driver, and smaller ones can accommodate four. You should not try to squeeze in more people than the legal limit since the driver will be fined if stopped by the police.

3) Contrary to most foreigners' expectations, a red sign "空車" (**kuusha,** or empty car) on the lower right side of the windshield—as seen from the front—indicates that the cab is unoccupied. Late at night, a green sign appears in the same place to indicate that the cab *is* occupied, even though the characters "割増" (**warimashi**) actually mean "fare increase". This is because there is usually a 20 percent surcharge between 11 p.m. and 5 a.m. When a driver is on radio call, he will put out a plaque—or switch on an orange sign— with the characters "迎車" (**geesha,** or "meet car"). If you have trouble hailing a cab on the street, you can always try one of the many taxi stands (タクシー乗り場 **takushii noriba**) located throughout Tokyo in front of hotels, department stores, bus and train terminals and other busy areas. You can of course also phone the taxi company directly (See below, Scenario 1).

4) You are required to pay only the amount that appears on the meter at the end of the ride. The only exceptions to this are when you use the expressways, in which case you are responsible for the toll; and when you carry on board four sets of golf clubs or excessive luggage that would require the driver to get out, open the trunk, or go through a number of other complex maneuvers. Even then, the driver will not expect more than the change from your fare—usually two or three hundred yen for his **tabako-dai** (タバコ代 , cigarette expenses).

5) If you forget something in the cab or if you have a complaint, e.g. you feel you were driven round in circles and charged in excess, you can call the **Tookyoo Takushii Kindaika Sentaa** (東京タクシー近代化センター , Tokyo Corporation for the Modernization of Taxi Operations) at 03-648-0300. In Osaka, the number is 06-933-5618. Most visitors, however, consider Japanese drivers exceedingly fair and honest, and few problems are ever encountered.

Useful Phrases When Riding Taxis

Scenario 1: Asking for and about cabs

#1:	Excuse me, where is the taxi stand?	**Sumimasen ga, takushii noriba wa doko desu ka.**

—151—

Lesson 11

#2:	Could (you) please call a taxi for me?	**Takushii o yonde kudasai.**
#3:	How long will it take (to get there) by taxi?	**Takushii de dono kurai jikan ga kakarimasu ka.**

Scenario 2: Instructing the driver

#1:	Could (you) please step on it?	**Isoide kudasai.**
#2:	(I)'m in a hurry, so please use the expressway.	**Isogimasu kara, koosoku-dooro ni notte kudasai.**
#3:	Please slow down.	**Yukkuri onegai-shimasu.**
#4:	Could (you) please ask someone for directions [lit. the road]?	**Dareka ni michi o kiite moraemasu ka.**
#5:	(I) have the phone number here, so could (you) please call (and get directions from them)?	**Koko ni denwa-bangoo ga arimasu kara, denwa-shite kiite kudasai.**
#6:	Could (I) have a receipt, please?	**Ryooshuusho o kudasai.**

Scenario 3: Calling to explain you will be late

Visitor:	(I)'m sorry, but (I)'ll be a little late.	**Mooshiwake arimasen ga, sukoshi okuremasu.**
Host:	How late?	**Dono kurai okuremasu ka.**
Visitor:	(I)'ll be late by about... minutes.	**...-hun/-pun kurai okure soo desu.**
Host:	Then, (you)'ll be here around [lit. it'll be around]...	**Soo suru to, ...-ji goro ni narimasu ne.**
Visitor:	That's right.	**Soo desu.**
Host:	All right, (we)'ll wait for (you).	**Wakarimashita. Omachi-shimasu.**

Scenario 4: Explaining a late arrival

#1:	(I) am terribly sorry to be late.	**Okuremashite makoto ni mooshiwake arimasen.**
#2:	There was an extremely heavy traffic jam... Moreover, (I) got a bit lost.	**Michi ga taihen komimashite... Sono ue, sukoshi michi ni mayoimashita.**

Lesson 12

At the Showroom

OBJECTIVES

1 to ask a clerk to explain what an exhibit is all about.

2 to politely ask someone to do something for you.

3 to negotiate for a reduction of the price.

Lesson 12

TARGET EXPRESSIONS AND PATTERNS

1 By doing..., (I)'ll do...   ...shite, ...shimasu.
2 (I)'ll try doing...   ...shite mimasu.
3 only «item X».   «X» shika... /+ negative/
4 Won't (you) please do...?   ...shite kudasaimasen ka.

SITUATION

Mr. Brown asks the clerk to explain how a word processor works at the showroom of Tokyo Machinery Ltd. After listening to the clerk's explanation, Mr. Brown asks the price of the word processor and requests a catalogue for reference.

DIALOGUE

	concerning, about	**ni tsuite**
	about a word processor	**waapuro ni tsuite**
	to explain	**setsumee-shimasu**
Brown	won't you...?	**kudasaimasen ka**

> **1** Won't you please explain this word processor? [lit. Concerning this word processor, won't you please explain?]
>
> **Kono waapuro ni tsuite, setsumee-shite kudasaimasen ka.**

	this one	**kochira**
Clerk	compact, small size	**kogata**

> **2** Certainly. This one is small, but very convenient.
>
> **Hai, kashikomarimashita. Kochira wa kogata desu ga, totemo benri desu yo.**

Brown	to be possible, to be able to do	**dekimasu**

> **3** Of course, it can handle the Japanese language too, can't it? [lit. the Japanese language is also possible.]
>
> **Mochiron, nihongo mo dekimasu ne.**

	both «item A» and «item B»	**«item A» mo «item B» mo**

—154—

Lesson 12

| | Japanese text | **wabun, nihonbun** |
| **Clerk** | English text | **eebun** |

4 | Yes, it can handle both Japanese and English text. | **Hai, wabun mo eebun mo dekimasu.** |

	to use	**tsukaimasu**
	way of using	**tsukaikata**
	to be probable	**deshoo**
Brown	it's probably difficult	**muzukashii deshoo nee**

5 | I guess it must be difficult to use. [lit. The way of using is probably difficult, isn't it?] | **Tsukaikata wa muzukashii deshoo nee.** |

	easy, simple	**kantan na**
	machine	**kikai**
Clerk	anyone, everyone	**dare demo**

6 | No, it is a very easy-to-use machine. Anyone can use it, so... [imp. you can, too.] | **Iie, totemo kantan na kikai desu yo. Dare demo dekimasu kara...** |

	however, but	**demo**
	a cursive script consisting of Japanese syllables	**hiragana**
	an angular script consisting	**katakana**
Brown	of Japanese syllables	

7 | However, in Japanese there are *kanji, hiragana* and *katakana,* so [imp. it must be difficult to use.] | **Demo, nihongo ni wa kanji, hiragana, katakana ga arimasu kara.** |

	type of machine	**kishu**
	Roman letters	**roomaji**
	by using Roman letters	**roomaji o tsukatte**
	to make, compose	**tsukurimasu**
	problem	**mondai**
Clerk	to try using	**tsukatte mimasu**

8 | This type of machine composes Japanese texts by using Roman letters, so there is no problem. (I)'ll try using it a little, so [imp. please watch.] | **Kono kishu wa roomaji o tsukatte, wabun o tsukurimasu kara, mondai (wa) arimasen yo. Chotto tsukatte mimasu kara...** |

Lesson 12

(Mr. Brown observes the clerk's demonstration)

		comparatively	**wari to**
Brown		price	**nedan, onedan** (polite)

9	It's comparatively easy, isn't it? How much is this? [lit. How much is the price?]	**Wari to yasashii desu nee. Onedan wa ikura desu ka.**

Clerk	to reduce the price	**benkyoo-shimasu**

10	This is 750,000 (yen), but (we will) discount it.	**Nanajuugo-man desu ga, benkyoo-shimasu yo.**

	staff	**sutahhu**
	to consult, talk	**soodan-shimasu**
Brown	catalogue	**katarogu**

11	Oh, is that so? Well then, (I) will also talk (this over) with our staff, so please give (me) a catalogue.	**Aa, soo desu ka. Jaa, uchi no sutahhu to mo soodan-shimasu kara, katarogu o kudasai.**

Clerk	nothing but, only	**shika** /+ negative/

12	Sorry, but (we) only have one in Japanese, but... [imp. would that be all right.]	**Sumimasen ga, wabun no shika arimasen ga...**

	to read	**yomimasu**
	to try reading	**yonde mimasu**
Brown	let me/us try to read	**yonde mimashoo**

13	Oh, that's fine. By using a dictionary, (I)'ll try reading (it).	**Aa, kekkoo desu yo. Jisho o tsukatte yonde mimashoo.**

JAPANESE WRITING

1 　ブラウン：　このワープロについて、説明してくださいませんか。

2 　店　員＊：　はい、かしこまりました。こちらは小型ですが、とても便利ですよ。

3 　ブラウン：　もちろん、 日本語もできますね。

4 　店　　員：　はい、和文も英文もできます。

5 　ブラウン：　使い方は難しいでしょうねえ。

Lesson 12

6 　店　員：　いいえ、とても簡単な機械ですよ。だれでもできますから…
7 　ブラウン：　でも、日本語には漢字、ひらがな、カタカナがありますから。
8 　店　員：　この機種はローマ字を使って和文を作りますから、問題（は）ありませんよ。ちょっと
　　　　　　　使ってみますから…
9 　ブラウン：　わりとやさしいですねえ。お値段はいくらですか。
10 　店　員：　七十五万ですが、勉強しますよ。
11 　ブラウン：　ああ、そうですか。じゃあ、うちのスタッフとも相談しますから、カタログをください。
12 　店　員：　すみませんが、和文のしかありませんが…
13 　ブラウン：　ああ、結構ですよ。辞書を使って、読んでみましょう。

NOTE:＊店員 (**ten'in**, clerk, salesperson)

READING

1 　Brown:　**Kono waapuro ni tsuite, setsumee-shite kudasaimasen ka.**
2 　Clerk:　**Hai, kashikomarimashita. Kochira wa kogata desu ga, totemo benri desu yo.**
3 　Brown:　**Mochiron, nihongo mo dekimasu ne.**
4 　Clerk:　**Hai, wabun mo eebun mo dekimasu.**
5 　Brown:　**Tsukaikata wa muzukashii deshoo nee.**
6 　Clerk:　**Iie, totemo kantan na kikai desu yo. Dare demo dekimasu kara…**
7 　Brown:　**Demo, nihongo ni wa kanji, hiragana, katakana ga arimasu kara.**
8 　Clerk:　**Kono kishu wa roomaji o tsukatte, wabun o tsukurimasu kara, mondai (wa) arimasen yo. Chotto tsukatte mimasu kara…**
9 　Brown:　**Wari to yasashii desu nee. Onedan wa ikura desu ka.**
10 　Clerk:　**Nanajuugo-man desu ga, benkyoo-shimasu yo.**
11 　Brown:　**Aa, soo desu ka. Jaa, uchi no sutahhu to mo soodan-shimasu kara, katarogu o kudasai.**
12 　Clerk:　**Sumimasen ga, wabun no shika arimasen ga…**
13 　Brown:　**Aa, kekkoo desu yo. Jisho o tsukatte yonde mimashoo.**

ADDITIONAL USEFUL EXPRESSIONS

1 At the store

(is) expensive	**takai**
(is) cheap	**yasui**

A:	This is expensive, isn't it? Don't (you) have a cheaper one?	**Kore wa takai desu nee. Motto yasui no wa arimasen ka.**

that one over there	**achira**
how would (it/that) be, how about	**ikaga deshoo ka**

B:	Well, how about that one over there? It's cheaper than this one.	**Jaa, achira wa ikaga deshoo ka. Kore yori yasui n desu ga…**

—157—

Lesson 12

2 At the store

	reduction in price	**nebiki**

A: Can (you) reduce the price for this?	**Kore wa nebiki dekimasu ka.**

	bargain-priced article	**tokkahin**
	(I)'m afraid not [lit. a little (difficult)]	**chotto**
	that one, those (near the listener)	**sochira**
	everything, everyone	**minna**
	counter for percentages (in units of ten)	**wari**
	20%	**ni-wari**
	20% off	**ni-wari-biki**

B: This is a bargain, so [imp. it won't be reduced]. Everything over there is 20% off, though [imp. so how about these instead?]	**Kore wa tokkahin desu kara, chotto…Sochira wa minna ni-wari-biki desu ga.**

3 At the showroom

	Japanese-made	**nihon-see**

A: This is made in Japan, isn't it?	**Kore wa nihon-see desu ne.**
B: Yes, it is.	**Hai, soo desu.**
A: Well then, how about that one over there?	**Jaa, sore wa.**

	American-made	**amerika-see**

B: Oh, this is made in America.	**Aa, kore wa amerika-see desu.**

4 At the store

	good(s), article(s)	**shinamono**
	(is) dirty	**kitanai**

A: This article is probably old, isn't it? It's a little dirty.	**Kono shinamono wa hurui desu nee. Chotto kitanai desu yo.**

	sample	**mihon**
	(is) pretty, clean	**kiree na**

—158—

Lesson 12

B: Oh, that is a sample. (We) have a clean one over here, so... [imp. please take a look at it.] | Aa, sore wa mihon desu. Kochira ni kiree na no ga arimasu kara...

5 At the office

what book	**nan no hon**

A: What book is that? | **Sore wa nan no hon desu ka.**

history	**rekishi**
(is) interesting	**omoshiroi**
(is) boring	**tsumaranai***

B: (It)'s a Japanese history book. (It)'s very interesting. | **Nihon no rekishi no hon desu. Totemo omoshiroi desu yo.**

**Does not appear in sample dialogue. Introduced for reference only.*

well, a great deal	**yoku** (adv. of **ii/yoi**)
to study	**benkyoo-shimasu**

A: You really study a lot, don't you? | **Hontoo ni anata wa yoku benkyoo-shimasu nee.**

REFERENCE

mini-kon	mini-computer	**ohu-kon**	office computer
poke-kon	pocket computer	**oo-ee**	office automation (OA)
paso-kon	personal computer	**sohuto'uea/**	software
bakachon	fool-proof	**sohuto**	
mai-kon	micro-computer, "my computer"	**haado'uea/ haado**	hardware
		puroguramu	program

NOTES

1 **-te mimasu** 'to try doing'

A verb gerund + **mimasu** means 'to do such-and-such and see' or 'to try doing such-and-such.'

Examples:
a) **Kinoo sake o non*de mima-shita.*** | "(I) tried drinking *sake* yesterday."
b) **Kono kikai o tsuka*tte mite* kudasai.** | "Please try using this machine."
c) **Ashita Tanaka-san no atarashii otaku e/ni it*te mimasu.*** | "Tomorrow, (I)'ll try to visit Mr. Tanaka's new house."

—159—

Lesson 12

2 **-te kudasaimasen ka**

A verb gerund + **kudasaimasen ka** [which literally means "Won't you (be kind enough to) give me such-and-such?"] is used for any very polite request. It is less direct than a verb gerund + **kudasai** "please do such-and-such."

Examples:
    a) **Michi o oshie*te kudasaimasen ka.***
        "Won't (you) be kind enough to show (me) the way?"
    b) **Ashita uchi e/ni irasshat*te kudasaimasen ka.***
        "Won't (you) be kind enough to come to my house tomorrow?"
    c) **Sore ni tsuite setsumee-shi*te kudasaimasen ka.***
        "Won't (you) be kind enough to explain about that?"

3 New Use of the Gerund (**-te** form)

A verb gerund is sometimes used to refer to the means by which something is or can be done. It can be translated as 'by doing such-and-such.'

Examples:
    a) **Jisho o tsukat*te*, nihongo no shinbun o yomimasu.**
        "(I) read Japanese newspapers by consulting [lit. using] a dictionary."
    b) **Mainichi chikatetsu ni not*te*, jimusho e/ni ikimasu.**
        "Everyday (I) go to the office by taking the subway."
    c) **Katarogu o mise*te*, setsumee-shimashita.**
        "(I) explained (it) by showing the catalogue."

Occasionally, it may be difficult to distinguish this use of the gerund from that which combines sentences, as introduced in Lesson 11. For example, the sentence, **Takada-san ni denwa-shite, chuushoku ni shootai-shimashita** can be translated as either, "(I) called Mr. Takada and invited him for lunch," or "(I) invited Mr. Takada for lunch by calling (him)."

4 **ni tsuite** 'about'

A noun + **ni tsuite** means 'about, concerning.'

Example: **Nyuuyooku *ni tsuite* setsumee-**   "(I) explained about New York."
                shimashita.

However, when it modifies a noun, the particle **no** occurs between **-tsuite** and the noun.

Example: **Nyuuyooku *ni tsuite no* hon o**   "(I) read a book about New York."
                yomimashita.
                [Nyuuyooku ni tsuite modifies **hon** 'book.']

5 Particle **shika** /+ negative/ 'only, nothing but'

Particle **shika** following a noun (or sometimes a noun + particle) always occurs with negative expressions and means 'only' or 'nothing but.'

Examples:
    a) **Biiru *shika* nomimasen.**   "(I) only drink beer."
    b) **Tanaka-san *shika* dekimasen.**   "Only Mr. Tanaka can do (it)."

Lesson 12

    c) **Kono ryoori wa Kyooto ni**   "This cuisine is available only in
       shika **arimasen.**   Kyoto."

6 **-kata** 'manner'
A verb stem (the affirmative non-past form without the **-masu** ending) + **kata** forms
a compound noun meaning 'manner of doing, way of doing.'

Examples:
a) **ikimasu** 'to go'   **iki +** *kata*   **iki***kata*   'way of going'
b) **kakimasu** 'to write' **kaki +** *kata* **kaki***kata* 'way of writing'
c) **tabemasu** 'to eat' **tabe +** *kata* **tabe***kata* 'way of eating'
d) **yomimasu** 'to read' **yomi +** *kata* **yomi***kata* 'way of reading'

7 **Na**-noun
Certain nouns, when followed by the particle **na,** can function as adjectives. For example:
kantan na kikai 'a simple machine' [lit. a machine of simplicity]. This kind of noun is
called a '**na**-noun.' Besides **kantan, na**-nouns introduced up to this point are:

genki	health, pep	**genki** *na* **kodomo**	a peppy child
kekkoo	goodness	**kekkoo** *na* **otaku**	a fine house
suki	liking	**suki** *na* **hon**	one's favorite book
benri	convenience	**benri** *na* **kikai**	a convenient machine
huben	inconvenience	**huben** *na* **uchi**	an inconvenient house

Na-nouns must be memorized as they occur in the text. Therefore, from now on all
na-nouns will be designated by the addition of the particle **na** when they are introduced.
Thus, **kantan /na/.**

8 **Kochira/sochira/achira/dochira** 'this one (these)/that one (those)/that one (those)
over there/which one(s)?'
These words have various meanings, depending upon the context. Carefully study the
following chart.

kochira	sochira	achira	dochira
this/these person(s) (Lesson 1)	that/those person(s)	that/those person(s) over there	which person(s)?
this side (Lesson 4)	the other side	over there	which side?
this way (Lesson 6)	that way	that way over there	which way?
this one/these (Lesson 12)	that one/those	that one/those over there	which one(s)?

—161—

Lesson 12

PRACTICE

1 Level Practice

Example: Teacher: **Setsumee-shite kudasai.**
            "Please explain (it)."
         Student: **Setsumee-shite kudasaimasen ka.**
            "Won't you be kind enough to explain (it)?"

a) **Ashita irasshatte kudasai.**   **Ashita irasshatte kudasaimasen ka.**
b) **Sore o misete kudasai.**   **Sore o misete kudasaimasen ka.**
c) **Yamada-san ni shookai-shite**   **Yamada-san ni shookai-shite**
    kudasai.   **kudasaimasen ka.**
d) **Ryooshuusho o kaite kudasai.**   **Ryooshuusho o kaite kudasaimasen**
     ka.

2 Transformation Practice

Example: Teacher: **Osake o nomimasu.**   "(I)'ll drink *sake.*"
         Student: **Osake o nonde mimasu.**   "(I)'ll try drinking *sake.*"

a) **Nihon-ryoori o tabemashita.**   **Nihon-ryoori o tabete mimashita.**
b) **Buchoo to soodan-shite kudasai.**   **Buchoo to soodan-shite mite kudasai.**
c) **Kono kikai o tsukaitai n desu.**   **Kono kikai o tsukatte mitai n desu.**
d) **Tanaka-san no atarashii kuruma ni**   **Tanaka-san no atarashii kuruma ni**
    norimashita ka.   **notte mimashita ka.**

3 Response Practice

Example: Teacher: **Taipuraitaa ga arimasu ka.**   "Is there a typewriter?"
         Student: **Taipuraitaa shika arimasen.**   "There is only a typewriter."

a) **Yamada-san ga kimashita ka.**   **Yamada-san shika kimasen deshita.**
b) **Wain o nomimashita ka.**   **Wain shika nomimasen deshita.**
c) **Buchoo to soodan-shimasu ka.**   **Buchoo (to) shika soodan-shimasen.**
d) **Katakana ga wakarimasu ka.**   **Katakana shika wakarimasen.**

4 Response Practice

Example: Teacher: **Nihongo to eego ga dekimasu ka.**
            "Can (you speak) Japanese and English?"
         Student: **Ee, nihongo mo eego mo dekimasu.**
            "Yes, (I) can (speak) both Japanese and English."

a) **Kanji to hiragana ga wakarimasu**   **Ee, kanji mo hiragana mo wakari-**
    ka.   **masu.**
b) **Oosaka to Kyooto e/ni ikimashita**   **Ee, Oosaka mo Kyooto mo ikimashita.**
    ka.

— 162 —

Lesson 12

c) Kore to sore wa itaria-see desu ka.   Ee, kore mo sore mo itaria-see desu.
d) Doitsugo to huransugo o benkyoo-   Ee, doitsugo mo huransugo mo
    shimashita ka.   benkyoo-shimashita.

5 Response Practice

Example: Teacher: **Nan ni tsuite hanashimasu ka. /Nihon no bijinesu/**
                "What are (you) going to talk about?" /Japanese business/
        Student: **Nihon no bijinesu ni tsuite hanashimasu.**
                "(I)'m going to talk about Japanese business."

a) **Nan ni tsuite soodan-shimashita**   **Nebiki ni tsuite soodan-shimashita.**
    ka. /nebiki/
b) **Nan ni tsuite setsumee-shimasu ka.**   **Kaisha no mondai ni tsuite setsumee-**
    /kaisha no mondai/   **shimasu.**
c) **Nan ni tsuite kikimashita ka.**   **Nihon no kuruma ni tsuite**
    /Nihon no kuruma/   **kikimashita.**

6 Communication Practice

Directions: Using the following patterns, inform the teacher of your own experiences.

a) **Watakushi wa «language» ga dekimasu.**
    "I can (speak) «language»."
b) **«Machine» no tsukaikata wa muzukashii desu.**
    "The use of «machine» is difficult."
c) **«Language» wa wari to kantan desu.**
    "«Language» is rather easy."
d) **Watakushi no «item» wa chuugoku-see desu.**
    My «item» is Chinese-made."
e) **Watakushi wa «subject» ni tsuite benkyoo-shimashita.**
    "I learned about «subject»."
f) **Watakushi wa ima «subject» ni tsuite yomitai n desu.**
    "Now I'd like to read about «subject»."
g) **«Company A» no kuruma wa «company B» no kuruma yori takai n desu.**
    "«Company A»'s car is more expensive than «company B»'s car."

— 163 —

Lesson 12

EXERCISES

a) Ask or tell the clerk at the showroom: The clerk replies:

1	Will you please explain about this machine?	Certainly.
2	Do you have an English catalogue?	We have only Japanese catalogues.
3	Do you have a smaller-size machine?	This is the smallest machine.
4	Is the operation of this machine difficult?	No, it isn't difficult. It's rather easy.
5	I'd like to try using this machine.	Please try using (it).
6	How much is it?	It's 280,000 yen.
7	Can you reduce the price?	No, I can't.
8	I'll go back to my office and consult with my staff.	Please come again.

b) Inform the teacher in Japanese that:
1. Mr. Tanaka explained about Japanese business to Mr. Brown.
2. Ms. Yamada wants to study how to use word processors.
3. In Japanese department stores they can't reduce the price.
4. Recently there are many Japanese-made typewriters in America.
5. You'll read a book about Japanese banks.
6. Mr. Takada wants to teach Mr. Brown how to write *katakana*.
7. Ms. Yamada bought a car after consulting Mr. Tanaka about it.

Model Answers:

a)
1	Kono kikai ni tsuite setsumee-shite kudasaimasenka.	Hai, kashikomarimashita.
2	Eebun no katarogu ga arimasu ka.	Wabun no katarogu shika arimasen.
3	Kogata no kikai wa arimasu ka.	Kore ga ichiban chiisai kikai desu.
4	Kono kikai no tsukaikata wa muzukashii desu ka.	Iie, muzukashiku arimasen. Wari to yasashii desu.
5	Kono kikai o tsukatte mitai n desu ga.	Doozo tsukatte mite kudasai.
6	(Nedan wa) ikura desu ka.	Nijuuhachi-man-en desu.
7	Benkyoo-dekimasu ka.	Iie, dekimasen.
8	Jimusho e/ni kaette sutahhu to soodan-shimasu.	Mata doozo.

b)
1. Tanaka-san wa nihon no bijinesu ni tsuite Buraun-san ni setsumee-shimashita.
2. Yamada-san wa waapuro no tsukaikata o benkyoo-shitai n desu.
3. Nihon no depaato de wa nebiki dekimasen.
4. Saikin Amerika ni wa nihon-see no taipuraitaa ga takusan arimasu.
5. Nihon no ginkoo ni tsuite no hon o yomimasu.
6. Takada-san wa Buraun-san ni katakana no kakikata o oshietai n desu.
7. Yamada-san wa Tanaka-san to soodan-shite kara kuruma o kaimashita.

Lesson 12

BUSINESS INFORMATION

Japanese Language Word Processors

Less than ten years ago, leading computer makers in the U.S. were convinced that the **nihongo** (日本語, Japanese language) word processor would never be widely used. Certainly, the very nature of the Japanese language posed formidable obstacles to word processing. Unlike the convenient 26-letter English alphabet, there are thousands of **kanji,** at least 2,000 of which are necessary to conduct daily business activities. Of these 2,000, many have exactly the same pronunciation, and some are composed of more than 20 individual strokes. To input such a complex 'alphabet' on a word processor was thought to be a programmer's nightmare. Even the traditional Japanese typewriter (和文タイプ**wabun taipu**) has such a complicated keyboard that only trained professionals can use it. Moreover, many people felt that the word processor, with its standardization and uniformity, would be incompatible with the traditional Japanese respect for the *written* word and the historical association of calligraphy with fine art. There is also the belief that an individual's handwriting is a mirror of his or her personality, and so people are expected to improve their writing and make it as attractive as possible—and not rely on convenient, standard forms.

To everyone's surprise, however, office automation—or **oo-ee** ("OA")—created an instant sensation in Japan, and the nation of erstwhile calligraphers took to **nihongo waapuro** like ducks to water. "OA" and **waapuro**—a contraction of **waado purocessa,** or word processor—are now household words, and endorsed by everyone from TV personalities to sumo wrestlers. According to recent MITI statistics, **waapuro** sales reached two million units in 1986—a whopping twenty-fold increase over 1984.

Numerous reasons have been cited for the sky-rocketing popularity of the Japanese language word processor. Certainly, a generation brought up with push-button conveniences and video games is bound to feel more comfortable with this new medium than with laboriously handwritten characters. And now that the familiar English keyboard has been adapted for use in Japanese word processing, **waapuro** have become much easier to program and operate. Also, curiously enough, the very preoccupation with calligraphy as a reflection of one's personality has worked in favor of the **waapuro** instead of against it, as predicted. Since only those with beautiful handwriting, according to popular belief, are likely to be decent, honorable and refined, it stands to reason that those with clumsy handwriting would embrace the **waapuro** with gratitude and relief.

Japanese word processors are also becoming popular among foreigners learning the language. Various models now feature **hiragana-kanji** or **roomaji-kanji** transformation. Using such machines, the student who can do no more than pronounce a certain word can type it in with **roomaji** (or **hiragana,** if he can read), and the computer will automatically transform these symbols into **kanji.** For example, if you type "**watashi wa gakko e ikimasu** (I go to school)," the sentence will appear as "私は学校へ行きます" on the monitor. All appropriate words, **watashi, gakkoo** and **i(kimasu),** will be rendered correctly in **kanji.**

—165—

Lesson 12

Waapuro and computers are getting more and more sophisticated, and prices are dropping all the time. As of the Spring of 1987, laptop word processors, usually called **handi waapuro** (ハンディワープロ , handy word processors) were priced under ¥40,000, and word processing software was selling for ¥10,000 and less. With the help of such machines, many foreigners are finding that the study of **kanji** is not nearly as difficult as they had thought. To make things even easier, there are now fully automatic English/ Japanese translation machines available, although these are still priced beyond the reach of individual students and all but the most well-endowed language schools. Still, at the present rate of computerization, it seems certain that translation machines will become standard equipment in language schools in the very near future, alongside the familiar tapes, cassettes and ubiquitous **waapuro.**

Lesson 13

Extending Invitations for a Party

OBJECTIVES

1   to discuss invitation arrangements.

2   to give one's own address.

3   to describe the rooms in one's house.

Lesson 13

TARGET EXPRESSIONS AND PATTERNS

1   (I)'m doing...   ...shite imasu.

2   (One's) address is 1-3, Roppongi   **Juusho wa Tookyoo-to, Minato-ku,**
    5-chome, Minato-ku, Tokyo.   **Roppongi go-choome, ichi no san desu.**

3   (One) is used to «item X».   **«X» ni narete imasu.**

SITUATION

Mr. Brown plans to have a party at his house and asks Ms. Yamada to prepare invitation cards.

DIALOGUE

	invitation card	shootaijoo
Brown	to complete	dekimasu

1 Ms. Yamada, are the invitation cards already completed?	**Yamada-san, shootaijoo wa moo deki-mashita ka.**

	mailing address	atena
	to be writing	kaite imasu
Yamada	to mail, put out	dashimasu

2 (I)'m writing the addresses now, so (I) will mail (them) this afternoon.	**Ima atena o kaite imasu kara, gogo dashimasu.**

Brown	address	juusho

3 Did (you) find out Mr. Kawamoto's address? [lit. As for Mr. Kawamoto's address, did (you) come to know?]	**Kawamoto-san no juusho wa waka-rimashita ka.**

Yamada

4 Yes, (I) asked (someone) by calling (his) office, so [imp. I found out.]	**Hai, jimusho ni denwa-shite, kiki-mashita kara...**

—168—

Lesson 13

	person	**kata** (respectful)
	that person	**ano kata** (respectful)
Brown	where	**dochira** (respectful)

5	Where is that person's residence?	**Ano kata no otaku wa dochira desu ka.**

	Tokyo Metropolitan District	**Tookyoo-to**
	Minato ward	**Minato-ku**
	a place name in Tokyo	**Roppongi**
	1-3 (street number and house number)	**ichi no san**
Yamada	section/district	**-choome**

6	(It) is 1-3, Roppongi 5-chome, Minato ward, Tokyo.	**Tookyoo-to, Minato-ku, Roppongi go-choome, ichi no san desu.**

Brown	(is) far	**tooi**

7	Well, it's not so far from my home.	**Jaa, uchi kara amari tooku arimasen nee.**

	party	**paatii**
	garden	**niwa**
Yamada	to do	**shimasu**

8	Will (you) have [lit. do] the party in the garden?	**Paatii wa niwa de shimasu ka.**

	this time	**kondo**
	guest, customer	**kyaku, okyakusama** (polite)
	(is) few, little	**sukunai**
Brown	living room	**ima**

9	No, there are few guests this time, so (I) will use the living room and the dining room.	**Iie, kondo wa okyakusama ga sukunai desu kara, ima to shokudoo o tsukaimasu.**

Yamada	preparation	**junbi**

10	How are the preparations (coming along)?	**Junbi wa ikaga desu ka.**

—169—

Lesson 13

	to prepare	**junbi-shimasu**
	life	**seekatsu**
	to get used to	**naremasu**
Brown	to be used to	**narete imasu**

> **11** My wife is preparing for it, but (she) is not used to Japanese life yet, so [imp. it's not easy.] — **Kanai ga junbi-shite imasu ga, mada Nihon no seekatsu ni narete imasen kara...**

	to help	**tetsudaimasu,**
Yamada		**otetsudai-shimasu** (polite)

> **12** Well then, shall (I) do something to help (her)? — **Jaa, nani ka otetsudai-shimashoo ka.**

	to be appreciated	**arigatai desu**
Brown	to be delighted	**yorokobimasu**

> **13** That would be (much) appreciated. My wife will also be delighted. — **Sore wa arigatai desu nee. Kanai mo yorokobimasu yo.**

	in that case	**sore de wa**
Yamada	weekend	**shuumatsu**

> **14** In that case, (I) will visit (you) next weekend, so [imp. I'll help you then.] — **Sore de wa, kondo no shuumatsu ni ukagaimasu kara...**

	to do so	**soo shimasu**
Brown		

> **15** Then, please do so. Thank you. — **Jaa, soo shite kudasai. Arigatoo.**

JAPANESE WRITING

1 **ブラウン**： 山田さん、招待状はもうできましたか。
2 **山　田**： 今、あて名を書いていますから、午後出します。
3 **ブラウン**： 川本さんの住所はわかりましたか。
4 **山　田**： はい、事務所に電話して聞きましたから…
5 **ブラウン**： あの方のお宅はどちらですか。
6 **山　田**： 東京都港区六本木5丁目1の3です。
7 **ブラウン**： じゃあ、うちからあまり遠くありませんねえ。
8 **山　田**： パーティは庭でしますか。

Lesson 13

9 ブラウン： いいえ、今度はお客様が少ないですから、居間と食堂を使います。
10 山　田： 準備はいかがですか。
11 ブラウン： 家内が準備していますが、まだ日本の生活に慣れていませんから…
12 山　田： じゃあ、何かお手伝いしましょうか。
13 ブラウン： それはありがたいですねえ。家内も喜びますよ。
14 山　田： それでは、今度の週末に伺いますから…
15 ブラウン： じゃあ、そうしてください。ありがとう。

READING

1 Brown: Yamada-san, shootaijoo wa moo dekimashita ka.
2 Yamada: Ima atena o kaite imasu kara, gogo dashimasu.
3 Brown: Kawamoto-san no juusho wa wakarimashita ka.
4 Yamada: Hai, jimusho ni denwa-shite kikimashita kara…
5 Brown: Ano kata no otaku wa dochira desu ka.
6 Yamada: Tookyoo-to, Minato-ku, Roppongi go-choome, ichi no san desu.
7 Brown: Jaa, uchi kara amari tooku arimasen nee.
8 Yamada: Paatii wa niwa de shimasu ka.
9 Brown: Iie, kondo wa okyakusama ga sukunai desu kara, ima to shoku-doo o tsukaimasu.
10 Yamada: Junbi wa ikaga desu ka.
11 Brown: Kanai ga junbi-shite imasu ga, mada Nihon no seekatsu ni narete imasen kara…
12 Yamada: Jaa, nani ka otetsudai-shimashoo ka.
13 Brown: Sore wa arigatai desu nee. Kanai mo yorokobimasu yo.
14 Yamada: Sore de wa, kondo no shuumatsu ni ukagaimasu kara…
15 Brown: Jaa, soo shite kudasai. Arigatoo.

ADDITIONAL USEFUL EXPRESSIONS

1 At the office

letter	**tegami**
to type	**taipu-shimasu**

A:	Type this letter, and mail (it) immediately, please.	**Kono tegami o taipu-shite, sugu dashite kudasai.**

express delivery service	**sokutatsu**
to send	**okurimasu**
to send by express	**sokutatsu de okurimasu**

B:	Shall (I) send (it) by express?	**Sokutatsu de okurimashoo ka.**
A:	Yes, please do so.	**Ee, soo shite kudasai.**

—171—

Lesson 13

2 At the office

	important	**taisetsu /na/**
	document	**shorui**
	registered mail	**kakitome**

| A: | This is an important document, so please send (this) by registered mail. | **Kore wa taisetsu na shorui desu kara, kakitome de okutte kudasai.** |

| | to go (and come back) | **itte kimasu** |

| B: | (I)'ll go to the post office right now (and come back.) | **Jaa, sugu yuubinkyoku e/ni itte kimasu.** |

| | stamp | **kitte** |
| | 60-yen stamp | **rokujuu-en (no) kitte** |

| A: | Are there any 60-yen stamps in the office now? | **Ima jimusho ni rokujuu-en (no) kitte ga arimasu ka.** |

| | postcard | **hagaki** |

| B: | (We) have postcards, but no stamps. | **Hagaki wa arimasu ga, kitte wa arimasen.** |

| | to buy (it and come back) | **katte kimasu** |

| A: | Then, please buy stamps too (and come back.) | **Jaa, kitte mo katte kite kudasai.** |

REFERENCE

kookuubin	air mail	**to, doa**	door
aeroguramu, kookuushokan	aerogram	**husuma**	sliding door
kozutsumi	parcel	**gareeji**	garage
hunabin	sea mail	**mon**	gate
denpoo	telegram	**hee**	fence
heya	room	**kakine**	hedge
nihonma	Japanese-style room	**ike**	pond
shinshitsu	bedroom	**suidoo**	water service
shosai	study	**denki**	electricity
oosetsuma	reception room	**gasu**	gas
kitchin, daidokoro	kitchen	**eyakon, eakon**	air conditioner
huroba	bathroom	**sutoobu**	stove
		hiitaa, danboo	heater

—172—

Lesson 13

kodomobeya	children's room	**ik-kai**	first floor
chikashitsu	basement	**ni-kai**	second floor
genkan	entrance	**san-gai**	third floor
rooka	corridor	**nan-gai**	which floor?

NOTES

1 **-te imasu** 'to be doing'
Verb gerund + **imasu** is generally used to indicate a present continuing action or state, while the non-past of a verb usually refers to habitual present and future action.

Examples:
    a) **Nihongo o benkyoo-shi*te* *imasu*.**   "(I)'m studying Japanese." (present continuing)
    b) **Ima made hon o yon*de* *imashita*.**   "(I) was reading a book up to now." (present continuing)
    c) **Nihongo o benkyoo-*shimasu*.**   "(I)'ll study Japanese." (future)
    d) **Boku wa doyoobi mo *hatarakimasu*.***   "I work on Saturdays too." (habitual present)

> *In Japanese a habitual action is sometimes also expressed by the **-te imasu** form. **Doyoobi mo hataraite imasu** can be used to mean "(I) work on Saturdays too" or "(I)'m working on Saturdays too." Whether the action is continuing in the present, or whether it will be repeated in the future, depends on the context.

Gerund + **imasu** may also mean that an action has been completed, and its effects are still being felt.

Examples:
    a) **Takada-san wa Oosaka e/ni it*te* *imasu*.**
    "Mr. Takada has gone to Osaka." [lit. He went to Osaka and is there.]
    b) **Kanai wa mada Nihon no seekatsu ni nare*te* *imasen*.**
    "My wife is not yet used to Japanese life." [lit. My wife has not become familiar with Japanese life and still isn't.]

2 **-te kimasu** 'to come back after doing (something)'
Verb gerund + **kimasu** is used to indicate that someone goes somewhere to do something, and comes back.

Example: **Kat*te* *kimasu*.**   "(I)'ll (go) buy (it and come back)."
                          or "(I)'ll come back after buying (it)."

However, **itte kimasu** means 'to come after having gone' or 'to go and come back.'

3 Compound Verb: Noun + **shimasu**
Some nouns directly followed by the verb **shimasu** 'to do' form compound verbs. For example, the noun **junbi** 'preparation' + **shimasu** becomes a compound verb,

—173—

Lesson 13

junbi-shimasu 'to prepare' [lit. to do/make preparations] (see DIALOGUE **11** of this Lesson). Among nouns introduced up to this point, the following nouns can occur with **shimasu** to form compound verbs. Note that in the following lessons, all nouns which can occur with **shimasu** will be designated accordingly **(-shimasu)**, i.e. **yakusoku (-shimasu).**

shitsuree	rudeness	**shitsuree-shimasu**	excuse me
denwa	telephone	**denwa-shimasu**	to call
yakusoku	promise	**yakusoku-shimasu**	to promise
shootai	invitation	**shootai-shimasu**	to invite
chuumon	order	**chuumon-shimasu**	to order
setsumee	explanation	**setsumee-shimasu**	to explain
benkyoo	study	**benkyoo-shimasu**	to study; discount
soodan	consultation	**soodan-shimasu**	to consult

Ohanashi-shimasu 'to talk' is also a compound verb consisting of the polite particle **o** + **hanashi** 'talking, story' + **shimasu.**
Words borrowed from other languages also may occur with **shimasu.**

Example: **taipu** 'typewriter'   **taipu-*shimasu*** 'to type'

4 How to give an address
In Japanese, an address begins with the largest area and ends with the smallest, usually a house number. Thus,

> **Tookyoo-to, Chuuoo-ku, Ginza roku-choome, juunana no ichi**
> "17-1, Ginza 6-chome, Chuo-ku, Tokyo"

-to in **Tookyoo-to** means 'the Metropolitan City (of) Tokyo,' **-ku** in **Chuuoo-ku** means 'ward,' and **-choome** in **roku-choome** means 'section/district.'

Additional Place Words

ken	prefecture	(e.g. **Kanagawa-*ken,*** Kanagawa Prefecture)
shi	city	(e.g. **Oosaka-*shi,*** Osaka City)
gun	county	(e.g. **Nishitama-*gun,*** Nishitama County)
machi	town	(e.g. **Yamada-*machi,*** Yamada Town)
mura	village	(e.g. **Yamamoto-*mura,*** Yamamoto Village)

PRACTICE

1 Transformation Practice

Example: Teacher: **Kakimasu.**   "(I)'ll write (it)."
                 Student: **Kaite imasu.**   "I'm writing (it)."

a) **Hatarakimasu.**   **Hataraite imasu.**
b) **Benkyoo-shimasu.**   **Benkyoo-shite imasu.**
c) **Tabemasu.**   **Tabete imasu.**
d) **Oshiemasu.**   **Oshiete imasu.**
e) **Tsukaimasu.**   **Tsukatte imasu.**
f) **Itadakimasu.**   **Itadaite imasu.**

Lesson 13

2 Response Practice

Example: Teacher: **Atena o kakimasu ka.**   "Are (you) going to write addresses?"
              Student: **Ima kaite imasu.**   "(I)'m writing (them) now."

a) **Taipuraitaa o tsukaimasu ka.**   Ima tsukatte imasu.
b) **Nihongo o benkyoo-shimasu ka.**   Ima benkyoo-shite imasu.
c) **Biiru o nomimasu ka.**   Ima nonde imasu.
d) **Kono zasshi o yomimasu ka.**   Ima yonde imasu.

3 Response Practice

Example: Teacher: **Kitte o kaimashoo ka.**   "Shall (I) buy stamps?"
              Student: **Ee, katte kite kudasai.**   "Yes, please buy (them and
                                                      come back)."

a) **Buchoo ni misemashoo ka.**   Ee, misete kite kudasai.
b) **Yamada-san to soodan-shimashoo   Ee, soodan-shite kite kudasai.
     ka.**
c) **Kono tegami o dashimashoo ka.**   Ee, dashite kite kudasai.
d) **Shachoo ni hanashimashoo ka.**   Ee, hanashite kite kudasai.
e) **Ginkoo e/ni ikimashoo ka.**   Ee, itte kite kudasai.

4 Communication Practice

Directions: For each of the following, indicate in Japanese that the person mentioned
                 is not used to the matter/item mentioned.

Example: **Kanai wa mada Nihon no seekatsu ni narete imasen.**
              "My wife is not yet used to Japanese life."

a) **Buraun-san, ano shigoto**
b) **Sumisu-san, Tookyoo no michi**
c) **Yamada-san, waapuro**
d) **Buraun-san no okusan, nihon-ryoori**

5 Communication Practice

Directions: Fill in the blanks « » with the appropriate addresses.

Example: **Kawamoto-san no juusho wa Tookyoo-to, Minato-ku, Roppongi, go
              no ichi no san desu.**

a) **Uchi no juusho wa** «address» **desu./Uchi wa** «address» **desu.**
b) **Jimusho no juusho wa** «address» **desu.**
c) **Honsha no juusho wa** «address» **desu.**
d) **Watakushi no** «native land» **no juusho wa** «address» **desu.**

6 Communication Practice

Directions: Using the vocabulary provided in the REFERENCE section, describe the
                 rooms in the following:

a) Your house in Japan   b) Your home in your native land.

—175—

Lesson 13

7 Communication Practice

Directions: Tell the teacher what you or others are doing, using the following patterns. patterns.

a) **Watakushi wa mainichi** «place» **de hataraite imasu.**
   "I work [lit. am working] at «place» everyday."
b) **Watakushi wa mainichi** «newspaper» **o yonde imasu.**
   "I read [lit. am reading] «newspaper» everyday."
c) **Kodomo** (or other person) **wa mainichi** «school» **de benkyoo-shite imasu.**
   "My child studies [lit. is studying] at «school» everyday."
d) **Watakushi wa** «school» **de benkyoo-shite imashita.**
   "I studied [lit. was studying] at «school»."

EXERCISES

a) Ask your secretary:
1   If she has gotten familiar with work in this office.
2   To send this letter by airmail.
3   If any letter has come from the head office today.
4   To type this document and mail it by noon.
5   If she sent the parcel by registered post.
6   To call JETRO and ask for Mr. Takada's address.

b) Inform the teacher in Japanese that:
1   Mr. Yamamoto is now teaching his staff how to use the word processor.
2   Mr. Brown is going to have a party this weekend at his house.
3   Mrs. Smith is already familiar with both the Japanese language and Japanese people.
4   Ms. Yamada is typing an important document, so please wait a while.
5   You know Mr. Kawamoto's company address, but not his home address.
6   Your wife studies Japanese every day.

Model Answers:

a) 1   **Kono jimusho no shigoto ni naremashita ka.**
   2   **Kono tegami o kookuubin de okutte kudasai.**
   3   **Kyoo honsha kara tegami ga kimashita ka.**
   4   **Kono shorui o taipu-shite, hiru made ni dashite kudasai.**
   5   **Kakitome de kozutsumi o okurimashita ka.**
   6   **Jetoro ni denwa-shite, Takada-san no juusho o kiite kudasai.**

b) 1   **Yamamoto-san wa ima sutahhu ni waapuro no tsukaikata o oshiete imasu.**
   2   **Buraun-san wa kono shuumatsu otaku de paatii o shimasu.**
   3   **Sumisu-san wa nihongo ni mo nihonjin ni mo moo narete imasu.**
   4   **Yamada-san wa taisetsu na shorui o taipu-shite imasu kara, shooshoo omachi-kudasai.**
   5   **Kawamoto-san no kaisha no juusho wa wakarimasu ga, otaku no wa waka-rimasen.**
   6   **Kanai wa nihongo o mainichi benkyoo-shite imasu.**

—176—

Lesson 13

BUSINESS INFORMATION

Giving a Business Party

Most Japanese parties take place in hotels or restaurants, but home parties are gaining popularity, especially among the younger generation. If you live in a spacious Western-style house or apartment and prefer home entertainment, the following guidelines will help ensure that all your guests—young and old—have an enjoyable time.

1   How to Get Them Here: Only a handful of Japan's major cities are laid out in the axial system familiar to Westerners, and even fewer have street names or an orderly system of numbering buildings. Most cities are like Tokyo—an endless snarl of nameless streets which are roughly grouped into wards (区 **ku**), districts, townships and neighborhoods. A detailed map enclosed with your invitation, therefore, is absolutely essential to make sure that your would-be guests do not spend the better part of the evening wandering around your neighborhood.

2   When to Get Them Here: The home party for business guests is best held on weekdays. Many of your guests may live far in the suburbs and will not relish the extra commute on their day off. For the same reason, your party should begin early, e.g. right after working hours, and end early so your guests can be well on their way before the trains stop running (usually around midnight).

3   Whom to Invite: The rules for business luncheons apply equally to parties. As much as possible, the guests on your list should be from the same business or company; they should be familiar with one another; they should be more or less of the same rank and from the same social background. The party should be small and cozy, with a certain light formality. You yourself may prefer grand, industry-wide extravaganzas to which everybody and his dog are invited. You may also think that by throwing such a party, you can take care of all your social obligations with one stroke. Or that everyone present at such a "bash" will have a wonderful time since they are all in the same line of business and have plenty in common to talk about. In fact, few things are more distressing to the Japanese businessman than to find himself thrown into a large group that includes friends and foes alike. Conversation will not flow smoothly, if at all, and little will be accomplished except general discomfort.

Note also that, as with the business lunch, spouses are generally not expected to attend parties unless the association between host and guest is a long and intimate one.

4   Playing the Host: If there are "new faces" among your guests, you should see to it that they are introduced to everyone early in the party. You yourself may think nothing of going up to a perfect stranger at a party and introducing yourself, but this goes quite against the grain of social protocol in Japan, particularly among the older generation. Unless you take the responsibility, some of your guests may remain strangers throughout the party—and thereafter—even if they do spend a good part of the evening seated next to each other. Finally, you should not assume that your guests will fend for themselves when it comes to food and drink since many Japanese can be quite inhibited when visiting others' homes for the first time. Some old-timers in Japan recommend that, if you

Lesson 13

must disappear on and off to supervise the dinner, you should have refreshments placed strategically around the room instead of in just one corner. This will give shy guests the opportunity to discreetly help themselves without having to get up and march conspicuously across your vast living room to the ''official'' refreshment table. Also, having several refreshment tables gives people that many more excuses to extricate themselves gracefully if they happen to be stuck with a particularly uninteresting fellow-guest.

5 What to Serve: Whisky and beer are probably the most popular alcoholic beverages in Japan, but your bar should also be well-stocked with soft drinks. Should you decide on a catered Japanese affair, or want to hold your business party in a Japanese restaurant, the following typical dishes are generally considered party-appropriate:

Dishes:

Kaiseki ryoori (懐石料理):	a full course dinner with soup, raw and broiled fish, and vegetables.
Sukiyaki (すき焼き):	thin slices of beef, various vegetables and bean curd cooked in a sweetened broth.
Tenpura (天ぷら):	deep fried shrimp, squid, fish and vegetables.
Shabu-Shabu (しゃぶしゃぶ):	very thin slices of beef, with vegetables and bean curd, dipped fondue-like into hot soup.
Sashimi (刺身):	slices of various raw fish.
Sushi (鮨):	oval-shaped rice balls, topped with slices of raw fish.
Yakitori (焼鳥):	barbecued chicken and vegetables, skewered.
Teppanyaki (鉄板焼):	seafood, vegetables and meat grilled on a hot-plate in front of you.
Robatayaki (炉端焼):	seafood, vegetables and beef cooked in an old farm-house-style fireplace.

Drinks:

Biiru (ビール):	beer.
Sake (酒):	rice wine, served warm **(Atsukan)** or cold **(Hiya).**
Shoochuu (焼酎):	spirits made from sweet potatoes or wheat, served on the rocks or with water **(Mizuwari),** with warm water **(Oyuwari),** or with soda **(Chuuhai).**
Uisukii (ウイスキー):	whisky, served on the rocks or with chilled water **(Mizuwari),** or with soda **(Soodawari).**
Wain (ワイン):	wine.

[Note: If you are invited to a home party, it is normal to bring along a small gift, usually flowers or store-bought confectionery, properly wrapped for the occasion. Home-baked goods, no matter how delicious, do not measure up to those with recognized brand names—at least in the eyes of most Japanese.]

Lesson 14

Messages

OBJECTIVES

1   to accept an invitation.

2   to decline an invitation politely.

3   to give a message.

4   to quote someone else's words.

5   to exchange greetings at a party.

Lesson 14

TARGET EXPRESSIONS AND PATTERNS

1	(He) said that...	...tte/to iimashita/osshaimashita.
2	(I) regret (to say) that...	**Zannen desu ga, ...**
3	(I) would/will do...gladly.	**Yorokonde...shimasu.**
4	(I)'ll introduce «person X» to «person Y».	**«X» o «Y» ni shookai-shimasu.**

SITUATION

Various people call Mr. Brown's office to reply to his invitation to the party.

DIALOGUE

	a little, a few	**sukoshi**
	a few minutes before	**sukoshi mae ni**
	to have a telephone (call)/	**denwa ga arimasu**
Yamada	there is a telephone (call)	

> **1** Good morning. There was a call for (you) from Mr. Yamamoto of Keidanren a few minutes ago.
>
> **Ohayoo gozaimasu. Sukoshi mae ni Keedanren no Yamamoto-san kara odenwa ga arimashita.**

	matter	**ken**
	(I) guess it's about the party	**paatii no ken deshoo**
	[lit. the matter of the party]	
	to say	**iimasu**
	what did (he) say?	**nan te/to iimashita ka**
	what did (he) say?	**nan te/to itte imashita ka**
Brown	[lit. what was he saying?]	

> **2** (I) guess it's about [lit. the matter of] the party. What did (he) say?
>
> **Aa, paatii no ken deshoo. Nan te itte imashita ka.**

	gladly	**yorokonde** (gerund of **yorokobu**)
Yamada	to say	**osshaimasu** (respectful)

> **3** (He) said that (he)'ll be glad to come.
>
> **Yorokonde ukagaimasu tte/to osshaimashita.**

(The telephone rings)

Brown	to answer (the phone)	**demasu**

—180—

Lesson 14

4	(I)'ll take it. [lit. (I)'ll go/come out.]	**(Boku ga) demasu.**

(Mr. Brown takes the call)

Brown

5	(This) is P & C.	**Pii-ando-shii desu.**

Kawamoto   invitation to a party   **paatii no goshootai**

6	Hello, Mr. Brown? (I)'m Kawamoto. Thank you very much for (your) invitation to the party.	**Moshimoshi, Buraun-san. Kawamoto desu. Paatii no goshootai, arigatoo gozaimashita.**

                     Not at all!   **tondemo arimasen,**
                                    tondemo gozaimasen (polite)

Brown   conditions   **tsugoo, gotsugoo** (respectful)

7	No, not at all! Is that convenient for (you)? [lit. How are the conditions for you?]	**Iie, tondemo gozaimasen. Gotsugoo wa ikaga desu ka.**

              well [lit. that is]   **sore ga**
                       regret   **zannen /na/**
       to my regret [lit. It is a regrettable thing, but...]   **zannen desu ga**
         actually [lit. the truth is...]   **jitsu wa**

Kawamoto   previous engagement   **sen'yaku**

8	Well, to my regret, (I) actually have a previous engagement, so [imp. I can't come.]	**Sore ga, zannen desu ga, jitsu wa sen'yaku ga gozaimashite...**

            way of doing   **shikata**
    it can't be helped [lit. There is no way of doing (it)]   **shikata ga arimasen**

Brown   opportunity, chance   **kikai**

9	Is that so? That's regrettable, isn't it? In that case, it can't be helped. By all means, please come the next (time you get a) chance.	**Soo desu ka. Sore wa zannen desu nee. Sore de wa, shikata ga arimasen. Tsugi no kikai ni wa zehi irasshatte kudasai.**

—181—

Lesson 14

Kawamoto

| 10 | Thank you very much. Well, good-bye. | **Doomo arigatoo gozaimasu. De wa, shitsuree-shimasu.** |

Brown

| 11 | Good-bye. | **Gomen-kudasai.** |

(To Ms. Yamada)

Brown
| | to attend | **shusseki-shimasu** |
| | can't attend | **shusseki-dekimasen** |

| 12 | Mr. Kawamoto can't attend. | **Kawamoto-san wa shusseki-dekima-sen.** |

Yamada
| | always | **itsumo** |
| | (is) busy | **isogashii, oisogashii** (respectful) |

| 13 | Is that so? He is always busy, isn't he? | **Soo desu ka. Ano kata wa itsumo oisogashii desu nee.** |

JAPANESE WRITING

1　山　田：　おはようございます。少し前に経団連の山本さんからお電話がありました。
2　ブラウン：　ああ、パーティの件でしょう。何て言っていましたか。
3　山　田：　喜んで伺いますっておっしゃいました。
4　ブラウン：　（ぼくが）出ます。
5　ブラウン：　ピー・アンド・シーです。
6　川　本：　もしもし、ブラウンさん。川本です。パーティの御招待、ありがとうございました。
7　ブラウン：　いいえ、とんでもございません。御都合はいかがですか。
8　川　本：　それが、残念ですが、実は先約がございまして…
9　ブラウン：　そうですか。それは残念ですねえ。それではしかたがありません。次の機会には、ぜひいらっしゃってください。
10　川　本：　どうもありがとうございます。では、失礼します。
11　ブラウン：　ごめんください。
12　ブラウン：　川本さんは出席できません。
13　山　田：　そうですか。あの方はいつもお忙しいですねえ。

—182—

Lesson 14

READING

1	Yamada:	Ohayoo gozaimasu. Sukoshi mae ni Keedanren no Yamamoto-san kara odenwa ga arimashita.
2	Brown:	Aa, paatii no ken deshoo. Nan te itte imashita ka.
3	Yamada:	Yorokonde ukagaimasu tte/to osshaimashita.
4	Brown:	(Boku ga) demasu.
5	Brown:	Pii-ando-shii desu.
6	Kawamoto:	Moshimoshi, Buraun-san. Kawamoto-desu. Paatii no goshootai, arigatoo gozaimashita.
7	Brown:	Iie, tondemo gozaimasen. Gotsugoo wa ikaga desu ka.
8	Kawamoto:	Sore ga, zannen desu ga, jitsu wa sen'yaku ga gozaimashite...
9	Brown:	Soo desu ka. Sore wa zannen desu nee. Sore de wa, shikata ga arimasen. Tsugi no kikai ni wa zehi irasshatte kudasai.
10	Kawamoto:	Doomo arigatoo gozaimasu. De wa, shitsuree-shimasu.
11	Brown:	Gomen-kudasai.
12	Brown:	Kawamoto-san wa shusseki-dekimasen.
13	Yamada:	Soo desu ka. Ano kata wa itsumo oisogashii desu nee.

ADDITIONAL USEFUL EXPRESSIONS

1 Greeting the guest

| | time | **tokoro** |
| | a busy time | **oisogashii tokoro** |

| A: | Mr. Yamamoto, (I)'m glad you could come at (such) a busy time. | **Yamamoto-san, oisogashii tokoro, yoku irasshaimashita.** |

| | today | **honjitsu** (formal) |

| B: | Thank you for (your) invitation today. | **Honjitsu wa goshootai arigatoo gozaimashita.** |

2 Small talk among guests

| | who | **donata** (respectful) |

| A: | Who is that person? | **Ano kata wa donata desu ka.** |

| | which person | **dono hito** |

| B: | Which person? | **Dono hito desu ka.** |

—183—

Lesson 14

	foreigner	**gaikokujin**
A:	That foreigner over there.	**Ano gaikokujin desu.**

	Morgan Bank	**Morugan-ginkoo**
	Mr. Hart	**Haato-san**
B:	Oh, that person is Mr. Hart of the Morgan Bank.	**Aa, ano kata wa Morugan-ginkoo no Haato-san desu.**

	some days ago, the other day	**senjitsu**
	another	**hoka no**
B:	Some days ago, (I) met (him) at another party.	**Senjitsu hoka no paatii de mo aimashita.**

	to introduce	**shookai-shimasu**
A:	(You) know (him)? Then, please introduce me to him.	**Shiriai desu ka. Jaa, boku o ano kata ni shookai-shite kudasai.**
B:	All right. Well then, let's go over there.	**Ii desu yo. De wa, achira e/ni ikimashoo.**

3 On the phone

	message	**kotozuke, okotozuke** (respectful)
A:	(I)'d like to leave a message for Mr. Brown.	**Buraun-san ni okotozuke o onegai-shimasu.**
B:	Certainly.	**Hai, doozo.**

	to report, convey	**tsutaemasu**
A:	I'm Main from the American Embassy. (I) can't attend the party, so please tell (him) so.	**Watakushi wa Amerika-taishikan no Mein desu. Paatii ni wa shusseki-dekimasen kara, soo tsutaete kudasai.**
B:	(I) understand.	**Wakarimashita.**

4 To decline an invitation

	unfortunately	**ainiku**

—184—

Lesson 14

	business trip	**shutchoo (-shimasu)**

A:	Unfortunately, (I) have a business trip scheduled [lit. business trip's schedule], so (I) regret that (I) cannot attend.	**Ainiku shutchoo no yotee ga gozaimashite zannen desu ga, shussekidekimasen.**

	(on) that day	**toojitsu**
	to travel	**ryokoo-shimasu**

B:	Unfortunately, on that day (I)'ll be traveling, so (I) won't be in Tokyo.	**Ainiku toojitsu wa ryokoo-shite imashite, Tookyoo ni orimasen.**

	friend	**yuujin, tomodachi**
	wedding ceremony	**kekkonshiki**

C:	My friend's wedding is on that day [lit. On that day, there's my friend's wedding ceremony], so [imp. I can't come.]	**Toojitsu tomodachi no kekkonshiki ga gozaimashite...**

NOTES

1 **-tte/to iimasu** 'to say that...'
-tte and its more formal equivalent **to** are used to indicate a quotation.

Examples:

   a) **Boku wa Yamada-san ni Kawamoto-san no juusho o oshiete kudasai *tte* iimashita.**
     "I asked Ms. Yamada to tell me Mr. Kawamoto's address."

   b) **Shachoo wa ii desu *to* osshaimashita.**
     "The president said that (it) was OK."

   c) **Tanaka-san wa paatii ni shusseki-dekimasen *te** iimashita.**
     "Mr. Tanaka said that (he) couldn't attend the party."

   d) **Takada-san ni boku wa Kyooto e/ni ikimasen *te** itte kudasai.**
     "Please tell Mr. Takada that I won't go to Kyoto."

   e) **Buchoo wa anata ni nan *te** iimashita ka.**
     "What did the general manager say to you?"
     *When **tte** is preceded by **n,** it is usually pronounced **te.**

Nan te/to iimashita ka means "What did he say?", while **nan te/to ii masu ka** which literally means "What do you say?", is often used to ask what something is called.

Example: **Kore wa *nan te/to iimasu ka.***
       "What do (you) call these?"
       Aa, sore wa hashi *tte/to iimasu.*
       "Oh, (we) call those chopsticks."

Lesson 14

This is a very convenient phrase for foreigners wishing to know the proper Japanese terms for articles.

2 Tentative Copula **deshoo**
Deshoo, the tentative form of **desu,** indicates probability.

Compare: **Sono kuruma wa Buraun-san no desu.**
          "That car is Mr. Brown's."
          and
          Sono kuruma wa Buraun-san no *deshoo.*
          "That car is probably Mr. Brown's."
          or
          "I guess that car is Mr. Brown's."

Deshoo is less direct than **desu,** so in questions, **deshoo** is a more polite form to use than **desu.**

Compare: **Ano kata wa Tanaka-san *desu* ka.**
          "Is he Mr. Tanaka?"
          and
          Ano kata wa Tanaka-san *deshoo* ka.
          "Do you suppose he is Mr. Tanaka?"

3 **Dekimasu** 'to be able to (do)'
The verb **dekimasu** introduced in Lesson 12 has two meanings: 'to be possible' and 'to be able to do.'

Examples: **Nihongo mo *dekimasu.***
          "(It) can also handle Japanese. [lit. Japanese language is also possible.]"
          Dare demo *dekimasu.*
          "Everyone can do (it)."

In both cases, **dekimasu** is used as an independent verb. However, in this lesson you have learned that **dekimasu** is used instead of **shimasu** to indicate potential.

Examples:
a) **shusseki-shimasu**   'to attend'   **shusseki-dekimasu**   'to be able to attend'
b) **benkyoo-shimasu**   'to study'   **benkyoo-dekimasu**   'to be able to study'
c) **yakusoku-shimasu**   'to promise'   **yakusoku-dekimasu**   'to be able to promise'

The potential form of other verbs will be discussed later.

4 Notes on Usage
A) **Yorokonde,** the gerund of **yorokobimasu** 'to be glad, to be pleased with' is used as an adverb in DIALOGUE **3** , and means 'gladly, joyfully [lit. being glad].'
B) **Demasu** in DIALOGUE **4** means 'to answer (the telephone),' e.g. ***denwa ni demasu*** [lit. get out on the phone], but it cannot be used in the sense of 'answering the question.'
C) **Donata** is a more polite equivalent of **dare** 'who?'

—186—

Lesson 14

D) **Tokoro** in **oisogashii tokoro** (ADDITIONAL USEFUL EXPRESSIONS **1** does not mean 'place, location' but 'time, occasion.'

E) As an equivalent of **gaikokujin** (外国人) 'foreigner [lit. foreign country person],' **gaijin** (外人) [lit. foreign person] is also used, but the latter usually refers to Westerners. It is recommended not to use the term **gaijin**, if possible, since its connotations are not always favorable.

F) **Honjitsu** is a more formal equivalent of **kyoo** 'today.'

G) Use of the Particle **ni** 'to'
   Note that the particle *ni* occurs in the following sentences to indicate destination of the action.
   i) **Paatii *ni* shusseki-shimasu.** "(I)'ll attend the party."
   ii) **«X» wa «Y» o «Z» *ni* shookai-shimasu.** "«person X» introduces «person Y» to «person Z»."

PRACTICE

1 Message Practice

Example:	Teacher:	**Yamamoto desu. Paatii ni yorokonde ukagaimasu.**
		"(I)'m Yamamoto. (I)'ll be glad to attend the party."
	Student:	**Yamamoto-san wa paatii ni yorokonde ukagaimasu tte/to osshaimashita.**
		"Mr. Yamamoto said that (he)'ll be glad to attend the party."

a) **Buraun desu. Ashita Oosaka e/ni ikimasu.**
    Buraun-san wa ashita Oosaka e/ni ikimasu tte/to osshaimashita.

b) **Yamada desu. Yo-ji goro made ni kaerimasu.**
    Yamada-san wa yo-ji goro made ni kaerimasu tte/to osshaimashita.

c) **Takada desu. Kinoo Kawamoto-san ni aimashita.**
    Takada-san wa kinoo Kawamoto-san ni aimashita tte/to osshaimashita.

d) **Sumisu desu. Ashita kaigi ni shusseki-dekimasen.**
    Sumisu-san wa ashita kaigi ni shusseki-dekimasen te/to osshaimashita.

e) **Tanaka desu. Konban denwa o kakemasu.**
    Tanaka-san wa konban denwa o kakemasu tte/to osshaimashita.

2 Message Practice

Example:	Teacher:	**Ano kikai wa benri desu. /kachoo/**
		"That machine is convenient." /manager/
	Student:	**Kachoo ni ano kikai wa benri desu tte/to itte kudasai.**
		"Please tell the manager that machine is convenient."

a) **Kono shorui wa taisetsu desu. /Yamada-san/**
    Yamada-san ni kono shorui wa taisetsu desu tte/to itte kudasai.

b) **Waapuro wa nebiki-dekimasen. /Buraun-san/**
    Buraun-san ni waapuro wa nebiki-dekimasen te/to itte kudasai.

c) **Zehi irasshatte kudasai. /Kawamoto-san/**
    Kawamoto-san ni zehi irasshatte kudasai tte/to itte kudasai.

Lesson 14

d) Yorokonde ukagaimasu. /Takada-san/	Takada-san ni yorokonde ukagaimasu tte/to itte kudasai.
e) Ashita hima desu. /Yamamoto-san/	Yamamoto-san ni ashita hima desu tte/to itte kudasai.

3 Response Practice

Example: Teacher: **Kono kuruma wa nihon-see desu ka.**
"Is this car Japanese-made?"
Student: **Ee, nihon-see deshoo.**
"Yes, (I) guess (it)'s Japanese-made."

a) Ano kata wa Haato-san desu ka.	Ee, Haato-san deshoo.
b) Buraun-san no jimusho wa Shinjuku desu ka.	Ee, Shinjuku deshoo.
c) Ano biru wa byooin desu ka.	Ee, byooin deshoo.
d) Kono densha wa Nakano-iki desu ka.	Ee, Nakano-iki deshoo.

4 Transformation Practice

Example: Teacher: **Buraun-san no paatii ni shusseki-shimasen.**
"(I)'ll not attend Mr. Brown's party."
Student: **Buraun-san no paatii ni shusseki-dekimasen.**
"(I) can't attend Mr. Brown's party."

a) Shachoo ni setsumee-shimasu ka.	Shachoo ni setsumee-dekimasu ka.
b) Kinoo benkyoo-shimashita.	Kinoo benkyoo-dekimashita.
c) Tanaka-san to soodan-shimasu.	Tanaka-san to soodan-dekimasu.
d) Waapuro wa nebiki-shimasu ka.	Waapuro wa nebiki-dekimasu ka.
e) Ano kikai wa chuumon-shimasen.	Ano kikai wa chuumon-dekimasen.

5 Communication Practice

Directions: Practice the following introductions, using real names.

a) **«Name A»-san wa watakushi o «name B»-san ni shookai-shimashita.**
"«Name A» introduced me to «name B»."
b) **Watakushi wa «name A»-san o «name B»-san ni shookai-shimashita.**
"I introduced «name A» to «name B»."
c) **Watakushi wa «name A»-san o «name B»-san ni shookai-shitai n desu.**
"I'd like to introduce «name A» to «name B»."

6 Communication Practice

Directions: Ask the teacher the Japanese names of things around you, using the following patterns, and write them down in Roman letters.
Note: You must ask about at least ten items.

—188—

Lesson 14

Pattern: **Kore wa nihongo de nan te/to iimasu ka.**
"What do (you) call this in Japanese?"

EXERCISES

Inform the teacher in Japanese that:
1   Mr. Yamamoto of Keidanren told Ms. Yamada that he would be glad to attend Mr. Brown's party.
2   Because Mr. Kawamoto has a previous engagement, he can't attend Mr. Brown's party.
3   Mr. Smith (Manager) told me that he wanted to come to Japan by September.
4   Mr. Tanaka called Mr. Brown and said that he met Mr. Takada at JETRO's party.
5   Mr. Brown introduced his secretary, Ms. Yamada, to Mr. Hart of Morgan Bank.
6   Mr. Yamamoto told me that he wanted to read that book, by all means.
7   Ms. Yamada said that she didn't know Mr. Brown's schedule for next week.
8   Mr. Takada (General Manager) couldn't attend today's meeting.
9   Mr. Brown is always very busy so he can't study Japanese.
10   Ms. Yamada told Mr. Brown that she wanted to buy a word processor, by all means.

Model Answers:

1   **Keedanren no Yamamoto-san wa Yamada-san ni Buraun-san no paatii ni yorokonde ukagaimasu tte/to iimashita/osshaimashita.**
2   **Kawamoto-san wa sen'yaku ga arimasu kara Buraun-san no paatii ni shusseki-dekimasen.**
3   **Sumisu-kachoo wa ku-gatsu made ni Nihon ni kitai tte/to iimashita/osshaimashita.**
4   **Tanaka-san wa Buraun-san ni denwa-shite Jetoro no paatii de Takada-san ni atta tte/to iimashita/osshaimashita.**
5   **Buraun-san wa hisho no Yamada-san o Morugan ginkoo no Haato-san ni shookai-shimashita.**
6   **Yamamoto-san wa zehi ano hon o yomitai tte/to iimashita/osshaimashita.**
7   **Yamada-san wa raishuu no Buraun-san no yotee wa wakarimasen te/to iimashita/osshaimashita.**
8   **Takada-buchoo wa kyoo no kaigi ni wa shusseki-dekimasen deshita.**
9   **Buraun-san wa itsumo totemo isogashii kara nihongo no benkyoo ga dekimasen.**
10   **Yamada-san wa Buraun-san ni zehi waapuro o kaitai tte/to iimashita/osshaimashita.**

Lesson 14

BUSINESS INFORMATION

Making Speeches

Social gatherings in Japan often feature individual or group singing, if the occasion is casual, or speech-making. If you are invited to an **enkai** (宴会, large Japanese-style party), whether by a client or as part of your own company outing, you will almost surely be asked after the meal to sing a solo or croon along to the sounds of **karaoke** (カラオケ, instrumental accompaniment). **Karaoke** [lit. empty orchestra] systems can be programmed to provide background music for a huge selection of both Western and Japanese popular tunes. In a country where almost everyone enjoys singing—regardless of ability—such systems can be found installed in many pubs, hotels, private homes and even sightseeing buses.

BUSINESS JAPANESE is regretfully unable to be of much help if you are invited to perform at **enkai.** However, if you are requested to make a speech at a more formal party or professional gathering, you may find the following lines useful.

1 The Prelude

Thank you for (your) introduction, Mr. Yoshida.

Yoshida-san, goshookai arigatoo gozaimashita.

As mentioned, (my name) is Williams and I'm Area Manager of ABC Trading for the Far East.

Tadaima goshookai itadakimashita Uiriamusu desu. Watakushi wa Ee-bii-shii Toreedingu no Kyokutoo-chiiki tantoo no maneejaa o shite orimasu.

May (I) say, first of all, how deeply (I) appreciate (your) invitation to this wonderful party today.

Honjitsu wa kono yoo ni subarashii seki ni omaneki itadakimashite, makoto ni arigatoo gozaimasu.

Now, (I)'d like to extend a few words of greeting on behalf of our company. But, to my regret, my Japanese is not good enough (to properly express these greetings.)

Toosha o daihyoo itashimashite, hitokoto goaisatsu o mooshiagetai to omoimasu. Tadashi, zannen desu ga, watakushi wa nihongo ga tokui de wa arimasen.

So, (I) ask your understanding for making the rest of this speech in English.

Desu kara, koko kara wa eego de hanasu koto o oyurushi itadakitai to omoimasu.

Now, ...

De wa, ...

—190—

Lesson 14

2 The Conclusion

Anyway, (I) would like to express my appreciation for being given the opportunity to talk to you at this time.	**Tonikaku, konkai goaisatsu no kikai o ataete itadakimashite, arigatoo gozaimashita.**

3 Other Useful Expressions for Party Small Talk

Scenario 1: Language

Guest A:	Your Japanese is very good!	**Nihongo ga ojoozu desu nee!**
Guest B:	No, not at all. (I) am just a beginner. (I) still have a lot to learn [lit. ...have to study a lot from now on].	**Iie, tondemo gozaimasen. Mada shoshinsha desu. Kore kara takusan benkyoo shinakute wa narimasen.**

Scenario 2: People and business

#1:	What sort of business are (you) in?	**Donna oshigoto o nasatte irasshaimasu ka.**
#2:	This is my colleague, Mr. Nakamura.	**Kochira wa dooryoo no Nakamura-san desu.**

[Note: Use **-san** when introducing a colleague to a member of the same group; omit **-san** when introducing the colleague to an outsider.]

#3:	He/she works in the same section as (I) do.	**Kare/kanojo wa onaji ka de shigoto o shite orimasu.**
#4:	He/she has also spent time in the U.S.	**Kare/kanojo mo Amerika ni ita koto ga arimasu yo.**
#5:	Please give my best regards to Mr. Yoshida.	**Yoshida-san ni zehi yoroshiku otsutae kudasai.**
#6:	Since (I) first met Mr. Yoshida in Paris, (I) have become very much indebted to (him).	**Pari de hajimete oaishite irai, Yoshida-san ni wa taihen osewa ni natte orimasu.**
#7:	How is (your) family?	**Gokazoku wa minasama ogenki de irasshaimasu ka.**

Lesson 14

Scenario 3: Sports and hobbies

\#1: Do (you) do any sports?

Supootsu o nani ka nasaimasu ka.

\#2: Do (you) ski/play golf/tennis?

Sukii/gorufu/tenisu o nasaimasu ka.

\#3: This year the Giants [Tokyo baseball team] are really doing poorly.

Kotoshi no Jaiantsu wa hontoo ni dame desu nee.

\#4: Do (you) have any hobbies?

Donna shumi o omochi desu ka.

\#5: (I) go to the theater/movies a lot.

Yoku shibai/eega o mi ni ikimasu.

\#6: Do (you) play chess/bridge?

Chesu/burijji o nasaimasu ka.

Scenario 4: Food and drink

\#1: What food do (you) like?

Tabemono de wa nani ga osukidesu ka.

\#2: (I) like Japanese cuisine, but (I) do not care for sashimi/eel/squid.

Nihonshoku wa suki desu ga, sashimi/unagi/ika wa dame desu.

\#3: What would (you) care for, tea, coffee or Japanese tea?

Koocha to koohii to nihoncha no uchi, nani ga yoroshii deshoo ka.

\#4: Please feel free to help yourself.

Doozo gojiyuu ni otori kudasai.

\#5: Please don't hesitate (to help yourself).

Doozo goenryo naku...

Scenario 5: Thanks and Goodbye

\#1: Thank you for inviting me to a lovely party.

(Suteki na paatii ni) omaneki itadaki arigatoo gozaimashita.

\#2: (I) had such a good time.

Taihen tanoshikatta desu.

\#3: (I)'m so sorry, but (I) have to leave now. (I) have an appointment early tomorrow morning, so...

Mooshiwake arimasen ga, oitoma shinakute wa narimasen. Ashita wa asa hayaku kara yakusoku ga aru mono desu kara...

\#4: How are (you) going home? Can (I) drop you off somewhere?

Okaeri wa doo saremasu ka. Dokoka made ookuri shimashoo ka.

\#5: Let's get together again soon.

Mata chikaku oai shimashoo.

Lesson 15

Hiring People

OBJECTIVES

1 to discuss employment terms.

2 to express an opinion.

3 to speak about educational backgrounds.

4 to describe age and personality.

Lesson 15

TARGET EXPRESSIONS AND PATTERNS

1	(I) think that...	...to omoimasu.
2	(It) gets/will get «description X».	«X» narimasu.
3	(She) becomes/will become «profession X».	«X» ni narimasu.
4	How/what shall (I/we) do?	Doo shimashoo ka.
5	At the time of...	...no toki.

SITUATION

After consulting with the president, Mr. Brown decides to increase his male staff, and he discusses how to employ someone with Ms. Yamada.

DIALOGUE

	and	**ga**
	male	**otoko, dansee**
	female	**onna, josee**
Brown	to hire, employ	**yatoimasu**

1 (I) also talked on the phone (about this) with the president, and (I) will hire one more male employee... — **Shachoo to mo denwa de soodan-shimashita ga, moo hitori dansee no shain o yatoimasu yo.**

	gradually	**dandan**
Yamada	to get busy	**isogashiku narimasu**

2 That's fine. (Our) business will also gradually get busy, so [imp. we need to hire one more employee.] — **Kekkoo desu nee. Shigoto mo dandan isogashiku narimasu kara...**

	(to) recruit	**boshuu (-shimasu)**
Brown	What/how shall (we/I) do?	**doo shimashoo ka**

3 Then, how shall (we) recruit [lit. how shall (we) do recruiting]? — **Jaa, boshuu wa doo shimashoo ka.**

capable person	**jinzai**
job bank	**jinzai-ginkoo**
advertisement	**kookoku**
newspaper advertisement	**shinbun-kookoku**

—194—

Lesson 15

Yamada	to think	**omoimasu**

4 There's also a job bank, but (I) think putting an ad in the newspapers is also good.

Jinzai-ginkoo mo arimasu ga, shinbun-kookoku mo ii to omoimasu.

	right away	**sassoku**
	newspaper	**shinbunsha**
	[lit. newspaper company]	
	to contact	**renraku-shimasu**
Brown	to contact newspapers	**shinbunsha ni renraku-shimasu**

5 Then, please try contacting newspaper (companies) right away.

De wa, sassoku shinbunsha ni renraku-shite mite kudasai.

	conditions, terms	**jooken**
Yamada	how shall (we/I) write?	**doo kakimashoo ka**

6 How shall (we) write up the conditions?

Jooken wa doo kakimashoo ka.

	university, college	**daigaku**
	to graduate	**sotsugyoo-shimasu**
Brown	age	**toshi**

7 (The applicant) should be a college graduate, up to age 30, and...

Daigaku-sotsugyoo de, toshi wa sanjuu made...

Yamada	experience	**keeken (-shimasu)**

8 How about job experience?

Shigoto no keeken wa.

	do not matter	**kamaimasen**
Brown	steady, serious	**majime /na/**

9 Experience does not particularly matter, but a steady person would be good, (don't you agree?)

Keeken wa betsu ni kamaimasen ga, majime na hito ga ii desu nee.

Lesson 15

		salary	**kyuuryoo**
		and the like	**ya**
Yamada		allowance	**teate**

10	What shall (we) do about salary, allowances, and the like?	**Kyuuryoo ya teate wa doo shima-shoo ka.**

		interview	**mensetsu (-shimasu)**
		time	**toki**
		at the time of interview	**mensetsu no toki ni**
		(anything) else, besides	**hoka ni**
Brown		necessary	**hitsuyoo /na/**

11	(We) will talk about it when (we) interview, so please write so in the ad. Is there anything else (we) need?	**Sore wa mensetsu no toki ni hana-shimasu kara, kookoku ni soo kaite kudasai. Hoka ni nani ka hitsuyoo desu ka.**

		only	**dake**
Yamada		that's all [lit. only that]	**sore dake**

12	No, that's all.	**Iie, sore dake desu.**

Brown

13	Then, please (do as I've requested.)	**Jaa, onegai-shimasu.**

JAPANESE WRITING

1 ブラウン：　社長とも電話で相談しましたが、もう一人、男性の社員を雇いますよ。

2 山　田：　結構ですねえ。仕事もだんだん忙しくなりますから…

3 ブラウン：　じゃあ、募集はどうしましょうか。

4 山　田：　人材銀行もありますが、新聞広告もいいと思います。

5 ブラウン：　では、さっそく新聞社に連絡してみてください。

6 山　田：　条件はどう書きましょうか。

7 ブラウン：　大学卒業で、年は三十まで…

8 山　田：　仕事の経験は。

9 ブラウン：　経験は別にかまいませんが、真面目な人がいいですねえ。

10 山　田：　給料や手当はどうしますか。

11 ブラウン：　それは面接の時に話しますから、広告にそう書いてください。

　　　　　　　他に何か必要ですか。

12 山　田：　いいえ、それだけです。

13 ブラウン：　じゃあ、お願いします。

Lesson 15

READING

1 Brown: Shachoo to mo denwa de soodan-shimashita ga, moo hitori dansee no shain o yatoimasu yo.
2 Yamada: Kekkoo desu nee. Shigoto mo dandan isogashiku narimasu kara...
3 Brown: Jaa, boshuu wa doo shimashoo ka.
4 Yamada: Jinzai-ginkoo mo arimasu ga, shinbun-kookoku mo ii to omoi-masu.
5 Brown: De wa, sassoku shinbunsha ni renraku-shite mite kudasai.
6 Yamada: Jooken wa doo kakimashoo ka.
7 Brown: Daigaku-sotsugyoo de, toshi wa sanjuu made...
8 Yamada: Shigoto no keeken wa.
9 Brown: Keeken wa betsu ni kamaimasen ga, majime na hito ga ii desu nee.
10 Yamada: Kyuuryoo ya teate wa doo shimashoo ka.
11 Brown: Sore wa mensetsu no toki ni hanashimasu kara, kookoku ni soo kaite kudasai. Hoka ni nani ka hitsuyoo desu ka.
12 Yamada: Iie, sore dake desu.
13 Brown: Jaa, onegai-shimasu.

ADDITIONAL USEFUL EXPRESSIONS

1 At the office

	to look for, seek	**sagashimasu**

A:	Is (your) daughter still seeking employment [lit. a job]?	**Musume-san wa mada shigoto o sagashite imasu ka.**
B:	Yes, (she)'s still looking.	**Ee, mada sagashite iru n desu yo.**

	what kind of...?	**donna**

A:	What kind of work does (she) want to do?	**Donna shigoto ga shitai n desu ka.**

	(not) easily to be found	**nakanaka** /+ negative/ **mitsukarimasu**

B:	(She) wants to work as [lit. become] a secretary, but a good job can't be found easily.	**Hisho ni naritai n desu ga, naka-naka ii shigoto ga mitsukarimasen.**
A:	Can (she) speak [lit. do] English?	**Eego ga dekimasu ka.**

—197—

Lesson 15

Junior college	**tandai**
English conversation	**eekaiwa**
one's strong point	**tokui /na/**

B: Because (she) studied English at (her) junior college, English conversation is (her) strong point.	**Tandai de eego o benkyoo-shimashita kara eekaiwa wa tokui desu.**

enterprise	**kigyoo**
of American origin	**Amerika-kee**
to work (for)	**tsutomemasu**
clerk, office worker	**jimuin**

A: My friend is working for an American company, and (they) are recruiting office workers there now.	**Boku no tomodachi ga Amerika-kee no kigyoo ni tsutomete imasu ga, ima soko de jimuin o boshuu-shite imasu yo.**

such	**sonna**
such a place	**sonna tokoro**

B: (My) daughter wants to work in such a company. By all means, please introduce that person (to her).	**Musume wa sonna tokoro de hatarakitai n desu yo. Zehi sono kata o shookai-shite kudasai.**
A: Yes, surely. (I)'ll try calling (him) now, so please wait a while.	**Ee, ii desu yo. Ima denwa-shite mimasu kara, chotto matte ite kudasai.**
B: Thank you. [lit. (I) request your good-will.]	**Yoroshiku onegai-shimasu.**

2 At the college

bank clerk	**ginkooin**

A: (I) guess you want to work as [lit. become] a bank clerk.	**Anata wa ginkooin ni naritai n deshoo.**

of foreign origin	**gaishi-kee**
to enter, join	**hairimasu**

B: Yes, (I) want to join a foreign bank, but [imp. do you have any ideas?]	**Ee, gaishi-kee no ginkoo ni hairitai n desu ga...**

—198—

Lesson 15

	English newspaper	**eeji-shinbun**
	Help Wanted ad	**kyuujin-kookoku**
	to come out, appear	**demasu**

A:	A Help Wanted ad from an American bank is [lit. appears] in today's English newspaper.	**Kyoo no eeji-shinbun ni Amerika no ginkoo no kyuujin-kookoku ga dete imasu yo.**

	to see	**mimasu**
	but, however	**shikashi**
	application	**oobo (-shimasu)**
	applicant	**oobosha**
	(is) many	**ooi**

B:	I saw (it) too. However, the terms are very favorable, so (I) guess there'll also be many applicants.	**Boku mo mimashita yo. Shikashi, totemo ii jooken desu kara, oobosha mo ooi deshoo nee.**

	to hold out, do one's best	**ganbarimasu**

A:	Well, good luck [lit. do your best]!	**Maa, ganbatte kudasai.**

REFERENCE

shoogakkoo	elementary school	**shiken (-shimasu)**	(to give) a test
chuugakkoo	middle school	**shiken o ukemasu**	to take a test
kookoo	high school	**nyuusha-shiken**	company's
senmongakkoo	professional/technical school		entrance exam.
daigakuin	graduate school	**hikki-shiken**	written exam.
gakushi	Bachelor (B.A./B.S.)	**mensetsu-shiken**	oral exam.
shuushi	Master (M.A./M.S.)	**gookaku (-shimasu)**	passing (an exam.)
hakushi	Doctor (Ph.D.)	**saiyoo (-shimasu)**	acceptance, employment
kinben /na/	diligent	**shuushoku (-shimasu)**	obtaining/starting
kappatsu /na/	active, cheerful		employment
humajime /na/	insincere	**taishoku (-shimasu)**	retirement, leaving employment
kichoomen /na/	methodical, punctual		
shinkeeshitsu /na/	nervous, sensitive	**tenshoku (-shimasu)**	changing one's
zubora /na/	negligent		occupation
sekkyokuteki /na/	positive, constructive		
shookyokuteki /na/	negative, passive		
yooki /na/	lively, joyful		
inki /na/	gloomy		

Lesson 15

NOTES

1 **-to omoimasu** 'to think that…'
A sentence + **to omoimasu** means 'to think that…'

Examples: a) **Boku mo raishuu ryokoo-shitai *to omoimasu*.***
"(I) think that I too would like to make a trip next week."
b) **Ano kuruma wa totemo takai *to omoimasu*.***
"(I) think that car over there is very expensive."
*Please note that, in each of the above sentences, the dependent clause uses the informal form: **ryokoo-shitai** 'want to travel' and **takai** '(is) expensive.' The informal form of verbs will be discussed in Lesson 18.

2 **Narimasu** 'to become, to get'
A) **-ku** form of adjectives + **narimasu**

Examples: a) **Ooki*ku* narimasu.**   "(It) gets/will become big."
b) **Taka*ku* narimashita.**   "(It) has gotten expensive."
c) **Yasu*ku* narimasen.**   "(It) doesn't/will not get cheap."
d) **Yo*ku* narimasen deshita.**   "(It) has not gotten better."
e) **Kaita*ku* narimashita.***   "(I) have gotten to the point where I want to buy (it)."

***Kaitaku** is the **-ku** form of **kaitai** 'to want to buy.'

B) A noun + **ni** + **narimasu** 'to become, to turn into'

Examples: a) **Ano hito wa keekan *ni narimashita*.**
"He became a policeman."
b) **Tanaka-san wa genki *ni narimashita*.**
"Mr. Tanaka became well." [lit. Mr. Tanaka turned into health.]
c) **Hisho *ni narimasen deshita*.**
"(She) didn't become a secretary."

3 **Doo** 'how?'
Doo is used to ask about the manner of doing something.

Examples: a) ***Doo* kakimashoo ka.**
"How shall (I) write it?"
b) ***Doo* setsumee-shimashita ka.**
"How did (you) explain it?"
c) ***Doo* shimasu ka.**
"How are (you) going to do (it)?"
d) **Kono kanji wa *doo* yomimasu ka.**
"How do (you) read this *kanji*?"

4 **Konna/sonna/anna/donna**
Konna 'this sort (of),' **sonna** 'that sort (of),' and **anna** 'that sort (of)… (over there)' precede the nouns they modify.

Examples: a) ***konna* taipuraitaa**   'this sort of typewriter'
b) ***sonna* zasshi**   'that sort of magazine'
c) ***anna* kaisha**   'that sort of company'

—200—

Lesson 15

Donna is usually used in questions about type and category.

Example: *donna* hon   'what sort of book?'

Please note that this group is different from the **kono/sono/ano/dono** group introduced in Lesson 6 and Lesson 8.

Compare: *Kono* kuruma ga kaitai n desu.
"(I) want to buy this car."
and
Konna kuruma ga kaitai n desu.
"(I) want to buy this sort of car."

Dono kuruma ga kaitai n desu ka.
"Which car do (you) want to buy?"
and
Donna kuruma ga kaitai n desu ka.
"What sort of car do (you) want to buy?"

5 **Dake** 'only'
A noun + **dake** means 'only/just...,' 'nothing/no one but...' and is usually used without a following particle.

Examples: a) **Jimusho ni wa Yamada-san *dake* imasu.**
"Only Ms. Yamada is in the office."
b) **Boku wa shinbun *dake* kaimashita.**
"I bought only a newspaper."
c) **Nichiyoobi *dake* hima desu.**
"(I)'m free only on Sunday(s)."
d) **Sore *dake* desu.**
"That's all."

6 Notes on Usage
A) **Kamaimasen,** which usually occurs in this negative form, has various meanings, such as "I don't care," "It makes no difference," "It doesn't matter," "It's all right," etc., depending upon the context.
B) **Toshi** 'age': To give a person's age, the same Japanese-origin numerals used for counting objects (see Lesson 8), e.g. **hito-tsu, huta-tsu,** etc., are used up through nine. From nine on, however, Chinese-origin numerals are used, e.g. **juu** (10), **juuichi** (11), etc. The exception, as when counting the days of the month, is twenty: **hatachi** 'twenty years old.'

Examples: **Musume wa ima *huta-tsu* desu.**
"(My) daughter is now two years old."
Kanojo no toshi wa *hatachi* desu.
"She [lit. Her age] is twenty years old."
Sugu *sanjuu* ni narimasu.
"(I)'m going to become thirty years old soon."

C) **-ni tsutomemasu:** The phrase **ni tsutomemasu** indicates that one is employed by or works for the organization whose name it follows. On the other hand, the phrase **de hatarakimasu** following the name of an organization/place indicates also the physical location at which one works.

—201—

Lesson 15

Compare:　**Jetoro *ni tsutomete* imasu.**
　　　　　　"(I)'m working for JETRO (the organization)."
　　　　　　and
　　　　　　Jetoro *de hataraite* imasu.
　　　　　　"(I)'m working at JETRO (the organization and the building)."

PRACTICE

1 Response Practice

Example:　　Teacher:　**Ano hoteru wa takai desu ka.**
　　　　　　　　　　"Is that hotel expensive?"
　　　　　　　Student:　**Ee, takai to omoimasu.**
　　　　　　　　　　"Yes, (I) think (it)'s expensive."

a) **Takada-san wa ima isogashii desu ka.**　　　**Ee, isogashii to omoimasu.**
b) **Oota-san wa sonna zasshi ga yomitai**　　　**Ee, yomitai to omoimasu.**
　　n desu ka.
c) **Ano kaisha wa oobosha ga ooi desu ka.**　　**Ee, ooi to omoimasu.**

2 Response Practice

Example:　　Teacher:　**Shigoto wa isogashii desu ka.**
　　　　　　　　　　"Are (you) busy at work?" [lit. Is (your) business busy?]
　　　　　　　Student:　**Ee, isogashiku narimashita.**
　　　　　　　　　　"Yes. (It) has gotten busy."

a) **Benkyoo wa tanoshii desu ka.**　　　**Ee, tanoshiku narimashita.**
b) **Kyuuryoo wa ii desu ka.**　　　　　**Ee, yoku narimashita.**
c) **Jinzai-ginkoo wa ooi desu ka.**　　　**Ee, ooku narimashita.**
d) **Shigoto wa omoshiroi desu ka.**　　　**Ee, omoshiroku narimashita.**
e) **Konna waapuro wa yasui desu ka.**　　**Ee, yasuku narimashita.**

3 Response Practice

Example:　　Teacher:　**Tanaka-san wa ima ginkooin desu ka.**
　　　　　　　　　　"Is Mr. Tanaka a bank clerk now?"
　　　　　　　Student:　**Ee, ginkooin ni narimashita.**
　　　　　　　　　　"Yes, (he) became a bank clerk."

a) **Anata wa ima sanjuugo desu ka.**　　　**Ee, sanjuugo ni narimashita.**
b) **Sumisu-san wa ima shachoo desu ka.**　　**Ee, shachoo ni narimashita.**
c) **Okusan wa ima genki desu ka.**　　　　**Ee, genki ni narimashita.**
d) **Shigoto wa ima hima desu ka.**　　　　**Ee, hima ni narimashita.**

4 Response Practice

Example:　　Teacher:　**Takada-san wa doko de hataraite imasu ka. /Jetoro/**
　　　　　　　　　　"Where is Mr. Takada working?" /JETRO/
　　　　　　　Student:　**Takada-san wa Jetoro ni tsutomete imasu.**
　　　　　　　　　　"Mr. Takada is working for JETRO."

—202—

Lesson 15

a) Yamamoto-san wa doko de hataraite imasu ka. /Keedanren/ — Yamamoto-san wa Keedanren ni tsutomete imasu.

b) Yamada-san wa doko de hataraite imashita ka. /shinbunsha/ — Yamada-san wa shinbunsha ni tsutomete imashita.

c) Musume-san wa doko de hataraki-masu ka. /Amerika-kee no kigyoo/ — Musume wa Amerika-kee no kigyoo ni tsutomemasu.

d) Jakku wa doko de hataraite imasu ka. /Pii-ando-shii no honsha/ — Jakku wa Pii-ando-shii no honsha ni tsutomete imasu.

e) Okusan wa doko de hataraite imashita ka. /tandai/ — Kanai wa tandai ni tsutomete imashita.

5 Response Practice

Example: Teacher: **Boshuu wa doo shimashoo ka.**
"How shall (we) invite (applicants)?" **/shinbun-kookoku/**
Student: **Shinbun-kookoku ga ii to omoimasu.**
"(I) think a newspaper ad is/will be good."

a) Ryokoo wa doko e/ni ikimashoo ka. /Kyooto/ — Kyooto ga ii to omoimasu.

b) Donna hito o yatoimashoo ka. /majime na hito/ — Majime na hito ga ii to omoimasu.

c) Nani o benkyoo-shimashoo ka. /eekaiwa/ — Eekaiwa ga ii to omoimasu.

d) Kyuujin-kookoku wa donna shinbun ni dashimashoo ka. /eeji-shinbun/ — Eeji-shinbun ga ii to omoimasu.

e) Kono mondai ni tsuite, dare to soodan-shimashoo ka. /Buraun-san/ — Buraun-san ga ii to omoimasu.

6 Response Practice

Example: Teacher: **Itsu kyuuryoo ni tsuite hanashimasu ka. /mensetsu/**
"When will (you) talk about the salary?" /interview/
Student: **Mensetsu no toki ni hanashimasu.**
"(I)'ll tell (the person) at the time of the interview."

a) Itsu Nihon no rekishi o benkyoo-shimashita ka. /daigaku/ — Daigaku no toki ni benkyoo-shimashita.

b) Itsu Haato-san ni aimashita ka. /Buraun-san no paatii/ — Buraun-san no paatii no toki ni aimashita.

c) Itsu sonna hon o yomimasu ka. /ryokoo/ — Ryokoo no toki ni yomimasu.

d) Itsu buchoo to soodan-shimasu ka. /kaigi/ — Kaigi no toki ni soodan-shimasu.

e) Itsu Jakku ni denwa-shimashita ka. /chuushoku/ — Chuushoku no toki ni denwa-shimashita.

Lesson 15

EXERCISES

Inform the teacher in Japanese that:

1 Because P & C has gotten busy, Mr. Brown wants to employ one more female secretary.
2 Mr. Ohta's daughter is seeking a job. She wants to work as a secretary in a foreign company.
3 Mr. Aoki has no experience in this sort of job, but he is a very earnest person, so I think he'll become a good staff member.
4 Mr. Yamamoto studied Chinese history at a university in Sendai.
5 What sort of word processor do you want to buy?
6 In Japanese newspapers, there are various Help Wanted ads, but I think that there are very few good jobs.
7 Mr. Brown said there had been many applicants, but there had been no qualified persons.
8 At the time of the interview, Mr. Imai said he was good at English conversation.

Model Answers:

1 **Pii-ando-shii no shigoto ga isogashiku narimashita kara Buraun-san wa moo-hitori josee no hisho o yatoitai n desu.**
2 **Oota-san no musume-san wa shigoto o sagashite imasu ga, gaishi-kee no kaisha no hisho ni naritai n desu.**
3 **Aoki-san wa konna shigoto no keeken wa arimasen ga, totemo majime na hito desu kara yoi sutahhu ni naru to omoimasu.**
4 **Yamamoto-san wa Sendai no daigaku de Chuugoku no rekishi o benkyoo-shimashita.**
5 **Donna waapuro ga kaitai n desu ka.**
6 **Nihon no shinbun ni wa iroiro na kyuujin-kookoku ga arimasu ga, ii shigoto wa totemo sukunai to omoimasu.**
7 **Buraun-san wa oobosha wa takusan imashita ga, ii hito wa imasen deshita tte/to iimashita.**
8 **Mensetsu no toki ni Imai-san wa eekaiwa wa tokui desu tte/to iimashita.**

Lesson 15

BUSINESS INFORMATION

The Recruitment Process

Finding qualified staff in any country can be a long and painstaking process. For the foreign employer in Tokyo, the difficulties are compounded by the language problem. It is not unusual to meet a candidate who has all the personal qualities and managerial experience you could possibly ask for, but who is also sadly lacking in English (or Japanese) conversational ability. If you are thinking of expanding your staff, or if you are looking for a position yourself, you should be aware of the following popular forms of recruitment.

1 Publications: Most foreign employers in Japan choose to advertise openings for bilingual staff in the various English-language newspapers, thinking that only job-hunters with a working knowledge of English would be reading them in the first place. However, it would be well worth your while to advertise positions in Japanese newspapers too, because their circulation is of course so much wider. A preliminary call to a local advertising agency will help confirm what the general readership of a given newspaper is, if you want to target a specific age group or profession.

There are also various Japanese magazines dedicated to the job market, including:

> **Shuukan Shuushoku Joohoo** (週刊就職情報, Weekly Employment News), which provides extensive coverage of openings in all types of businesses, for both males and females and all age groups.
> **Nikkan Arubaito Nyuusu** (日刊アルバイトニュース , "Daily Arbeit [German for 'work'] News") and **Huromu Ee** (フロム・エー , "From A"), both of which are aimed at students and list primarily part-time openings.
> **Torabaayu** (とらば～ゆ, "Travail" [or 'work' in French]), which is dedicated exclusively to the female job market.
> **Beruuhu** (ベルーフ, "Beruf" [or 'vocation' in German]), which specializes in technical, scientific and research-related fields.

2 Universities: By far the most extensive, systematic and effective recruitment programs are those which large Japanese companies conduct at the major universities. As elsewhere in the world, job descriptions are sent to various university departments to be posted on their respective bulletin boards. Unlike other countries, however, the competition for talented freshman staff is so fierce that an official schedule has been set up for the recruitment process so that all companies throughout the nation will be competing on equal footing. If a graduate were applying for a post through this program, he would begin by attending formal **setsumeekai** (説明会, explanatory sessions) at the company between August 20 and September 5. Any contact with universities prior to August 20 would be considered foul play on the part of the company. The candidate would then move on to the interview phase, generally referred to as **kobetsu hoomon** (個別訪問, personal visiting), and after that to the written examinations. Applicants are notified officially of their success or failure after October 15, and they enter their new company—sometimes for life—in April of the following year.*

—205—

Lesson 15

In a society which places so much emphasis on personal relationships, the value and persuasive power of alumni in this recruitment process should not be underestimated. All things being equal, the graduate will almost always choose a company where a former college-mate is gainfully employed over another firm where he knows no one. Joining a company with friends not only provides a sense of continuity, but may also ensure that the new employee will be personally looked after in his new career. Alumni are therefore included as much as possible in all phases of a company's recruitment program. And it is also easy to see how foreign firms in Japan are at a basic disadvantage in university recruiting, since they are usually not as established as their Japanese competitors and do not have this **oo-bii** (オービー , "O.B." or "old boy") network operating on their behalf.

3   Recruitment Firms: If you have trouble finding qualified applicants on your own, you can always turn to the various recruiting firms and temporary placement agencies which now specialize in meeting the needs of foreign employers in Japan. Fees vary according to the nature of the assignment, of course, but usually amount to 30% of the candidate's annual salary if he or she is successfully placed. If your needs are extremely specialized, however, the agency may stipulate a minimum annual salary, especially in the case of executive positions.

4   Other: At some point in their careers, most employers will be forced to release an employee or two. Because of the tradition of life-employment (終身雇用制度 **shuu-shin koyoo seedo**) in Japan, it is much more difficult to dismiss staff here than in other countries. Large conglomerates in fact often "recycle" employees by shifting them from one company to another within their own group rather than dismiss them outright. If you are faced with this delicate task, you may be interested to know that some recruitment firms also offer "outplacement" services. If someone in your company simply *must* go, you can always approach such agencies to find suitable employment elsewhere for him and also count on them to notify the employee tactfully of these "other opportunities."

*Dates provided here are subject to change.

Lesson 16

Interviews

OBJECTIVES

1   to interview applicants for job openings.

2   to find out about someone's education and work experience.

3   to discuss family background.

4   to discuss employment-related matters.

5   to learn forms of polite/formal speech.

Lesson 16

TARGET EXPRESSIONS AND PATTERNS

1 (It)'s this one.   **Kore de gozaimasu.**

2 (I) live in «place X».   **«X» ni sunde orimasu.**

3 Why did (you) do...?   **Doo shite...shimashita ka.**

4 (I) work as «profession X».   **«X» o shite imasu.**

5 (I) receive «item X» from Mr./Ms.   **«X» o «Y»-san ni/kara moraimasu.**
   «name Y».

6 (I) give «item X» to Mr./Ms. «name Y».   **«X» o «Y»-san ni agemasu.**

7 Mr./Ms. «name X» gives (me) «item Y».   **«X»-san ga «Y» o kuremasu.**

SITUATION

Mr. Brown selects a few applicants from the many who answered the ad in the newspaper. Now the first candidate, Mr. Imai, comes to the office for an interview.

DIALOGUE

	personal history	**rirekisho**
Brown	to bring	**motte kimasu**

> **1** Did (you) bring (your) personal history? **Rirekisho o motte kimashita ka.**

	to bring	**motte mairimasu** (modest)
Imai	this is it	**kore de gozaimasu** (polite)

> **2** Yes, (I) brought it. Here it is. [lit. this is it.] **Hai, motte mairimashita. Kore de gozaimasu.**

	home, dwelling	**sumai**
Brown	a place name (near Tokyo)	**Kawasaki**

> **3** (Your) home is in Kawasaki, isn't it? **Aa, sumai wa Kawasaki desu ne.**

	relatives	**shinseki**
	to live	**sumimasu**
Imai	to be living	**sunde imasu, sunde orimasu** (modest)

—208—

Lesson 16

4	Yes, (I)'m living in my relative's house in Kawasaki.	**Hai, Kawasaki no shinseki no uchi ni sunde orimasu.**

	specialty	**senmon**
	economics	**keezai**
	Stanford	**Sutanhoodo**
	business school	**bijinesu-sukuuru**
Brown	to study abroad	**ryuugaku-shimasu**

5	(Your) major subject [lit. specialty] at university was economics, right? And then (you) studied at Stanford University Business School?	**Daigaku no senmon wa keezai deshita ne. Sore kara Sutanhoodo no bijinesu-sukuuru ni ryuugaku-shimashita ka.**

	business administration	**kee'eegaku**
Imai	to receive	**moraimasu**

6	Yes, (I) received a master's degree in business administration there.	**Hai, soko de kee'eegaku no shuushi o moraimashita.**

	to return to one's country	**kikoku-shimasu**
Brown	teacher	**sensee**

7	(You) became a university teacher after coming back (to Japan) right? [lit. ...returning to your home country.]	**Kikoku-shite kara, daigaku no sensee ni narimashita ne.**

	(one's) Alma Mater	**bokoo**
	lecturer	**kooshi**
Imai	to work as a lecturer	**kooshi o shimasu**

8	Yes, (I) was a lecturer at (my) Alma Mater.	**Hai, bokoo no kooshi o shite orimashita.**

	how come?, why?	**doo shite, naze**
Brown	to quit, resign	**yamemasu**

9	Why did (you) resign from the university?	**Naze daigaku o yamemashita ka.**

—209—

Lesson 16

	world	**sekai**
	spring	**haru**
	to resolve	**omoikirimasu**
Imai	resolutely, boldly	**omoikitte**

10 (I) thought (I)'d like to work in the business world, so this spring, (I) resolved to resign from the university. [lit. I resolutely resigned from the university.]

Bijinesu no sekai de hatarakitai to omoimashite, kono haru, omoikitte daigaku o yamemashita.

	thanks for your trouble [lit. (you) suffered a lot]	**gokuroosama deshita**
Brown	within this week	**konshuu-chuu ni**

11 (I) see. Thanks for your trouble. (We)'ll contact (you) within this week by phone, so [imp. please wait].

Wakarimashita. Gokuroosama deshita. Konshuu-chuu ni denwa de renraku-shimasu kara...

Imai	to request	**onegai-itashimasu** (modest)

12 Thank you very much. [lit. May (I) ask that (you) kindly extend (your) good-will (toward me).]

Yoroshiku onegai-itashimasu.

JAPANESE WRITING

1 **ブラウン**： 履歴書を持って来ましたか。

2 **今　井**： はい、持ってまいりました。これでございます。

3 **ブラウン**： ああ、住まいは川崎ですね。

4 **今　井**： はい、川崎の親戚の家に住んでおります。

5 **ブラウン**： 大学の専門は経済でしたね。それから、スタンフォードのビジネス・スクールに
　　　　　　留学しましたか。

6 **今　井**： はい、そこで 経営学の修士をもらいました。

7 **ブラウン**： 帰国してから、大学の先生になりましたね。

8 **今　井**： はい、母校の講師をしておりました。

9 **ブラウン**： なぜ大学をやめましたか。

10 **今　井**： ビジネスの世界で働きたいと思いまして、この春　思い切って大学をやめました。

11 **ブラウン**： わかりました。御苦労さまでした。今週中に電話で連絡しますから…

12 **今　井**： よろしくお願いいたします。

—210—

Lesson 16

READING

1 Brown: Rirekisho o motte kimashita ka.
2 Imai: Hai, motte mairimashita. Kore de gozaimasu.
3 Brown: Aa, sumai wa Kawasaki desu ne.
4 Imai: Hai, Kawasaki no shinseki no uchi ni sunde orimasu.
5 Brown: Daigaku no senmon wa keezai deshita ne. Sore kara Sutanhoodo no bijinesu-sukuuru ni ryuugaku-shimashita ka.
6 Imai: Hai, soko de kee'eegaku no shuushi o moraimashita.
7 Brown: Kikoku-shite kara, daigaku no sensee ni narimashita ne.
8 Imai: Hai, bokoo no kooshi o shite orimashita.
9 Brown: Naze daigaku o yamemashita ka.
10 Imai: Bijinesu no sekai de hatarakitai to omoimashite, kono haru, omoi-kitte daigaku o yamemashita.
11 Brown: Wakarimashita. Gokuroosama deshita. Konshuu-chuu ni denwa de renraku-shimasu kara...
12 Imai: Yoroshiku onegai-itashimasu.

ADDITIONAL USEFUL EXPRESSIONS

1 At the interview

to graduate [lit. get out] **demasu**

A:	When did (you) graduate from college?	**Itsu daigaku o demashita ka.**

Hokkaido University **Hokkaidoo-daigaku**

B:	(I) graduated from Hokkaido University in 1982.	**Sen-kyuuhyaku-hachijuuni-nen ni Hokkaidoo-daigaku o sotsugyoo-shimashita.**

to get married **kekkon-shimasu**

A:	Are (you) married?	**Kekkon-shite imasu ka.**

single **dokushin, hitori**

B:	No, (I)'m still single.	**Iie, mada dokushin desu.**

—211—

Lesson 16

2 At the interview

	English typewriter	**eebun-taipu**

A: Can (you) use [lit. do] an English typewriter?	**Eebun-taipu wa dekimasu ka.**

	student	**gakusee**
	40 words	**yonjuu waado**

B: It was (my) strong point when (I) was a student, but recently (I) don't do (it) very much, so I guess (I type) around 40 words (per minute).	**Gakusee no toki wa tokui deshita ga, kono goro wa amari shite orimasen kara, yonjuu waado gurai deshoo.**

	test	**tesuto, shiken**
	to give a test	**tesuto o shimasu**
	(newspaper/magazine) article	**kiji**
	to translate	**hon' yaku-shimasu**
	to give	**agemasu**

A: (I) want to give (you) an English test. Please try translating the article in this magazine into English. Shall (I) give (you) some paper?	**Eego no tesuto o shitai n desu ga, kono zasshi no kiji o eego ni hon'-yaku-shite mite kudasai. Kami o age-mashoo ka.**
B: Yes, please.	**Hai, onegai-shimasu.**

3 At the interview

	previous company	**mae no kaisha**
	monthly salary	**gekkyuu**

A: About how much was (your) monthly salary in (your) previous company?	**Mae no kaisha de wa gekkyuu wa ikura gurai deshita ka.**

	take-home pay	**tedori**

B: The take-home pay was about 250,000 (yen).	**Tedori ga nijuugoman gurai deshita.**

	bonus	**boonasu**

A: How about bonuses?	**Boonasu wa.**

Lesson 16

summer	**natsu**
autumn	**aki***
winter	**huyu**
two months' salary	**ni-kagetsubun**
[lit. two months' worth/portion]	
three months' salary	**san-kagetsubun**
to give	**kuremasu**

B:	(The company) gave (me) the equivalent of about two months' salary in summer and three months' salary in winter.	**Natsu wa gekkyuu no ni-kagetsubun, huyu wa san-kagetsubun gurai kuremashita.**

Does not appear in sample dialogue. Introduced for reference only.

REFERENCE

hooritsu	law	**kinmujikan**	working hour
seejigaku	political science	**zangyoo**	overtime
bungaku	literature	**shakai-hoken**	social insurance
shakaigaku	sociology	**koyoo-hoken**	unemployment insurance
koogaku	engineering		
kagaku	science	**nenkin**	pension
igaku	medical science	**taishokukin**	retirement allowance, severance pay
shinrigaku	psychology		
kyooju	professor	**shuushin-koyoo-seedo**	lifetime employment system
jokyooju	assistant professor	**nenkoo-joretsu-seedo**	seniority system

NOTES

1 More about polite/formal expressions

De gozaimasu is a polite equivalent of the copula **desu** 'to be,' and it is used only with nouns and certain particles. In the negative, the particle **wa** usually occurs between **de** and **gozaimasen**: ...**de wa gozaimasen** 'isn't...'

Examples:
  a) **Kore wa watakushi no rirekisho *de gozaimasu*.**
     "This is my personal history."
  b) **Ano kata wa uchi no shain *de wa gozaimasen*.**
     "That person is not one of our (company's) staff."
  c) **Kono tegami wa shachoo kara *de gozaimasu*.**
     "This letter is from the president."
  d) **Kono tegami wa shachoo kara *de wa gozaimasen*.**
     "This letter is not from the president."

Be careful not to confuse **de gozaimasu** with **gozaimasu**, the polite form of **arimasu** 'to have, exist.' (see Lesson 8).

—213—

Lesson 16

Compare: **Kore wa watakushi no rirekisho *de gozaimasu.***
"This is my personal history."

and

Koko ni watakushi no rirekisho ga *gozaimasu.*
"My personal history is here."

Orimasu 'to be,' introduced in Lesson 6, is also used as a modest equivalent of **imasu** in the structure **-te imasu.** Therefore, **-te orimasu** is most commonly used when the speaker is referring to himself or to members of the speaker's group.

Example: **Shujin wa ima tegami o kai*te orimasu.***
"My husband is writing a letter now."

2 Verbs of Giving and Receiving: **agemasu/kuremasu/moraimasu**
Agemasu is used when the speaker or someone else gives to an equal or a superior.

Examples: a) **Boku wa Buraun-san ni pen o *agemashita.***
"I gave a pen to Mr. Brown."
 b) **Kono haizara o *agemashoo* ka.**
"Shall (I) give (you) this ashtray?"
 c) **Buraun-san wa Takada-san ni kono hon o *agemashita.***
"Mr. Brown gave this book to Mr. Takada."

Note that when someone gives to an inferior (or to animals) **yarimasu** is used.

Example: **Kanai wa neko ni sakana o *yarimasu.***
"My wife gives fish to the cat."

Kuremasu is used when someone gives to the speaker, or to the person being addressed by the speaker.

Note that the giver is designated by the particle **ga** or **wa,** and the recipient by the particle **ni.**

Examples: a) **Buraun-san *ga* kono jisho o boku *ni kuremashita.***
"Mr. Brown gave me this dictionary."
 b) **Dare *ga* anata *ni* kono chizu o *kuremashita* ka.**
"Who gave you this map?"
 c) **Kaisha *wa* dono gurai anata *ni* boonasu o *kuremasu* ka.**
"How much money will the company give you as a bonus?"

Moraimasu is used when something is received by the speaker, the person being addressed by the speaker, or a third person. When using the verb **moraimasu,** the recipient is designated by **ga** or **wa,** and the giver by **ni** or **kara.**

Examples: a) **Boku *wa* Tanaka-san *kara* kono zasshi o *moraimashita.***
"I received this magazine from Mr. Tanaka."
 b) **Dare *ni* sono pen o *moraimashita* ka.**
"Whom did (you) get that pen from?"
 c) **Buraun-san *wa* kono goro Jakku *kara* tegami o *moraimasen.***
"Mr. Brown doesn't receive any letters from Jack these days."

—214—

Lesson 16

3 **-chuu ni** 'within'

-chuu ni is used to indicate a time limit or target date, and means 'within...' or 'someday/sometime in...'

Examples: a) **Kongetsu-*chuu ni* shachoo ga Nihon e/ni kimasu.**
             "The president will come to Japan within this month."
           b) **Kotoshi-*chuu ni* Igirisu e/ni ikitai n desu ga...**
             "(I) want to go to England within this year."
           c) **Kyoo-*juu ni* * kono shigoto ga dekimasu ka.**
             "Can (you) complete this work sometime today?"

              ***-chuu** sometimes changes into **-juu** depending upon the preceding vowel: in general, '**u**' and '**i**' are followed by **-chuu,** while '**a**' and '**o**' may occur with **-juu.**

4 Notes on Usage

A) **Motte kimasu** literally means 'to hold and come.'

B) **Kooshi o shimasu:** A noun indicating one's profession/occupation + **o** + **shimasu** is used to mean 'to work as such-and-such.'

Example: **Chichi wa Hukuoka de ginkooin *o shite* imasu.**
               "My father works as a bank clerk in Fukuoka."

C) **Omoikitte,** the gerund of **omoikirimasu** 'to resolve,' is usually used as an adverb meaning 'resolutely, boldly.'

Example: **Sono mondai ni tsuite, *omoikitte* shachoo ni soodan-shimashita.**
               "Concerning that problem, I resolutely consulted with the president."

D) **Hon'yaku-shimasu** is commonly used in the following pattern:

Example: «language A» **o** «language B» **ni *hon'yaku-shimasu.***
               "To translate «A» into «B»."

PRACTICE

1 Level Practice

Example: Teacher: **Rirekisho wa kore desu.**
                    "Here is (my) personal history." [lit. My personal history is this one]
           Student: **Rirekisho wa kore de gozaimasu.**

a) **Ano kata ga Takada-buchoo desu.**	**Ano kata ga Takada-buchoo de gozaimasu.**
b) **Buraun-san no paatii wa ashita desu.**	**Buraun-san no paatii wa ashita de gozaimasu.**
c) **Mae no shigoto wa daigaku no kooshi deshita.**	**Mae no shigoto wa daigaku no kooshi de gozaimashita.**
d) **Daigaku no senmon wa keezai ja arimasen deshita.**	**Daigaku no senmon wa keezai de wa gozaimasen deshita.**

—215—

Lesson 16

2 Level Practice

Example: Teacher: **Daigaku no kooshi o shite imasu.**
"(I)'m working as a lecturer at a university."
Student: **Daigaku no kooshi o shite orimasu.** (modest)

a) **Musume wa Amerika ni ryuugaku-shita imashita.**   **Musume wa Amerika ni ryuugaku-shita orimashita.**

b) **Mainichi nihongo o benkyoo-shite imasu.**   **Mainichi nihongo o benkyoo-shite orimasu.**

c) **Ima watakushi wa Yokohama ni sunde imasu.**   **Ima watakushi wa Yokohama ni sunde orimasu.**

d) **Kesa jimusho de shorui o taipu-shite imashita.**   **Kesa jimusho de shorui o taipu-shite orimashita.**

3 Transformation Practice

Example: Teacher: **Buraun-san ga pen o kuremashita.**
"Mr. Brown gave (me) a pen."
Student: **Buraun-san ni/kara pen o moraimashita.**
"(I) got a pen from Mr. Brown."

a) **Chichi ga hon o kuremashita.**   **Chichi ni/kara hon o moraimashita.**

b) **Dare ga sono hon o kuremashita ka.**   **Dare ni/kara sono hon o morai-mashita ka.**

c) **Yamada-san ga chizu o kuremashita.**   **Yamada-san ni/kara chizu o moraimashita.**

d) **Buraun-san ga shootaijoo o kuremashita.**   **Buraun-san ni/kara shootaijoo o moraimashita.**

e) **Takada-san ga kono katarogu o kuremashita.**   **Takada-san ni/kara kono katarogu o moraimashita.**

4 Communication Practice

Directions: For each of the following, inform the teacher in Japanese that you will give the item indicated to the person indicated.

Example: Teacher: **Yamada-san, kono jisho**
Student: **Watakushi wa Yamada-san ni kono jisho o agemasu.**
"I'll give this dictionary to Ms. Yamada."

a) **Takada-san, Nyuuyooku no chizu**   **Watakushi wa Takada-san ni Nyuuyooku no chizu o agemasu.**

b) **Takada-buchoo, wain**   **Watakushi wa Takada-buchoo ni wain o agemasu.**

c) **Sumisu-san, nihon-see no haizara**   **Watakushi wa Sumisu-san ni nihon-see no haizara o agemasu.**

d) **Kawamoto-san, kee'eegaku no hon**   **Watakushi wa Kawamoto-san ni kee'eegaku no hon o agemasu.**

e) **Kachoo no ojoosan, taipuraitaa**   **Watakushi wa kachoo no ojoosan ni taipuraitaa o agemasu.**

—216—

Lesson 16

5 Transformation Practice

Example: Teacher: **Bijinesu no sekai de hatarakitai desu kara, daigaku o yamemashita.**
"Because (I)'d like to work in the business world, (I) resigned from the university."

        Student: **Bijinesu no sekai de hatarakitai to omoimashite, daigaku o yamemashita.**
"Thinking (I)'d like to work in the business world, (I) resigned from the university."

a) **Chizu ga kaitai desu kara, hon'ya e/ni ikimashita.**   **Chizu ga kaitai to omoimashite, hon'ya e/ni ikimashita.**

b) **Shuushi ni naritai desu kara, daigakuin ni hairimashita.**   **Shuushi ni naritai to omoimashite, daigakuin ni hairimashita.**

c) **Ryuugaku-shitai desu kara, sensee ni soodan-shimashita.**   **Ryuugaku-shitai to omoimashite, sensee ni soodan-shimashita.**

d) **Doitsu-ryoori ga tabetai desu kara, Ginza e/ni kimashita.**   **Doitsu-ryoori ga tabetai to omoimashite, Ginza e/ni kimashita.**

e) **Nihongo o benkyoo-shitai desu kara, kono jisho o kaimashita.**   **Nihongo o benkyoo-shitai to omoimashite, kono jisho o kaimashita.**

6 Communication Practice

Directions: Using the following patterns, describe your own experiences to the teacher.

a) **Watakushi wa «name» -daigaku de benkyoo-shimashita.**
"I studied at «name» university."

b) **Watakushi wa «year» ni sono daigaku o sotsugyoo-shimashita.**
"I graduated from the university in «year»."

c) **Watakushi no senmon wa «subject» deshita.**
"My major was «subject»."

d) **Watakushi wa sono daigaku de «gakushi, shuushi or hakushi» o moraimashita.**
"I received «a Bachelor's, Master's or Doctor's» degree from the university."

e) **Watakushi wa «year» ni ima no kaisha ni hairimashita.**
"I joined the present company in «year»."

f) **Chichi wa ima «profession» o shite imasu.**
"My father is now working as «profession»."

g) **Chichi no sumai wa «place» desu.**
"My father's dwelling is «place»."

EXERCISES

a) Ask the job applicant in Japanese the following: Reply to the interviewer in Japanese as follows:

1	Are you married?	Yes, I'm married
2	Do you have any children?	Yes, I have a daughter.
3	How old is she?	She is 12 years old.
4	What was your major?	I studied law.

— 217 —

Lesson 16

5	Why did you resign from the previous company?	The job wasn't interesting.
6	Have you any experience in working for a bank?	Yes, I have.
7	Can you speak English?	I'm not so good.
8	Can you type?	Yes, I can.
9	Do you read English newspapers daily?	No, I don't.

b) Inform the teacher in Japanese that:
  1 Mr. Brown translates Japanese news articles into English daily.
  2 Mr. Takada worked as a professor at Tokyo University until 1980.
  3 Mr. Tanaka will become General Manager some time this week.
  4 Mr. Yamamoto got an American-made car from his old friend.
  5 Ms. Yamada received an English magazine from Mr. Kawamoto.
  6 Mr. Ohta's company isn't giving any bonuses this year.

Model Answers:

a)
1	Kekkon-shite imasu ka.	Hai, shite imasu.
2	Okosan wa irasshaimasu ka.	Hai, musume ga hitori orimasu.
3	Ojoosan wa oikutsu desu ka.	Juuni desu.
4	Senmon wa nan deshita ka.	Hooritsu deshita.
5	Dooshite mae no kaisha o yamemashita ka.	Shigoto ga omoshiroku nakatta n desu.
6	Ginkoo de no (shigoto no) keeken wa arimasu ka.	Hai, gozaimasu.
7	Eego ga dekimasu ka.	Amari yoku dekimasen.
8	Taipu-dekimasu ka.	Hai, dekimasu.
9	Mainichi eego no shinbun o yonde imasu ka.	Iie, yonde imasen.

b) 1 Buraun-san wa mainichi nihongo no shinbun-kiji o eego ni hon' yaku-shite imasu.
  2 Takada-san wa sen-kyuuhyaku-hachijuu-nen made Tookyoo-daigaku no kyooju o shite imashita.
  3 Tanaka-san wa konshuu-chuu ni buchoo ni narimasu.
  4 Yamamoto-san wa hurui tomodachi kara amerika-see no kuruma o morai-mashita.
  5 Yamada-san wa Kawamoto-san kara eego no zasshi o moraimashita.
  6 Oota-san no kaisha wa kotoshi wa boonasu o kuremasen.

Lesson 16

BUSINESS INFORMATION

The Interview

Joining a new company is sometimes compared in Japan to marrying into a powerful clan. The bride may not be very pretty, but this is hardly significant if the family is an old and famous one, if it can provide protection for you and your relatives, and if theirs is a name you can carry with pride. Although Japan certainly has its share of fast-track yuppies and entrepreneurs, there are still many Japanese who will put up with modest salaries and long hours, as long as their company provides for them like a family and has a good reputation in professional society. Some foreign companies try to make up for their lack of "paternal" assistance by offering higher pay, but this alone is not always enough to dispel the sense of insecurity their employees may feel.

If you are thinking of employing additional Japanese staff, or if you hope to join a Japanese company, the following points may help ensure a successful interview and a smooth professional relationship thereafter.

1 **The Personal Touch:** In Japan, personal details in many cases take precedence over business and scholastic accomplishments. If you are being interviewed for a position in a local company, you may be asked what sort of work your brothers and sisters are doing, for example, in addition to all the standard questions about job experience and language skills. Likewise, if you are the employer, you should not be surprised if a candidate's resume describes his passion for golf, along with other facts and figures you would normally consider irrelevant. In fact, it would be a good idea to inquire into such "unrelated" matters, as this may reassure him that you have as much interest in his non-professional life as any Japanese employer.

Note too, that in contrast to many Western resumes, your Japanese candidate's curriculum vitae may be quite vague about his academic record. This does not necessarily imply that he wishes to evade the subject. Rather, Japanese employers are seldom concerned about grades; they feel it is much more important that the candidate show a cooperative spirit and that he be receptive to the company's training and ideals. The general assumption on both sides is that the *really* pertinent training for the position will take place only after the applicant has entered the company.

You may also find it useful to know that, once an employee in a Japanese firm gets noticed for performance, he is often rotated to a different department. If, in the West, you are moved to a different—but not higher—position, you may safely assume your days in that firm are numbered. In Japan, however, such a move is usually promising. The corporate promotion system is one of spiraling rather than vertical ascent, i.e. every step upwards involves several to the side. Employees marked for managerial posts will be shifted from job to job so that they can acquire a wide exposure to different responsibilities and develop a well-rounded view of the corporation and its needs. In contrast to the West, the lateral move is sometimes welcomed here as the first step on the round-about, "scenic" route to the top.

—219—

Lesson 16

2 Conditions: Working conditions, social benefits and salaries for company employees in Japan must conform to the standards set by the Ministry of Labor. Questions regarding these standards—as well as complaints about violations—may be directed to the **Roodo Kijun Kantokusho** (労働基準監督署, Labor Standards Administration Office). If you are being interviewed for a position by a Japanese firm, you should make sure you know exactly what the company's *own* standards are, too. Many firms are quite flexible about working conditions for foreigners, but some adhere firmly to one standard for all employees, foreign or Japanese. For your own protection, you should "check the fine print"* to make sure you and your employer are really speaking the same language, e.g. that the net figure you expect on your paycheck doesn't equal the gross figure on his payroll, and that you're not stuck with ten days' vacation when the cheap ticket you already bought for your home leave stipulates that you stay there for thirty. A little advance preparation will help avoid rocking the boat later—with possible loss of face for your personnel director.

*A figure of speech, since there is seldom a written contract between employer and employee.

Lesson 17

Business Negotiations I

OBJECTIVES

1 to start business negotiations.

2 to explain what your company does.

3 to explain about your products.

4 to ask for another opportunity to negotiate.

Lesson 17

TARGET EXPRESSIONS AND PATTERNS

1 (Someone) does… for (me/you). **…shite kuremasu.**

2 to have (someone) do… **…shite moraimasu.**

3 to do… for (someone). **…shite agemasu.**

4 (I)'ll do… in advance. **…shite okimasu.**

5 Because… **…no de, …**

6 Mr./Ms. «name X»'s background [lit. matters concerning Mr./Ms. «name X»]. **«X»-san no koto.**

SITUATION

P & C, Ltd. becomes the agent in Japan for the American industrial robot maker, USM, Ltd. To sell robots to Japanese companies, Mr. Brown asks Mr. Kawamoto of Japan Automobile Manufacturers Association Inc. to introduce him to Japanese companies. Through Mr. Kawamoto's mediation, Mr. Brown calls on Mr. Ohyama, General Manager of the Purchasing Administration Department of Nissan Motor Co., Ltd. Mr. Brown meets Mr. Ohyama and his assistant, Mr. Suzuki.

DIALOGUE

(After exchanging initial greetings)

thing, fact, matter	**koto**
Mr. Brown's background [lit. things/matters concerning Mr. Brown]	**Buraun-san no koto**
Ohyama to inform for (my/your) benefit	**hanashite kuremasu**

> **1** Mr. Kawamoto has spoken a lot to (me) about (you). [lit. As for matters concerning Mr. Brown, Mr. Kawamoto has spoken of various things (for my benefit).]
>
> **Buraun-san no koto wa, Kawamoto-san ga iroiro hanashite kuremashita yo.**

business	**shoobai, bijinesu**
business in Japan	**Nihon de no shoobai/bijinesu**
way of doing	**yarikata**
Brown to have (someone) teach	**oshiete moraimasu**

> **2** Is that so? (I)'m always having Mr. Kawamoto teach (me) how to do business in Japan.
>
> **Soo desu ka. Kawamoto-san ni wa itsumo Nihon de no shoobai no yarikata o oshiete moratte orimasu.**

—222—

Lesson 17

Ohyama	fluent, skilled	**joozu, ojoozu** (respectful)

> **3** He too mentioned (this), but you [lit. Mr. Brown] are really fluent in Japanese.
>
> **Kare mo itte imashita ga, Buraun-san wa hontoo ni nihongo ga ojoozu desu nee.**

	still	**madamada**
	poor (at ...)	**heta /na/**
Brown	because (I) am poor (at ...)	**heta desu no de**

> **4** No, not at all! Because (I)'m still poor at (it), (it) bothers (me). Studying Japanese is more difficult than business.
>
> **Iie, tondemo gozaimasen. Madamada heta desu no de, komatte orimasu. Nihongo no benkyoo wa shoobai yori muzukashii desu.**

(Both laugh)

Ohyama	matter, business	**yooken, goyooken** (respectful)

> **5** By the way, what can (I) do for (you) today [lit. what's today's business matter]?
>
> **Tokoro de, kyoo no goyooken wa.**

	we, our company	**watakushidomo** (modest)
	U.S.A.	**Beekoku**
	USM, Ltd.	**Yuu-esu-emu-sha**
Brown	agent	**dairiten**

> **6** The fact is that our company lately has become an agent for USM, Ltd. in the U.S.A.
>
> **Jitsu wa, watakushidomo (no kaisha) wa kondo Beekoku no Yuu-esu-emu-sha no dairiten ni narimashita.**

	robot	**robotto**
Ohyama	maker	**meekaa**

> **7** Oh, USM (Ltd.) is a robot maker, isn't it?
>
> **Aa, Yuu-esu-emu wa robotto no mee-kaa desu nee.**

	industry	**sangyoo**
Brown	for industry-use	**sangyoo-yoo**

> **8** Yes, (it) manufactures industrial robots.
>
> **Hai, sangyoo-yoo no robotto o tsu-kutte orimasu.**

—223—

Lesson 17

Ohyama

| 9 | Where is the company located? | **Kaisha wa dochira ni arimasu ka.** |

	Ohio	**Ohaio**
	Texas	**Tekisasu**
Brown	description, explanation	**setsumeesho, gaiyoo**

| 10 | The head office is in New York, but there are factories in Ohio and Texas. Here is (their) company's brochure [lit. description]. | **Honsha wa Nyuuyooku desu ga, koojoo wa Ohaio to Tekisasu ni arimasu. Kochira ga kaisha no gaiyoo desu.** |

| | (to have the honor) of looking over | **haiken-shimasu** (modest) |
| **Ohyama** | manufactured goods | **seehin** |

| 11 | (I)'ll (be honored to) look it over. (They) are making a lot of different products, aren't they? | **Haiken-shimasu. Iroiro na seehin o tsukutte imasu nee.** |

	new products	**shinseehin**
	very, awfully	**taihen /na/**
	wonderful	**subarashii**
	wonderful things	**subarashii mono**
	examination	**kentoo (-shimasu), gokentoo** (respectful)
Brown		

| 12 | Yes, in particular, this new product is really wonderful, so by all means, won't (you) please take a look (at it) [lit. examine (it)]. | **Hai, toku ni kono shinseehin wa taihen subarashii mono desu kara, zehi gokentoo kudasaimasen ka.** |

	NC robot	**Enu-shii robotto**
	to go out	**dekakemasu**
Ohyama	some day, one of these days	**izure**

| 13 | It's an NC robot, isn't it? | **Enu-shii robotto desu nee.** |

(Pause)

| | To be frank with (you), (I)'m going out at three today, so (I)'d like to hear about the details again some other day. | **Jitsu wa watakushi, kyoo wa san-ji kara dekakemasu no de, kuwashii koto wa izure mata ukagaimasu.** |

—224—

Lesson 17

	respects, greeting	aisatsu, goaisatsu (polite)
Brown	only to pay (my) respects	goaisatsu ni dake

14 (I) see. (I) came only to pay (my) respects today, so (I'll visit) again some day in the near future. — **Soo desu ne. Kyoo wa goaisatsu ni dake ukagaimashita no de izure mata chikai uchi ni.**

	to examine	kentoo-shimasu
Ohyama	to examine for future reference	kentoo-shite okimasu

15 Well then, we'll also examine (this) by then, so [imp. we'll talk to you later.] — **De wa, watakushidomo mo kentoo-shite okimasu kara…**

Brown

16 Thank you very much (for taking time to see me) when (you) are so busy. — **Doomo, taihen oisogashii tokoro o arigatoo gozaimashita.**

JAPANESE WRITING

1 　大　山：　ブラウンさんのことは、川本さんがいろいろ話してくれましたよ。

2 　ブラウン：　そうですか。川本さんにはいつも日本での商売のやり方を教えてもらっております。

3 　大　山：　彼も言っていましたが、ブラウンさんは本当に日本語がお上手ですねえ。

4 　ブラウン：　いいえ、とんでもございません。まだまだ下手ですので、困っております。
　　　　　　　　日本語の勉強は商売よりむずかしいです。

5 　大　山：　ところで、今日の御用件は。

6 　ブラウン：　実は、私共の会社は今度米国のユー・エス・エム社の代理店になりました。

7 　大　山：　ああ、ユー・エス・エムはロボットのメーカーですねえ。

8 　ブラウン：　はい、産業用のロボットをつくっております。

9 　大　山：　会社はどちらにありますか。

10 　ブラウン：　本社はニューヨークですが、工場はオハイオとテキサスにあります。
　　　　　　　　こちらが会社の概要です。

11 　大　山：　拝見します。いろいろな製品を作っていますねえ。

12 　ブラウン：　はい、特にこの新製品は大変すばらしいものですから、是非御検討下さいませんか。

13 　大　山：　エヌ・シーロボットですねえ。実は私、今日は三時から出かけますので、
　　　　　　　　詳しいことはいずれまた伺います。

14 　ブラウン：　そうですね。今日はごあいさつにだけ伺いましたので、いずれまた近いうちに。

15 　大　山：　では、私共も検討しておきますから…

16 　ブラウン：　どうも、大変お忙しいところをありがとうございました。

Lesson 17

READING

1 **Ohyama:** Buraun-san no koto wa, Kawamoto-san ga iroiro hanashite kure-mashita yo.
2 **Brown:** Soo desu ka. Kawamoto-san ni wa itsumo Nihon de no shobai no yarikata o oshiete moratte orimasu.
3 **Ohyama:** Kare mo itte imashita ga, Buraun-san wa hontoo ni nihongo ga ojoozu desu nee.
4 **Brown:** Iie, tondemo gozaimasen. Madamada heta desu no de, komatte orimasu. Nihongo no benkyoo wa shoobai yori muzukashii desu.
5 **Ohyama:** Tokoro de, kyoo no goyooken wa.
6 **Brown:** Jitsu wa, watakushidomo (no kaisha) wa kondo Beekoku no Yuu-esu-emu-sha no dairiten ni narimashita.
7 **Ohyama:** Aa, Yuu-esu-emu wa robotto no meekaa desu nee.
8 **Brown:** Hai, sangyoo-yoo no robotto o tsukutte orimasu.
9 **Ohyama:** Kaisha wa dochira ni arimasu ka.
10 **Brown:** Honsha wa Nyuuyooku desu ga, koojoo wa Ohaio to Tekisasu ni arimasu. Kochira ga kaisha no gaiyoo desu.
11 **Ohyama:** Haiken-shimasu. Iroiro na seehin o tsukutte imasu nee.
12 **Brown:** Hai, toku ni kono shin-seehin wa taihen subarashii mono desu kara, zehi gokentoo kudasaimasen ka.
13 **Ohyama:** Enu-shii robotto desu nee. Jitsu wa watakushi, kyoo wa san-ji kara dekakemasu no de, kuwashii koto wa izure mata ukagaimasu.
14 **Brown:** Soo desu ne. Kyoo wa goaisatsu ni dake ukagaimashita no de izure mata chikai uchi ni.
15 **Ohyama:** De wa, watakushidomo mo kentoo-shite okimasu kara...
16 **Brown:** Doomo, taihen oisogashii tokoro o arigatoo gozaimashita.

ADDITIONAL USEFUL EXPRESSIONS

1 At the office

business talk | **shoodan**

A:	How was yesterday's negotiation? [lit. business talk.]	**Kinoo no shoodan wa doo deshita ka.**

hopeful, promising | **yuuboo /na/**

B:	It looks quite promising.	**Nakanaka yuuboo desu yo.**

probably | **tabun**
no good, useless | **dame /na/**

A:	That's good, isn't it? Mine will probably be useless/no good.	**Sore wa ii desu nee. Boku no hoo wa tabun dame desu yo.**

—226—

Lesson 17

transactions, business	**torihiki**
time	**jikan**
to take time	**jikan ga kakarimasu**

B: Big transactions take time, don't they.	**Ookii torihiki wa jikan ga kakarimasu kara nee.**

2 At the party

to handle, deal with	**atsukaimasu**

A: What are (you) handling now?	**Ima nani o atsukatte imasu ka.**

to sell	**urimasu**

B: I'm selling NC robots.	**Enu-shii robotto o utte imasu.**

business conditions	**keeki**

A: How's business?	**Keeki wa doo desu ka.**
B: It's not very brisk, so [imp. I would like to make some changes.]	**Sore ga amari yoku arimasen no de...**

to introduce (someone) to (you)	**shookai-shite agemasu**

A: Well, shall (I) introduce a good company to (you)?	**Jaa, ii kaisha o shookai shite agemashoo ka.**
B: Really? By all means, please do so.	**Hontoo desu ka. Zehi onegai-shimasu.**

REFERENCE

shoohin	article(s)/good(s) for sale	**koosaku-kikai, kooki**	machine tool
shoogyoo	commerce	**sentan-gijutsu, hai-teku**	high-tech
koogyoo	mining	**soodairiten**	general agent
koogyoo	industry	**shijoo**	market
noogyoo	agriculture	**kaitsuke**	buying
gyogyoo	fisheries	**urikomi**	canvassing for selling
saabisugyoo	service industry	**yunyuu (-shimasu)**	import
		yushutsu (-shimasu)	export
		koobai-kanri-bu	purchasing administration department

—227—

Lesson 17

NOTES

1 Verb Gerund + **agemasu/kuremasu/moraimasu**

A verb gerund + **agemasu** is used to indicate that someone does something to/for someone else. The person benefiting from the action is indicated by the particle **ni.**

Examples:
    a) **Buraun-san ni chizu o kai*te* *agemashita*.**
        "(I) drew a map for Mr. Brown."
    b) **Takada-san ni ano hon o mise*te* *agemashita* ka.**
        "Did (you) show that book to (and for the benefit of) Mr. Takada?"
    c) **Tetsudat*te* *agemashoo* ka.**
        "Shall (I) help (you)?"
    d) **Kanai wa nihon-ryoori ni tsuite Buraun-san ni setsumee-shi*te* *agemasu*.**
        "My wife will explain Japanese cuisine to Mr. Brown (for his benefit)."

Note that like the pattern, noun + **agemasu** (Lesson 16) the speaker can't be the person who receives the service.

Verb gerund + **kuremasu** is used to indicate that someone does something to/for the speaker. However, in questions, the person addressed is usually the one who receives the service.

Examples:
    a) **Sensee ga sono hon o yon*de* *kuremashita*.**
        "The teacher read that book to me (for my benefit)."
        or
        "The teacher read that book on my behalf."
    b) **Dare ga setsumee-shi*te* *kuremashita* ka.**
        "Who explained (it) to (you)?"
    c) **Tanaka-san wa Haato-san o shookai-shi*te* *kuremasen* deshita.**
        "Mr. Tanaka didn't introduce (me) to Mr. Hart (for my benefit)."

Verb gerund + **moraimasu** is used to indicate that someone has something done by someone else. The person providing the service is indicated by **ni.**

Examples:
    a) **Boku wa tomodachi *ni* tetsudat*te* *moraimashita*.**
        "I had my friend help me."
    b) **Dare *ni* kono pen o kat*te* *moraimashita* ka.**
        "Who bought this pen for you/on your behalf?
        [lit. Whom did you have this pen bought by?]"
    c) **Mise no hito *ni* ryooshuusho o kai*te* *moraimashoo ka*.**
        "Shall (I) have the store's clerk write a receipt?"

Verb gerund + **moraitai n desu ga** is often used in an indirect request.

Compare:
    Ashita hachi-ji made ni jimusho ni ki*te* *moraitai n desu ga*.
    "(I)'d like to have (you) come to the office by eight tomorrow, but [imp. can you come?]"
    and
    Ashita hachi-ji made ni jimusho ni ki*te* *kudasai*.
    "Please come to the office by eight tomorrow."

—228—

Lesson 17

2 Verb Gerund + **okimasu**

Verb gerund + **okimasu** means 'to do... beforehand/in advance/for future reference/for the time being.'

Examples: a) **Raishuu shiken o ukemasu kara, konshuu-chuu ni kono hon o yonde *okimasu*.**
"(I)'ll take a test next week, so (I)'ll read this book within the week (for future benefit)."

           b) **Konban tomodachi ga kimasu kara, ima biiru o katte *okimashoo*.**
"(My) friends will come (to my home) this evening, so (I)'ll buy some beer now (in advance)."

           c) **Hiru made ni kono shorui o taipu-shite *oite* kudasai.**
"Please have this document typed (for future use) by noon."

3 Particle **no de** 'because'

The particle **no de** is used at the end of a clause to indicate a reason or a cause, and is normally translated as 'because,' 'since.'

Examples: a) **Ryokoo-shite imashita *no de*, sono paatii ni shusseki-dekimasen deshita.**
"Because (I) was travelling, (I) couldn't attend that party."

           b) **Anata ga setsumee-shite kuremashita *no de*, yoku wakarimashita.**
"Because you explained (it to me), (I) understood (it) very well."

           c) **Amerika e/ni ikitai* *no de*, eego o benkyoo-shite imasu.**
"Because (I) want to go to America, (I)'m studying English."

              ***No de** often follows informal forms of adjectives, *-tai* forms and verbs.

4 **Koto** 'thing, matter, fact'

Koto, a noun always preceded by a modifier, is used to refer to things, matters or facts which are intangible, in contrast to the term, **mono,** which is used to indicate some tangible, concrete thing or person.

«noun X» + **no koto** usually means 'things concerning/about «X»,' or '«X»'s background.' Thus, **anata no koto** '(matters) about you, your background'; **shigoto no koto** '(things) about work.'

When preceded by an adjective, **koto** is usually translated as 'fact' or 'thing.' Thus, **kuwashii koto** 'detailed facts, details,'; **omoshiroi koto** 'interesting fact(s), interesting thing(s).'

5 Notes on Usage

A) **Joozu** 'good at (it), skillful' and **heta** 'poor at (it), unskillful'

Joozu desu and **heta desu** are usually used as follows:

Kare wa eego ga *joozu desu*.   "He speaks English well."
Musume wa taipu ga *heta desu*.   "(My) daughter is poor at typing."

B) **Watakushidomo** is a modest expression meaning 'we,' and **watakushidomo (no kaisha)** is a modest expression meaning 'our company.' **Toosha** is a more formal term used for the same meaning: 'our company.'

—229—

Lesson 17

C) **Aisatsu** usually means 'greeting(s),' but it is sometimes used to refer to the courtesy calls which one is expected to pay when assuming a new position or job. In this lesson, Mr. Brown calls on Mr. Ohyama to pay his respects prior to starting business negotiations. This type of courtesy call is absolutely necessary to conduct business in Japan. **Goaisatsu ni dake ukagaimashita** (DIALOGUE **14**) means "(I) called on (you) only as a courtesy (and I'll not start negotiations)." It can be said that this indirect approach is the typical Japanese way of taking the initial step toward serious business negotiations. Note that the particle **ni** in the sentence above means 'for (the purpose of),' like the **ni** in **yuushoku ni** 'for dinner' in Lesson 9, ADDITIONAL USEFUL EXPRESSIONS.

PRACTICE

1 Response Practice

Example: Teacher: **Dare ga hanashimashita ka. /Kawamoto-san/**
"Who told (you that)?" /Mr. Kawamoto/
Student: **Kawamoto-san ga hanashite kuremashita.**
"Mr. Kawamoto told (me) [lit. ...for my benefit]"

a) **Dare ga chizu o kakimashita ka. /Yamada-san/**   **Yamada-san ga kaite kuremashita.**

b) **Dare ga Haato-san o shookai-shimashita ka. /Takada-san/**   **Takada-san ga shookai-shite kuremashita.**

c) **Dare ga shorui o misemashita ka. /Oota-san/**   **Oota-san ga misete kuremashita.**

2 Response Practice

Example: Teacher: **Dare ga nihongo o oshiemasu ka. /sensee/**
"Who teaches (you) Japanese?" /the teacher/
Student: **Sensee ni oshiete moraimasu.**
"(I) have (my) teacher teach (me Japanese)."

a) **Dare ga taipu-shimashita ka. /Yamada-san/**   **Yamada-san ni taipu-shite moraimashita.**

b) **Dare ga renraku-shimasu ka. /Tanaka-san/**   **Tanaka-san ni renraku-shite moraimasu.**

c) **Dare ga nebiki-shimashita ka. /Buraun-san/**   **Buraun-san ni nebiki-shite moraimashita.**

3 Response Practice

Example: Teacher: **Anata ga michi o oshiemashita ka.**
"Did you show [lit. teach] (him/her/them) the way?"
Student: **Ee, watakushi ga oshiete agemashita.**
"Yes, I showed (him/her/them the way)."

a) **Anata ga sono zasshi o misemasu ka.**   **Ee, watakushi ga misete agemasu.**

b) **Anata ga tegami o kakimashita ka.**   **Ee, watakushi ga kaite agemashita.**

—230—

Lesson 17

c) Anata ga ojoosama ni kono taipuraitaa o kaimasu ka.

Ee, katte agemasu.

d) Anata ga sono shigoto o tetsudai-
mashita ka.

Ee, tetsudatte agemashita.

4 Response Practice

Example: Teacher: **Kono seehin ni tsuite kentoo-shimasu ka.**
"Will (you) look into matters concerning this product?"
Student: **Ee, kentoo-shite okimasu.**
"Yes, (I)'ll look into (it for future use)."

a) **Shachoo ni denwa-shimashita ka.**   **Ee, denwa-shite okimashita.**
b) **Ano shorui o kakimashita ka.**   **Ee, kaite okimashita.**
c) **Sutahhu to soodan-shimasu ka.**   **Ee, soodan-shite okimasu.**
d) **Moo biiru o kaimashita ka.**   **Ee, katte okimashita.**
e) **Ano tegami o dashimashita ka.**   **Ee, dashite okimashita.**

5 Transformation Practice

Example: Teacher: **Takai desu kara, kaimasen.**
"(It)'s expensive, so (I) won't buy (it)."
Student: **Takai desu no de, kaimasen.**
"Because (it)'s expensive, (I) won't buy (it)."

a) **Ima kentoo-shite imasu kara, moo
sukoshi matte kudasai.**

**Ima kentoo-shite imasu no de, moo
sukoshi matte kudasai.**

b) **Kyoo wa isogashii desu kara,
paatii ni shusseki-dekimasen.**

**Kyoo wa isogashii desu no de, paatii
ni shusseki-dekimasen.**

c) **Kuruma o atsukatte imasu kara,
kuruma no koto wa yoku
wakarimasu.**

**Kuruma o atsukatte imasu no de,
kuruma no koto wa yoku
wakarimasu.**

d) **Yuu-esu-emu no dairiten ni narimashita kara, yoroshiku onegai-
shimasu.**

**Yuu-esu-emu no dairiten ni narima-
shita no de, yoroshiku onegai-
shimasu.**

6 Communication Practice

Directions: Using the following patterns, inform the teacher in Japanese of the goods
handled by your, or your friend's company. Request additional vocabulary
if necessary.

Examples: a) **Watakushi no kaisha wa** «names of articles A, B, and C» **o atsukatte
imasu.**
"My company handles «names of articles A, B, and C»."

b) **Tomodachi no** «name X» **-san no kaisha wa** «names of articles A,
B, and C» **o atsukatte imasu.**
"My friend, «X»'s company handles «names of articles A, B, and C»."

—231—

Lesson 17

EXERCISES

Inform the teacher in Japanese that:

1 Because Mr. Kawamoto told Mr. Ohyama about Mr. Brown, Mr. Ohyama knows a little about Mr. Brown.
2 Mr. Brown has Mr. Kawamoto teach him how to do business in Japan.
3 Because P & C became the agency for USM, Ltd., Mr. Brown is selling industrial robots.
4 USM, Ltd. is manufacturing NC robots.
5 Mr. Brown said he came to Nissan just as a courtesy.
6 In Japan large business transactions always take considerable time.
7 Mr. Kawamoto introduced Mr. Brown to Mr. Ohyama, General Manager of the Purchasing Administration Department of Nissan Motor Co., Ltd. (for Mr. Brown's sake).
8 Mr. Tanaka isn't good at English, but he is very good in business.

Model Answers:

1 **Kawamoto-san wa Buraun-san no koto o Ooyama-san ni hanashimashita no de, Ooyama-san wa Buraun-san no koto wa sukoshi wakarimasu.**
2 **Buraun-san wa Kawamoto-san ni Nihon de no bijinesu no yarikata o oshiete moratte imasu.**
3 **Pii-ando-shii wa Yuu-esu-emu no dairiten ni narimashita no de, Buraun-san wa sangyoo-yoo robotto o utte imasu.**
4 **Yuu-esu-emu wa Enu-shii robotto o tsukutte imasu.**
5 **Buraun-san wa Nissan ni goaisatsu ni dake ukagaimashita tte/to iimashita.**
6 **Nihon de wa ookii torihiki wa itsumo jikan ga kakarimasu.**
7 **Kawamoto-san wa Buraun-san o Nissan no koobai-buchoo no Ooyama-san ni shookai-shite agemashita.**
8 **Tanaka-san wa eego wa amari joozu ja arimasen ga, bijinesu wa taihen joozu desu.**

—232—

Lesson 17

BUSINESS INFORMATION

Starting Negotiations

1 Introductions: By the time you buckle down to serious negotiations, you will probably have visited your prospective client company a number of times and established a few contacts there. Nevertheless, the guidelines about **shookai** (紹介, introductions) that apply to first-time visits are still valid at this stage. If possible, you should have a third party put in a good word for you to your prospective client although, of course, the objective of the **shookai** this time is not so much to help get your foot inside the door but to get the client himself to open up to your business proposal. Sometimes, the **shookai** will consist of nothing more than a simple **"yoroshiku onegai-shimasu"** (よろしくお願いします , lit. "I ask for your good will in this matter"), but even that may be enough to start your ball rolling. The ideal candidate to put in this good word on your behalf would be a strategically-ranked mutual friend in the industry. However, if you are new in Japan and do not know a soul, you can call on the PR section, the International Division or such contacts as you may already have established within the company itself for assistance. If all else fails, you can try one of the industrial or professional associations, e.g. Japan Automobile Manufacturers Association Inc. (to which Mr. Kawamoto in the DIALOGUE belongs).

2 The Courtesy Call: As with business lunches, it is best to take negotiations with Japanese companies one step at a time. Preliminary phone calls and introductions are usually followed by a courtesy call. Although high-ranking officials may show up at your courtesy call, it will do you and your cause no good whatsoever to plunge right into serious talk about figures, dates and schedules at this point. This would not only be a violation of normal practices but a waste of your time, since the high-ranking officials attending the first meeting usually do so only for **aisatsu** (挨拶, paying respects). It is not unusual for Japanese directors to be quite removed from the normal day-to-day affairs of their company, being far more involved in long-range strategic planning. Whatever detailed explanation you choose to launch into about your product may be absolutely Greek to them; the more sensitive among them may even be slighted by your implication that it is they who have to deal with the nitty-gritty of business transactions. It is normally only after the **aisatsu** have been taken care of that the person(s) most qualified for the task will be assigned to handle your business. Consequently, if you are used to getting to the heart of the matter right from the start, you should try to control your impatience. Concentrate instead on creating a positive impression and setting a mood conducive to mutual cooperation in the future.

3 The Conversation: Sometimes, meetings with Japanese businessmen may seem rather stiff to the foreign visitor, especially when you are talking for the first time. No matter how hard you try, your counterparts just don't seem to respond. There may be all these painful gaps in the conversation during which you rack your brains for appropriate small talk. From time to time, you will probably wonder what you did wrong and despair of ever getting your project off the ground. However, you should not be intimidated by the awkwardness of your courtesy call or subsequent meetings. The painful silences may not be due to any *faux pas* on your part at all. Rather, your hosts may simply be shy or

—233—

Lesson 17

reluctant to speak English—not so much to you, a native speaker, but in front of their colleagues who will then know for once and for all the low (or so they fear) level of their conversational ability. At times like this, a little Japanese on your part will certainly come as a big relief. You should try not to worry unduly about whether you sound clumsy or funny. In fact, drawing a little laughter—whether intentional or not—will not only break the ice but maybe also help clear the way for future discussions.

4 Major Economic Organizations in Japan: Below are a few economic organizations in the private sector that may be able to assist you during your stay in Japan.

Japan Federation of Economic Organizations, or KEIDANREN (経団連, short for 経済団体連合会 *Keezai Dantai Rengookai*): The spokesman for big business, with considerable influence in political circles. Keidanren is very active in trying to ease international trade friction between governments and industries. In addition to providing useful information to foreign business persons, it can be a source of valuable contacts with individual industries. Keidanren is moreover receptive to foreign inquiries and business complaints.

Japan Federation of Employers' Associations, or NIKKEIREN (日経連, short for 日本経営者団体連盟 *Nihon Kee'eesha Dantai Renmee*): The representative organization for private management all across the nation. Nikkeiren is the spokesman for management interests in labor disputes.

The Japan Chamber of Commerce and Industry, or NISSHO (日商, short for 日本商工会議所 *Nihon Shookookaigisho*): The spokesman for small and medium-sized companies. Nissho can be especially helpful to the foreign business person in organizing exhibitions and trade fairs, and assisting with import procedures.

Japan External Trade Organization, or JETRO (ジェトロ, acronym for 日本貿易振興会 *Nihon Booeki Shinkoo Kai*): Semi-governmental body which provides market information and assistance to foreign companies and governments entering the Japanese market. JETRO is the first place most foreigners go to for advice about business regulations and trade procedures, as it is far more accessible than other government offices and has an extensive library of foreign language publications on the Japanese business environment. JETRO also has 79 offices in 57 countries overseas.

Lesson 18

Business Negotiations II

OBJECTIVES

1   to discuss a product.

2   to discuss a factory.

3   to discuss patents and utility models.

4   to learn the use of informal verbs.

Lesson 18

TARGET EXPRESSIONS AND PATTERNS

1 to be able to do…   …suru koto ga dekiru.

2 It is the fact of doing…   …suru n desu.

3 until (one) does…   …suru made.

SITUATION

Mr. Brown visits Nissan Motor Co., Ltd. again, and discusses the NC robot with Mr. Suzuki of the Purchasing Administration Department.

DIALOGUE

Brown

1	Today, (I) thought (I)'d like to talk about the NC robot (which I mentioned) the other day. [imp. that's why I came here.]	**Kyoo wa, senjitsu no Enu-shii robotto ni tsuite ohanashi-shitai to omoimashite…**

Suzuki   after that   **sono go**

2	After that we also had a look at (it), [lit. we also tried examining (it),] but it is a wonderful robot, isn't it?	**Watakushidomo mo sono go kentooshite mimashita ga, are wa subarashii robotto desu nee.**

one unit	**ichi-dai**
various	**iron /na/** (informal form of **iroiro /na/**)
to do	**suru** (informal form of **shimasu**)
to be able	**dekiru** (informal form of **dekimasu**)
to be able to (do)	**(suru) koto ga dekiru**
your company	**onsha** (respectful)
to be suited for	**muku** (informal)*
to be	**iru** (informal form of **imasu**)

Brown

3	Yes, with one unit, (this robot) can do various jobs, so (I) think (it) is suited for your company's factories.	**Hai, ichi-dai de iron na shigoto o suru koto ga dekimasu kara, onsha no koojoo ni muite iru to omoimasu.**

Hereafter, verbs will be introduced in their informal forms (citation forms).

Suzuki   to be using   **tsukatte iru n desu**

—236—

Lesson 18

| 4 | In the U.S.A., what kinds of factories are using (it)? [lit. ...in what kinds of factories are (they) using (it)?] | Amerika de wa donna koojoo de tsukatte iru n desu ka. |

Brown   mainly   **omo ni**

| 5 | Mainly, airplane manufacturers are using (this robot). [lit. in airplane factories (they) are using (this robot).] | Omo ni, hikooki no koojoo de tsukatte imasu. |

       data, materials   **shiryoo**
Suzuki   to want   **hoshii**

| 6 | (I)'d like more detailed information, but [imp. do you have any?] | Motto kuwashii shiryoo ga hoshii n desu ga... |

Brown

| 7 | This is a catalogue for that robot. | Kore ga ano robotto no katarogu desu. |

(While looking over the catalogue)

       patent   **tokkyo**
Suzuki   to take out, obtain   **toru**

| 8 | (USM) took out a patent ten years ago, didn't they? | Tokkyo wa juu-nen mae ni totta n desu ne. |

Brown until (someone/something) can do   **dekiru made**

| 9 | Yes, that's right. After that, it took eight years before we could finish the product. | Hai, soo desu. Sore kara, seehin ga dekiru made, hachi-nen kakari-mashita. |

       technology   **gijutsu**
Suzuki   technical   **gijutsuteki /na/**

| 10 | Can you give a technical explanation, too? | Gijutsuteki na setsumee mo anata ga dekimasu ka. |

—237—

Lesson 18

	specialist	**senmonka**
Brown	to call for	**yobu**

11 No, but (I)'ll call for a specialist from USM, Ltd. [imp. can you wait?] | **Iie, sore wa Yuu-esu-emu kara senmonka o yobimasu ga...**

	one time	**ichi-do**
	one more time	**moo ichi-do**
Suzuki	within the company	**shanai**

12 (I) understand. Well then, (I) will contact (you) again after I also consult (people in) the company one more time. | **Wakarimashita. De wa, watakushi mo moo ichi-do shanai de soodan-shite kara, mata renraku-shimasu.**

	to wait	**matsu**
Brown	to wait	**omachi-suru** (polite)

13 Well then, (I) will be expecting [lit. waiting for] (your reply), so [imp. please do as you say.] | **De wa, omachi-shite orimasu kara...**

JAPANESE WRITING

1　ブラウン：　今日は、先日のエヌ・シーロボットについてお話ししたいと思いまして…

2　鈴　　木：　私共もその後検討してみましたが、あれはすばらしいロボットですねえ。

3　ブラウン：　はい、一台でいろんな仕事をすることができますから、御社の工場にむいていると思います。

4　鈴　　木：　アメリカではどんな工場で使っているんですか。

5　ブラウン：　主に、飛行機の工場で使っています。

6　鈴　　木：　もっと詳しい資料が欲しいんですが…

7　ブラウン：　これがあのロボットのカタログです。

8　鈴　　木：　特許は十年前にとったんですね。

9　ブラウン：　はい、そうです。それから、製品ができるまで、八年かかりました。

10　鈴　　木：　技術的な説明もあなたができますか。

11　ブラウン：　いいえ、それはユー・エス・エムから専門家を呼びますが…

12　鈴　　木：　わかりました。では、私ももう一度社内で相談してから、又連絡します。

13　ブラウン：　では、お待ちしておりますから…

READING

1　**Brown: Kyoo wa, senjitsu no Enu-shii robotto ni tsuite ohanashi-shitai to omoimashite...**

Lesson 18

2 Suzuki: Watakushidomo mo sono go kentoo-shite mimashita ga, are wa subarashii robotto desu nee.
3 Brown: Hai, ichi-dai de iron na shigoto o suru koto ga dekimasu kara, onsha no koojoo ni muite iru to omoimasu.
4 Suzuki: Amerika de wa donna koojoo de tsukatte iru n desu ka.
5 Brown: Omo ni, hikooki no koojoo de tsukatte imasu.
6 Suzuki: Motto kuwashii shiryoo ga hoshii n desu ga…
7 Brown: Kore ga ano robotto no katarogu desu.
8 Suzuki: Tokkyo wa juu-nen mae ni totta n desu ne.
9 Brown: Hai, soo desu. Sore kara, seehin ga dekiru made, hachi-nen kakari-mashita.
10 Suzuki: Gijutsuteki na setsumee mo anata ga dekimasu ka.
11 Brown: Iie, sore wa Yuu-esu-emu kara senmonka o yobimasu ga…
12 Suzuki: Wakarimashita. De wa, watakushi mo moo ichi-do shanai de soo-dan-shite kara, mata renraku-shimasu.
13 Brown: De wa, omachi-shite orimasu kara…

ADDITIONAL USEFUL EXPRESSIONS

1	obtaining a patent	tokkyo o toru no

A: In Japan, is it difficult to obtain a patent?	**Nihon de tokkyo o toru no wa muzu-kashii desu ka.**

well…	**saa**
to come to know	**shiru**
does not know	**shirimasen**
friend	**yuujin**
lawyer	**bengoshi**

B: Well, (I) don't know. My friend who is a lawyer is doing that kind of work, so shall (I) introduce (him to you)?	**Saa shirimasen. Yuujin no bengoshi ga sonna shigoto o shite iru kara shookai-shimashoo ka.**
A: Yes, please.	**Ee, onegai-shimasu.**

2 At a law office

way, procedure	hoohoo

A: (I)'d like to obtain a patent for a new machine. Please tell (me what the) procedure (is).	**Atarashii kikai no tokkyo o toritai n desu ga… Hoohoo o oshiete kuda-sai.**

—239—

Lesson 18

let me see	**soo desu nee**
written application	**gansho**
Patent Office	**Tokkyochoo**
application	**shinsee (-suru)**
drawing	**zumen**
to attach	**soeru**

B: Well, let me see. Prepare an application and apply to the Patent Office, but (you should) attach a detailed description and drawings.	**Soo desu nee. Gansho o tsukutte Tokkyochoo ni shinsee-suru n desu ga, kuwashii setsumeesho to zumen o soemasu.**

approximately	**yaku, oyoso**

A: After applying for it, about how many years will it take till (I) receive the patent?	**Shinsee-shite kara tokkyo o toru made yaku nan-nen kakarimasu ka.**

at least	**sukunaku tomo**
a year and a half	**ichi-nen han**

B: Well, it will take at least a year and a half.	**Soo desu nee. Sukunaku tomo ichi-nen han kakarimasu yo.**

REFERENCE

shoohyoo	trademark	**hatsumee (-suru)**	invention
ishoo	design	**kenri**	right
jitsuyoo shin'an	utility model	**dokusen (-suru)**	monopoly
tooroku (-suru)	registration	**sankoo shiryoo**	reference material
tokkyoryoo	patent fee	**kaikeeshi**	accountant

NOTES

1 Informal Verbs, Non-Past

The informal (non-past affirmative) form of verbs is called the "citation form" because it is usually the only form cited in dictionaries. The informal form of verbs is identical in meaning to the **-masu** form, but it is used mainly in casual situations.

There are four groups of verbs in Japanese:

A) **-ru** verbs (verbs ending in **-ru,** which is replaced with **-masu** in formal usage)

Examples (informal/formal): **deki*ru*/deki*masu*** 'can do'
                         kake*ru*/kake*masu* 'make a call'

—240—

Lesson 18

> **hajime*ru*/hajime*masu*** 'start'
> **oshie*ru*/oshie*masu*** 'teach'

Note that the **-ru** ending is always preceded by the vowels **e** or **i**.

B) **-u** verbs (verbs ending in **-u,** which is replaced with **-imasu** in formal usage)

Examples (informal/formal): **muk*u*/muk*imasu*** 'be suitable'
kak*u*/kak*imasu* 'write'
mots*u*/moch*imasu* 'have, hold'*
tor*u*/tor*imasu* 'take'
yom*u*/yom*imasu* 'read'

*When **-imasu** is preceded by **ch, ch** is changed into **ts** in the informal form.

C) **-aru** verbs (verbs ending in **-aru,** which is replaced with **-aimasu** in formal usage)
There are only five verbs in this category, all of which are polite forms.

Example (informal/formal): **irasshar*u*/irasshai*masu*** 'come/go/be'

D) irregular verbs (two only)

Examples (informal/formal): *suru/shimasu* 'do'
kuru/kimasu 'come'

2 Informal Verbs, Past

The informal past tense of a verb is formed by replacing the final **-e** of the gerund form (introduced in Lesson 8) with **-a,** as indicated in the table below:

meaning	**-masu** form	citation form (informal, non-past)	gerund form	informal past
start	hajimemasu	hajimeru	hajimete	hajime*ta* 'started'
teach	oshiemasu	oshieru	oshiete	oshie*ta* 'taught'
can do	dekimasu	dekiru	dekite	dekita 'was able to do'
be suitable	mukimasu	muku	muite	muita 'was suitable'
buy	kaimasu	kau	katte	katta 'bought'
come/go/be	irasshaimasu	irassharu	irasshatte	irasshatta 'came/went/was'
do	shimasu	suru	shite	shita 'did'
come	kimasu	kuru	kite	kita 'came'

All verbs introduced in this text are listed in the APPENDIX with their inflected forms.

3 **-koto ga dekiru**

The informal form of verbs (non-past tense) + **koto ga dekiru,** is used to indicate that ''«the subject» is able to do such-and-such.'' [lit. «the subject» is capable of the act of such-and-such.] The particle **ga** may be replaced with **wa,** depending on the context of the sentence. (Refer to Lesson 6 for explanation of **ga** and **wa** usage.)

Examples: a) **Kono robotto wa iron na shigoto o suru *koto ga dekimasu.***
''This robot can do various jobs.''
b) **Buraun-san wa Tookyoo e/ni iku *koto wa dekimasen.***
''Mr. Brown cannot go to Tokyo.''

—241—

Lesson 18

4 Verb + **n desu,** meaning literally, 'it is the fact of such-and-such'
Verbs used for this are the informal forms of non-past or past tense.

Compare: **Atarashii kuruma o kaimasu.**
"(I) will buy a new car."

and

Atarashii kuruma o *kau n desu*.
"(I) will buy a new car. [lit. it is the fact of buying a new car.]"

Atarashii kuruma o kaimashita.
"(I) bought a new car."

and

Atarashii kuruma o *katta n desu*.
"(I) bought a new car. [lit. It is the fact of having bought a new car.]"

There is no difference in meaning between **kaimasu/kaimashita** and **kau n desu/katta
n desu,** but this **n desu** pattern is used simply to soften the directness of the statement.
-tai n desu introduced in Lesson 9 is another example of this pattern. Not only **-tai** but
also other adjectives can be used with **n desu.**

Examples: a) **Kono kuruma wa takai *n desu*.**
"This car is expensive."
b) **Sumisu-san wa sashimi wa tabenai *n desu*.**
"Mr. Smith does not eat sashimi."

5 Informal form of verbs (non-past tense) + **made**
Informal form of verbs may be used with **made** to indicate 'until «subject*» does/did
such-and-such.'

Examples: a) **Buraun-san ga kuru *made* machimashita.**
"(I) waited until Mr. Brown came."
b) **Kaigi ga owaru *made* denwa-suru koto ga dekimasen.**
"(I) cannot make a phone call till the conference is over."

Please note that only the non-past informal form is used in this pattern, even though the
action described in the sentence may be in the past.

-made ni is also used with the non-past informal form of verbs to mean 'by the time
«subject*» does/did.'
*Note that the subject may not always be the subject of the whole sentence, but may be
the subject of the subordinate clause, as in the above examples.

Example: **Ooyama san ga kuru *made ni* kaigi wa owarimashita.**
"By the time Mr. Ohyama came, the conference was over."

6 Informal form of verbs + **no**
The noun **no** 'the one(s), the fact(s)' can be preceded by the informal form of verbs (non-
past or past) in an adjective clause modifying **no.**
No may refer to a person, thing, place, time or action depending on the context of the
sentence.

Examples: a) **Tokkyo o toru *no* wa muzukashii desu ne.** (action)

—242—

Lesson 18

"To obtain a patent is difficult, isn't it? [lit. The fact of obtaining...]"
b) **Tokkyo o totta *no* wa itsu deshita ka.** (time)
"When did you obtain the patent?"
c) **Tokkyo o toritai *no* wa Ooyama san desu.** (person)
"The person who wants to obtain a patent is Mr. Ohyama."

7 Hoshii

Hoshii is an adjective, meaning 'to be desirable.' It is used to mean 'to desire' or 'to want' in the following pattern:

Person who desires	that which is desired	
Watakushi wa	**shigoto ga**	**hoshii.**
I want a job. [lit. As for me, a job is desirable.]		

8 Notes on Usage

A) Counters: **-dai** is the counter for machines such as vehicles, typewriters, television sets, robots, etc.
                     -do is the counter for the number of times/occasions.

B) Note that the affirmative of **shirimasen** 'doesn't know' is **shitte imasu** 'know,' and **shirimasu** 'come to know.'

Compare: **Watakushi wa ano hito o *shirimasen.***
                    "I don't know that person"
                    Watakushi wa ano hito o *shitte imasu.*
                    "I know that person."
                    Watakushi wa ano hito o *shirimasu.* [rarely used]
                    "I will come to know that person."

PRACTICE

1 Transformation Practice

Example: Teacher: **Ooyama-san wa kono waapuro o tsukaimasu.**
                         "Mr. Ohyama will use this word processor."
           Student: **Ooyama-san wa kono waapuro o tsukau koto ga dekimasu.**
                         "Mr. Ohyama can use this word processor."

a) **Senjitsu atarashii kikai no tokkyo o torimashita.**   **Senjitsu atarashii kikai no tokkyo o toru koto ga dekimashita.**

b) **Wain to oodoburu o omochi-shimasu.**   **Wain to oodoburu o omochi-suru koto ga dekimasu.**

c) **Amari osake o nomimasen.**   **Amari osake o nomu koto ga dekimasen.**

d) **Buraun san wa nihongo o hanashimashita.**   **Buraun san wa nihongo o hanasu koto ga dekimashita.**

Lesson 18

2 Transformation Practice

Example: Teacher: **Ashita Tokkyochoo e/ni ikimasu.**
"Tomorrow (I) will go to the Patent Office."
Student: **Ashita Tokkyochoo e/ni iku n desu.**
[lit. "It is a matter of going to the Patent Office tomorrow."]

a) **Kee'eegaku ni tsuite hanasu koto ga dekimasu.** **Kee'eegaku ni tsuite hanasu koto ga dekiru n desu.**
b) **Senjitsu denwa de renraku-shima-shita.** **Senjitsu denwa de renraku-shita n desu.**
c) **Amerika no daigaku ni ryuugaku shimasu.** **Amerika no daigaku ni ryuugaku suru n desu.**
d) **Ima shootaijoo no atena o kaite imasu.** **Ima shootaijoo no atena o kaite iru n desu.**

3 Communication Practice

Directions: For each of the following, combine the separate sentences by using the particle **no.**

Example: Teacher: **Ginza de shokuji o shimasu. + Totemo takai desu.**
"(I)'ll have a meal at Ginza. + It's very expensive."
Student: **Ginza de shokuji o suru no wa, totemo takai desu.**
"To have a meal at Ginza is very expensive."

a) **Ima tokkyo o shinsee-shite imasu. + Yamada-san desu.** **Ima tokkyo o shinsee-shite iru no wa Yamada-san desu.**
b) **Migi ni magarimasu. + Nibanme no yotsukado desu.** **Migi ni magaru no wa nibanme no yotsukado desu.**
c) **Kee'eegaku no shuushi o morai masu. + Muzukashii desu.** **Kee'eegaku no shuushi o morau no wa muzukashii desu.**
d) **Kinoo Buraun-san ga tabemashita. + Tenpura desu.** **Kinoo Buraun-san ga tabeta no wa tenpura desu.**
e) **Senmonka ga sochira no kaisha ni ukagaimasu. + Raishuu desu.** **Senmonka ga sochira no kaisha ni ukagau no wa raishuu desu.**

4 Response Practice

Example: Teacher: **Itsu made imashoo ka. /shachoo ga kaerimasu/**
"Until when shall (I) stay? /The company president comes back./"
Student: **Shachoo ga kaeru made ite kudasai.**
"Please stay until the company president comes back."

a) **Itsu made matte imashoo ka. /kaigi ga owarimasu/** **Kaigi ga owaru made matte ite kudasai.**
b) **Doko made setsumee-shimashoo ka. /waapuro o tsukau koto ga dekimasu/** **Waapuro o tsukau koto ga dekiru made setsumee-shite kudasai.**
c) **Itsu made otetsudai shimashoo ka. /Nihon no seekatsu ni naremasu/** **Nihon no seekatsu ni nareru made tetsudatte kudasai.**

—244—

Lesson 18

d) Itsu made oshiemashoo ka. /Nihongo no shinbun ga wakari-masu/

Nihongo no shinbun ga wakaru made oshiete kudasai.

5 Response Practice

Directions: Based on your experiences, respond in Japanese to each of the following questions.

a) **Itsu Nihon e irasshaimashita ka.**
b) **Nan-do Kyooto e ikimashita ka.**
c) **Moo ichido itte mitai desu ka** (If the student has been to Kyoto before).
d) **Otaku kara ichiban chikai eki made dono kurai kakarimasu ka.**
e) **Taipuraitaa o tsukatte imasu ka.**
f) **Donna taipuraitaa o tsukatte imasu ka** (If the student uses a typewriter).
g) **Nani ga ichiban hoshii desu ka.**
h) **Nihon wa «your name» -san ni muite imasu ka.**
i) **Kaisha ni tsuite setsumee-suru koto ga dekimasu ka.**

EXERCISES

Inform the teacher in Japanese that:
1   Mr. Yamamoto can explain the new machine to Mr. Ohta.
2   As Mr. Brown would like to obtain a patent, he wants various data concerning patents.
3   Ms. Ohyama will be in the office till the conference is over.
4   This typewriter is suitable for your secretary.
5   Your company president came to Japan three years ago, but he will come once more next month.
6   There is no specialist in Japanese law within your company.
7   You cannot give a detailed technical explanation.
8   Making a telephone call in Japan is very difficult.
9   It will take three years till you obtain an M.A.
10   You'll send an application form to the university.
11   There are now 19,000 robots in Japan.

Model Answers:

1   **Yamamoto-san wa atarashii kikai ni tsuite Oota-san ni setsumee-suru koto ga dekimasu.**
2   **Buraun-san wa tokkyo o toritai no de, tokkyo ni tsuite iroiro na shiryoo ga hoshii n desu.**
3   **Ooyama-san wa kaigi ga owaru made jimusho ni imasu.**
4   **Kono taipuraitaa wa watakushi no hisho ni muite imasu.**
5   **Shachoo wa san-nen mae ni Nihon ni kimashita ga, raigetsu moo ichi-do kimasu.**
6   **Shanai ni Nihon no hooritsu no senmonka wa imasen.**
7   **Kuwashii gijutsuteki na setsumee o suru koto wa dekimasen.**
8   **Nihon de denwa o kakeru no wa taihen muzukashii desu.**
9   **Shuushi o toru made san-nen kakarimasu.**
10   **Daigaku ni gansho o okurimasu.**
11   **Nihon ni ima ichiman-kyuusen-dai no robotto ga arimasu.**

—245—

Lesson 18

BUSINESS INFORMATION

Negotiations

As you have probably already discovered, negotiations in Japan are conducted along different lines from those abroad. A little understanding of these lines may help you discuss business with greater ease, and a minimum of frustration.

1 The Mood, or "Beating around the Bush": Many executives in the West make no bones about the fact that they are very busy people. It has been observed that they often arrive at the negotiation table with an itemized list of all the goals they intend to achieve, and then expect to proceed at a brisk pace right down this list so as not to waste everyone's precious time. In fact, they like to get a straight yes or no to their proposal that same day—if not immediately. Meetings in Japan are of a more exploratory nature, however. Questions are asked, interest may or may not be expressed, but certainly no commitments are made. In the DIALOGUE, for example, Mr. Brown hints that his robots would be ideal for Japanese factories, but the only response this elicits from his counterpart is another question. There is in fact nothing at all in the conversation to indicate that Mr. Suzuki is genuinely interested in the product. He did of course take the trouble to read the company brochure that Mr. Brown gave him the last time they met, but this may have been as much out of obligation to the intermediary, Mr. Kawamoto, as out of real interest in industrial robots. Besides, even if he does show some interest in today's meeting, he may change his mind tomorrow after further consultation with his superiors. To avoid disappointment, therefore, you should remember that in many negotiations in Japan, it is information that is being sought (directly or indirectly) rather than a hard and fast conclusion. No matter how enthusiastic you think your listeners are, it is always best not to count your chickens until they are hatched.

2 The Size of the Negotiating Team, or "Safety in Numbers": Many companies in the West prefer to send just one person to represent them at negotiations with other firms. One traveling businessman is certainly cheaper than two and, besides, who needs a crowd of colleagues cramping one's style at the negotiating table? In Japan, however, it is far more common to negotiate in groups of two or more. Sometimes, the extra participant is there because of his superior English ability. But more often, he attends in order to provide that extra pair of eyes and ears—the better to observe and to listen to you. In contrast to the West, extra opinions are considered an advantage rather than an interference. There is also the notion that the size of the negotiating team indicates the seriousness of a company's commitment to the transaction being discussed. Consequently, you might consider adding to your retinue if the business you are going to negotiate in Japan is an ambitious one.

3 Learning from Each Other, or "Doing Your Fair Share": You may think at this point that you are doing more than your fair share in trying to learn Japanese ways. After all, negotiation is a two-way street and your counterparts could just as well exert themselves to learn *your* way of negotiating, for a change. If you are beginning to feel this way, then it would be a good time to recall that your Japanese counterparts were actually some of the world's most avid students of things Occidental —and still are. Most Japanese have not quite adjusted to the idea that their country is a world leader and will insist that there

—246—

Lesson 18

is still plenty that they must learn from the West. But just how much Japan still expects to learn from the U.S. and Europe will not be apparent until you glance at the long list of foreign publications that are translated into Japanese almost as soon as they roll off the press in their home country. Indeed, the hunger of the Japanese people for Western ideas and their curiosity—some say obsession—about others' opinion of *themselves* find no parallel anywhere in the industrialized world.

If you ever think that you have had your fill of the continuing "boom" in Japan-related books, therefore, it would be helpful to remember that this is still a mere drop in the bucket compared to the flood of foreign publications in Japan—and that your hosts are indeed as devoted students of Western management practices as you are of their language and customs.

Popular Foreign Books in Japan: The following is a sampling of foreign books that have been made available in Japanese in the years indicated. Japanese titles are given below the originals.

Title	Authors
1987	
Kaisha: The Japanese Corporation **(Kaisha)**	James C. Abegglen George Atalk, Jr.
Innovation: The Attacker's Advantage **(Inobeeshon)**	Richard Foster
XEROX: American Samurai **(Zerokkusu)**	Gary Jacobson John Hillkirk
McDonald's: Behind The Arches **(Makudonarudo)**	John F. Love
Breakthrough! **(Bureekusuruu!)**	P. Ranganath Nayak John M. Ketteringham
Letters of a Businessman to his Son **(Bijinesuman no chichi yori musuko e no sanju-tsuu no tegami)**	G. Kingsley Ward
1986	
The Frontiers of Management **(Manejimento hurontia)**	Peter F. Drucker
The Japanese School **(Japaniizu sukuuru)**	Benjamin C. Duke
Interest Rates, the Markets, and the New Financial World **(Kauhuman no keekoku)**	Henry Kaufman
The Real Coke, The Real Story **(Koka-koora no eedan to gosan)**	Thomas Oliver
Made in America **(Yuberosu)**	Peter Ueberroth

—247—

Lesson 18

Title	Authors
1985	
The Media Monopoly	Ben H. Bagdikian
(Media no shihaisha)	
The One Minute Manager Gets Fit	Kenneth Blanchard
(Ip-punkan fittonesu)	D.W. Edington
	Marjorie Blanchard
Iacocca: An Autobiography*	Lee Iacocca
(Aiakokka)	
The Good War: An Oral History of World War Two	Studs Terkel
(Yoi sensoo)	
1984	
The Art of Corporate Success	Ken Auletta
(Paafekuto kanpanii)	
The Japanese Mind:	Robert C. Christopher
The Goliath Explained	
(Japaniizu maindo)	
KGB	Brian Freemantle
(Kee-jii-bii)	
The Anatomy of Power	John Kenneth Galbraith
(Kenryoku no kaiboo)	
Megatrends	John Naisbitt
(Megatorendo)	
A Whack on the Side of the Head	Roger Von Oech
(Atama ni gatsun to ichi-geki)	
In Search of Excellence	Thomas J. Peters
(Ekuserento kanpanii)	Robert H. Waterman, Jr.
The Next American Frontier	Robert B. Reich
(Nekusuto hurontia)	

The best-selling title throughout Japan for that year.

Lesson 19

Business Negotiations III

OBJECTIVES

1 to engage in business negotiations.

2 to discuss trade terms.

3 to report in business talks on what you have heard.

Lesson 19

TARGET EXPRESSIONS AND PATTERNS

1	to decide to do...	...suru koto ni suru.
2	«modifying verb» + «noun»	...suru «noun».
3	to be expected/supposed to do	...suru hazu desu.
4	to intend to do	...suru tsumori desu.
5	It is said that...	...suru soo desu.

SITUATION

Mr. Brown visits Mr. Ohyama again and has further discussions about business conditions and other matters. As a result, Mr. Brown promises to request USM, Ltd. to dispatch a specialist to Nissan Motor Co., Ltd. to explain the robots.

DIALOGUE

Ohyama   to discuss   **hanashiau**

> **1** Today, (I)'d like to discuss business conditions, [imp. is that all right?]
>
> **Kyoo wa torihiki no jooken ni tsuite hanashiaitai n desu ga...**

Brown

> **2** Yes. Thank you very much.
>
> **Hai. Arigatoo gozaimasu.**

Ohyama   first of all   **hajime ni**
     price   **kakaku**

> **3** First of all, (let me ask about) the price. How much will (it) be for one unit?
>
> **Hajime ni kakaku desu ga, ichi-dai ikura ni narimasu ka.**

Brown   dollar   **doru**

> **4** (It will cost) $10,000 a unit.
>
> **Ichi-dai, ichiman-doru desu.**

Ohyama   payment   **shiharai**
     dollar base   **doru-date**
     It is said to be on a dollar base   **doru-date da soo desu**

—250—

Lesson 19

| 5 | (I) understand that the payment should be in dollars? [lit. It is said that payment is on a dollar base?] | **Shiharai wa doru-date da soo desu ne.** |

| **Brown** | to hope for, prefer | **nozomu** |

| 6 | Well , USM hopes for payment in dollars, but [imp. do you foresee any problem?] | **Ee, Yuu-esu-emu wa doru-date o nozonde iru n desu ga...** |

	denomination, currency	**tatene**
	to decide to do	**...suru koto ni suru**
	trade term, invoice term	**shikiri-jooken**
Ohyama	to think	**kangaeru**

| 7 | Then, let's talk [lit. let's decide to talk] later about the currency. Next, what are the trade terms? [lit. what are you thinking about the trade terms?] | **Sore de wa tatene ni tsuite wa mata ato de soodan-suru koto ni shima-shoo. Tsugi ni shikiri-jooken wa doo kangaete imasu ka.** |

| **Brown** | ordinarily | **hutsuu** |
| | FOB | **ehu-oo-bii** |

| 8 | Ordinarily, USM('s term) is FOB. | **Yuu-esu-emu wa hutsuu ehu-oo-bii desu.** |

| **Ohyama** | insurance | **hoken** |
| | to bear the cost | **hutan-suru** |

| 9 | Then, (that means) we are bearing the cost of insurance. [lit. the one who bears the cost of insurance is us.] | **De wa, hoken o hutan-suru no wa uchi desu ne.** |

| **Brown** | as a rule, in principle | **gensokuteki ni** |
| | buyer | **kaite** |

| 10 | In principle, the buyer bears the cost for that. [lit. (it) is the buyer's burden.] | **Gensokuteki ni, kaite no hutan desu.** |

—251—

Lesson 19

		(is) severe, strict	**kibishii**
Ohyama		specialist who can explain	**setsumee no dekiru senmonka**

11 (Those) are stiff (terms), aren't they? [lit. (It)'s severe, isn't (it).] And then, when is the specialist who can give the technical explanation coming? — **Kibishii desu nee. Sore kara, gijutsu-teki na setsumee no dekiru senmonka wa itsu kimasu ka.**

		telex	**terekkusu**
		intention	**tsumori**
		to intend to send	**okuru tsumori desu**
		reply	**henji**
		expectation of doing	**suru hazu**
Brown		to be expected to come	**kuru hazu desu**

12 (I) intend to send a telex tonight, so a reply should come immediately. [lit. a reply is expected to come immediately.] — **Konban terekkusu o okuru tsumori desu kara, sugu henji ga kuru hazu desu.**

		to hear	**kiku**
Ohyama		concrete	**gutaiteki /na/**

13 Then, after hearing that person's explanation, (I)'d like to discuss this in more concrete terms, but [imp. is that OK?] — **Jaa, sono hito no setsumee o kiite kara, gutaiteki na jooken ni tsuite hanashiaitai n desu ga...**

Brown

14 That's fine. Well, (I)'ll contact (you) again. — **Kekko desu. De wa mata renraku-shimasu.**

JAPANESE WRITING

1 　大　山：　今日は取り引きの条件について話し合いたいんですが…

2 　ブラウン：　はい。ありがとうございます。

3 　大　山：　初めに価格ですが、一台いくらになりますか。

4 　ブラウン：　一台、一万ドルです。

5 　大　山：　支払いはドル建てだそうですね。

6 　ブラウン：　ええ、ユー・エス・エムはドル建てを望んでいるんですが…

7 　大　山：　それでは、建値については、また後で相談する事にしましょう。
　　　　　　　　次に、仕切り条件はどう考えていますか。

Lesson 19

8　ブラウン：　ユー・エス・エムは普通エフ・オー・ビーです。

9　大　山：　では、保険を負担するのはうちですね。

10　ブラウン：　原則的に、買い手の負担です。

11　大　山：　きびしいですねえ。それから、技術的な説明のできる専門家はいつ来ますか。

12　ブラウン：　今晩テレックスを送るつもりですから、すぐ返事が来るはずです。

13　大　山：　じゃあ、その人の説明を聞いてから、具体的な条件について話し合いたいんですが…

14　ブラウン：　結構です。ではまた連絡します。

READING

1　Ohyama:　Kyoo wa torihiki no jooken ni tsuite hanashiaitai n desu ga…
2　Brown:　Hai. Arigatoo gozaimasu.
3　Ohyama:　Hajime ni kakaku desu ga, ichi-dai ikura ni narimasu ka.
4　Brown:　Ichi-dai, ichiman-doru desu.
5　Ohyama:　Shiharai wa doru-date da soo desu ne.
6　Brown:　Ee, Yuu-esu-emu wa doru-date o nozonde iru n desu ga…
7　Ohyama:　Sore de wa, tatene ni tsuite wa, mata ato de soodan-suru koto ni shimashoo. Tsugi ni, shikiri-jooken wa doo kangaete imasu ka.
8　Brown:　Yuu-esu-emu wa hutsuu ehu-oo-bii desu.
9　Ohyama:　De wa, hoken o hutan-suru no wa uchi desu ne.
10　Brown:　Gensokuteki ni, kaite no hutan desu.
11　Ohyama:　Kibishii desu nee. Sore kara, gijutsuteki na setsumee no dekiru senmonka wa itsu kimasu ka.
12　Brown:　Konban terekkusu o okuru tsumori desu kara, sugu henji ga kuru hazu desu.
13　Ohyama:　Jaa, sono hito no setsumee o kiite kara, gutaiteki na jooken ni tsuite hanashiaitai n desu ga…
14　Brown:　Kekko desu. De wa mata renraku-shimasu.

ADDITIONAL USEFUL EXPRESSIONS

1　Concerning payment

payment in installments　**bunkatsu-barai**

A: Can (we) pay in installments?	**Bunkatsu-barai wa dekimasu ka.**

12-month payment plan　**juuni-kagetsu-barai**

B: Yes, 12-month and 24-month plans are (available).	**Ee, juuni-kagetsu-barai to nijuuyon-kagetsu barai ga arimasu.**

interest　**rishi**

A: How much is the interest?	**Rishi wa ikura desu ka.**

Lesson 19

	percent	**paasento**
	8%	**hachi-paasento**

B:	It is 8% for a 12-month plan and 15% for a 24-month plan. [imp. which do you prefer?]	**Juuni-kagetsu-barai wa hachi-paa-sento de nijuuyon-kagetsu-barai wa juugo-paasento desu ga...**

2 Over the telephone

	to start selling	**uridasu**

A:	(I) would like to have [lit. have you send] a description of the machine which started selling recently.	**Saikin uridashita kikai no setsu-meesho o okutte moraitai n desu ga.**

	handling charge	**tesuuryoo**
	to not need, to be unnecessary	**iranai** (informal form of **irimasen**)
	shipping charge	**sooryoo**

B:	Handling charges are not required, but shipping charges are. [imp. would that be a problem?]	**Tesuuryoo wa irimasen ga, sooryoo ga irimasu ga...**
A:	(I) understand. How much is it?	**Wakarimashita. Oikura desu ka.**

	ten copies	**juu-bu**

B:	The shipping charge is 140 yen for up to ten copies.	**Sooryoo wa juu-bu made hyaku-yonjuu-en desu.**

REFERENCE

noohinsho	statement of delivery	**kawase reeto**	exchange rate
seekyuusho	invoice	**ryoogae (-suru)**	money exchange
meesaisho	detailed statement	**kooza**	(bank) account
tsuke	charge account	**hurikomi**	transferring to another
teeka	fixed price		bank account
genka	cost price	**en-date**	yen base
urite	seller	**waribiki (-suru)**	discount
eru-shii, shin'yoojoo	L/C (letter of credit)	**haitatsu (-suru)**	delivery
denpyoo	sales slip, voucher	**kawase**	money order
nooki	date/time of delivery	**yokin (-suru)**	deposit
		kessai (-suru)	settlement of account

Lesson 19

NOTES

1 Copula **da**, and **datta**

Da is an informal equivalent of **desu**; **datta** is of the informal equivalent of **deshita**.

Examples:	Informal: **Kakaku wa gojuu-doru *da*.**
	Formal: **Kakaku wa gojuu-doru *desu*.**
	"It's worth $50. [lit. The price is $50.]"
	Informal: **Sanjuu-en wa sooryoo *datta*.**
	Formal: **Sanjuu-en wa sooryoo *deshita*.**
	"30 yen was the shipping charge."

2 Informal Verbs: Negative form

To form the negative of informal verbs, observe the following rules:

A) **-ru** verb: change **-ru** to **-nai**
   Example: **oshie*ru*** "(I) teach" → **oshie*nai*** "(I) don't teach"
B) **-u** verb: change **-u** to **-anai**
   Example: **kak*u*** "(I) write" → **kak*anai*** "(I) don't write"
C) **-aru** verb: change **-aru** to **-aranai**
   Example: **irassh*aru*** "(you) come/go/are" → **irassh*aranai*** "(you) don't come/go/aren't"
D) Irregular verb:
   Example: ***suru*** "(I) do" → ***shinai*** "(I) don't do"
   kuru "(I) come" → ***konai*** "(I) don't come"

3 Informal Negative Form: Past Tense

To form the past informal negative, replace the **-i** of the non-past negative with **-katta**.

Examples:	a) **oshiena*i*** "(I) don't teach" →	**oshiena*katta*** "(I) didn't teach"
	b) **shina*i*** "(I) don't do" →	**shina*katta*** "(I) didn't do"

In Japanese, these informal non-past negative forms are actually adjectives ending in **i**. Note that the past informal forms of all adjectives follow the same rule:

Examples:	a) **taka*i*** 'is expensive' →	**taka*katta*** 'was expensive'
	b) **hoshi*i*** 'is desirable' →	**hoshi*katta*** 'was desirable'
	c) **chiisa*i*** 'is small' →	**chiisa*katta*** 'was small'

4 Informal Form in Adjective Clauses ("Sentence Modifier")

Informal forms are usually used in adjective clauses ("sentence modifiers") to modify the noun or nouns which follow in the sentence.

Adjective Clause		
informal verb adjective noun + **no/na**	+	noun(s) to be modified

Examples:	a) **Kinoo *katta* taipuraitaa** "the typewriter which I bought yesterday." (informal verb in adjective clause modifying **taipuraitaa**)
	b) **Setsumee ga *dekiru* senmonka** "the specialist who can explain (it)." (informal verb in adjective clause modifying **senmonka**)

—255—

Lesson 19

    c) **Yuu-esu-emu ga nozonde *iru* kakaku** "the price which USM is hoping for." (informal verb in adjective clause modifiying **kakaku**)

    d) **Tsukatte *inai* denwa** "a telephone which (someone) is not using." (adjective in clause modifying **denwa**)

    e) **Okutte *hoshii* seehin** "the goods which (someone) wants to send." (adjective in clause modifying **seehin**)

    f) **Imai-san ga *kooshi no* gakkoo** "the school in which Mr. Imai is a lecturer." (noun + **no** in clause modifying **gakkoo**)

Note that the particle **ga,** indicating that the preceding noun is the subject of an adjective clause, is sometimes replaced with **no.** The above clause **b)** for example, may be changed as follows:

    Setsumee *no* dekiru senmonka. "the specialist who can explain (it)."

When a sentence ending with the non-past copula, **da** or **desu,** is to be embedded as an adjective clause, the copula is replaced with **na** or **no** depending on the preceding noun. (Refer to Lesson 12 for usage of **na** nouns.)

Examples: a) **Imai-san ga kooshi *desu*. + Kore wa gakkoo desu.**

            Kore wa Imai-san ga kooshi *no* gakkoo desu.
            "This is the school in which Mr. Imai is a lecturer."

    b) **Nooki ga taisetsu *desu*. + Kore wa torihiki desu.**

            Kore wa nooki no taisetsu *na* torihiki desu.
            "The business in which timely delivery [lit. date of delivery] is important"

When a sentence with the past copula, **datta** or **deshita,** is to be used as an adjective clause, the informal copula, **datta,** (but never **deshita**), precedes the noun being described.

Example: **Ni-nen mae wa sen-en *deshita*. + Kore wa hon desu.**

            Kore wa ni-nen mae wa sen-en *datta* hon desu.
            "This is the book which cost 1,000 yen two years ago."

Please remember that **no** can function as a noun (See Lesson 18). In such a case, the copula is always changed to **na,** regardless of the preceding noun.

Compare: **Imai-san ga kooshi no gakkoo wa kore desu.**
            Imai-san ga kooshi no *no* [noun 'the one'] wa kore desu.
            [incorrect]
            Thus: **Imai-san ga kooshi *na* no wa kore desu.** [correct: first **no** becomes **na**]
            "The one at which Mr. Imai is a lecturer is this (one)."

5 **hazu desu** 'to be expected to do such-and-such [lit. it is the expectation]'
An adjective clause (sentence modifier) + **hazu desu** means 'to be expected/supposed to do.'

Examples: a) **Oota-san wa ano gakkoo no kooshi no *hazu desu*.**
            "Mr. Ohta is supposed to be a lecturer at that school."

—256—

Lesson 19

    b) **Kono hon no hoo ga takai *hazu desu*.**
        "This book should be more expensive."
    c) **Buraun-san wa sugu kuru *hazu desu*.**
        "It is expected that Mr. Brown will come soon."
    d) **Kaigi ga owaru made konai *hazu desu*.**
        "It is expected that (he/she) will not come till the meeting is over."

6   **soo desu** 'It is said that/(I) heard that...'
soo desu is used with the informal form of verbs and with adjectives to report on what has been said or heard, or to pass on information.

Examples: a) **Kakaku wa gojuu-doru da* *soo desu*.**
          "It is said that the price is $50."
         b) **Ooyama-san wa kono kaisha o yameta *soo desu*.**
          "It is said that Mr. Ohyama has quit this company."
         c) **Buraun-san wa tokkyo ni tsuite hanashiaitai *soo desu*.**
          "I heard that Mr. Brown wanted to discuss the patent."

          *Note that the copula **da** can occur before **soo desu,** without changing to **no** or **na.**

Compare: **Kakaku wa gojuu-doru *da* soo desu.**
          "It is said that the price is $50."
         Kakaku wa gojuu-doru *da* to omoimasu.
          "I think the price is $50."
         Kakaku wa gojuu-doru *na* n desu.
          "The price is $50. [lit. It is the fact that the price is $50.]"
         Kakaku wa gojuu-doru *no* hazu desu.
          "The price is expected to be $50."

7   **tsumori desu** 'to intend to do such-and-such' [lit. It is the intention that].
tsumori desu is always preceded by a modifying word(s) or clause(s).

Examples: a) **Tokkyo o shinsee-suru *tsumori desu*.**
          "(I) intend to apply for a patent."
         b) **Kyoo wa gakkoo e ikanai *tsumori desu*.**
          "Today, (I) intend not to go to school."

8   **koto ni suru** 'to decide to do such-and-such'
A clause with informal form + **koto ni suru** is used to express a decision.

Examples: a) **Wain o nomu *koto ni shimashoo*.**
          "Let's decide to drink wine."
         b) **Senmonka no iken o kiku *koto ni shimashita*.**
          "(We) decided to hear the specialist's opinion."
         c) **Moo kono seehin wa tsukuranai *koto ni shimashita*.**
          "We decided not to manufacture this product any more."

When a clause with a noun + non-past copula **da** or **desu** is to be used in this pattern, both the copula and the **koto** of this pattern drop to become: noun + **ni suru.** E.g. **Kyoo wa biiru desu *koto ni shimashita*** [erroneous] becomes:

         Kyoo wa biiru *ni shimashita*. (noun + **ni suru**)
         "Today I decided on beer."

Lesson 19

9 Hajime ni 'first,' tsugi ni 'next' and **sore kara** 'and then'

The above phrases are used when describing the order of events, or when requesting things in a certain sequence.

Example: *Hajime ni onamae o kaite kudasai.*
"First, please write your name."
Tsugi ni juusho.
"Next, your address."
Sore kara ima shitai koto.
"And then, (write) what (you) want to do now."

Note: **Tsugi ni** and **sore kara** are interchangeable.

PRACTICE

1 Response Practice

Example: Teacher: **Kinoo donna hon o kaimashita ka. /rekishi no hon/**
"What kind of book did (you) buy yesterday?" /history book/
Student: **Kinoo katta hon wa rekishi no hon deshita.**
"The book (I) bought yesterday was a history book."

a) **Yuu-esu-emu wa donna jooken o nozonde imasu ka. /juuni-kagetsu-barai/**

Yuu-esu-emu no nozonde iru jooken wa juuni-kagetsu-barai desu.

b) **Kinoo donna henji ga kimashita ka. /ii henji/**

Kinoo kita henji wa ii henji deshita.

c) **Yamamoto-san wa donna kikai o atarashiku uridashimashita ka. /kogata no maikon/**

Yamamoto-san no atarashiku uridashita kikai wa kogata no maikon deshita.

d) **Dono hito ga kono kikai no setsumee ga dekimasu ka. /inai/**

Kono kikai no setsumee no dekiru hito wa inai n desu.

e) **Ima wa dono waapuro o tsukatte imasen ka. /akai no/**

Ima tsukatte inai waapuro wa akai no desu.

f) **Dono seehin ga nebiki dekimasu ka. /nihonsee/**

Nebiki dekiru seehin wa nihonsee desu.

g) **Ooyama-san wa dono kaisha no hisho deshita ka. /Tookyoo-kiki/**

Ooyama-san ga hisho datta kaisha wa Tookyoo-kiki desu.

h) **Dono jisho ga ichiban taisetsu desu ka. /kono eego no jisho/**

Ichiban taisetsu na jisho wa kono eego no jisho desu.

2 Response Practice

Example: Teacher: **Nakano-iki wa itsu kimasu ka. /sugu/**
"When does the train for Nakano come?" /soon/
Student: **Sugu kuru hazu desu.**
"(It) is expected to come soon."

a) **Yuubinkyoku wa doko ni arimasu ka. /ano biru no ura/**

Ano biru no ura ni aru hazu desu.

b) **Seehin ga dekiru made ni nannen gurai kakari masu ka. /hachi nen/**

Hachi-nen gurai kakaru hazu desu.

—258—

Lesson 19

c) Ano hito no shigoto wa nan desu ka. /daigaku no kooshi/ — **Daigaku no kooshi no hazu desu.**

d) Hoken wa onsha ga hutan shimasu ka. /iie shimasen/ — **Iie, toosha wa hutan shinai hazu desu.**

e) Ootasan wa doru-date to endate to dochira ga ii deshoo ka. /doru-date/ — **Doru-date ga ii hazu desu.**

3 Communication Practice

Directions: Inform the teacher in Japanese that it is your intention to do each of the following.

Example: Teacher: **Amerika e terekkusu o okurimasu.**
"(I) will send a telex to the USA."
Student: **Amerika e terekkusu o okuru tsumori desu.**
"(I) intend to send a telex to the USA."

a) **Kyoo no paatii e/ni (wa) ikimasen.** — **Kyoo no paatii e/ni ikanai tsumori desu.**

b) **Shinbun kookoku o dashimasu.** — **Shinbun kookoku o dasu tsumori desu.**

c) **Gonenkan Nihon ni imasu.** — **Gonenkan Nihon ni iru tsumori desu.**

d) **Kono seehin wa nebiki-shimasen.** — **Kono seehin wa nebiki-shinai tsumori desu.**

4 Communication Practice

Directions: Inform the teacher in Japanese that you have decided on/to do each of the following.

Example: Teacher: **Moo biiru wa nomimasen.**
"(I) don't drink beer any more."
Student: **Moo biiru wa nomanai koto ni shimashita.**
"(I) decided not to drink beer any more."

a) **Moo ichido gutaiteki na jooken ni tsuite hanashiaimasu.** — **Moo ichido gutaiteki na jooken ni tsuite hanashiau koto ni shimashita.**

b) **Ashita no paatii e/ni wa ikimasen.** — **Ashita no paatii e/ni wa ikanai koto ni shimashita.**

c) **Kono kikai no kakaku wa gohyaku-doru desu.** — **Kono kikai no kakaku wa gohyaku-doru ni shimashita.**

d) **Moo ichi-do shanai de kentoo shimasu.** — **Moo ichi-do shanai de kentoo suru koto ni shimashita.**

5 Transformation Practice

Example: Teacher: **Kono kaisha wa robotto o tsukutte imasu.**
"This company is making robots."
Student: **Kono kaisha wa robotto o tsukutte iru soo desu.**
"It is said that this company is making robots."

—259—

Lesson 19

a) Ashita katarogu o okutte kuremasu. | Ashita katarogu o okutte kureru soo desu.
b) Kono shinseehin wa benri desu. | Kono shinseehin wa benri da soo desu.
c) Mada senmonka wa kimasen. | Mada senmonka wa konai soo desu.
d) Yamamoto-san no nozonde iru no wa doru-date desu. | Yamamoto-san no nozonde iru no wa doru-date da soo desu.
e) Moo ichi-do torihiki jooken ni tsuite hanashiaitai n desu. | Moo ichi-do torihiki jooken ni tsuite hanashiaitai soo desu.

EXERCISES

Inform the teacher in Japanese that:

1 You heard that USM would examine it beforehand one more time.
2 You heard that the president was out of the office.
3 You decided to try using the product which USM newly produced.
4 You intend to obtain a patent for this technology.
5 It is said that the buyer bears the cost for shipping.
6 It is expected that Mr. Tanaka can pay in installments.
7 After receiving a reply from New York, let's decide to discuss trade terms one more time.
8 The lecturer who is teaching Japanese economics at this college is Mr. Ohyama.

Model Answers:

1 Yuu-esu-emu wa moo ichi-do kentoo-shite oku soo desu.
2 Shachoo wa gaishutsu-chuu da soo desu.
3 Yuu-esu-emu ga atarashiku tsukutta seehin o tsukatte miru koto ni shima-shita.
4 Kono gijutsu no tokkyo o toru tsumori desu.
5 Kaite ga sooryoo o hutan-suru soo desu.
6 Tanaka-san wa bunkatsu-barai ga dekiru hazu desu.
7 Nyuuyooku kara henji o moratte kara, moo ichi-do shikiri-jooken ni tsuite hanashiau koto ni shimashoo.
8 Kono daigaku de Nihon no keezai o oshiete iru kooshi wa Ooyama-san desu.

Lesson 19

BUSINESS INFORMATION

Reading Business and Financial Documents

Many shipping and trade terms have transferred "as is" from English into Japanese, e.g. "CIF" (Cost, Insurance and Freight) is simply pronounced **"Shii-ai-ehu,"** "FOB" (Free on Board) becomes **"Ehu-oo-bii,"** and "L/C" (Letter of Credit) becomes **"Eru-shii."** When it comes to financial jargon, however, the original Japanese terms and **kanji** prevail—except for certain recent financial instruments like swaps (スワップ **suwappu**). If you can recognize a few very basic **kanji,** along with some of the business-related terms in which they appear, you may be able to make out the contents of general financial statements, articles and business correspondence.

I "ROOT" KANJI

 貝 = **kai**
meaning: SHELL
(Note: In ancient times, shells were used as currency.)

Kanji containing "ROOT"	Pronunciation / Meaning		Related Business/Financial Terms
A	費	= tsuiya(su); hi SPENDING, EXPENSE	交際費, **koo-sai-hi** (exchange) + (occasion) + (expense) = ENTERTAINMENT EXPENSE
			消費, **shoo-hi** (extinguish) + (expense) = CONSUMPTION
B	財	= zai TREASURE, PROPERTY FINANCE	消費財, **shoo-hi-zai** (extinguish) + (expense) + (property) = CONSUMER GOOD(S)
			財界, **zai-kai** (finance) + (world) = FINANCIAL CIRCLES, BUSINESS WORLD
			財源, **zai-gen** (finance) + (source) = FINANCIAL RESOURCES, SOURCE OF REVENUE

Lesson 19

	Kanji containing "ROOT"	Pronunciation Meaning		Business Meaning/Financial Terms
C	資	=shi FUNDS, CAPITAL	資金，	shi-kin (fund) + (money) =FUNDS
			投資，	too-shi (throw) + (fund) =INVESTMENT
			資本，	shi-hon (fund) + (source) =CAPITAL
			資産，	shi-san (fund) + (property) =ASSETS
D	貯	=takuwa(eru); cho RESERVE, SAVE	貯金，	cho-kin (save) + (money) =SAVINGS
			貯蓄，	cho-chiku (save) + (store) =SAVING, STORING UP
E	債	=sai DEBT	債券，	sai-ken (debt) + (ticket) =BOND
			債権，	sai-ken (debt) + (right) =CREDIT, ASSET
			債務，	sai-mu (debt) + (duty) =DEBT, LIABILITY

II "ROOT" KANJI

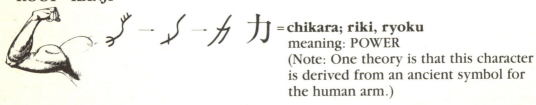

=chikara; riki, ryoku
meaning: POWER
(Note: One theory is that this character is derived from an ancient symbol for the human arm.)

—262—

Lesson 19

Kanji con-taining "ROOT"	Pronunciation Meaning	Related Business/Financial Terms
A 働	= hatara(ku); doo LABOR, WORK	労働者， **roo-doo-sha** (labor) + (work) + (person) = LABORER 労働組合， **roo-doo-kumi-ai** (labor) + (work) + (group) + (put together) = LABOR UNION
B 勤	= tsutome(ru); kin SERVICE, WORK	勤務， **kin-mu** (work) + (service) = DUTY, WORK 勤務先， **kin-mu-saki** (work) + (service) + (destination) = WORK PLACE
C 協	= kyoo COOPERATION	協議， **kyoo-gi** (cooperation) + (deliberation) = CONFERENCE, COUNCIL 協同， **kyoo-doo** (cooperation) + (same) = COLLABORATION 協力， **kyoo-ryoku** (cooperation) + (power) = COOPERATION
D 動	= ugo(ku); doo MOVE	動機， **doo-ki** (move) + (opportunity) = MOTIVE, MOTIVATION 動向， **doo-koo** (move) + (turn) = TREND, TENDENCY
E 効	= ki(ku); koo EFFECT	効果， **koo-ka** (effect) + (result) = EFFECT, RESULT 効率， **koo-ritsu** (effect) + (ratio) = EFFICIENCY

Lesson 19

III "ROOT" KANJI

= kuruma; sha
meaning: WHEEL

Kanji containing "ROOT"	Pronunciation Meaning		Related Business/Financial Terms
A	輸	= yu TRANSPORT	輸出,	**yu-shutsu** (transport) + (go out) = EXPORT
			輸入,	**yu-nyuu** (transport) + (come in) = IMPORT
			輸送,	**yu-soo** (transport) + (send) = TRANSPORTATION, CONVEYANCE
B	運	= hako(bu); un CARRY, BEAR	資産運用,	**shisan-unyo** (fund) + (property) + (carry) + (use) = ASSETS MANAGEMENT
			運輸,	**un-yu** (carry) + (transport) = TRANSPORTATION
			運営,	**un'ee** (carry) + (conduct) = OPERATION, MANAGEMENT
			運転,	**un-ten** (carry) + (revolve) = DRIVE, OPERATE
C	転	= koro(bu); ten ROLL, REVOLVE	回転,	**kai-ten** (go around) + (revolve) = ROTATE
			転職,	**ten-shoku** (revolve) + (job) = JOB CHANGE
			転換,	**ten-kan** (revolve) + (substitute) = CONVERSION

Lesson 20

Japanese Business Practices

OBJECTIVES

1   to discuss how business negotiations are going.

2   to discuss Japanese companies and their customs.

3   to understand the Japanese decision-making process *(nemawashi)*.

4   to learn the use of the noun *yoo,* 'like, as.'

Lesson 20

TARGET EXPRESSIONS AND PATTERNS

1	It seems that...		...suru yoo desu.
2	When/at the time of...		...toki (ni)
3	For the purpose of...		...tame (ni)
4	Mr./Ms. «name X» is satisfied with «name Y».		«X»-san wa «Y» ga ki ni iru.

SITUATION

A USM, Ltd. specialist arrives in Japan to give detailed technical explanations about the robots, and he starts discussions with Nissan. Negotiations are progressing smoothly, but they have not yet reached a final conclusion on the contract.

DIALOGUE

		Nissan (Motor Co., Ltd.)	Nissan
		negotiation	kooshoo
Yamamoto		to go well	umaku iku

1	Are negotiations with Nissan going well?	**Nissan to no kooshoo wa umaku itte imasu ka.**

		to be satisfied with	ki ni iru
		it seems to be satisfactory	ki ni itte iru yoo da
Brown		conclusion	ketsuron

2	(They) seem to be very satisfied with the robots, but the conclusion isn't coming [lit. does not come out easily], so [imp. I'm a bit worried.]	**Robotto wa taihen ki ni itte iru yoo desu ga, nakanaka ketsuron ga denai no de...**

Yamamoto		opinion	iken

3	(It) is a big transaction, so there must also be various opinions within the company.	**Ookii torihiki desu kara, shanai ni mo iron na iken ga aru n desu yo.**

—266—

Lesson 20

Brown

4	Right. Mr. Ohyama [lit. General Manager Ohyama] was also saying that, but [imp. it does take time.]	**Ee. Ooyama-buchoo mo soo itte imashita ga...**

something new	**nani ka atarashii koto**
the time(s) (when)	**toki**
at the times when	**toki ni wa**
first of all	**mazu**
Yamamoto laying the groundwork	**nemawashi**

5	In Japanese enterprises, laying the groundwork is first of all important when doing something new.	**Nihon no kigyoo de wa, nani ka atarashii koto o suru toki ni wa, mazu 'nemawashi' ga taisetsu na n desu yo.**

consensus	**konsensasu**
«noun» for the purpose of	**tame no «noun»**
Brown preparation for a consensus	**konsensasu no tame no junbi**

6	It is to prepare for a consensus [lit. preparation for the sake of a consensus].	**Konsensasu no tame no junbi desu ne.**

person in charge	**tantoosha**
post	**busho**
superior (official)	**jooshi**
director	**juuyaku**
Yamamoto persuasion	**settoku (-suru)**

7	That's right. The person in charge consults with (people in) various positions, and his superior then persuades the directors.	**Soo desu. Tantoosha ga iroiro na busho to soodan-shite, sono jooshi wa juuyaku o settoku-suru n desu.**

Yamamoto «verb» for the purpose of	**tame ni «verb»**

8	It takes time to reach that consensus. [lit. For the sake of that consensus, time is being taken.]	**Sono konsensasu no tame ni jikan ga kakatte iru n desu yo.**

—267—

Lesson 20

	like, similar to	yoo /na/
	American (-like) way of doing	amerika no yoo na yarikata
	considerably	kanari
Brown	to differ	chigau

9 It seems quite different from the American way of doing (things).

Amerika no yoo na yarikata to wa kanari chigau yoo desu ne.

	Japanese-like	nihon-teki
Yamamoto	point	ten

10 But there are also good points in the Japanese way of doing (things).

Demo, nihon-teki na yarikata ni mo ii ten ga aru n desu yo.

Brown

11 Of course I agree with you, but (I) am not yet used to (that), so [imp. I'm still troubled.]

Mochiron soo deshoo ga, mada narete inai no de...

	to worry	shinpai-suru
Yamamoto	there is nothing/no matter	koto wa nai

12 Well, (I) think there is nothing much to worry about.

Maa, amari shinpai-suru koto wa nai to omoimasu yo.

Brown	without worrying	shinpai-shinai de

13 (I) agree with (you). Let's just wait [lit. Let's decide to wait] without worrying so much.

Soo desu ne. Amari shinpai-shinai de matsu koto ni shimashoo.

JAPANESE WRITING

1　山　本：　日産との交渉はうまくいっていますか。

2　ブラウン：　ロボットは大変気に入っているようですが、なかなか結論が出ないので…

3　山　本：　大きい取り引きですから、社内にもいろんな意見があるんですよ。

4　ブラウン：　ええ。大山部長もそう言っていましたが…

5　山　本：　日本の企業では、何か新しい事をする時には、まず「根回し」が大切なんですよ。

6　ブラウン：　コンセンサスのための準備ですね。

7　山　本：　そうです。担当者がいろいろな部署と相談して、その上司は重役を説得するんです。

8　山　本：　そのコンセンサスのために時間がかかっているんですよ。

Lesson 20

9	ブラウン：	アメリカのようなやり方とはかなり違うようですね。
10	山　本：	でも、日本的なやり方にもいい点があるんですよ。
11	ブラウン：	もちろんそうでしょうが、まだ慣れていないので…
12	山　本：	まあ、あまり心配する事はないと思いますよ。
13	ブラウン：	そうですね。あまり心配しないで待つことにしましょう。

READING

1	Yamamoto:	Nissan to no kooshoo wa umaku itte imasu ka.
2	Brown:	Robotto wa taihen ki ni itte iru yoo desu ga, nakanaka ketsuron ga denai no de…
3	Yamamoto:	Ookii torihiki desu kara, shanai ni mo iron na iken ga aru n desu yo.
4	Brown:	Ee. Ooyama-buchoo mo soo itte imashita ga…
5	Yamamoto:	Nihon no kigyoo de wa, nani ka atarashii koto o suru toki ni wa, mazu 'nemawashi' ga taisetsu nan desu yo.
6	Brown:	Konsensasu no tame no junbi desu ne.
7	Yamamoto:	Soo desu. Tantoosha ga iroiro na busho to soodan-shite, sono jooshi wa juuyaku o settoku-suru n desu.
8	Yamamoto:	Sono konsensasu no tame ni jikan ga kakatte iru n desu yo.
9	Brown:	Amerika no yoo na yarikata to wa kanari chigau yoo desu ne.
10	Yamamoto:	Demo, nihon-teki na yarikata ni mo ii ten ga aru n desu yo.
11	Brown:	Mochiron soo deshoo ga, mada narete inai no de…
12	Yamamoto:	Maa, amari shinpai-suru koto wa nai to omoimasu yo.
13	Brown:	Soo desu ne. Amari shinpai-shinai de matsu koto ni shimashoo.

ADDITIONAL USEFUL EXPRESSIONS

1 Before concluding the agreement

A:	Please, just for a minute, listen to my opinion.	**Chotto, boku no iken o kiite kudasai.**
B:	Do you have something you want to say?	**Nani ka iitai koto ga aru n desu ka.**

	to be anxious	**ki ni naru**

A:	Yes. I'm anxious about the transaction this time.	**Ee, boku wa kondo no torihiki ga ki ni naru n desu.**
B:	Why is that?	**Doo shite desu ka.**

—269—

Lesson 20

counterpart	**aite**
somehow	**doomo**
to trust	**shin'yoo-suru**

| A: (I) can't trust (my) counterpart, somehow. | **Torihiki aite ga doomo shin'yoo-de-kimasen.** |

2 Following the negotiations

| A: Did the negotiation [lit. business talk] with Nissan go well? | **Nissan to no shoodan wa umaku ikimashita ka.** |

| finally | **yatto** |
| to contract | **keeyaku-suru** |

| B: Yes, (I) finally signed the contract [lit. contracted] yesterday. | **Ee, kinoo yatto keeyaku-shimashita.** |

| congratulations | **omedetoo** |

| A: That's good, isn't it? Congratulations. | **Sore wa yokatta desu nee. Omedetoo.** |

REFERENCE

haki (-suru)	abolition	**keeyakusho**	contract document
seeritsu (-suru)	conclusion	**dakyoo (-suru)**	compromise
kaiyaku (-suru)	cancellation	**jooho (-suru)**	concession
kooshin (-suru)	renewal	**booeki (-suru)**	trade
henkoo (-suru)	change		
shuusee (-suru)	correction		
ringi-see	the system of circulating proposals for general approval		

NOTES

1 **-yoo** 'appearance'
Yoo is a **na** -noun, used in combination either with clauses, or with a noun + **no/na,** informal verbs and adjectives.
Note carefully the following combinations:
A) **-yoo da** 'it seems...', 'it is the appearance that...' (used with clauses)
This is used to state your impression.

—270—

Lesson 20

Examples: a) **Ano hito wa taihen ki ni itte iru *yoo desu.***
"That person seems to be very satisfied. [lit. It is the appearance that...]"
b) **Kono kaisha no seehin wa sukoshi takai *yoo desu.***
"The products of this company seem to be a bit expensive."
c) **Yamamoto-san wa Nissan no kuruma o tsukatte iru *yoo desu.***
"It seems that Mr. Yamamoto is using a Nissan (model). [lit. a car (manufactured) by Nissan]."

B) **«noun X» + no yoo na «noun Y»** 'Y like X, Y in the manner of X,'
«informal verb, adjective» + yoo na Y 'Y that seems like...'

Examples: a) **hisho *no yoo na* shigoto** (noun + **no**)
'work like that of a secretary'
b) **sugu kau *yoo na* henji** (informal verb)
'a reply that seems like (someone is) to buy immediately'
c) **ki ni itte inai *yoo na* tegami** (adjective)
'a letter giving an impression of dissatisfaction'

C) **...(no) yoo ni** 'as ..., in the manner of..., in the same way as...'

Examples: a) **Buchoo no itta *yoo ni,* moo ichi-do hanashiaimashoo.**
"As the general manager said, let's discuss (it) one more time."
b) **Oota-san *no yoo ni* Ooyama-san mo daigaku no kooshi ni narimashita.**
"Like Mr. Ohta, Mr. Ohyama also became a lecturer at the college."

D) **...yoo ni iu** 'instruct/advise (to do)'

a) **Shinpai-shinai *yoo ni* itte kudasai.**
"Please tell (him) not to worry."
b) **Hisho ni kaeru *yoo ni* iimashita.**
"(Someone) asked a secretary to go home."

2 Toki 'time'
Toki is a noun frequently modified by an informal verb, an adjective, or a noun + **no/na**:

A) **«the modifier» + toki no «noun X»** '«X» during/in/for the time of...'

Examples: a) **Chuugakkoo *no toki no* hon** (noun + **no**)
'the book (used) during the time of middle-school days.'
b) **Genki *na toki no* shashin** (noun + **na**)
'a picture (taken) in healthy times.'
c) **Keeyaku-suru *toki no* junbi** (informal verb)
'preparation for the time of making a contract.'

B) **«the modifier» + toki (ni)** 'when (doing), when (someone does)'
Ni is optionally used. The combination of **toki (ni) wa** indicates repeated action, meaning 'at times when...', as in the following:

—271—

Lesson 20

Examples: a)   **Paatii wa okyaku-sama ga sukunai *toki (ni) wa* ima de shimasu.**
     "Party will be held in the living room at a time when there are few guests."

     b)   **Kaisha ni denwa-shita *toki (ni)* Ooyama-san ga demashita.**
     "When I called the company, Mr. Ohyama answered."

3 **«Noun X»** + **no tame** 'for the purpose of «X», on the account of «X»'

A) **«noun X» no tame no «noun Y»** «Y» for the purpose of «X»

Examples: a)   **setsumee *no tame no* tegami**
     'a letter for the purpose of explaining'

     b)   **konsensasu *no tame no* junbi**
     'preparation for the sake of consensus'

B) **«noun X» no tame (ni), ...** 'for the purpose of «X», ...'

Example: **Kuwashii kentoo *no tame ni,* motto shiryoo ga irimasu.**
     "For a detailed examination, I need more data."

Note: an informal verb or an adjective can also precede **tame,** e.g. **benkyoo suru tame. Tame,** in this case, means 'purpose' or 'reason' depending upon the context: 'for the purpose of studying' or 'because of the studying'.

4 **Nani ka** + **«adjective clause»** + **koto/mono** 'something/anything...'
As explained in Lesson 17, the term **mono** *is* used to refer to concrete 'things,' while **koto** is used in reference to abstract 'things.'

> informal verb
> adjective   }   **koto/mono** 'thing'
> noun + **no/na**

Examples: a)   ***Nani ka dekiru koto* ga arimasu ka.** (abstract)
     "Is there anything (I) can do? [lit. Is there anything to be done?]"

     b)   ***Nani ka tsumetai mono* ga irimasu.** (concrete)
     "I need something cold."

     c)   ***Nani ka taisetsu na koto* o iimashita ka.** (abstract)
     "Did (someone) say something important?"

5 **Ki ni iru** 'to be satisfied with' and **ki ni naru** 'to be anxious about'
Ki ni iru and **ki ni naru** are used in the same pattern as the verbs **dekiru** 'can do,' **wakaru** (know/understand), and **iru** (need), which have been previously introduced:

—272—

Lesson 20

Person who is satisfied/anxious	What the person is satisfied with/anxious about	be satisfied with be anxious about
Yamamoto-san wa	**kono kaisha ga**	**ki ni irimashita.** **ki ni narimashita.**
Mr. Yamamoto was satisfied with this company. Mr. Yamamoto was anxious about this company.		

PRACTICE

1 Response Practice

Example: Teacher: **Buraun-san wa Nissan to keeyaku-shimasu ka. /hai/**
"Will Mr. Brown make a contract with Nissan?" /Yes/
Student: **Hai, keeyaku-suru yoo desu.**
"Yes, it seems that (he) will make a contract."

a) **Sono kaisha to no shoodan wa umaku itte imasu ka. /iie/**   **Iie, umaku itte inai yoo desu.**

b) **Sugu ketsuron ga demasu ka. /iie/**   **Iie, sugu denai yoo desu.**

c) **Ano kaisha no tesuuryoo wa motto takai desu ka. /hai/**   **Hai, motto takai yoo desu.**

d) **Ano hito wa Buraun-san no hisho desu ka. /hai/**   **Hai, hisho no yoo desu.**

e) **Ooyama-san wa ashita moo ichi-do hanashiau koto ni shimashita ka. /hai/**   **Hai, moo ichi-do hanashiau koto ni shita yoo desu.**

f) **Yamada-san wa paatii ni ikanai tsumori deshita ka. /hai/**   **Hai, ikanai tsumori datta yoo desu.**

2 Combination Practice

Directions: Combine the following sentences, using **toki (ni)** or **toki (ni) wa.**

Example: Teacher: **Nissan to keeyaku-shimashita.**
"(I) signed the contract with Nissan."
Kanari jikan ga kakarimashita.
"It took quite a long time."
Student: **Nissan to keeyaku-shita toki (ni), kanari jikan ga kakarimashita.**
"When (I) signed the contract with Nissan, it took quite a long time."

a) **Kaigi ga owaru no o matte imasu. Uchi ni denwa-shimashita.**   **Kaigi ga owaru no o matte iru toki, uchi ni denwa-shimashita.**

—273—

Lesson 20

b) Amerika-kee kigyoo ni tsutomete imashita. Eego o benkyoo-shimashita.

Amerika-kee kigyoo ni tsutomete ita toki, eego o benkyoo-shimashita.

c) San-nen mae kono kaisha no shain deshita. Tedori nijuuman-en deshita.

San-nen mae kono kaisha no shain datta toki, tedori nijuuman-en deshita.

3 Response Practice

Example: Teacher: **Nan no junbi o shite imasu ka. /konsensasu/**
"For what are (you) preparing?" /consensus/
Student: **Konsensasu no tame no junbi o shite imasu.**
"(I)'m preparing for a consensus."

a) Nan no benkyoo o shite imashita ka. /Nihon no kaisha to no kooshoo/

Nihon no kaisha to no kooshoo no tame no benkyoo o shite imashita.

b) Nan no hanashiai o shite imasu ka. /kondo no torihiki/

Kondo no torihiki no tame no hanashiai o shite imasu.

c) Nan no kookoku o dashitai n desu ka. /shain boshuu/

Shain boshuu no tame no kookoku o dashitai n desu.

d) Nan no otetsudai o shimashoo ka. /paatii/

Patii no tame no tetsudai o shite kudasai.

4 Transformation Practice

Example: Teacher: **Kinoo atarashii kikai o kaimashita.**
"Yesterday, (I) bought a new machine."
Student: **Kinoo katta atarashii kikai ga ki ni irimashita.**
"(I)'m satisfied with the machine (I) bought yesterday."

a) Pii-ando-shii to keeyaku o shimashita.

Pii-ando-shii to shita keeyaku ga ki ni irimashita.

b) Kinoo eego no jisho o moraimashita.

Kinoo moratta eego no jisho ga ki ni irimashita.

c) Senjitsu doitsu wain o nomimashita.

Senjitsu nonda doitsu wain ga ki ni irimashita.

d) Senmonka ga setsumee-shite kure-mashita.

Setsumee-shite kureta senmonka ga ki ni irimashita.

e) Shinbun ni kookoku ga dete imashita.

Shinbun ni dete ita kookoku ga ki ni irimashita.

5 Communication Practice

Directions: Using **nani ka** + «a modifying word (or words)» + **mono/koto wa arimasen ka,** ask the teacher in Japanese if he/she has the following.

a) something Mr. Yamamoto likes (concrete)

Nani ka Yamamoto-san ga suki na mono

—274—

Lesson 20

b) something important (abstract)   **Nani ka taisetsu na koto**
c) something the manager is satisfied   **Nani ka kachoo ga ki ni iru mono**
     with (concrete)
d) something (he/she) wants to say   **Nani ka iitai koto**
     (abstract)
e) something to prepare (abstract)   **Nani ka junbi-suru koto**

EXERCISES

Inform the teacher in Japanese that:
1 The negotiations for buying new robots are going well.
2 It seems that Mr. Brown is not worrying so much about yesterday's contract with Nissan Motor Co., Ltd.
3 When Mr. Yamamoto is not satisfied with his business counterpart, he does not conclude the contract.
4 When you have something you want to say, please tell us (what it is) without worrying so much.
5 When I graduated from college, the American company was recruiting new staff.
6 In Japan, after business negotiations are started, it seems to take time before a contract is concluded.
7 That company's way of doing (things) is good, but your company's way also has good points.
8 It's expected that a conclusion will come in the near future.
9 Due to the fact that there are various opinions within the company, it's very hard to reach [lit. make] a consensus, so it takes time.
10 It seems that the study of Japanese is going well, but it takes time.
11 It is expected that everybody will be satisfied with this book.

Model Answers:

1 **Atarashii robotto o kau tame no kooshoo wa umaku itte imasu.**
2 **Buraun-san wa kinoo no Nissan to no keeyaku ni tsuite amari shinpai-shite inai yoo desu.**
3 **Yamamoto-san wa torihiki aite ga ki ni iranai toki ni wa keeyaku-shimasen.**
4 **Nani ka iitai koto ga aru toki ni wa amari shinpai-shinai de itte kudasai.**
5 **Daigaku o deta toki, Amerika no kaisha ga atarashii sutahhu o boshuu-shite imashita.**
6 **Nihon de wa shoodan o hajimete kara keeyaku-suru made, jikan ga kakaru yoo desu.**
7 **Sono kaisha no yarikata wa ii desu ga, onsha no yarikata mo ii ten ga arimasu.**
8 **Chikai uchi ni ketsuron ga deru hazu desu.**
9 **Shanai ni iroiro na iken ga aru no de, konsensasu o tsukuru no wa totemo muzukashii desu kara jikan ga kakarimasu.**
10 **Nihongo no benkyoo wa umaku itte iru yoo desu ga, jikan ga kakarimasu.**
11 **Dare demo kono hon ga ki ni iru hazu desu.**

Lesson 20

BUSINESS INFORMATION

Dealing with Failure—or with Success

Sometimes, despite all good intentions, the contract you hoped for fails to materialize. This would of course be frustrating in any country, but perhaps more so in Japan since—as many foreigners feel—your counterparts give you so little indication all along about just how the negotiation is progressing. Once you do come to recognize the telltale signs of difficulty, you will be in a better position to remedy the situation—or at least keep your business relationship intact for the "next time."

1 The Loaded Silence: A pause in the discussion can sometimes indicate that an impasse has been reached. Foreigners often interpret this silence as a sign of hesitation, and will attempt to fill the gap with yet another incentive or with a better offer, thinking that they still have a chance. This can be a waste of breath. Not only do you end up compromising your position, but your persuasion will be falling on the wrong ears since the opinion being expressed to you usually also reflects those of superiors consulted at length prior to the meeting. It is important to understand, therefore, that no matter how subtle or vague your counterpart's negative replies are, e.g. "It is difficult..." or "Well, I don't know..."—or even if he says nothing at all—these may all add up to the same thing: "No." On your part, you are expected to read the signs and not make things more awkward by insisting.

The following conversation is a good example of a tactful negotiator at work:

Negotiator A:
Well, may (we) understand then that there is no problem concerning the price?

Soo shimasu to, kakaku ni tsuite wa mondai wa nai to kangaete ii n deshoo ka.

Negotiator B:
(Silence) Well...(we) are not saying that there's no problem concerning the price—(we) are saying that there are other factors which are more important than the price.

Soo desu nee...kakaku ni tsuite wa mondai ga nai wake ja nai n desu ga, sore yori mo jyuuyoo na mondai ga aru to mooshiagete iru wake desu.

Negotiator A:
The delivery period and after-sales service, right? But (we) would like your (respected) company to clarify its position on these points a little more...

Nooki to ahutaa-saabisu no mondai desu ne. Shikashi, kono ten ni tsuite wa onsha no okangae o moo sukoshi hakkiri sasete itadakitai n desu ga...

Negotiator B:
Well...as (we) have already told (you), it is not possible for our department alone to decide on these points either, so...(we) cannot say more.

Ee to desu nee, kono ten ni tsuite mo sude ni mooshiagemashita ga, toobu dake de wa kimerare nai koto desu no de, kore ijyoo mooshiageraremasen.

—276—

Lesson 20

Negotiator A:
When may (we) expect a decision?

Ketsuron ga deru no ni dono kurai kakarimasu ka.

Negotiator B:
(Silence)

Negotiator A:
Well, (I) guess it's impossible to proceed any further until your consultation with the appropriate departments at the end of the month, is that right?

Wakarimashita. Soo shimasu to, kongetsu-matsu no onsha de no kanren-busho to no kyoogi made wa kore ijyoo susumemasen nee.

Negotiator B:
That's about right.

Maa, soo yuu koto ni narimasu.

Note that, although it was not specifically mentioned that the delivery time and after-sales services were not suitable, Negotiator A perceived that the talk was deadlocked on these issues. He confirms this by asking additional questions, conveys his understanding of the problem, and finally retreats gracefully by proposing a recess until the end of the month. The anticipated deal did not come through, therefore, and this proposed new meeting may never take place. But as any experienced foreign businessman will tell you, it was far more important for Negotiator A to maintain harmony between the two parties because this will serve as the vital link to future business opportunities.

2   Success: If all goes well, then there is little to say except, **"Omedetoo gozaimasu"** (おめでとうございます, Congratulations!). May we then suggest that you kindly refer to Lessons 9 and 10 of this text for entertainment guidelines so you can cement your new alliance with an appropriate lunch or dinner. A final word of advice is that you should be discreet about the timing of this celebration. It should not be arranged so soon after the deal is concluded as to seem over-anxious, but neither should it take place so much later that your new partners forget how much effort you put into mastering the Japanese language and customs during the negotiation process.

Ganbatte kudasai!
(Good Luck!)

APPENDIX

Verbs

Verbs are divided into 4 groups according to their endings: **-ru, -u, -aru,** and irregular verbs. Most verbs belong to the first two groups. In the third group (**-aru**), there are only five verbs all of which are polite: **gozaru*, irassharu, kudasaru, nasaru,** and **ossharu.** There are only two irregular verbs: **kuru, suru.** Furthermore, **-u** verbs are divided into nine sub-groups depending on the sound immediately preceding **u: -ku, -gu, -bu, -mu, -nu, -su, -ru, -tsu** and a vowel + **-u.**

*Rarely used in Modern Japanese, except for its Formal forms.

Types of verbs		Non-past Informal	Non-past Formal	Gerund (-te form)	Past Informal	Negative Non-past Informal	Meaning
-ru Verbs		-ru tabe*ru*	-masu tabe*masu*	-te tabe*te*	-ta tabe*ta*	-nai tabe*nai*	eat
-u Verbs	**-ku**	-ku i*ku*	-kimasu i*kimasu*	-tte i*tte*	-tta i*tta*	-kanai i*kanai*	go
	-gu	-gu oyo*gu***	-gimasu oyo*gimasu*	-ide oyo*ide*	-ida oyo*ida*	-ganai oyo*ganai*	swim
	-bu	-bu yo*bu*	-bimasu yo*bimasu*	-nde yo*nde*	-nda yo*nda*	-banai yo*banai*	call
	-mu	-mu yo*mu*	-mimasu yo*mimasu*	-nde yo*nde*	-nda yo*nda*	-manai yo*manai*	read
	-nu	-nu shi*nu***	-nimasu shi*nimasu*	-nde shi*nde*	-nda shi*nda*	-nanai shi*nanai*	die
	-su	-su da*su*	-shimasu da*shimasu*	-shite da*shite*	-shita da*shita*	-sanai da*sanai*	put out
	-ru	-ru u*ru*	-rimasu u*rimasu*	-tte u*tte*	-tta u*tta*	-ranai u*ranai*	sell
	-tsu	-tsu ma*tsu*	-chimasu ma*chimasu*	-tte ma*tte*	-tta ma*tta*	-tanai ma*tanai*	wait
	vowel	-u i*u*	-imasu i*imasu*	-tte i*tte*	-tta i*tta*	-wanai i*wanai*	say
-aru Verbs (polite)		-aru irassh*aru*	-imasu irassha*imasu*	-atte irassh*atte*	-atta irassh*atta*	-aranai irassh*aranai*	be/come/go
Irregular Verbs		kuru suru	kimasu shimasu	kite shite	kita shita	konai shinai	come do

****shinu** and **oyogu** have not been introduced in this text.

—278—

Adjectives

Inflections for adjectives (ending with **-i**) are as follows:

Non-past	Adv. (+nai)	Gerund	Past
-i	-ku	-kute	-katta
taka*i*	taka*ku (nai)*	taka*kute*	taka*katta*

Counters

	Lesson	Counter for	Combined with
-ban	3	number in series	C*
-bu	19	printed materials	C
-dai	18	machines	C
-do	18	number of times	C
-doru	19	dollar	C
-en	6	yen	C
-gatsu	6	months of the year	C
-hai/-pai/-bai	10	glassfuls/cupfuls	C
-hon/-pon/-bon	10	long and cylindrical objects	C
-hun/-pun	4	minutes	C
-ji	4	the time of day (hours)	C
-jikan	4	number of hours	C
-ka	6	days (2 through 10, and 20)	J**
-kagetsu	6	number of months	C
-kai/-gai	13	floors	C
-nen	6	years	C
-nichi	6	days (except 2 through 10, and 20)	C
-nin	10	persons (3 and more)	C
-ninmae	10	portions of food	C
-ri	10	persons (only for 1 or 2)	J
-tsu	8	units (only for 1 through 9)	J
-wari	12	percentages (in units of ten)	C

*C indicates Chinese-origin numerals.
**J indicates Japanese-origin numerals.

Verb Inflections

All the verbs introduced in this text and their inflections are as follows:

Citation	Stem (-masu)	Gerund	Informal Past	Informal Negative	Meaning
ageru	age	agete	ageta	agenai	give
aru	ari	atte	atta	nai	have
au	ai	atte	atta	awanai	meet
chigau	chigai	chigatte	chigatta	chigawanai	be wrong; differ
dasu	dashi	dashite	dashita	dasanai	mail; put out
dekakeru	dekake	dekakete	dekaketa	dekakenai	go out
dekiru	deki	dekite	dekita	dekinai	be possible; be able to do
deru	de	dete	deta	denai	answer (the phone); come out (graduate)
ganbaru	ganbari	ganbatte	ganbatta	ganbaranai	hold out; stand out
(gozaru)*	gozai	(gozatte)	(gozatta)	(gozaranai)	have (polite)
hairu	hairi	haitte	haitta	hairanai	enter; join
hajimeru	hajime	hajimete	hajimeta	hajimenai	begin; start
hanashiau	hanashiai	hanashiatte	hanashiatta	hanashiawanai	discuss
hanasu	hanashi	hanashite	hanashita	hanasanai	talk
hataraku	hataraki	hataraite	hataraita	hatarakanai	work
iku	iki	itte	itta	ikanai	go
irassharu	irasshai	irasshatte**	irasshatta	irassharanai	go; come; be (respectful)
iru	iri	itte	itta	iranai	need
iru	i	ite	ita	inai	be; exist
itadaku	itadaki	itadaite	itadaita	itadakanai	take; receive (modest)
itasu	itashi	itashite	itashita	itasanai	do (modest)
iu	ii	itte	itta	iwanai	say
kaeru	kaeri	kaette	kaetta	kaeranai	return; go back
kau	kai	katte	katta	kawanai	buy
kakaru	kakari	kakatte	kakatta	kakaranai	take
kakeru	kake	kakete	kaketa	kakenai	place (a telephone call)
kaku	kaki	kaite	kaita	kakanai	write; draw
kamau	kamai	kamatte	kamatta	kamawanai	care about
kangaeru	kangae	kangaete	kangaeta	kangaenai	think
kiku	kiki	kiite	kiita	kikanai	ask; hear
ki ni iru	ki ni iri	ki ni itte	ki ni itta	ki ni iranai	be satisfied
komaru	komari	komatte	komatta	komaranai	be troubled
kureru	kure	kurete	kureta	kurenai	give
kuru	ki	kite	kita	konai	come
magaru	magari	magatte	magatta	magaranai	turn
mairu	mairi	maitte	maitta	mairanai	come (modest)
matsu	machi	matte	matta	matanai	wait
miru	mi	mite	mita	minai	see
miseru	mise	misete	miseta	misenai	show
mitsukaru	mitsukari	mitsukatte	mitsukatta	mitsukaranai	be found
morau	morai	moratte	moratta	morawanai	receive
motsu	mochi	motte	motta	motanai	have
muku	muki	muite	muita	mukanai	be suited for
nareru	nare	narete	nareta	narenai	get used to
naru	nari	natte	natta	naranai	become
nozomu	nozomi	nozonde	nozonda	nozomanai	hope for

—280—

Citation	Stem (-masu)	Gerund	Informal Past	Informal Negative	Meaning
okuru	okuri	okutte	okutta	okuranai	send
omoikiru	omoikiri	omoikitte	omoikitta	omoikiranai	resolve
omou	omoi	omotte	omotta	omowanai	think
oru	ori	otte	otta	oranai	be (modest)
oshieru	oshie	oshiete	oshieta	oshienai	teach
ossharu	osshai	osshatte	osshatta	ossharanai	say (respectful)
owaru	owari	owatte	owatta	owaranai	end
sagasu	sagashi	sagashite	sagashita	sagasanai	look for; seek
shiru	shiri	shitte	shitta	shiranai	come to know
soeru	soe	soete	soeta	soenai	attach
suru	shi	shite	shita	shinai	do
taberu	tabe	tabete	tabeta	tabenai	eat
tanomu	tanomi	tanonde	tanonda	tanomanai	ask; order
tetsudau	tetsudai	tetsudatte	tetsudatta	tetsudawanai	assist
tomeru	tome	tomete	tometa	tomenai	stop
toru	tori	totte	totta	toranai	take out; obtain
tsukau	tsukai	tsukatte	tsukatta	tsukawanai	use
tsukuru	tsukuri	tsukutte	tsukutta	tsukuranai	make
tsutaeru	tsutae	tsutaete	tsutaeta	tsutaenai	report; convey
tsutomeru	tsutome	tsutomete	tsutometa	tsutomenai	work
ukagau	ukagai	ukagatte	ukagatta	ukagawanai	visit; ask (modest)
ukeru	uke	ukete	uketa	ukenai	receive
uridasu	uridashi	uridashite	uridashita	uridasanai	start selling
uru	uri	utte	utta	uranai	sell
wakaru	wakari	wakatte	wakatta	wakaranai	know; understand
yameru	yame	yamete	yameta	yamenai	quit; resign
yatou	yatoi	yatotte	yatotta	yatowanai	hire; employ
yomu	yomi	yonde	yonda	yomanai	read
yorokobu	yorokobi	yorokonde	yorokonda	yorokobanai	be delighted

*The forms in parentheses are rarely used in Modern Japanese.
****irashite** is also used as the gerund form.

BIBLIOGRAPHY

Some selected books and periodicals in English

On Japanese

Nihongo Notes 1-5
(Osamu and Nobuko MIZUTANI, The Japan Times, Ltd., ¥1,000 each)
Japanese phrase book series which explain in plain terms not only the usage but also the Japanese way of life and thinking.

Nihonjingo, Zoku Nihonjingo
(Mitsubishi Corporation, Toyo Keizai Shinposhya, ¥880 each)
Two series which cover expressions frequently used among Japanese. The title, *Nihonjingo,* is made up of two words, *Nihonjin* (Japanese person) and *go* (the language), implying that these are inseparable.

On Business

JETRO Marketing Series
(Japan External Trade Organization, ¥500 each)
A series of booklets which provide basic information about Japan as an export market. Titles in this series include 'Japan as an Export Market,' 'The Role of Trading Companies in International Commerce,' 'Planning for Distribution in Japan,' and 'The Japanese Consumer.' A recent release, 'Retailing in the Japanese Consumer Market,' is available at ¥1,000. For further information, contact JETRO offices abroad or the head office (see below).

On Life in Japan

Gaijin's Guide: Practical Help for Everyday Life in Japan
(Janet ASHBY, The Japan Times, Ltd., ¥1,200)
A handbook for daily life in Japan, with explanations and illustrations for everything from Japanese product labels to train schedules to telegraphic transfers at the bank.

Now You Live in Japan
(Research Committee for Bi-cultural Life in Japan, The Japan Times, Ltd., ¥1,200)
A handbook for foreign residents which covers Japanese regulations and procedures concerning immigration, housing, education, insurance and taxation, among other things.

Tokyo Shopping & Dining
(Japan Travel Bureau, Inc., ¥1,200)
Guide to the city's stores and restaurants, with emphasis on traditional Japanese cuisine and gifts, and complete with maps and photos.

"Salaryman" in Japan
(Japan Travel Bureau, Inc., ¥880)
Volume 8 in JTB's popular illustrated "pocketbook" series. Provides concise information about the average salaried worker's life at home and at work, including useful insights into language, etiquette and office politics.

On Statistics and Other Basic Information

Japan 1986: An International Comparison
(Toshio MATSUOKA, Keizai Koho Center, ¥880)
A handy booklet which provides essential statistics comparing Japan with other countries. Useful review of current status of Japan.

Nippon: A Chartered Survey of Japan 1986/87
(The Tsuneta Yano Memorial Society, Kokusai-sha, ¥4,200)
An annual review of statistics on a wide range of activities, including economy, finance, industry and society.

Encyclopedia of Japan I-IX
(Gen ITASAKA, Kodansha International, ¥140,000)
Nine-volume encyclopedia which includes information on almost everything Japanese, ranging from cultural and historical matters to recent progress in research and development. A supplement is available at ¥3,000.

Nippon: The Land and Its People
(Nippon Steel Corporation, Gakuseisha Publishing Co., Ltd., ¥1,200)
"Japan at a glance"—a handbook of basic information on Japan. Well-organized to give you concise answers for most questions concerning Japan.

Directories and Other References

Japan Directory 1987
(The Japan Press, Ltd., ¥50,000)
An annual two-volume directory.
Volume I: Foreign residents, government agencies, embassies, churches, clubs, schools, hospitals, banks and other organizations in Tokyo.
Volume II: Business firms.

Japan Yellow Pages: Japan Telephone Book
(Japan Yellow Pages Ltd., ¥2,000)
Published twice a year.

Economic Survey of Japan (1984—1985)
(Economic Planning Agency, Japanese Government, ¥6,800)
The official English version of Japan's 'The Annual Economic Report (White Paper on the Economy) for FY 1985.' An analysis of the nation's economic performance for the year, copiously illustrated with charts and tables.

Periodicals

The Japan Economic Journal (weekly)
(Nihon Keizai Shimbun, Inc., ¥400/copy; Subscription ¥9,900/half year, ¥16,800/a year)
Weekly review of Japan's economic, trade, financial and political activities. Information on economic indicators, stock, corporate records and research and development is also provided. English version of the Nihon Keizai Shimbun, a leading economic daily in Japan.

Tokyo Business Today (monthly)
(Toyo Keizai Shinposha [The Oriental Economist], ¥950/copy; Subscription ¥11,400/a year)
Topical articles on Japanese marketing, finance, technology and politics written by leading foreign businessmen and authorities on Japan, or translated from articles by Japanese journalists. With regular features and monthly cover story.

The Nihongo Journal (monthly)
(ALC Press, ¥580/copy; Subscription ¥30,960/ a year)
Topical articles on Japan in both English and Japanese, designed to expose readers to living, non-textbook-like Japanese while also providing news on culture, sports and other aspects of life in Japan.

Speaking of Japan (monthly)
(Keizai Koho Center, ¥800/copy; Subscription ¥9,600/a year)
A magazine containing speeches by distinguished foreign and Japanese individuals from public and private sectors as well as the academic world. The speakers discuss a variety of topics which concern Japan and, in many cases, her relations with foreign countries.

The Journal of Japanese Trade and Industry (bimonthly)
(Japan Economic Foundation, ¥1,200/copy; Subscription ¥7,200/a year)
A bimonthly magazine which focuses on trade, industrial and technological issues.

Tokyo News Letter (bimonthly)
(Mitsubishi Corporation, free of charge)
A bimonthly easy-to-read newsletter which features timely topics on new technology and contemporary life and culture in Japan.

Contact Addresses

Japan External Trade Organization (JETRO)
2-5, Toranomon 2-chome, Minato-ku, Tokyo 105
Tel: 03 (582) 5511
Keizai Koho Center
(Japan Institute for Social and Economic Affairs)
Otemachi Bldg. 6-1, Otemachi 1-chome, Chiyoda-ku Tokyo 100
Tel: 03 (201) 1416
Government Publications Service Center
2-1, Kasumigaseki 1-chome, Chiyoda-ku, Tokyo 100
Tel: 03 (504) 3885

INDEX

The number in parentheses indicates where the word appears for the first time in the book.

Example:
(4, 5)   Lesson 4, Dialogue **5**
(15, Ad. 2) Lesson 15, Additional Useful Expressions **2**
(10, Ref.) Lesson 10, Reference

A

aa oh (1, 6)
achira there, the other side (4, 4)
  that way (11, Ad. 3)
  that one over there (12, Ad. 1)
aeroguramu aerogram (13, Ref.)
ageru /-ru/ to give (16, Ad. 2)
  shookai-shite ageru to introduce (someone) to (you) (17, Ad. 2)
aimasu formal form of *au*
ainiku unfortunately (14, Ad. 4)
aisatsu respects, greeting (17, 14)
aite counterpart (20, Ad. 1)
aka (noun) red (10, 3)
akai (is) red (8, Ad. 2)
aki autumn (16, Ad. 3)
amari /+ neg./ not so much (8, 6)
Amerika America, USA (2, Ad. 4)
amerika-see of American origin (15, Ad. 1)
Amusuterudamu Amsterdam (2, Ref.)
anata you (1, Ad. 2)
ane older sister (9, Ref.)
ani older brother (9, Ref.)
ano /+ noun/ that (one) over there (6, 4)
  ano hito that person (he/she) (2, Ad. 2)
aoi (is) blue (8, Ad. 2)
Aoyama Aoyama (5, 4)
are that one over there (8, 7)
arigatai (is) appreciated (13, 13)
arigatoo gozaimasu (polite) thank you (1, 5)
arimasu formal form of *aru*
aru /-u/ to have (6, 10)
asa morning (4, 4)
asa-gohan breakfast (9, Ref.)
Asakusa Asakusa (11, 2)
asatte day after tomorrow (5, Ad. 2)
ashita tomorrow (4, Ad. 2)
atarashii (is) new (7, 3)
atena mailing address (13, 2)
ato de later (3, Ad. 4)
atsukaimasu formal form of *atsukau*
atsukau /-u/ to handle, deal with (17, Ad. 2)
au /-u/ to meet (9, 6)

B

bakachon fool-proof (12, Ref.)
ban-gohan supper (9, Ref.)
-ban counter for naming numbers in series (3, Ad. 2)
bangoo number (3, 1)
-barai —payment plan (19, Ad. 1)
  juuni-kagetsu-barai 12 month payment plan (19, Ad. 1)
basu bus (5, Ad. 4)
basu-tee bus stop (11, Ref.)
Beekoku U.S.A. (17, 6)
bengoshi lawyer (18, Ad. 1)
benjo toilet (11, Ref.)
benkyoo (-suru) reduction of the price (12, 10)
  studying (12, Ad. 5)
benri /na/ convenient (7, 12)
Berurin Berlin (2, Ref.)
betsu ni particularly (9, Ad. 1)
bijinesu business (17, 2)
bijinesu-sukuuru business school (16, 5)
-biki —off (12, Ad. 2)
  ni-wari-biki 20% off (12, Ad. 2)
biru building (6, 4)
bokoo one's Alma Mater (16, 8)
boku I (male only) (7, 11)
booeki (-suru) trade (20, Ref.)
boonasu bonus (16, Ad. 3)
boorupen ball-point pen (7, Ref.)
boshuu (-suru) recruit (15, 3)
botchan (respectful) son (9, Ref.)
-bu department (2, 5)
  eegyoo-bu business department (2, 5)
-bu counter for printed materials (19, Ad. 2)
  juu-bu ten copies (19, Ad. 2)
buchoo general manager (2, 5)
buin staff of a department (2, 5)
-bun text (12, 4)
bungaku literature (16, Ref.)
bunkatsu-barai payment in installments (19, Ad. 1)
busho post (20, 7)
butaniku pork (10, Ref.)
byooin hospital (11, Ref.)

C

chairoi (is) brown (8, Ad. 2)
chichi father (9, Ref.)
chigaimasu formal form of *chigau*
chigau /-u/ to be wrong (3, Ad. 3)
  to differ (20, 9)
chiisai (is) small (7, 9)
chiizu cheese (10, 7)
chikai uchi ni within the near future (9, Ad. 3)
chikaku ni near (9, 8)

chikashitsu

chikashitsu basement (13, Ref.)
chikatetsu subway (5, Ad. 1)
chizu map (7, 5)
choodo just, exactly (8, 8)
choome section/district (13, 6)
chooshoku breakfast (9, Ad. 1)
chotto a little (7, 3)
  I'm afraid that it won't do— (12, Ad. 2)
-chuu ni within (16, 11)
chuugakkoo middle school (15, Ref.)
Chuugoku China (2, Ref.)
chuugokugo Chinese (language) (7, Ad. 5)
chuuka-ryoori Chinese food (9, Ref.)
chuumon (suru) order (10, 5)
chuushoku lunch (9, 3)

D

da (non-past copula) to be (19, 5)
-dai counter for machines
  ichi-dai one unit (18, 3)
daidokoro kitchen (13, Ref.)
daigaku university, college (15, 7)
daigakuin graduate school (15, Ref.)
dairiten agent (17, 6)
daisuki /na/ very pleasing (9, Ad. 4)
dake only (15, 12)
  sore dake that's all (15, 12)
  goaisatsu ni dake only to pay (my) respects (17, 14)
dakyoo (-suru) compromise (20, Ref.)
dame /na/ no good, useless (17, Ad. 1)
danboo heater (13, Ref.)
dandan gradually (15, 2)
dansee male (15, 1)
dare who (4, Ad. 4)
dare demo anyone, everyone (12, 6)
dashimasu formal form of *dasu*
dasu /u/ to mail, put out (13, 2)
-date -base (19, 5)
  doru-date dollar base (19, 5)
  en-date yen base (19, Ref.)
de at, in (11, 2), by (5, 2)
  kuruma de by car (5, 2)
  kogitte de by a check (8, Ad. 3)
  sokutatsu de by express (13, Ad. 1)
dekakeru /-ru/ to go out (17, 13)
dekimasu formal form of *dekiru*
dekiru /-ru/ to be possible, to be able to do (12, 3)
  to complete (13, 1)
  (-suru) koto ga dekiru to be able to (do) (18, 3)
demasu formal form of *deru*
demo however (12, 7)
-demo
  dare demo anybody (12, 6)

— 284 —

denki electricity (13, Ref.)
denkiya electric appliance shop (11, Ref.)
denpoo telegram (13, Ref.)
denpyoo sales slip, voucher (19, Ref.)
densha local train (5, Ad. 4)
dentaku electric calculator (7, Ref.)
denwa (-suru) telephone (3, 1)
   denwa ga aru to have a telephone (call) (14, 1)
denwa-bangoo telephone number (3, 1)
denwa-choo telephone book (7, 1)
denwa o kakemasu formal form of *denwa o kakeru*
denwa o kakeru /-ru/ to place a telephone call (4, 1)
depaato department store (11, Ref.)
deru /-ru/ to answer (the phone) (14, 4)
   to come out, appear (15, Ad. 2)
   to graduate (16, Ad. 1)
deshita (coupla: formal past) was (2, 4)
deshoo to be probable (12, 5)
   muzukashii deshoo it's probably difficult (12, 5)
desu formal form of *da*
desu kara therefore (4, 6)
Detoroito Detroit (4, 2)
de wa well then (9, 12)
-do counter for number of times
   ichi-do one time (18, 12)
doa door (13, Ref.)
dochira which (10, 3)
   where (13, 5)
dochirasama Who? (3, 6)
Doitsu Germany (2, Ref.)
doitsugo German (language) (7, Ad. 5)
doko where (2, 6)
   doko ni (4, Ad. 1)
dokusen (-suru) monopoly (18, Ref.)
dokushin single (16, Ad. 1)
donata (respectful) who (14, Ad. 2)
donna what kind of—? (15, Ad. 1)
donogurai about how long? (5, 3)
dono which (14, Ad. 2)
dono hito which person (14, Ad. 2)
doo how (15, 3)
   doo shimashoo ka what/how shall we/I do? (15, 3)
doo itashimashite you're welcome (1, Ad. 1)
   that's OK (3, Ad. 3)
doomo thanks (1, 7)
   doomo arigatoo thank you very much (3, 3)
doomo somehow (20, Ad. 1)
doo shite how come?, why? (16, 9)
doozo please (1, 5)

doozo yoroshiku pleased to meet you. (1, 4)
dore which one (8, 3)
-doru counter for dollar (19, 4)
   ichiman-doru $10,000 (19, 4)
doyoobi Saturday (5, Ad. 3)

E

e /particle/ to (someplace) (5, 1)
eakon air conditioner (13, Ref.)
ee yes, that's right (1, 8)
eebun English text (12, 4)
eebun-taipu English typewriter (16, Ad. 2)
eeji-shinbun English newspaper (15, Ad. 2)
eekaiwa English conversation (15, Ad. 1)
eeto well (4, 4)
eego English (language) (7, 2)
eegyoo-bu sales and marketing department (2, 5)
eegyoo-buin staff member of the sales and marketing department (2, 5)
Ehu-oo-bii FOB (19, 8)
eki station (6, 2)
-en counter for yen (6, 6)
   kyuuhyaku-gojuu-en ¥950 (6, 6)
en-date yen base (19, Ref.)
Enu-shii robotto N.C. robot (17, 13)
enpitsu pencil (7, Ref.)
eru-sii L/C (Letter of Credit) (19, Ref.)
eyakon air conditioner (13, Ref.)

G

ga but (1, Ad. 4)
   and (15, 1)
gaikokujin foreigner (14, Ad. 2)
gaishi-kee of foreign origin (15, Ad. 2)
gaishutsu-chuu away from home or office (3, Ad. 4)
gaiyoo description, explanation (17, 10)
gakkoo school (11, Ref.)
gakusee student (16, Ad. 2)
gakushi Bachelor (univ. grad.) (15, Ref.)
ganbarimasu formal form of *ganbaru*
ganbaru /-u/ to hold out, do one's best (15, Ad. 2)
gansho written application (18, Ad. 2)
gareeji garage (13, Ref.)
gasu gas (13, Ref.)
-gatsu counter for naming the months of the year (6, 18)

-gawa —side (11, 11)
gekkyuu monthly salary (16, Ad. 3)
genka cost price (19, Ref.)
genkan entrance (13, Ref)
genki /na/ (in good) health (1, 7)
gensokuteki ni as a rule, in principle (19, 10)
getsuyoobi Monday (5, 1)
gijutsu technology (18, 10)
gijutsuteki /na/ technical (18, 10)
ginkooin bank clerk (15, Ad. 2)
go five (3, 2)
-go —language (7, Ad. 5)
go after
   sono go after that (18, 2)
goaisatsu (polite) respects, greeting (17, 14)
gochisoosama (deshita) it was a feast (10, Ad. 1)
go-gatsu May (6, 18)
gogo p.m. (4, Ad. 5)
gohan food, meal (9, Ref.)
   cooked rice (10, Ref.)
gokazoku (respectful) family (9, Ref.)
gokentoo (respectful) examination (17, 12)
gokuroosama deshita thanks for your trouble (16, 11)
gokyoodai (respectful) brothers/ sisters (9, Ref.)
gomen-kudasai excuse me (9, 14)
gookaku (-suru) passing (an exam) (15, Ref.)
gookee total (8, 13)
goro about (4, 4)
goryooshin (respectful) parents (9, Ref.)
goshootai (polite) invitation (14, 6)
goshujin husband (9, Ref.)
gotsugoo (respectful) conditions (14, 7)
goyooken (respectful) matter, business (17, 5)
gozaimasu formal form of *gozaru*
gozaru (polite) /-aru/ to have (8, 7)
   -de gozaru (polite) polite equivalent of the copula *desu* (16, 2)
gozen a.m. (4, Ad. 5)
gurai about (4, Ad. 6)
gutaiteki /na/ concrete (19, 13)
gyogyoo fisheries (17, Ref.)
gyuuniku beef (10, Ref.)
gyuunyuu milk (10, Ref.)

H

haado (uea) hardware (12, Ref.)
Haato-san Mr. Hart (14, Ad. 2)
hachi eight (3, 2)
hagaki postcard (13, Ad. 2)
haha mother (9, Ref.)

—285—

-hai counter for glassful/cupful (10, Ad. 1)
hai yes (3, 2)
haiken (-suru) having the honor to look it over (17, 11)
hairimasu formal form of *hairu*
hairu /-u/ to enter, join (15, Ad. 2)
haitatsu (-suru) delivery (19, Ref.)
hai-teku high-tech (17, Ref.)
haizara ash tray (8, Ad. 2)
hajimemashite How do you do? (1, 2)
hajime ni first of all (19, 3)
hajimemasu formal form of *hajimeru*
hajimeru /-ru/ to start (10, 15)
haki (-suru) abolition (20, Ref.)
hakushi doctor (Ph.D.) (15, Ref.)
hamu ham (10, 7)
-han
   ichi-ji han 1:30 (4, Ad. 5)
   hachi-jikan han 8 and a half hours (4, Ad. 6)
   ichi-nen han a year and a half (18, Ad. 2)
hanashi (-suru) talk, conversation (9, 5)
hanashiaimasu formal form of *hanashiau*
hanashiau /-u/ to discuss (19, 1)
hanashimasu formal form of *hanasu*
hanasu /-u/ to talk (9, 5)
hantai opposite (11, Ad. 3)
haru spring (16, 10)
hasami scissors (7, Ref.)
hatarakimasu formal form of *hataraku*
hataraku /-u/ to work (9, 2)
hatsumee (-suru) invention (18, Ref.)
hazu expectation (19, 12)
   kuru hazu to be expected to come (19, 12)
hee fence (13, Ref.)
hen area (11, 6)
   kono hen this area (11, 6)
henji reply (19, 12)
henkoo (-suru) change (20, Ref.)
heta /na/ poor (at ...) (17, 4)
heya room (13, Ref.)
hidari left (11, 11)
hidari-gawa left side (11, 11)
hiitaa heater (13, Ref.)
hikki-shiken written exam (15, Ref.)
hikooki airplane (5, Ad. 2)
hima /na/ free time, leisure (9, Ad. 1)
hiragana *hiragana* (12, 7)
hiru noon (5, 1)
hiru-gohan lunch (9, Ref.)
hisho secretary (2, Ad. 1)
hito person (2, Ad. 2)
hitori single (16, Ad. 1)

hitotsu one unit (8, Ad. 1)
hitsuyoo /na/ necessary (15, 11)
hoka ni (anything) else, besides (15, 11)
hoka no another (14, Ad. 2)
hoken insurance (19, 9)
Hokkaidoo-daigaku Hokkaido Univ. (16, Ad. 1)
hon book (7, Ad. 5)
-hon counter for long and cylindrical objects (10, 6)
hondana bookshelf (7, 2)
honjitsu (formal) today (14, Ad. 1)
honsha head office (2, Ad. 4)
hontoo ni really (3, 11)
hon'ya book store (11, Ref.)
hon'yaku (-suru) translation (16, Ad. 2)
hoo the alternative (10, 4)
   akai hoo the red one (10, 4)
   direction (11, Ad. 3)
   kochira no hoo in this direction (11, Ad. 3)
hoohoo way, procedure (18, Ad. 2)
hooritsu law (16, Ref.)
hoshii to want (18, 6)
hotchikisu stapler (7, Ref.)
huben /na/ inconvenient (7, 7)
Hukuoka Fukuoka (2, Ref.)
humajime /na/ insincere
-hun counter for minutes (4, Ad. 5)
hunabin sea mail (13, Ref.)
hune ship (5, Ad. 4)
Huransu France (2, Ref.)
huransugo French (language) (7, Ad. 5)
huransu-ryoori French food (9, Ref.)
hurikomi transferring to another bank account (19, Ref.)
huroba bathroom (13, Ref.)
hurui (is) old (7, 3)
husuma sliding door (13, Ref.)
huta-tsu two units (8, Ad. 1)
hutsuu ordinarily (19, 8)
huutoo envelope (7, Ref.)
huyu winter (16, Ad. 3)
hyaku 100 (3, Ad. 1)

I

ichi one (3, 2)
ichiban the most, the best (10, 12)
ichiman-en-satsu 10,000 yen note (8, Ad. 4)
igaku medical science (16, Ref.)
Igirisu U.K. (2, Ref.)
ii (is) good (7, 7)
ii desu ka is it all right? (8, Ad. 3)
iie no (1, Ad. 4)
iimasu formal form of *iu*

ikaga how? (6, Ad. 3)
ikaga desu ka would you care for— (6, Ad. 3)
   how about (8, 7)
   ikaga deshoo ka how would (it/that) be (12, Ad. 1)
ike pond (13, Ref.)
iken opinion (20, 3)
-iki -bound (11, 2)
   Asakusa-iki Asakusa-bound (11, 2)
ikimasu formal form of *iku*
ik-kai first floor (13, Ref.)
iku /-u/ to go (5, 1)
   umaku iku go well (19, Ref.)
ikura how much (6, 5)
ikutsu how many units (8, Ad. 1)
ima now (2, 5)
ima living room (13, 9)
imasu formal form of *iru*
imooto younger sister (9, Ref.)
imootosan (respectful) younger sister (9, Ref.)
inki /na/ gloomy (15, Ref.)
intaa-chenji interchange (11, Ref.)
irasshaimase welcome (8, 1)
irasshaimasu (respectful) formal form of *irassharu*
irassharu /-aru/ (respectful) to go (5, 2)
   to be, stay (5, 7)
   to come (5, Ad. 3)
irimasu formal form of *iru*
iroiro /na/ various (9, 5)
iron /na/ informal form of *iroiro na* (18, 3)
iru /-ru/ to be, exist (4, 2)
   kaite iru to be writing (13, 2)
iru /-u/ to need (7, 1)
ishoo design (18, Ref.)
isogashii (is) busy (14, 13)
issho ni together with (9, 5)
itadakimasu formal form of *itadaku*
itadaku /-u/ (modest) to receive, accept (6, 16)
Itaria Italy (2, Ref.)
itariago Italian (language) (7, Ad. 5)
itaria wain Italian wine (10,1)
itashimasu formal form of *itasu*
itasu /-u/ modest form of *suru* (16, 12)
   onegai-itasu /-u/ (modest) to request (16, 12)
itoko cousin (9, Ref.)
itsu when (5, Ad. 3)
itsu made until when? (6, Ad. 4)
itsumo always (14, 13)
itsu-tsu five units (8, Ad. 1)
iu /-u/ to say (14, 2)
izen formerly (2, 5)
izure some day, one of these days (17, 13)

J

jaa well (3, Ad. 4)
-ja arimasen be not—(1, Ad. 4)
-ja arimasen deshita was not—
(2, Ad. 3)
Jetoro JETRO (2, 1)
-ji counter for the time of day in
hours (4, 3)
jikan time (17, Ad. 1)
-jikan counter for number of hours
(4, 8)
jimuin clerk, office worker
(15, Ad. 1)
jimu-kiki office machine (11, 6)
jimusho office (2, 6)
jinja shrine (11, Ref.)
jinzai capable person (15, 4)
jinzai-ginkoo job bank (15, 4)
jisa time difference (4, 7)
jisho dictionary (7, Ad. 2)
jitsu wa actually, frankly (14, 8)
[lit. the truth is—]
jitsuyoo shin'an utility model
(18, Ref.)
jokyooju assistant professor
(16, Ref.)
-joo letter (1, 6)
shookaijoo a letter of introduction (1, 6)
shootaijoo invitation letter
(13, 1)
joogi ruler (7, Ref.)
jooho (-suru) concession (20, Ref.)
jooken conditions, terms (15, 6)
jooshi superior (official) (20, 7)
joozu fluent, skilled (17, 3)
josee female (15, 1)
junbi(-suru) preparation (13, 10)
juu ten (3, Ad. 1)
juubun /na/enough, fully (10, Ad. 1)
juusho address (13, 3)
juuyaku director (20, 7)

K

ka /particle/ (question) (1, 1)
ka /particle/ or (11, 4)
kabushikigaisha corporation, Ltd.
(8, 16)
kachoo section chief, manager (4, 1)
kado corner (11, 10)
kaerimasu formal form of *kaeru*
kaeru /-u/ to return, go back
(5, Ad. 4)
kagaku science (16, Ref.)
-ka counter for days (6, Ref.)
-kagetsu counter for number of
months (6, 19)
-kagetsu-bun
ni-kagetsu-bun two months
salary (16, Ad. 3)

-kai counter for naming/counting
floors
ik-kai first floor (13, Ref.)
kaigi meeting (10, 11)
kaikee bill, check (10, Ad. 3)
kaikeeshi accountant (18, Ref.)
kaimashoo ka shall (I/we) buy?
(7, 8)
kaimasu formal form of *kau*
kau /-u/ to buy (7, 4)
kaisha company (1, Ad. 3)
kaite buyer (19, 10)
kaitsuke buying (17, Ref.)
kaiyaku (-suru) cancellation
(20, Ref.)
kakaku price (19, 3)
kakarimasu formal form of *kakaru*
kakaru /-u/ to take (time) (5, 3)
jikan ga kakaru to take time
(17, Ad. 1)
kakimasu formal form of *kaku*
kakine hedge (13, Ref.)
kakitome registered mail (13, Ad. 2)
kaku /-u/ to write (8, 14)
to draw (11, Ad. 2)
kamaimasen do not matter (15, 9)
kami paper (7, Ref.)
Kanada Canada (2, Ref.)
kanai my wife (9, Ad. 1)
kanari considerably (20, 9)
kanji Chinese character (7, 12)
kangaemasu formal form of
kangaeru
kangaeru /-ru/ to think (19, 7)
Kankoku South Korea (2, Ref.)
kanojo she (2, Ad. 1)
kanpai toast, cheers (10, 16)
kantan /na/ easy, simple (12, 6)
kappatsu /na/ active, cheerful
(15, Ref.)
kara so (4, 2)
from (5, 4)
irasshatte kara after arriving
(10, 8)
kare he (2, 4)
kashikomarimashita certainly [lit. I
have respectfully obeyed] (10, 7)
kata (respectful) person (13, 5)
ano kata that person (13, 5)
(V. stem)+kata way (12, 5)
tsukaikata how to use (12, 5)
shikata how to do (14, 8)
yarikata way of doing (17, 2)
katakana *katakana* (12, 7)
katarogu catalogue (12, 11)
kau /-u/ to buy (7, 4)
Kawasaki Kawasaki (16, 3)
kawase money order (19, Ref.)
kawase reeto exchange rate
(19, Ref.)
kayoobi Tuesday (5, Ad. 4)
kazoku family (9, Ref.)
-kee —origin (15, Ad. 2)

gaishi-kee of foreign origin
(15, Ad. 2)
Amerika-kee of American origin
(15, Ad. 1)
kee'eegaku business administration
(16, 6)
keekan policeman (11, 7)
keeken experience (15, 8)
keeki business condition (17, Ad. 2)
keesatsu (sho) police station
(11, Ref.)
keeyaku (-suru) contract (20, Ad. 2)
keeyakusho contract document
(20, Ref.)
keezai economics (16, 5)
kekkoo /na/ fine (6, Ad. 3)
kekko desu to be fine (6, Ad. 3)
kekkon (-suru) getting married
(16, Ad. 1)
kekkonshiki wedding ceremony
(14, Ad. 4)
ken matter (14, 2)
paatii no ken matter of the party
(14, 2)
kenri right (18, Ref.)
kentoo (-suru) examination (17, 15)
kesa this morning (4, Ad. 4)
keshigomu eraser (7, Ref.)
kessai (-suru) settlement of account
(19, Ref.)
ketsuron conclusion (20, 2)
kibishii (is) severe, strict (19, 11)
kichoomen /na/ methodical,
punctual (15, Ref.)
kigyoo enterprise (15, Ad. 1)
kiiroi (is) yellow (8, Ad. 2)
kiji (newspaper/magazine) article
(16, Ad. 2)
kikai machine (12, 6)
kikai opportunity, chance (14, 9)
kikimasu formal form of *kiku*
kikoku (-suru) returning to one's
home country (16, 7)
kiku /-u/ to ask (11, 7)
to hear (19, 13)
kimasu formal form of *kuru* (5, 1)
kinben /na/ diligent (15, Ref.)
ki ni iru /-u/ to be satisfied with
(20, 2)
ki ni naru /-u/ to be anxious
(20, Ad. 1)
kinmujikan working hour (16, Ref.)
kinoo yesterday (4, Ad. 3)
kin'yoobi Friday (5, Ad. 7)
kirai /na/ displeasing (9, Ad. 4)
kiree /na/ pretty, clean (12, Ad. 4)
kisha train (for long distance)
(5, Ad. 4)
kishu type of machine (12, 8)
kissaten tea room, coffee shop
(10, Ref.)
Kita-Choosen North Korea (2, Ref.)
Kita-Kyuushuu Kita-Kyushu (2, Ref.)

—287—

kitanai (is) dirty (12, Ad. 4)
kitte stamp (13, Ad. 2)
  rokujuu-en (no) kitte 60-yen stamp (13, Ad. 2)
kochira this person (1, Ad. 3)
  here, this side (4, 4)
  this way (6, 13)
  this one (12, 2)
kochira koso it is I (who should say so) (10, 16)
kodomo child(ren) (9, Ref.)
kodomobeya children's room (13, Ref.)
kogata small size, compact (12, 2)
kogitte check (8, Ad. 3)
koko here (5, 1)
kokono-tsu nine units (8, Ad. 1)
kokusai-bu International Department (6, 10)
kokusai-denwa international call (4, Ad. 4)
kokusai-kooryuu-bu International Communication Department (2, 5)
komarimasu formal form of *komaru*
komaru /-u/ to be troubled (8, Ad. 3)
konban this evening (4, 6)
konban wa good evening (1, Ad. 1)
kondo this time (13, 9)
kongo from now on (10, 15)
kongo tomo also from now on (10, 15)
konnichi wa hello (1, 1)
kono this (one) (6, Ad. 2)
  kono kuruma this car (6, Ad. 2)
kono goro recently (10, 13)
kono hen this area (11, 6)
konsensasu consensus (20, 6)
konshuu this week (5, Ad. 2)
koobai kanri-bu Purchasing Administration Department (17, Ref.)
kooban police box (11, 7)
Koobe Kobe (2, Ref.)
koocha black tea (10, Ref.)
kooen park (11, Ad. 4)
koogaku engineering (16, Ref.)
koogyoo mining (17, Ref.)
koogyoo industry (17, Ref.)
koohii coffee (6, Ad. 3)
koojoo factory (11, Ad. 4)
kooki machine tool (17, Ref.)
kookoku advertisement (15, 4)
kookoo high school (15, Ref.)
kookuubin air mail (13, Ref.)
kookuushokan aerogram (13, Ref.)
koosaku-kikai machine tool (17, Ref.)
koosaten intersection (11, 9)
kooshi lecturer (16, 8)
kooshin (-suru) renewal (20, Ref.)

kooshoo negotiation (20, 1)
koosoku-dooro highway (11, Ref.)
kooza (bank) account (19, Ref.)
kore this (1, 4)
koto thing, fact, matter (17, 1)
  Buraun-san no koto Mr. Brown's background (17, 1)
  (...suru) koto ni suru to decide (to do) (19, 7)
  koto wa nai there is nothing/no matter (20, 12)
kotoshi this year (6, Ad. 7)
kotozuke message (14, Ad. 3)
koyoo-hoken unemployment insurance (16, Ref.)
kozutsumi parcel (13, Ref.)
ku nine (3, Ad. 1)
-ku ward (13, 6)
  Minato-ku Minato ward (13, 6)
kudamono fruit (10, Ref.)
kudasai please give— (8, 8)
  misete kudasai please show me (8, 2)
kudasaimasen ka won't you—? (12, 1)
«name» kun Mr. «name» (10, 10)
kurejitto-kaado credit card (8, Ad. 3)
kuremasu formal form of *kureru*
kureru /-ru/ to give (16, Ad. 3)
  hanashite kureru to inform for my/your benefit (17, 1)
kurippu clip (7, Ref.)
kuroi (is) black (8, Ad. 2)
kuru /irr./ to come (5, 1)
  itte kuru to go and come back (13, Ad. 2)
kuruma car (5, 2)
kusuriya drugstore (11, Ref.)
kuwashii (is) detailed (8, 6)
kyabinetto cabinet (7, 6)
kyaku guest, customer (10, 8)
kyonen last year (6, Ad. 7)
kyoo today (4, Ad. 2)
kyoodai brothers/sisters (9, Ref.)
kyooju professor (16, Ref.)
kyookai church (11, Ad. 4)
Kyooto Kyoto (2, Ref.)
kyuu nine (3, Ad. 1)
kyuujin-kookoku help wanted ad (15, Ad. 2)
kyuuryoo salary (15, 10)

M————————

machimasu formal form of *matsu*
mada /+negative/ not yet (9, Ad. 2)
madamada still (17, 4)
made to (5, 4)
  dekiru made until (someone/something) can (do) (18, 9)
made ni by (5, Ad. 6)

mae before, ago (4, Ad. 5)
  front (11, Ad. 1)
  ginkoo no mae in front of the bank (11, Ad. 1)
  mae no kaisha previous company (16, Ad. 3)
  sukoshi mae ni a few minutes before (14, 1)
magarimasu formal form of *magaru*
magaru /-u/ to turn (11, 9)
mago grandchild (9, Ref.)
maido every time (8, 17)
mai-kon micro-computer, my computer (12, Ref.)
mainichi everyday (4, Ad. 6)
mairimasu formal form of *mairu*
mairu /-u/ (modest) to come (6, 12)
majime /na/ steady, serious (15, 9)
man ten thousand (3, Ad. 1)
manshon apartment (usually a rather good one) (11, Ad. 4)
Marunouchi a place name in Tokyo (2, Ad. 4)
-mashoo let's— (7, Ad. 4)
  ikimashoo let's go (7, Ad. 4)
-mashoo ka shall (I/We)—? (7, 8)
  kaimashoo ka shall (I) buy? (7, 8)
massugu straight (11, 9)
mata again (8, 17)
matsu /-u/ to wait (18, 13)
mazu first of all (20, 5)
-me suffix for ordinal number (11, 9)
  ni-ban-me the second (11, 9)
mee niece (9, Ref.)
meegosan (respectful) niece (9, Ref.)
meekaa maker (17, 7)
meesaisho detailed statement (19, Ref.)
meeshi business card (1, 4)
Mein Main (14, Ad. 3)
memo-choo memo pad (7, Ref.)
mensetsu (-suru) interview (15, 11)
mensetsu-shiken oral exam (15, Ref.)
michi way, street, road (11, 8)
migi right (11, 9)
mihon sample (12, Ad. 4)
mimasu formal form of *miru*
Minato-ku Minato ward (13, 6)
mini-kon mini computer (12, Ref.)
minna everything, everyone (12, Ad. 4)
miru /-ru/ to see (15, Ad. 2)
  tsukatte miru to try using (12, 8)
miruku milk (10, Ref.)
mise store (10, 1)
misemasu formal form of *miseru*
miseru /-ru/ to show (8, 2)
Mitaka Mitaka (11, 4)
mitsukarimasu formal form of *mitsukaru*
mitsukaru /-u/ to be found (15, Ad. 1)

—288—

mit-tsu three units (8, Ad. 1)
mizu cold water (10, Ref.)
mo (particle) also (7, 8)
«item A» mo «item B» mo both «item A» and «item B» (10, 4)
mochimasu formal form of *motsu*
mochiron of course (10, Ad. 2)
mokuyoobi Thursday (5, Ad. 7)
mon gate (13, Ref.)
mondai problem (12, 8)
mono thing(s) (concrete) (17, 12)
　subarashii mono wonderful thing(s) (concrete) (17, 12)
mono person (3, 7)
moo already (9, 3)
moo one more (10, 8)
　moo hitori one more person (10, 8)
　moo ip-pai one more glassful/cupful (10, Ad. 1)
　moo ichi-do one more time (18, 12)
moraimasu formal form of *morau*
morau /-u/ to receive (16, 6)
　oshiete moraimasu to have (someone) teach (17, 2)
Morugan-ginkoo Morgan Bank (14, Ad. 2)
moshimoshi hello (3, 9)
motsu /-u/ to have, bring (10, 9)
motte kimasu formal form of *motte kuru*
motte kuru /irr./ to bring (16, 1)
motte mairu /-u/ (modest) to bring (16, 2)
motto more (7, 9)
muku /-u/to be suited for (18, 3)
musuko son (9, Ref.)
musukosan (respectful) son (9, Ref.)
musume daughter (9, Ref.)
musumesan (respectful) daughter (9, Ref.)
mut-tsu six units (8, Ad. 1)
muzukashii (is) difficult (7, Ad. 5)

N_____

n contraction of *no* (9, 5)
　ohanashi shitai n desu it is the matter of wanting to talk (9, 5)
　tsukatte iru n desu it is the matter of using (18, 4)
Nagoya Nagoya (2, Ref.)
nai to be not
　iranai do(es) not need (19, Ad. 2)
　shinpai shinai de without worrying (20, 11)
naisen (telephone) extension (3, Ad. 2)
naka inside (7, 6)
nakanaka fairly (9, 8)

nakanaka /+ negative/ (not) easily (15, Ad. 1)
Nakano Nakano (11, 4)
namae name (8, 15)
nan contraction of *nani* (3, Ad. 2)
nana seven (3, Ad. 1)
nana-tsu seven units (8, Ad. 1)
nan-ban what number (3, Ad. 2)
nan de by means of what (5, Ad. 1)
nan-gai what floor? (13, Ref.)
nani what? (10, 1)
nani-go what language? (7, Ad. 5)
nani-iki train for where (11, 3)
nani ka something (10, 6)
　nani ka atarashii koto something new (20, 5)
nan-ji what time? (4, 3)
　nan-ji ni at what time (5, 5)
　nan-ji kara from what time (5, Ad. 5)
　nan-ji made till what time (5, Ad. 5)
nan-jikan how many hours? (4, 7)
nan-nen what year?
　how many years? (6, Ad. 7)
nan-nichi what date?
　How many days? (6, Ad. 6)
nan no hon what book (12, Ad. 5)
nan-yoobi what day of the week? (5, Ad. 7)
naremasu formal form of *nareru*
nareru /-ru/ to get used to (13, 11)
narete iru /-ru/ to be used (13, 11)
narimasu formal form of naru
naru /-u/ to become (15, 2)
　isogashiku naru /-u/ to become busy (15, 2)
　«N» + ni + naru to become «N» (15, Ad. 1)
natsu summer (16, Ad. 3)
naze why? (16, 9)
ne Isn't that right? (sentence particle for confirmation) (5, Ad. 2)
nebiki (-suru) reduction in price (12, Ad. 2)
nedan price (12, 9)
nemawashi laying the groundwork (20, 5)
-nen counter for naming and counting years (6, Ad. 4)
nenkin pension (16, Ref.)
nenkoo-joretsu-seedo seniority system (16, Ref.)
ni in, at, on (place) (4, 2)
　to (4, 1)
　at (time) (5, 5)
　for (9, Ad. 1)
　yuushoku ni for dinner (9, Ad. 1)
ni two (3, 2)
-nichi counter for days (6, 6)
nichiyoobi Sunday (5, Ad. 2)
Nihon Japan (2, Ad. 4)
Nihonbashi Nihonbashi (11, 2)

nihon-bun Japanese text (12, 4)
nihongo Japanese (language) (7, 2)
nihonma Japanese-style room (13, Ref.)
nihon-ryoori Japanese food (9, Ad. 4)
nihon-see Japanese-made (12, Ad. 3)
Nikkeeren Nikkeiren (5, 1)
niku meat (10, Ad. 2)
nikuya meat store (11, Ref.)
-nin counter for people (10, Ad. 3)
-ninmae counter for portions of food (10, Ad. 3)
Nippon Japan (2, Ad. 4)
Nissan Nissan Motor Co., Ltd. (20, 1)
niwa garden (13, 8)
no (particle) of, from, located in, related to (1, 2)
　go-hachi-ni no go-go-ichi-ichi 582-5511 (telephone number) (3, 2)
　paatii no shootai invitation to a party (14, 6)
　one (7, 2)
　eego no English one (7, 2)
　atarashii no new one (7, 3)
　kaisha no company's (8, 14)
　tokkyo o toru no obtaining a patent (18, Ad. 1)
no de because (17, 4)
　heta desu no de because (I) am poor (17, 4)
nomimasu formal form of *nomu*
nomimono drink(s) (10, 1)
nomu /-u/ to drink (10, 13)
noogyoo agriculture (17, Ref.)
noohinsho statement of delivery (19, Ref.)
nooki date/time of delivery (19, Ref.)
nori glue, paste (7, Ref.)
norikaemasu formal form of *norikaeru*
norikaeru /-ru/ to transfer (11, 3)
norimasu formal form of *noru*
noru /-u/ to get on, take (a vehicle) (11, 3)
nozomimasu formal form of *nozomu*
nozomu /-u/ to hope for, prefer (19, 6)
nyuusha-shiken company's entrance exam (15, Ref.)
Nyuuyooku N.Y. (2, Ref.)

O_____

oaiso bill, check (10, Ad. 3)
oba aunt (9, Ref.)
obaasama (respectful) grandmother (9, Ref.)
obaasan (respectful) grandmother (9, Ref.)
obasama (respectful) aunt (9, Ref.)

obasan (respectful) aunt (9, Ref.)
ocha (polite) tea (6, 15)
odenwa kudasai give (me) a call (3, Ad. 5)
ogenki /na/ (respectful) (in good) health (1, 7)
Ohaio Ohio (17, 10)
ohanashi (-suru) (polite) talk (9, 5)
ohayoo (gozaimasu) good morning (1, Ad. 1)
ohima (polite) free time (9, Ad. 1)
ohiru lunch [lit. noonday] (9, 5)
ohu-kon office computer (12, Ref.)
oi nephew (9, Ref.)
oigosan (respectful) nephew (9, Ref.)
oishii (is) delicious (10, Ad. 1)
oisogashii (respectful) (is) busy (4, 13)
oitokosan (respectful) cousin (9, Ref.)
oji uncle (9, Ref)
ojiisama (respectful) grandfather (9, Ref.)
ojiisan (respectful) grandfather (9, Ref.)
ojisama (respectful) uncle (9, Ref.)
ojisan (respectful) uncle (9, Ref.)
ojoosan (respectful) daughter (9, Ref.)
ojoozu (respectful) fluent, skilled (17, 3)
okaasama (respectful) mother (9, Ref.)
okaasan (respectful) mother (9, Ref.)
okagesama de thank you (for asking) (1, Ad. 2)
okamai naku don't bother (6, Ad. 3)
okashi cake, sweets (10, Ref.)
okimasu formal form of *oku*
okosan (respectful) child(ren) (9, Ref.)
okotozuke (respectful) message (14, Ad. 3)
oku /-u/
  kentoo-shite okimasu to examine for future reference (17, 15)
okurimasu formal form of *okuru*
okuru /-u/ to send (13, Ad. 1)
okusama (respectful) your wife (9, Ad. 1)
okusan your wife (9, Ad. 1)
okyakusama (polite) guest, customer (10, 8)
omachi kudasai please wait (3, 8)
omachi (-suru) (polite) to wait (18, 13)
omagosan (respectful) grandchild (9, Ref.)
omatase-shimashita thank you for your waiting (10, 14)
omedetoo congratulations (20, Ad. 2)

ome ni kakarimasu formal form of *ome ni kakaru*
ome ni kakaru /-u/ to meet (polite) (9, 12)
omoikirimasu formal form of *omoikiru*
omoikiru /-u/ to resolve (16, 10)
omoikitte resolutely, boldly (16, 10)
omoimasu formal form of *omou*
omo ni mainly (18, 5)
omoshiroi (is) interesting (12, Ad. 5)
omochi (-suru) (respectful) to have, bring (10, 9)
omou /-u/ to think (15, 4)
onamae (respectful) name (8, 15)
onedan (polite) price (12, 19)
oneesama (respectful) older sister (9, Ref.)
oneesan (respectful) older sister (9, Ref.)
onegai (-suru) (polite) may I speak to [lit. please] (3, 5) please do so (7, 12)
oniisama (respectful) older brother (9, Ref.)
oniisan (respectful) older brother (9, Ref.)
onna female (15, 1)
onsha (respectful) your company (18, 3)
oobo (-suru) application (15, Ad. 2)
oobosha applicant (15, Ad. 2)
oodoburu hors d'oeuvres (10, 7)
Oo-Ee office automation (12, Ref.)
ooi (is) many (15, Ad. 2)
ookii (is) big (7, 7)
Oosaka Osaka (2, Ref.)
oosetsuma reception room (13, Ref.)
Oosutoraria Australia (2, Ref.)
Ootemachi Otemachi (11, 1)
Oranda Holland (2, Ref.)
orimasu formal form of *oru*
oru /-u/ (modest) to be (6, Ad. 1)
  sunde oru to be living (16, 4)
osake (polite) Japanese *sake* (10, 13)
oshiemasu formal form of *oshieru*
oshieru /-ru/ to teach (11, 8)
oshiriai (respectful) acquaintance (2, 1)
osoi (is) late (10, 10)
osoreirimasu (modest) thank you [lit. I'm overwhelmed.] (6, 14)
osshaimasu formal form of *ossharu*
ossharu /-aru/ (respectful) to say (14, 3)
osuki (respectful) liking (10, 1)
  osuki desu ka (respectful) do you like? (10, 1)
otaku your house (3, Ad. 3)
otearai (polite) toilet (11, Ref.)
otera (polite) temple (11, Ref.)
otetsudai (-suru) to help (polite) (13, 12)

otoko male (15, 1)
otoosan (respectful) father (9, Ref.)
otooto younger brother (9, Ref.)
otootosan (respectful) younger brother (9, Ref.)
ototoi day before yesterday (5, Ad. 1)
otsumami (polite) snack (to go with drinks) (10, 6)
otsuri (polite) change (6, 8)
owarimasu formal form of *owaru*
owaru /-u/ to finish (10, 11)
oyakusoku (respectful) appointment (6, Ad. 5)
oyasumi nasai good night (1, Ad. 1)
oyoso approximately (18, Ad. 2)
oyu hot water (10, Ref.)

P

paasento percent (19, Ad. 1)
  hachi-paasento 8% (19, Ad. 1)
paatii party (13, 8)
-pai counter for glassful/cupful (10, Ad. 1)
pan bread (10, Ref.)
Pari Paris (2, Ref.)
paso-kon personal computer (12, Ref.)
Pekin Beijing (2, Ref.)
pen pen (7, Ref.)
Pii-and-shii P & C (Ltd.) (1, 3)
poke-kon pocket computer (12, Ref.)
-pon counter for long and cylindrical objects (10, 6)
-pun counter for minutes (4, Ad. 5)
puroguramu program (15, Ref.)

R

rainen next year (6, Ad. 7)
raishuu next week (5, Ad. 4)
ree zero (3, Ad. 1)
rekishi history (12, Ad. 5)
renraku (-suru) contact (15, 5)
resutoran restaurant (9, 8)
-ri counter for people (10, 8)
ringi-see the system of circulating proposals for general approval (20, Ref.)
  rirekisho personal history (16, 1)
rishi interest (19, Ad. 1)
robotto robot (17, 7)
roku six (3, Ad. 1)
Rondon London (2, Ref.)
rooka corridor (13, Ref.)
Rooma Rome (2, Ref.)
roomaji Roman alphabet (12, 8)
Roppongi Roppongi (13, 6)
roshiago Russian (language) (7, Ad. 5)
Rosu L.A. (2, Ref.)
rusu out of home (3, Ad. 5)

ryokoo (-suru) travel (14, Ad. 4)
ryoogae (-suru) money exchange (19, Ref.)
ryookinjo tollgate (11, Ref.)
ryoori (-suru) cooking, cuisine (9, 8)
ryooriya restaurant (9, 8)
ryooshin parents (9, Ref.)
ryooshuusho receipt (8, 14)
ryuugaku (-suru) studying abroad (16, 5)

S

saa well (18, Ad. 1)
saabisugyoo service industry (17, Ref.)
sagashimasu formal form of *sagasu*
sagasu /-u/ to look for, seek (15, Ad. 1)
saiyoo (-suru) acceptance, employment (15, Ref.)
sakana fish (10, Ad. 2)
sakanaya fish store (11, Ref.)
sake Japanese *sake* (10,13)
saki from now, future (6, Ad. 4)
«name» -sama (respectful) Mr./Ms. «name» (3, 5)
san three (3, Ad. 1)
«name» -san Mr./Ms. «name» (1, 1)
san-gai third floor (13, Ref.)
sangyoo industry (17, 8)
sankoo shiryoo reference (18, Ref.)
Sapporo Sapporo (2, Ref.)
sashimi raw fish (10, Ad. 2)
sassoku right away (15, 5)
-satsu —note (8, Ad. 4)
   ichiman-en-satsu 10,000 yen note (8, Ad. 4)
sayoonara good-bye (1, Ad. 1)
-see —made
   nihon-see Japanese-made (12, Ad. 3)
seehin manufactured goods (17, 11)
seejigaku political science (16, Ref.)
seekatsu life (13, 11)
seekyuusho invoice (19, Ref.)
seeritsu (-suru) conclusion (20, Ref.)
sekai world (16, 10)
seki o hazushite imasu (he) has just stepped out for a moment (3, Ad. 5)
sekkyokuteki /na/ positive, constructive (15, Ref.)
sen thousand (3, Ad. 1)
Sendai Sendai (2, Ref.)
senjitsu some days ago, the other day (14, Ad. 2)
senmon specialty (16, 5)
senmongakkoo professional/technical school (15, Ref.)
senmonka specialist (18, 11)

sensee teacher (16, 7)
senshuu last week (5, Ad. 3)
sentan-gijutsu high-tech (17, Ref.)
senyaku previous engagement (14, 8)
seroteepu Scotch tape (7, Ref.)
setsumee (-suru) explanation (12, 1)
setsumeesho description, explanation (17, 10)
settoku (-suru) persuasion (20, 7)
shaapupen mechanical pencil (7, Ref.)
shachoo the president (4, 2)
shain company employee (2, 4)
shakaigaku sociology (16, Ref.)
shakai-hoken social insurance (16, Ref.)
shanai within the company (18, 12)
shi four (3, Ad. 1)
shibaraku for a long time (3, 10)
shichi seven (3, Ad. 1)
Shidonii Sydney (2, Ref.)
shigoto (-suru) work, job (9, 1)
shiharai payment (19, 5)
Shii-bii-emu CBM (company name) (2, 4)
shijoo market (17, Ref.)
shika /+ neg./ nothing but, only (12, 12)
Shikago Chicago (2, Ad. 4)
shikashi but, however (15, Ad. 2)
shikata way of doing (14, 9)
   shikata ga nai it can't be helped (14, 9)
shiken (-suru) test (15, Ref.)
shiken o ukemasu formal form of *shiken o ukeru*
shiken o ukeru /-ru/ to take a test (15, Ref.)
shikiri-jooken trade term, invoice term (19, 7)
shimasu /irr./ formal form of *suru*
shin lead (7, Ref.)
shinamono goods, article (12, Ad. 4)
shinbun newspaper (7, Ad. 1)
shinbun-kookoku newspaper advertisement (15, 4)
shinbunsha newspaper company (15, 5)
shingoo signal (11, Ref.)
Shinkansen Shinkansen Line (5, Ad. 2)
shinkeeshitsu /na/ nervous, sensitive (15, Ref.)
shinpai (-suru) worry (20, 12)
shinrigaku psychology (16, Ref.)
shinsee (-suru) application (18, Ad. 2)
shinseehin new products (17, 12)
shinseki relatives (16, 4)
shinshitsu bedroom (13, Ref.)
shin'yoo (-suru) trust (20, Ad. 1)
shin'yoojoo L/C (letter of credit) (19, Ref.)

shiriai acquaintance (2, 1)
shirimasu formal form of *shiru*
shiro (noun) white (10, 3)
shiroi (is) white (8, 4)
shiru /-u/ to come to know (18, Ad. 1)
shiryoo data, materials (18, 6)
shisha branch office (2, Ad. 4)
shita under (7, Ad. 2)
   zasshi no shita under the magazine (7, Ad. 2)
shitsuree excuse me (1, Ad. 4)
   shitsuree desu ga excuse me, but— (1, Ad. 4)
   shitsuree-shimasu good-bye (1, Ad. 1)
shizuka /na/ quiet (11, Ad. 4)
shokudoo dining room (10, Ref.)
shokuin staff (2, Ad. 2)
shoobai business (17, 2)
shooboosho fire station (11, Ref.)
shoodan business talk (17, Ad. 1)
shoogakkoo elementary school (15, Ref.)
shoogyoo commerce (17, Ref.)
shoohin article(s)/good(s) for sale (17, Ref.)
shoohyoo trademark (18, Ref.)
shookai (-suru) introduction (1, 6)
shookaijoo letter of introduction (1, 6)
shookyokuteki /na/ negative, passive (15, Ref.)
shooruumu showroom (7, 1)
shooshoo a little, for a while (3, 8)
shootaijoo invitation card (13, 1)
shootai (-suru) invitation (9, 10)
Shoowa Showa (6, Ad. 7)
shorui document (13, Ad. 2)
shosai study room (13, Ref.)
shujin husband (9, Ref.)
shusseki (-suru) attend (14, 12)
shutchoo (-suru) business trip (14, Ad. 4)
shuumatsu weekend (13, 14)
shuusee (-suru) modification (20, Ref.)
shuushi Master (M.A., M.S.) (15, Ref.)
shuushoku (-suru) /-irr./ obtaining/starting employment (15, Ref.)
shuushin-koyoo-seedo lifetime employment system (16, Ref.)
soba vicinity (11, Ad. 4)
soba noodle (10, Ref.)
sobaya *soba* shop (10, Ref.)
Sobieto USSR (2, Ref.)
sobo grandmother (9, Ref.)
sochira the person addressed (3, Ad. 4)
   that way (near the hearer) (11, Ad. 3)
   that one, those (near the hearer) (12, Ad. 2)

—291—

soemasu formal form of *soeru*
soeru /-ru/ to attach (18, Ad. 2)
sohu grandfather (9, Ref.)
sohuto (uea) software (12, Ref.)
soko there, that place (5, Ad. 4)
sokutatsu express delivery service (13, Ad. 1)
sonna such (15, Ad. 1)
   sonna tokoro such a place (15, Ad. 1)
sono that (one) (6, Ad. 2)
   sono kuruma that car (6, Ad. 2)
   sono go after that (18, 2)
soo so (1, 9)
   soo suru do so (13, 15)
   soo desu it is said (19, 5)
   soo desu nee let me see (18, Ad. 2)
soodan (-suru) consulting, talk (12, 11)
soodairiten general agent (17, Ref.)
sooryoo shipping charge (19, Ad. 2)
sore dake only that (15, 12)
sore de wa in that case (13, 14)
sore ga well [lit. that is] (14, 8)
sore kara and then (7, 5)
sotsugyoo (-suru) graduation (15, 7)
Souru Seoul (2, Ref.)
subarashii (is) wonderful (17, 12)
sugi after (4, Ad. 5)
sugu soon, immediately, right now (6, 12)
   sugu soba immediate vicinity (11, Ad. 4)
suidoo water service (13, Ref.)
suiyoobi Wednesday (5, Ad. 7)
suki desu to like (9, 9)
sukiyaki sukiyaki (10, Ref.)
sukoshi a few, a little (14, 1)
sukunai (is) few, little (13, 9)
sukunaku tomo at least (18, Ad. 2)
sumai home, dwelling (16, 3)
sumimasen ga— sorry to bother you, but— (11, 1)
sumimasu formal form of *sumu*
sumu /-u/ to live (16, 4)
supeingo Spanish (language) (7, Ad. 5)
suru /irr/ to do (13, 8)
   denwa o suru to place a phone call (4, 6)
   doo shimashoo ka what/how shall we/I do? (15, 3)
   kooshi o suru to work as a lec-turer (16, 8)
   tesuto o suru to give a test (16, Ad. 1)
sushiya *sushi* shop (10, Ref.)
Sutanhoodo Stanford (16, 5)
sutoobu stove (13, Ref.)
sutahhu staff (12, 11)
suupaa super market (11, Ref.)

T

tabako cigarette, tobacco (6, Ad. 3)
tabemasu formal form of *taberu*
taberu /-ru/ to eat (9, Ad. 4)
tabun probably (17, Ad. 1)
(V. stem) tai to want to (do) (9, 5)
   ohanashi-shitai to want to talk (9, 5)
taihen /na/ very, awfully (17, 12)
taipu typewriter (16, Ad. 2)
taipu (-suru) typing (13, Ad. 1)
taipuraitaa typewriter (7, Ref.)
taisetsu /na/ important (13, Ad. 2)
taishikan embassy (11, Ad. 2)
taishoku (-suru) retirement, leaving employment (15, Ref.)
taishokukin retirement allowance, severance pay (16, Ref.)
taitee usually (4, Ad. 6)
Takada-san Mr./Mrs./Ms. Takada (2, 1)
takai (is) expensive (12, Ad. 1)
takusan many (8, Ad. 2)
takushii taxi (5, 3)
tamago egg (10, Ref.)
tame
   tame ni «verb» «verb» for the purpose of (20, 8)
   tame no for the purpose of (20, 6)
   konsensasu no tame no junbi preparation for consensus (20, 6)
tandai junior college (15, Ad. 1)
tanomimasu formal form of *tanomu*
tanomu /-u/ to ask, order (10, 8)
tanoshii (is) happy, gay (9, 11)
tantoosha person in charge (20, 7)
tatene denomination, currency (19, 7)
(t)te quotation
   nan te iu what does (someone) say? (14, 2)
teate allowance (15, 10)
tedori take-home pay (16, Ad. 3)
teeka fixed price (19, Ref.)
tegami letter (13, Ad. 1)
-teki —like (20, 10)
   Nihon-teki Japanese-like (20, 10)
Tekisasu Texas (17, 10)
ten point (20, 10)
tenpura tempura (10, Ad. 3)
tenpuraya tempura shop (10, Ref.)
tenshoku (-suru) changing one's occupation (15, Ref.)
tera temple (11, Ref.)
terekkusu telex (19, 12)
tesuto test (16, Ad. 2)
tesuuryoo handling charge (19, Ad. 2)
tetsudaimasu formal form of *tetsudau*
tetsudau /-u/ to assist (13, 12)
to door (13, Ref.)

-to Metropolitan District (13, 6)
   Tokyoo to Tokyo Metropolitan District (13, 6)
to with (6, 10)
   and (7, 11)
   quotative (14, 2)
   or (10, 3)
   shiro to aka to white or red (10, 3)
toki time (15, 11)
   mensetsu no toki ni at the time of interview (15, 11)
   toki ni wa at the time when (20, 5)
tokkahin bargain-priced article (12, Ad. 2)
tokkyo patent (18, 8)
Tokkyochoo Patent Office (18, Ad. 2)
tokkyoryoo patent fee (18, Ref.)
tokoro location, place (11, Ad. 4)
tokoro time (14, Ad. 1)
   oisogashii tokoro a busy time (14, Ad. 1)
tokoro de by the way (2, 1)
toku ni especially (10, Ad. 2)
tokui /na/ one's strong point (15, Ad. 1)
tomemasu formal form of *tomeru*
tomeru /-ru/ to stop (11, Ad. 1)
tomodachi friend (2, 3)
tonari next door (11, 11)
tondemo arimasen not at all (14, 7)
tondemo gozaimasen (respectful) not at all (14, 7)
tonkatsu pork cutlet (10, Ad. 3)
too ten units (8, Ad. 1)
tooi (is) far (13, 7)
toojitsu (on) that day (14, Ad. 4)
Tookyoo Tokyo (6, 2)
Tookyoo-eki Tokyo Station (6, 2)
Tookyoo-kiki Tokyo Machinery, Ltd. (11, 8)
Tookyoo-to Tokyo Metropolitan District (13, 6)
toori street, road (11, 8)
tooroku (-suru) registration (18, Ref.)
toosha our company (9, 8)
Toozaisen Tozai Line (11, 2)
Toranomon Toranomon (2, 7)
torihiki transactions, business (17, Ad. 1)
torimasu formal form of *toru*
toriniku fowl, chicken (10, Ref.)
Toronto Toronto (2, Ref.)
toru /-u/ to take out, obtain (18, 8)
toshi age (15, 7)
totemo very (1, 8)
-tsu counter for units (8, Ad. 1)
tsugi next (9, 3)
tsugoo conditions (14, 7)
(ni) tsuite concerning, about (12, 1)
   waapuro ni tsuite about a word processor (12, 1)

— 292 —

tsukaikata way of using (12, 5)
tsukaimasu formal form of *tsukau*
tsukau /-u/ to use (12, 5)
tsuke charge account (19, Ref.)
tsukiatari end of a street (11, Ad. 1)
tsukue desk (7, Ad. 1)
tsukurimasu formal form of *tsukuru*
tsukuru /-u/ to make, compose (12, 8)
tsumami snack (to go with drinks) (10, 6)
tsumaranai (is) boring (12, Ad. 5)
tsumori intention (19, 12)
　okuru tsumori desu to intend to send (19, 12)
tsuri change (6, 8)
tsutaemasu formal form of *tsutaeru*
tsutaeru /-ru/ to report, convey (14, Ad. 3)
tsutomemasu formal form of *tsutomeru*
tsutomeru /-ru/ to work (for) (15, Ad. 1)
Tsuusan-shoo MITI (7, 11)

U

uchi my house (3, Ad. 3)
uchi de among (10, Ad. 2)
uchi no our (9, 8)
　uchi no kaisha our company (9, 8)
udon noodle (10, Ref.)
ue on (7, Ad. 1)
　tsukue no ue on the desk (7, Ad. 1)
uisukii whisky (10, 13)
ukagaimasu formal form of *ukagau*
ukagau /-u/ (modest) to visit, call (9, 7)
　to ask, inquire (11, 6)
　chotto ukagaimasu ga excuse me, but (11, 6)
ukemasu formal form of *ukeru*
ukeru /-ru/ to receive, take (15, Ref.)
　shiken o ukeru to take a test (15, Ref.)
umaku iku /-u/ go well (20, 1)
ura back side (11, Ad. 3)
uridashimasu formal form of *uridasu*
uridasu /-u/ to start selling (19, Ad. 2)
urikomi canvassing for selling (17, Ref.)
urimasu formal form of *uru*
urite seller (19, Ref.)
uru /-u/ to sell (17, Ad. 2)
ushiro back, rear, behind (11, Ad. 4)

W

waado word
　yonjuu waado 40 words (16, Ad. 2)
waapuro word processor (7, 1)
wabun Japanese text (12, 4)
wain wine (10, 1)
　Itaria-wain Italian wine (10, 1)
wakarimasu formal form of *wakaru*
wakaru /-u/ to know, understand (3, 1)
-wari counter for percentages in units of ten (12, Ad. 2)
　ni-wari 20% (12, Ad. 2)
waribiki (-suru) discount (19, Ref.)
wari to comparatively (12, 9)
washoku Japanese food (9, Ref.)
watakushi I (1, 4)
　watakushi no my (1, 4)
watakushidomo we, our company (17, 6)

Y

ya and the like (15, 10)
yakamashii (is) noisy (11, Ad. 4)
yakitori yakitori (10, Ref.)
yakusoku appointment (6, 10)
yaku approximately (18, Ad. 2)
yamemasu formal form of *yameru*
yameru /-ru/ to quit, resign (16, 9)
yaoya vegetable store (11, Ref.)
yasai vegetable (10, Ad. 2)
yarikata way of doing (17, 2)
yasashii (is) easy (7, Ad. 5)
yasui (is) cheap (12, Ad. 1)
yatoimasu formal form of *yatou*
yatou /-u/ to hire, employ (15, 1)
yatto finally (20, Ad. 2)
yat-tsu eight units (8, Ad. 1)
yo /sentence particle of emphasis/ (4, 2)
yobu to call for (18, 11)
yokin (-suru) deposit (19, Ref.)
Yokohama Yokohama (2, Ref.)
yoku (adv. of *ii/yoi*) frequently, often (10, 13)
　well, a great deal (12, Ad. 5)
yoku irasshaimashita welcome! (6, 13)
yomimasu formal form of *yomu*
yomu /-u/ to read (12, 13)
yon four (3, Ad. 1)
-yoo for the purpose of (17, 8)
　sangyoo-yoo for industry use (17, 8)
yoo da (it) seems (to be)—(20, 2)
　kini itte iru yoo da (he) seems to be satisfied with (20, 2)
yoo /na/ like, similar to (20, 9)
yooken matter, business (17, 5)

yooki /na/ lively, joyful (15, Ref.)
yooshoku western food (9, Ref.)
yori more than (10, Ad. 2)
yorokobimasu formal form of *yorokobu*
yorokobu /-u/ to be delighted (13, 13)
yorokonde gladly (14, 3)
yoroshii /-ku/ (is) good, fine, all right
　doozo yoroshiku pleased to meet you (1, 4)
yoroshiku onegai-shimasu your good-will, please (10, 15)
yoru night (4, 2)
yotee plan, schedule (9, 3)
yotsukado intersection (11, 9)
yot-tsu four units (8, Ad. 1)
yunyuu (-suru) import (17, Ref.)
yushutsu (-suru) export (17, Ref.)
yuubinkyoku post office (11, 11)
yuuboo /na/ hopeful, promising (17, Ad. 1)
Yuu-esu-emu-sha U.S.M., Ltd. (17, 6)
yuujin friend (14, Ad. 4)
yuushoku dinner (9, Ad. 1)

Z

zangyoo overtime (16, Ref.)
zannen /na/ regret (14, 8)
　zannen desu ga to my regret (14, 8)
zasshi magazine (7, Ad. 2)
zehi by all means (9, Ad. 3)
zero zero (3, Ad. 1)
zubora /na/ negligent (15, Ref.)
zumen drawing (18, Ad. 2)